I0817479

ARMORED FORCES OF RUSSIA AND THE SOVIET UNION

Tanks and Armored Vehicles

Victor Schunkow

Originally published as *Die Geschichte der russischen Panzerwaffe: 1919 bis heute* by Motorbuch Verlag, Stuttgart, © 2021 Motorbuch Verlag
Translated from the German by David Johnston

Library of Congress Control Number: 2025930713

Production design by Kate North
Cover design by Molly Shields
Type set in Dystopian/Myriad Pro (OTF)/Adobe Garamond Pro

ISBN: 978-0-7643-6967-4
ePub: 978-1-5073-0586-7

Printed in India
10 9 8 7 6 5 4 3 2 1

Published by Schiffer Publishing, Ltd.
4880 Lower Valley Road
Atglen, PA 19310
Phone: (610) 593-1777; Fax: (610) 593-2002
Email: Info@schifferbooks.com
Web: www.schifferbooks.com

CONTENTS

Introduction

Armored forces are one of the youngest branches of service in the world's armies. Tanks were first used in combat by the British on September 15, 1916, during their Somme offensive. Having withstood days of grueling barrage fire, the German infantry in their trenches had bloodily beaten off every British attack; however, they were powerless against the rumbling steel monsters. On this day, in the space of five hours the British managed to achieve a 3-mile-deep penetration, with just one-twentieth the casualties suffered in previous attacks. Although only eighteen of the provided thirty-two vehicles took part in the attack due to the technical vulnerability of the tanks, the new weapon proved to be extremely effective. Although the Germans quickly sealed off the breakthrough, this did not prevent the commander of the British forces in France, encouraged by the results, from telegraphing to London that he should be sent a further one thousand tanks. The French also began building their own tanks, and finally the Germans as well. While just twenty examples of the A7V Sturmpanzer were built in 1918, it was regarded as the most advanced tank of the First World War. Most German tank battalions were equipped with captured British tanks, however.

British tanks also saw action during the Russian Civil War. They served with the Entente forces who came to the aid of the Whites. The tank battalions of the White Russian forces were also equipped with British tanks. The crews of these battalions were made up of British officers

A T-34/85 during an event on Liberation Day in the Czech Republic. *Ralf Weinreich*

plus Russian officers and men who were trained at the School of British Tanks in Taganrog.

The tank units of the Reds were formed using captured British and French vehicles. They received their first vehicles in April 1919, French Renault FT-17 light tanks. They were combined in a special battalion that was under the command of the Council of People's Commissars of the Ukraine.

On May 28, 1920, the Revolutionary Military Council of the Republic (RVSR) officially issued the order for the formation of the Red Army's first tank battalions. It laid the foundation for the development of the later Soviet-Russian tank forces.

The goal of this book is to describe to the reader the organizational development of the Russian armored forces. In general, military organizational forms and structures depend on current tactics and strategies, which in turn depend on the state of weapons development, equipment, and training. The tanks of the First World War could hardly travel faster than walking speed and were characterized by limited range and poor technical reliability. They were intended mainly to support the infantry and were organized in independent battalions and companies. As technical improvements came about, the tank became increasingly important in tactical and operational terms, expanding the tactical successes of the infantry and cavalry or making them possible in the first place.

The theory of deep operations developed in the USSR in the 1930s envisaged the deployment of shock armies equipped with armored fighting vehicles and motorized transport vehicles as well as modern means of communication. The Red Army was an offensive army, and the shock armies were to be deployed in the main directions of attack. Independent mechanized brigades and mechanized corps were created to achieve breakthroughs of the enemy front. The latter consisted of formations of tanks, motorized infantry, artillery, and various combat support and supply units.

Brigades and mechanized corps intended for strategic use were equipped with fast BT-2, BT-5, and BT-7 wheeled/tracked tanks. Brigades that were to break through the enemy's defenses together with the infantry at the tactical level (in the first phase of a deep operation) received less fast but better-armored T-26 tanks. T-28 medium and T-35 heavy tanks equipped the tank brigades of the Soviet High Command Reserve, which supported the advancing mechanized brigades and corps at focal points of the attack.

In the late 1930s, as part of the Stalinist purges, many pioneers and supporters of the theory of deep operations in the Red Army were liquidated or imprisoned. This had a negative impact on the further expansion of the mechanized (tank) corps: The prevailing opinion in the People's Commissariat of Defense was now that these were theories and structures that were far removed from practice and wrong and should be abandoned.

In November 1939, the High Command decided to disband the corps and instead create fifteen motorized divisions as part of the infantry. Even though each of the divisions was to receive a tank regiment with 275 tanks and be deployed operationally, the formation of divisions instead of much more powerful corps was a clear step backward for an armed force that, according to Communist ideas, was by no means intended to serve only for defense. The leadership of the People's Commissariat of Defense was forced to realize this when, during the Western campaign in May and June 1940, fast German tank units, in conjunction with infantry, artillery, and air force, crushed the French, British, and Belgian forces within a few weeks. It drew immediate conclusions from this: As early as July 6, 1940, the Council of People's Commissars of the USSR passed a resolution on the recommendation of the People's Commissariat of Defense, which provided for the formation of eight mechanized corps and two independent tank divisions. In March 1941, it was decided to set up twenty more mechanized corps. These formations were equipped with tanks from disbanded brigades and armored battalions from rifle divisions. However, the corps were to draw their main striking power from the new T-34 medium and KV heavy tanks, which were more heavily armed and armored than any previous tank.

When the Great Patriotic War—the war between Germany and the Soviet Union that began in June 1941—began, the process of forming mechanized corps was far from complete, but the existing powerful tank brigades had already been disbanded. For this and other reasons, the Red Army suffered enormous losses in tanks in the initial phase of the war. As a result, the Soviet command disbanded the mechanized corps and their tank divisions to form independent tank brigades and battalions in their place—the new main organizational forms of the Soviet tank forces.

However, costly experiences during the counteroffensive in the winter of 1942 led the Red Army to again create larger armored formations. At that time the Soviet tank industry had significantly increased its production of modern tank types, which made it possible to again form tank corps in the spring of 1942. The first tank armies followed in May and June. The formation of mechanized corps with a new organizational structure began in

September 1942. They were envisaged for combined breakthrough operations by the fronts (army groups); they were thus basically copied from the German example.

A tank corps consisted of three tank brigades, a motorized infantry brigade, a reconnaissance battalion, antiaircraft and antitank regiments, a rocket-launcher battalion, and support units. According to official information, a corps consisted of a total of one hundred tanks (KV, T-34, T-60, or T-70), which was later increased to 168 vehicles.

A mechanized corps consisted of three mechanized brigades (each brigade included a tank regiment), a tank brigade, antiaircraft and antitank regiments, a rocket artillery battalion, and support units. The corps thus had 175 tanks. This organization into tank and mechanized corps was very successful in principle. During the war, they were changed only by improving their firepower and mobility and increasing their strategic and tactical independence.

Tank armies initially consisted of two tank corps, several rifle divisions, independent tank brigades, antiaircraft regiments, antitank regiments, and rocket artillery. Lessons learned in using tank armies in the summer of 1942 showed that the presence of tank corps and rifle divisions with different equipment and levels of mobility tended to make command and control as well as material and technical support difficult. At the end of January 1942, a special meeting of the State Defense Committee (GKO) was held on the formation of tanks armies with a new structure. It was decided to remove nonmotorized rifle divisions from the tank armies and to separate the "tank core" organizationally from other formations. It was considered expedient to equip an army with two tank corps and one mechanized corps. In addition, there would be an antiaircraft artillery division as well as rocket-launcher, mortar, howitzer, antitank, and motorcycle regiments. The support troops included an aviation regiment for close air support and liaison tasks (Po-2 aircraft), a transport regiment, a combat engineer battalion, two repair battalions, and various supply units. With their new structure, the tank armies were very mobile and possessed great striking power. The highest commands reinforced the fronts (army groups) intended for offensive operations with tank armies.

The tank forces of the USSR were reorganized after the end of the Second World War. Unlike the reorganization at the end of the 1930s, the tank and mechanized corps were reorganized into tank and mechanized divisions; the tank, motorized rifle, and mechanized brigades became tank, motorized rifle, and mechanized regiments.

In addition to three tank and motorized infantry regiments, the tank division was given a heavy self-propelled artillery regiment. The armored forces lost none of their striking power because of this restructuring; on the contrary, it increased significantly. By order no. 10 of the People's Commissar for Defense of June 10, 1945, a tank division now had 314 tanks and 24 self-propelled guns.

The reorganization of 1945 also affected the tank armies. They were renamed mechanized armies and as a rule consisted of two tank and two mechanized divisions. In 1957 the mechanized armies were reorganized and became tank armies with increased numbers of tanks.

As per a guideline issued by the general staff on March 12, 1957, rifle and mechanized divisions were turned into motorized rifle divisions. In the late 1980s the Soviet armed forces had six tank armies. With the

beginning of perestroika, in several tank divisions the ratio of tank and motorized divisions was changed from 3:1 to 2:2 to reduce their offensive potential.

That meant that a division was now made up of two tank and two motorized regiments. The most-important organizational structures of the modern Russian armored forces are tank brigades and the tank battalions of the motorized rifle regiments. At the same time, the number of main battle tanks in a division was reduced from 326 to 250. As a result, almost all tank and motorized rifle divisions were disbanded, and their equipment was transferred to training bases (BNI) and weapons and equipment depots (BNVT).

In modern Russia, the tank forces are no longer an independent branch of the land forces. The Main Armored Directorate (GABTU) in the Ministry of Defense does not exercise a command function but instead deals with equipping the armed forces with armored vehicles and their operation and maintenance. The tank arm is still considered the main weapon of the Russian army. The most-important forms of organization are tank brigades and tank battalions within the motorized rifle brigades.

On November 13, 2014, the 1st Guards Tank Army was reestablished by decree of the president of the Russian Federation. It consists mainly of the newly formed 2nd Guards Motorized Rifle Division and the 4th Guards Tank Division.

The further development and improvement of its combat capability will be achieved mainly by equipping it with advanced types of battle tanks and further modernizing the organization.

Russian T-72 of the Czech armed forces during a public display. *Ralf Weinreich*

CHAPTER 1
THE TANK TAKES TO THE BATTLEFIELD

In the first battles of movement of the First World War—before the fronts froze into trench warfare—various armies employed a new means of waging war: wheeled armored vehicles. The Russian Tsarist army, too, formed companies equipped with wheeled armored vehicles armed with machine guns. They were converted civilian automobiles, meaning that they had converted the chassis of automobiles and trucks into armored cars. The companies were employed quite successfully in the reconnaissance, liaison, communications, and patrol roles; some were also used to support cavalry and infantry units. Since the war in the east remained more "mobile" than in the west, these wheeled armored vehicles, like the cavalry, were used more widely even after 1914–15 than, for example, on the Western Front.

French Renault FT-17 tank in service with the "White" forces (*above and below*)

However, the limited cross-country capabilities and the technical vulnerability of the gasoline-powered armored vehicles seriously limited their usefulness on the battlefield. With rare exceptions, their use in support of infantry attacks ended in disproportionately heavy losses. They were incapable of negotiating trenches, shell holes, and other obstacles, which were often encountered in large numbers on or near the battlefield. Disabled vehicles were also easy targets for enemy weapons. And let us not forget the poor condition or lack of a developed road network in the east.

The use of wheeled armored vehicles proved to be most difficult for the warring parties on the Western Front. Even more so than in the east, artillery was used en masse there, its notorious barrage fire transforming the battlefield into a veritable moonscape, which was practically insurmountable for wheeled armored vehicles. To solve this problem, first the British, then the French and Germans, created armored combat vehicles with greater off-road mobility. They drove on caterpillar tracks (i.e., two continuous bands of track plates driven by two or more wheels). The hinged track links distributed the weight of the vehicle much more evenly over the ground than wheels and ensured a low specific ground pressure, which prevented the vehicle from sinking deeply, even in soft ground. This meant that these "tanks" could overcome even difficult terrain. It was a principle with potential—all main battle tanks and most infantry fighting vehicles still roll on tracks today.

The British began working on their first tracked armored vehicle in early 1915. It was based on the Killen Strait tractor, with three tracks, and was fitted with a wire cutter as "armament." In June 1915 the vehicle was demonstrated to members of the British government, on whom it made a good impression. The superstructure of the Austin wheeled armored car was subsequently mounted on the tractor chassis and tests were carried out, but the military was not convinced and rejected the vehicle due to its inadequate off-road capabilities. A short time later, engineer William Tritton and a naval officer, Lieutenant Commander Walter Gordon Wilson, presented their own version of a tracked vehicle. It consisted of the tracks of a Bullock Creeping Grip Tractor, on which a box-shaped armored body was mounted. Testing of the machine, called "Little Willie," took place in September

1915. One report stated, "Sailors have succeeded in building the first tracked vehicle. They used it to cross trenches about 1.32 m (4.3 ft.) in width and 1.35 m (4.4 ft.) deep. The vehicle turned on its axis like a dog with something stuck to its tail."

Since the military wanted a vehicle that could cross 8-foot trenches, it also rejected "Little Willie." Tritton and Wilson next presented "Big Willie," and it was a success. They dispensed with a tractor chassis and instead used an armored body in the form of a diamond-shaped box that was attached to the hull with spindle-shaped springs. The use of cast track links with integrated center guide teeth, which held the track on the running gear, proved to be decisive for cross-country mobility. The armor protected the eight-man crew from rifle bullets; the vehicle's armament initially consisted only of machine guns. The Tank Mark I derived from this was then created with two armament options: The so-called "male" version was armed with two 57 mm guns and four machine guns, while the "female" version carried only machine guns (6 MGs). The "male" was intended to take on machine gun nests and fortified positions, while the "female" engaged the infantry.

The BA-10 armored car was a descendant of the armored automobile of the First World War. Large numbers of these vehicles were captured or destroyed by the German armed forces in 1941.

British Tank Mark I

A 105 hp carburetor engine gave the 27-metric-ton (26.6 ton) vehicle a top speed of 6.4 kph (4 mph); the driving range on a well-surfaced road was 38 km (23.6 mi.). On uneven terrain, the vehicle negotiated slopes, walls up to 1 m (3.3 ft.) high, and trenches up to 3.5 m (11.5 ft.) wide.

The development of "Big Willie" took place in the strictest secrecy under the guise of the production of liquid containers (water tanks) for the Russian Empire. The camouflage name "Tank" was later applied to all tracked armored vehicles of the First World War.

Inside an assembly plant for tanks Mk. I

Remarkably, in Russia the word "tank" was translated as "tub," so that Russian newspapers reported British tank attacks as follows: "English tubs attacked German positions near . . ."

British tanks first saw action on September 15, 1916, near Flers on the Somme. Although only thirty-two of forty-six vehicles reached their starting positions and a further fourteen of these broke down or got stuck in the mud before the attack began, the rest managed to break through to a depth of 5 km (3.1 mi.). The losses suffered by the accompanying British infantry were much lower than usual.

Although the Germans quickly sealed off the breakthrough, this success inspired the British generals, and the leadership in London saw the tanks as a miracle weapon. British industry received an order for the quantity production of tanks. As early as the beginning of 1917, fifty of the improved Tanks Mk. III and Mk. IV were built, followed by 1,220 examples of the heavy Tank Mk. IV derivative and 400 Tank Mk. V variants.

At first, the tank units were attached to the British Machine Gun Corps. There were initially six tank companies of four platoons each, with each platoon comprising three "male" or "female" vehicles and a reserve tank. A tank company consisted of 28 officers and 255 noncommissioned officers and men. In total, the tank contingent in the machine gun corps had 184 officers and 1,610 noncommissioned officers and enlisted men.

British tank Mark I in Russian service

In November 1916, the establishment of four tank battalions began, which were based on four companies in France; the two companies remaining in England formed the basis for a further five tank battalions. In January 1917, the 1st Tank Brigade was formed with two battalions, followed by the 2nd Tank Brigade in February and the 3rd Tank Brigade in April. The steady increase in tank production made it possible to set up the 4th Tank Brigade at the end of 1917, and the 5th Tank Brigade was finally added in March 1918.

On July 28, 1917, the first three brigades were combined to form the Tank Corps, and by September 1918 it already comprised five brigades. Each consisted of three tank battalions of three companies and a transport unit. According to plan, the corps was to consist of 24,653 troops as well as 864 heavy and 610 light tanks. The Tank Corps put the British army in a position to launch large-scale operations, since only the mass deployment of tanks promised decisive successes in the war.

Tank Mk. I moving up into attack position

The French began producing tanks at almost the same time as the British. At the end of December 1915, Colonel Jean-Baptiste Etienne submitted a proposal to the general staff of the French army with the support of the Schneider Group, which envisaged the creation of an armored fighting vehicle based on the Baby Holt tracked vehicle.

The proposal was accepted, and a prototype was successfully tested in February 1916. On February 25, Schneider received an order to produce over four hundred vehicles by November 25, 1917.

And that was not all. FAMH was awarded a contract to build a further four hundred tanks based on a design by Colonel Emile Rimayo. These vehicles were named after the town in which the FAMH company was located, Saint-Chamond.

The Schneider and the Saint-Chamond models were considered medium tanks. They differed significantly in design from the English types. Their tracks did not extend the entire height of the hull but were much flatter and ended in recesses in the hull. The track drive and steering of the Saint-Chamond were provided by separate electric motors.

The French tanks were armed with a 75 mm gun and several machine guns. The Schneider reached a marching speed of 4 kph (2.5 mph); the Saint-Chamond was slightly faster, at 8 kph (5 mph).

In 1916, the automobile company Renault entered the tank development business. In contrast to the heavy and expensive Schneider and Saint-Chamond tanks, Renault opted for a lightweight model suitable for mass production for direct support of the infantry. A wooden model was available by December 30, 1916, and the prototype began trials at the end of January 1917.

The French Char Renault FT-17

With the Char FT (*char* = tank), the Renault designers succeeded in creating an armored vehicle that was outstanding for its time and anticipated the design of modern main battle tanks: engine at the rear, fighting compartment and driver at the front, armament in a 360° rotating turret. The running gear, which included the suspension and tracks, also showed new approaches. Thanks to the turret, however, the weapon(s) could be employed in any direction; no additional weapon stations were required, which in turn had a positive effect on the strength of the crew and the vehicle as a whole. The 16 mm thick (0.6 in.) armor protection was sufficient for the intended use. The armor plates were sloped and could therefore withstand armor-piercing rifle bullets. The vehicle was powered by a four-cylinder 18 CV carburetor engine with an output of 39 hp, which gave the FT (also known as the FT-17) a top speed of 7.8 kph (4.8 mph). Range on paved roads was 65 km (40 mi.). To increase mobility, it was planned to transport the tank, which weighed just 6.5 tons, on trucks anyway. The only thing the military did not like about the FT was that it was armed with only one machine gun. There were also doubts that it would be able to cross trenches, due to its small size. Nevertheless, Renault received an order for an initial batch of one hundred vehicles. The initial combat experience with the Schneider and Saint-Chamond tanks showed that only a concentrated deployment made sense. From the French point of view, this could be achieved only through mass production of lightweight Renault FTs. As a result, the companies Berliet, SOMUA, and Delaunay-Belleville were included in the production program alongside Renault. By November 1918, at the time of the armistice, the French had produced 3,177 Renault FTs, followed by a further 570 after the end of the war.

FT-17: a view of the driver's position

The French army divided the Schneider and Saint-Chamond medium tanks into batteries of four vehicles each, based on the artillery model. Four batteries formed a group, and three to four groups formed a battalion. In February, there were already four battalions each of Schneider and Saint-Chamond tanks. The battalions had a total of 245 Schneider and 222 Saint-Chamond tanks.

French FT-17 light tank

In contrast to the medium tanks, which were organized like artillery, the light tanks were assigned to the infantry since these were intended to provide direct support during an attack. The basic tactical unit was the platoon of three gun-armed and two machine gun FTs. A company comprised three combat platoons, a reserve of five vehicles, a maintenance platoon, a supply squadron, and a repair workshop. Three companies formed a battalion. In November 1918, the French army had twenty-six battalions with Renault FTs and four more were in formation. The largest unit was the mixed regiment, which consisted of one battalion of medium and two battalions of light *chars*. The German general staff did not immediately recognize the importance of the tank; although it caused a brief scare when it first appeared, the situation was quickly brought under control again. In addition, the tanks could be engaged with artillery and machine guns firing armor-piercing composite rigid ammunition; in any case, several tanks broke down for technical reasons even without being fired upon, or got stuck in rough terrain. Nonetheless, their successes finally persuaded the German general staff to also play the tank card and develop their own vehicles. The Supreme Army Command assigned the development task to a commission set up in November 1916 under General Friedrichs, head of Department 7 (Transport) of the General War Department in the Prussian War Ministry. The official abbreviation A7V (Department 7, Transportation) gave the new combat vehicle, developed under the leadership of Chief Engineer Joseph Vollmer, its name.

A Renault FT-17 demonstrates its ability to cope with difficult terrain.

The German Sturmpanzer A7V

The first model was unveiled as early as January 1917. On January 20, the War Ministry ordered one hundred chassis. Trials with the A7V prototype took place in the spring and summer of 1917; the first production model built by Daimler-Motoren-Gesellschaft (DMG) was available at the end of October.

The design of the German tank differed greatly from the British and French designs. The Germans had not failed to notice that many British tanks could be put out of action simply by firing at their tracks. For this reason, they placed the undercarriage of the A7V protected under the hull, which was to be groundbreaking for future tank design. However, this was at the expense of the trench-crossing capability and also affected the superstructure, which consisted mainly of straight steel plates. But no tank design of the First World War could be described as ideal anyway. However, unlike the British tanks, for example, the A7V had spring-loaded road wheels, which gave it significantly better handling characteristics.

The A7V was designed to be an assault tank for the support of infantry and assault troops (the legendary "storm troops"), which was the basis for its unusual design. There were two engines in the middle, each driving a track, which allowed the A7V to turn on its vertical axis. The two Daimler carburetor engines each produced 100 hp and provided a top speed of 12 kph (7.5 mph). The interior was divided into three areas: the forward fighting compartment, with the main gun and two machine guns, the commander's and driver's platform above the engines, and the rear fighting compartment, with four machine guns. This resulted in an excellent weight distribution, to which the placement of the fuel tanks under the floor panels of the forward fighting compartment and—to balance the weight—the gearboxes in the underfloor of the rear fighting compartment contributed. The armor measured 30 mm (1.18 in.) at the front, 15 mm (0.6 in.) at the sides and rear, and 6 mm (0.24 in.) in the roof. Overall, the vehicle, which was 3.35 m (11 ft.) in height, 3.06 m (10 ft., 0.5 in.) wide, and 7.3 m (23 ft., 11 in.) in length, weighed 30 tons. The main forward armament consisted of a 57 mm gun. It was a Maxim-Nordenfeldt casemate rapid-fire cannon, several of which had been captured in Belgium and which fired armor-piercing and high-explosive shells and canister shot. The ammunition load was initially 180 and then 300 rounds. In addition, there were six water-cooled 7.9 mm type 08 machine guns with 15,000 rounds. As a rule, the crew consisted of an officer as commander

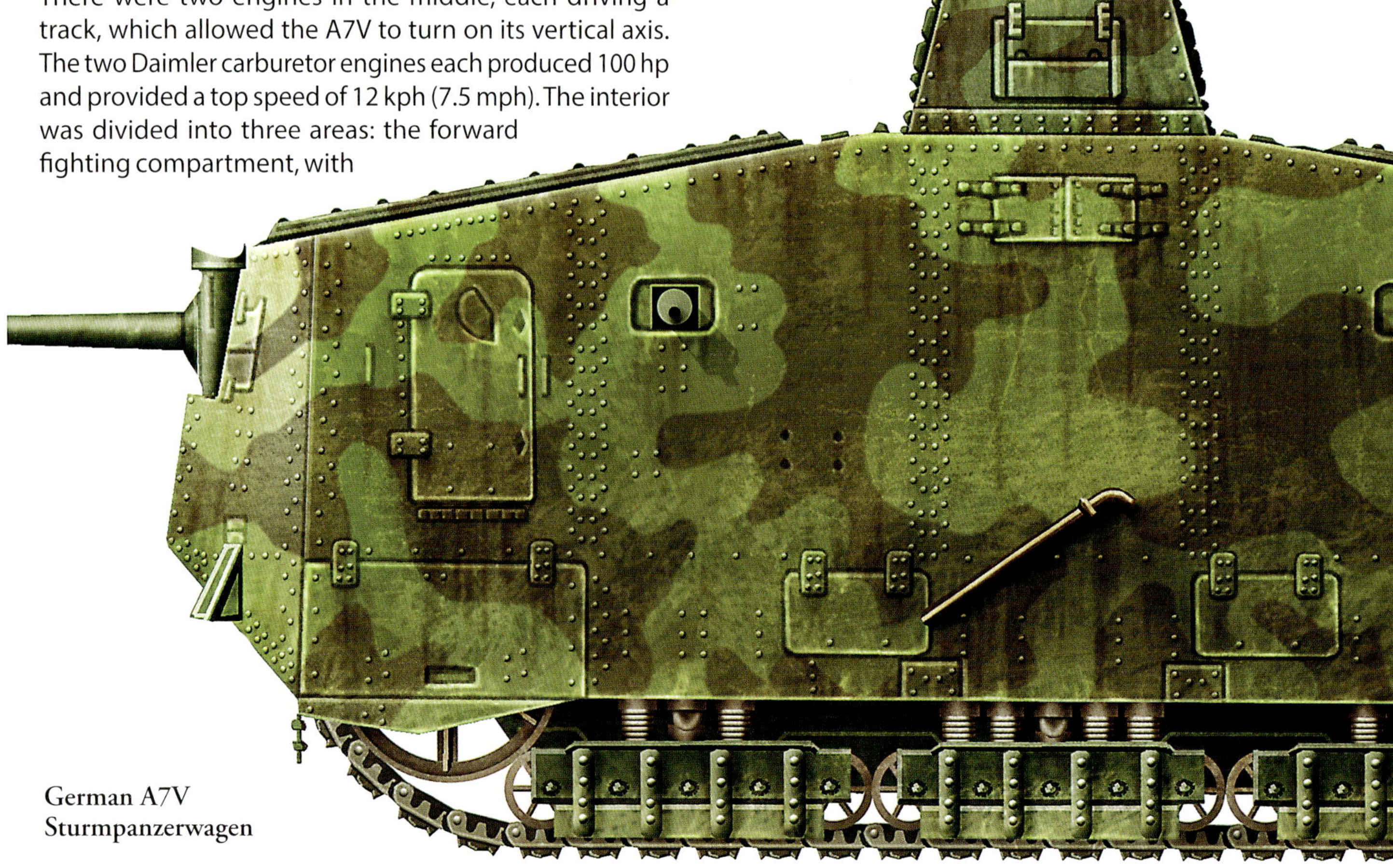

German A7V Sturmpanzerwagen

and seventeen men, made up of a second sergeant, a driver, an assistant driver, two mechanics, a signalman, two gunners, and nine machine gunners. No other tank of the First World War had a larger crew or greater firepower.

The plans of the German Ministry of War envisaged the construction of one hundred A7Vs, but this did not happen due to material shortages and the industry being overloaded with other orders. In the end, only twenty vehicles were built, which were divided between the Sturm-Panzer-Kraftwagen Battalions Nos. 1 and 2, established on September 29, 1917. Each battalion consisted of ten vehicles, five of which were in reserve. It is remarkable that the Germans were able to form six further battalions using captured British tanks.

The A7V experienced its baptism of fire during a counterattack on the banks of the Saint-Quentin Canal on March 21, 1918, when the German armored vehicles succeeded in penetrating 8 km (5 mi.) into the British front line. Their appearance had the same shocking effect on the British as the first use of tanks by the British in 1916.

Due to their small numbers alone, the German tanks did not leave the same impression as the British and French tanks in the First World War: according to production figures, the German produced 20 A7Vs compared to 800 medium and 3,177 light French tanks, as well as 2,370 heavy, 250 medium, and 35 British special tanks.

In Russia, the tank weapon went its own way. In August 1916, the Putilov factory presented an experimental half-track vehicle, the so-called Polutank. The design was developed by the Frenchman Adolphe Kégresse, who served as an ensign in a technical unit of the Tsarist army. It was a standard Austin, which had a caterpillar drive instead of rear wheels and widened front wheels. There were small rollers at the front for crossing trenches.

During tests, the vehicle demonstrated much-better off-road capability than existing wheeled armored vehicles. It overcame 5-foot-wide trenches and gradients of up to 30° and could also cope with swampy terrain. With speeds of up to 25 mph, it also reached a remarkable top speed.

On the basis of the test results, the GVTU decided to equip all the Russian army's Austins (with the exception of those of the first series) with a half-track drive. The conversions were carried out by the Putilov factory. Prior to the October Revolution, the factory completed thirty-four sets of parts for the conversion of the armored cars. Actual production of the vehicle did not begin until the summer of 1919. From July 1919 to March 1920, a total of twelve vehicles, which were referred to as "Austin Kegress" in the documents, were completed. The Red Army placed them in service with its armored battalions.

An A7V on a railcar (probably handed over to the French after 1918)

Gulikevich Armored Vehicle

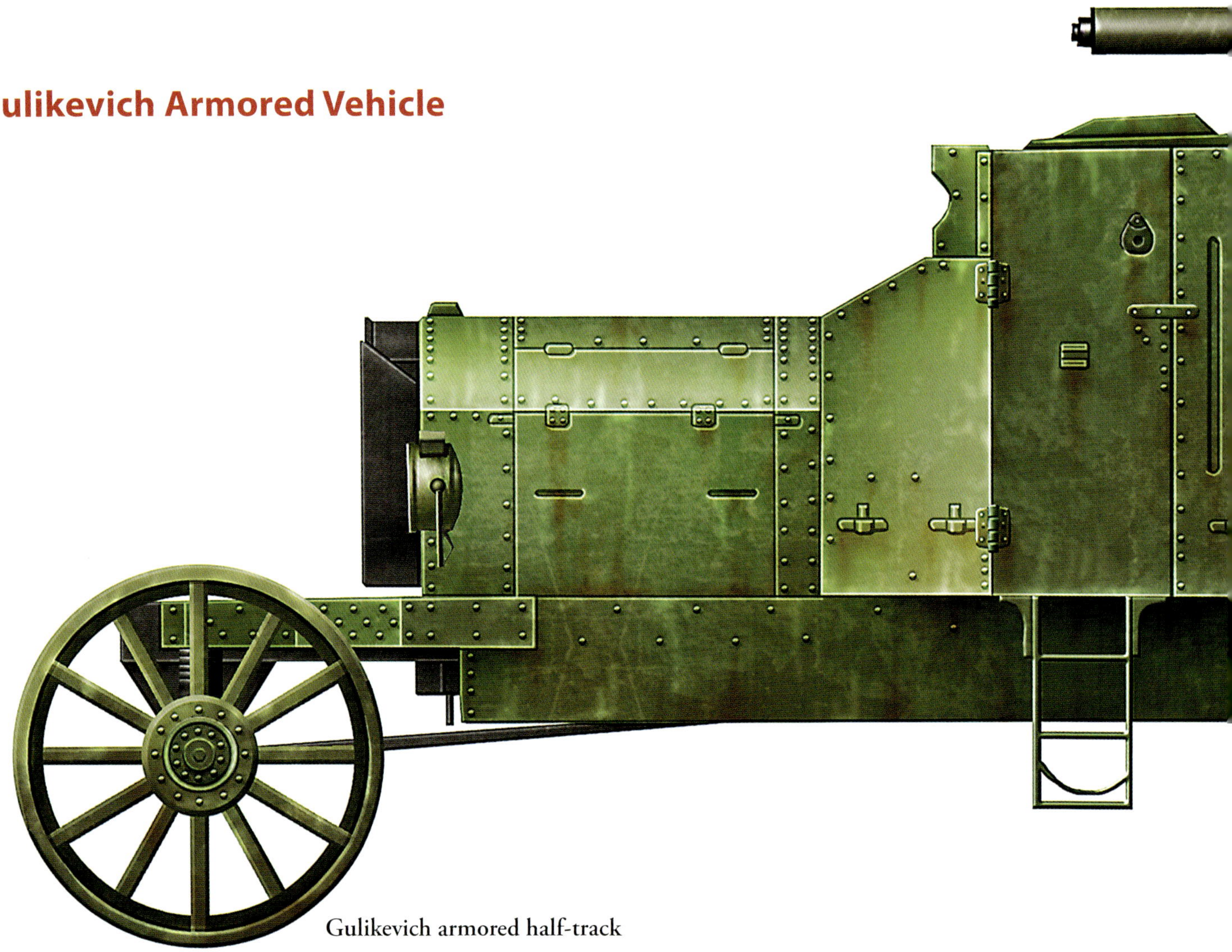

Gulikevich armored half-track

Another significant project involving an all-terrain and armored half-track vehicle was the "armored tractor" of artillery colonel N. A. Gulikevich, which was based on the chassis of a caterpillar tractor from the American Allis Chalmers company.

The Gulikevich armored half-track took part in the revolutionary battles in Moscow in November 1917.

The body was made of 6.5 mm (0.25 in.) armor plates, and the drive was provided by a 68 hp carburetor engine and a transmission with four forward and one reverse gears. The running gear consisted of two crawler tracks with large metal link rails, whereby both sides of the running gear were each connected to the chassis frame with a horizontal axle pivot arranged transversely to the direction of travel. This allowed the undercarriage to tilt longitudinally—a great advantage in difficult terrain. There were two unsprung wheels with steel rims on the front axle, which was also powered.

The driver's and fighting compartments were not separated. In the forward part was the driver's seat and a rotating turret with two Maxim machine guns, as well as the fuel and ammunition supply. A 76 mm gun was installed in the rear, and a reverse driver also sat there.

For the gun to be used, the Gulikevich armored car had to be backed into firing position and "parked," especially since the horizontal field of fire could not drop below the horizontal.

The Commission for Armored Vehicles approved the Gulikevich armored car and provided the designer with a loan to build a prototype at the Putilov plant. The vehicle was completed in November 1916, and the military began trials in early 1917. Remarkably, even before the tests had been completed, the factory received an order to build another model. Gulikevich proposed equipping several battalions of thirty to forty vehicles each with his half-track vehicle and attaching them to the army corps as breakthrough weapons. This plan did not come to fruition for two reasons: in the spring of 1916, the War Ministry had only ten Allis Chalmers tractors procured as tractors for heavy guns. The main reason, however, was the October Revolution, which thwarted any further procurement of tractors in the United States.

Chassis of the Gulikevich half-track

The only armored vehicle built by Gulikevich was named Akhtyrets and was handed over to the Reserve Armored Car Battalion. During the October Revolution, like other combat vehicles of the battalion, it was used by units of the Red Guard during the upheaval in Petrograd and then in Moscow. During the Civil War, the vehicle was named Red Petersburg and saw service with the 3rd Armored Car Battalion of the Red Army, which operated in eastern Russia.

The Porokhovschikov Armored Vehicle

Porokhovschikov's Vezdekhod ("anywhere goer") tracked vehicle

Kégress's armored car and Gulikevich's armored tractor were by no means the only armored-vehicle projects developed in Russia. The project for a tracked vehicle offered by engineer A. A. Porokhovschikov in January 1915 was a somewhat bizarre design. The vehicle, named Vezdekhod (meaning "anywhere goer") by its inventor, was designed to move where other vehicles could not—through sand, mud, or snow and ditches, as well as overcoming small water obstacles. The unusual design was based on a welded frame, and this, wrapped in plywood, rested on a wide track made of rubberized fabric. The track was stretched over four drums, while a fifth drum pushed from above and provided the necessary track tension during travel. The rear drum acted as the drive wheel, which drew its power from a 10 hp carburetor engine via a driveshaft and gearbox. Rotating struts with wheels were mounted on both sides. They were intended to steer the vehicle in one direction or the other. When driving on a paved road or on firm ground, the "anywhere goer" rested on these wheels and the rear drive drum,

A. A. Porokhovschikov with his "anywhere goer"

with most of the track surface above the surface of the road. Off-road testing of the "anywhere goer" began on May 13, 1915, and continued until the end of the year. Numerous defects in the design came to light: the glued rubber coating of the track came loose, the track jumped out of the guide, the vehicle's off-road mobility on soft ground and snow left much to be desired, and this also applied to the steering. On the other hand, the vehicle, which could allegedly transport up to fifteen people, developed a top speed of 42.6 kph (26.5 mph) on paved roads. The test report noted, among other things, "After a year of work, at a cost of 8,500 rubles and repeated trials during this time, the vehicle did not meet the desired requirements during testing and generally did not display any particularly positive characteristics."

In view of this result, the decision was made not to pursue the project any further. Porokhovschikov nevertheless received an offer to hand over the prototype to the GVTU.

The Lebedenko Armored Vehicle

In 1915, the head of the War Ministry's testing department, N. N. Lebedenko, offered an improved version of the "anywhere goer" with wheel drive. Lebedenko clearly recognized that off-road capabilities improved with an increase in wheel diameter. Monstrous front wheels with a diameter of around 9 m (29.5 ft.), each driven by a 240 hp engine, were to ensure excellent off-road mobility. The engines came from captured German airships. At the rear, on the other hand, was a roller-like castor that took over the steering.

N. N. Lebedenko first made a working miniature wooden model and presented it to the czar. In his palace office, the model demonstrated remarkable "cross-country mobility" and easily climbed over the thick volumes of the *Laws of the Russian Empire*. The czar was impressed and arranged for the necessary funds to be approved for its construction. In addition, a joint-stock company was set up to build the vehicle in a clearing in a dense forest near Moscow, for reasons of camouflage and testing. Construction of the Lebedenko vehicle began at the end

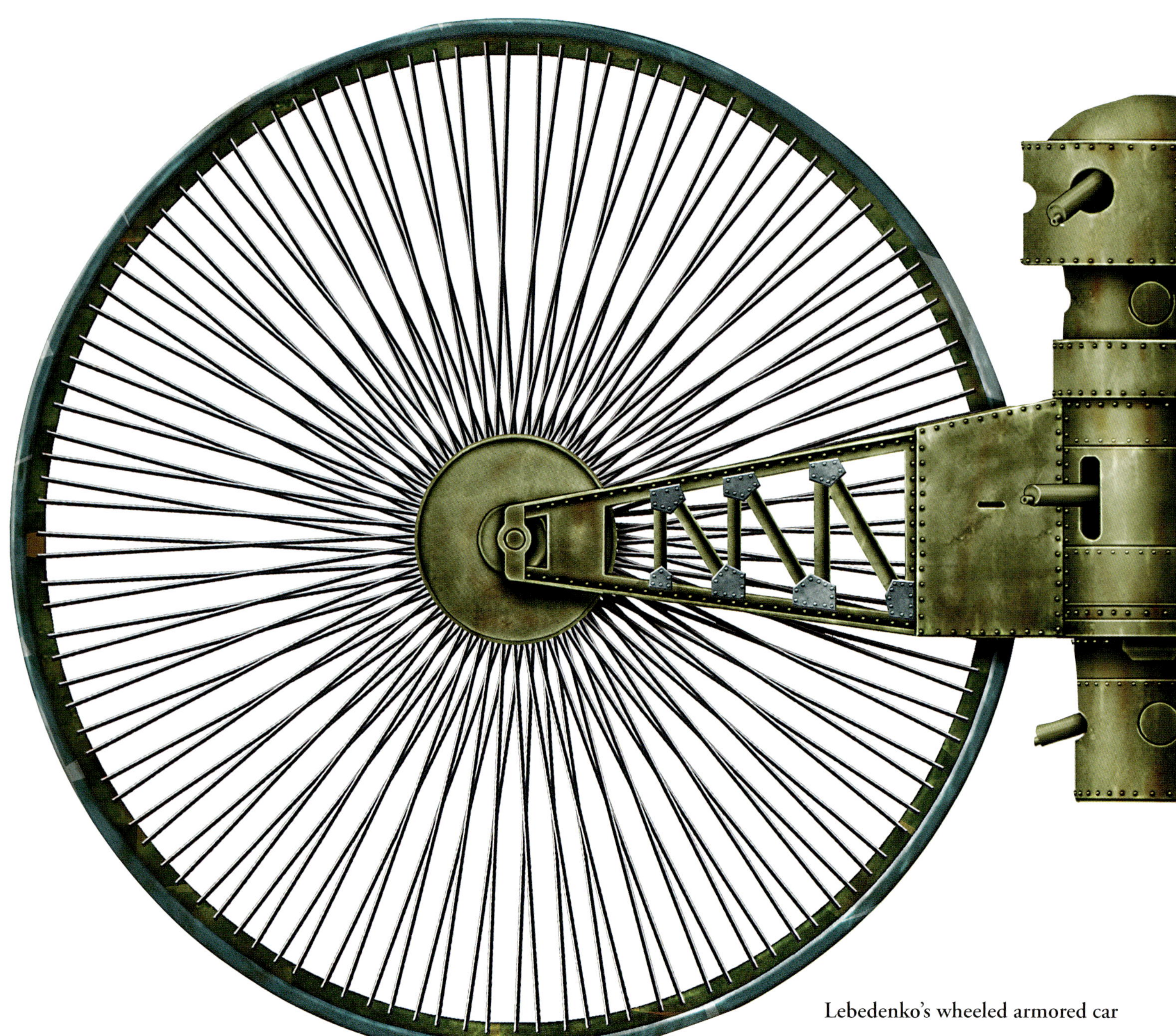

Lebedenko's wheeled armored car

Lebedenko's "giant wheel" during testing

of July 1915 and underwent its first tests in August 1917, in the aforementioned forest clearing. After starting the engines, the wheels turned only briefly and the car rolled over a young birch tree and then got stuck in the swampy forest floor. All further attempts to get it moving again failed miserably. Attempts were made to remedy the situation by widening the wheels and increasing the contact surface (thereby reducing the ground pressure), but the War Ministry refused to relent and stopped allocating funds for improvements. And so, the Lebedenko large-wheeled automobile was simply left in the woods with the foxes and hares and was finally scrapped in 1923.

Among the unrealized projects were the so-called armored car by shipbuilding engineer V. D. Mendelev and the 20-ton tank from the Rybinsk plant.

W. D. Mendeleev submitted his draft to the War Ministry on August 24, 1916. Basically, the 10 m long vehicle with a superstructure of 100–150 mm thick armor plates can be classified as a self-propelled gun platform or "landship." The armor offered protection against almost all field artillery shells of the time. The armament was also unusually powerful. A 120 mm naval gun on a pedestal mount was installed in the front section. The ammunition supply of forty-six rounds was stored in the middle, and the heavy shells were fed by means of a rail roller. The caliber was clearly too large for the mobile fire support of the infantry. The French Saint-Chamond tank was equipped with a 75 mm field gun, and British tanks were content with 57 mm guns. Incidentally, Mendeleev's "armored car" could hardly deny a certain outward resemblance to the French vehicle. The angular, chunky, and heavy Mendeleev vehicle was best suited as a mobile coastal defense or fortress weapon.

But it also scored with several unusual features. The design of the track drive was quite original—the upper track section ran covered under the hull, which offered protection from enemy fire. Another feature was its pneumatic-piston suspension. In addition, the suspension of each road wheel was attached to the end of a piston inserted into a vertical cylinder. All cylinders on one side were combined into one pneumatic system. The design of the running gear not only ensured suspension during travel. It even allowed the entire armored box to be lowered to the ground to absorb the enormous recoil forces when the 120 mm gun was fired. The drive consisted of a carburetor engine with an output of 250 hp, which was unusual for the time. The transmission consisted of a main clutch, a manual transmission, and a differential as a steering device. Mendeleev calculated that the vehicle should be able to reach a top speed of 24.8 kph (15.4 mph) on roads.

In addition to its strong armor protection, multiple driver's seats were also intended to ensure survivability on the battlefield. In addition to the two driver's seats for forward and reverse travel in the front and rear, there were two reserve driver's seats that each crew member could take over if the main driver was unavailable.

Mendeleev went to great lengths to plan his "armored car" as carefully as possible. He drew up meticulous specifications, weight tables, and calculations (e.g., for the size of the track and bearing surface). Despite innovative technical solutions, the project did not really fit in with the times; due to its size, it could have been produced only by the shipbuilding industry. However, it was never realized in metal. The main arguments against it were the high costs and the monstrous weight of 173.2 tons (just for comparison: the German Maus tank, built as a prototype in 1944–45, weighed 188 tons).

After the War Ministry had failed in its attempts to put its own Russian tank on the tracks, it decided to procure 360 Schneider tanks from France. Delivery was scheduled for 1917–18, and the vehicles were to be put into service with the first tank units of the Russian army, which were planned to be deployed at the end of 1917. The October Revolution thwarted these plans.

While the Reds had a significant superiority in wheeled armored vehicles and armored trains during the civil war, the Whites had the edge in tracked armored vehicles. The first arrived in Odessa on December 12, 1918, with French and Greek troops. To be precise, these were twenty Renault FT-17s from the 3rd Company of the French 303rd Assault Artillery Regiment. On March 18, 1919, the company and its *chars* took part in battles on the outskirts of Odessa for the first time. However, the advancing units of the 1st Zadneprovshchaya Rifle Division of the 2nd Ukrainian Soviet Army inflicted a defeat on the troops of the intervention forces and the White volunteers near Berezovka and captured a rich booty of war materiel. A report by division commander P. E. Dybenko stated the following: "The enemy—Greeks, French, and volunteers—were driven out of their positions and fled in panic and complete disorder. Within a few minutes we made rich booty: about one hundred machine guns, four guns, two of them long-range cannons, a lot of equipment, seven steam locomotives, an armored train, four tanks, and two staff quarters: those of the Greeks and French."

One of the four captured tanks was sent to revolutionary leader Lenin with the following accompanying letter: "Without sufficient guns and rifles, the Ukrainian proletariat took up arms against weapons of modern technology, but as you can see, even tanks, those modern monsters that the last war produced, did not withstand the struggle for independence. Today the 2nd Ukrainian Soviet Army is lucky enough to present you, dear teacher, with one of these dangerous weapons. We are sending you one of these tanks, which will be the best proof of the power of the proletarian revolution."

However, the tank in question arrived in Moscow dismantled, so Lenin turned to the People's Commissar for Military and Naval Affairs of Ukraine with the request to "send a tank to show it off at the May Day parade in Moscow." Lenin's request was granted, and on May 1, 1919, a French Char FT established the Soviet-Russian tradition of holding tank parades on Red Square at every available opportunity. Russian politicians—but also Western politicians, think of France—still seem to take great pleasure in regularly rattling their sabers and parading troops in the capital.

In the meantime (1919), the Council of People's Commissars of the Ukraine had an armored-car battalion set up in Kharkov, which also took in captured vehicles. Its existence was short-lived: on June 26, 1919, it was completely routed in a battle against units of the White Volunteer Army. Some of the Red infantry deserted to the enemy or took flight, and so the vehicles suddenly found themselves without infantry escort. Some were knocked out, while others were simply abandoned by their crews and captured by the enemy.

The Renault FT that took part in the military parade on Red Square on May 1, 1919, was assigned to the tank division of the All-Russian Central Executive Committee. This consisted of the following vehicles:

- 2 Austin armored cars
- 1 Fiat 1.5-ton truck
- 1 Fiat ambulance
- 1 Pierce Arrow workshop vehicle
- 1 White tanker truck
- 1 Packard mobile field kitchen
- 4 motorcycles, two armed with machine guns

Personnel strength was 52.

In mid-May 1919 the battalion was attached to the Eighth Army. All that is known about the further fate of the division is that it was in the Boguchar region on May 27 and was preparing to move to Kalach. The "Information on the Tank Divisions of the Southern Front on June 12, 1919" stated only that the battalion in question "was handed over on May 26."

Deliveries of British tanks to the Whites began in the spring of 1919. The first batch of tanks, six Tank Mark Vs and six Mark As, was delivered to the armed forces in the south of Russia on March 22, 1919. Since the vehicles were to be operated by Russian crews, the British sent twenty-nine instructors with them. They established the School of British Tanks in Yekaterinodar, and it later moved to Taganrog. For the most part, former artillery officers, gunners, machine gunners, and military drivers were sent to the school for training, and they were to form the core of the later tank battalions. About two hundred tank officers were trained from June to December 1919. The course of training was supposed to last six months, but the situation at the front led to abbreviated training—for example, the first course left the school after just four weeks.

On April 14, 1919, the I Tank Battalion was formed by order no. 674 of the commander in chief of the Armed Forces of Southern Russia, with the following organization:

- Battalion headquarters
- 1st Tank Unit (3 Mk. Vs)
- 2nd Tank Unit (2 Mk. Vs)
- 3rd Tank Unit (2 Mk. As)
- 4th Tank Unit (3 Mk. As)

Plans called for each unit to also have one tractor, one workshop vehicle, one tanker truck, four trucks, three cars, and several motorcycles, which would ensure them a certain independence in action.

The tanks were transported by rail. Each unit was assigned a train, which as a rule consisted of a steam locomotive and several cars, including three or four flatcars for tanks and other vehicles, two passenger coaches for officers and crews, and several boxcars for spare parts, workshop supplies, fuel and lubricants, and ammunition.

The Russian 1st Tank Battalion

The units of the 1st Tank Battalion were allocated to the infantry divisions of the volunteer army. For example, on May 9, 1919, the 1st Tank Unit joined the 3rd Infantry Division and, the following day, took part in the attack on the Chorunsk station. Tank commander A. Zechov reported: "In front of the tanks was flat terrain that rose slightly in the direction of the enemy. The trenches were at the top of the hill, and beyond them the terrain descended toward Chorunsk. The tanks quickly overtook the infantry and rolled toward the Red trenches. At about a thousand paces, they were met by heavy rifle and machine gun fire. Bullets crashed like peas against the armor protection without causing any damage. The tanks in turn opened fire from their weapons. When we reached the trenches, they were already empty. The enemy infantry had left them so hastily that we did not even see the fleeing men once we reached the ridge. They had already disappeared into the village of Chorunsk. As the tanks crossed the ridge, enemy batteries opened fire on them. The shells fell very close, some exploding only three or four steps in front of the tanks. The Reds' batteries fired accurately, but they could not stop the tanks. When the Reds realized this, they withdrew and the Chorunsk station was occupied by us. The fact that the enemy could not put a single tank out of action in our first battle was of great importance to us—the Reds now believed in the invincibility of these machines."

The situation was similar for the other tank units. At the beginning of June 1919, all tank units were subordinated to the Caucasian army, which was advancing toward Tsaritsyn. The 1st and 4th Units (two Mk. Vs and two Mk. As, respectively) took part in the battles for the city. Two days before the attack, the tank commanders carried out a reconnaissance of the terrain and the approach routes. The attack began at 02:00 on June 16. One of the crews commanded by Captain Cox consisted exclusively of British personnel, all the others of Russians. The tanks were followed by armored wheeled vehicles, cavalry, and

Captured tank Mark V of the Russian 1st Tank Battalion, in service with the Reds

units of the 7th Infantry Division. Artillery support was provided by an armored train with long-range naval guns. The defenders of Tsaritsyn assumed that they would be able to repel the White attack from their positions, which were fortified with barbed-wire entanglements and machine gun nests. But they were wrong. With artillery support, the tanks approached the barbed-wire entanglements and stopped. Volunteers from the crews disembarked under enemy fire and threw grappling hooks over the entanglements, after which the tanks went into reverse and tore away the entanglements while Red machine gun fire poured down on them—without inflicting any damage. Then the tanks rolled over the trenches. Soon the first position was taken. Panic spread among the Bolsheviks. They threw their weapons away and fled in droves. Within three hours, the 37th Division smashed the Red Army, the remnants of which retreated to Tsaritsyn in complete disarray, leaving all their equipment behind. The Whites made rich pickings. In Tsaritsyn, the Bolsheviks

Tank Mark V in use by the White armed forces in southern Russia

General Anton Ivanovich Denikin, one of the most important commanders of the White Army, in conversation with tank crews

built their last hope on four armored trains with guns. However, these fired so poorly that none of the tanks were damaged. Three of the armored trains made off; the fourth covered the retreat. One tank managed to tear apart the tracks, cutting off the armored train's retreat. Two shots into the locomotive did the rest. In the meantime, the White infantry had caught up and forced the crew of the armored train to surrender after a short battle. The next day, June 17, 1919, units of the White Caucasus army marched into Tsaritsyn.

In the meantime, more and more tanks arrived at the port of Novorossisk aboard transport ships:

- on July 16: 24 tanks
- on September 10: 6 tanks
- on October 6: 29 tanks
- on October 10: 4 tanks
- on October 13: 2 tanks

From Novorossisk, they traveled by train to Taganrog, where transport and other damage was first repaired at the Nef-Wilde factory. The School of British Tanks then used the tanks to form the II Tank Battalion. As a result, on November 18, 1919, the AFSR had an impressive tank force consisting of a "tank group" (I and II Battalions) plus three additional units:

I Tank Battalion consisting of
- 1st Tank Unit (3 tanks)
- 2nd Tank Unit (3 tanks)
- 3rd Tank Unit (4 tanks)
- 4th Tank Unit (4 tanks)

II Tank Battalion consisting of
- 5th Tank Unit (3 tanks)
- 6th Tank Unit (4 tanks)
- 7th Tank Unit (4 tanks)
- 8th Tank Unit (4 tanks)

Plus:
- 9th Tank Unit (in the formation process)
- 10th Tank Unit (4 tanks)
- 11th Tank Unit (in the formation process)

Meanwhile, the School of British Tanks received a further eleven tanks, while sixteen vehicles were undergoing repair work at the Nef-Wilde factory and another eleven tanks were waiting to be picked up at the port of Novorossisk.

To manage the tank units, the Office for Armored Car and Tank Units was established on August 26 (September 8) by order no. 2173 of the commander in chief of the Armed Forces of Southern Russia. In addition to the formation of new units, its tasks included the training of personnel; the supplying of spare parts, fuel, and lubricants; and the repair of combat vehicles.

The hostilities extended over large parts of southern Russia, which required corresponding mobility. Wherever possible, the slow tanks were moved by rail. The later colonel G. Benois, leader of a White tank battalion,

British tank Mark V before being sent to the front

commented: "When I think back to our tank units and operations, I believe that our superiors regarded us as a very valuable weapon; too valuable to be used in operations other than focal-point operations. Therefore, the high command kept us in reserve most of the time and exposed us to imminent danger only in difficult or decisive situations. Since the tank units were on the railroad, the fronts were constantly on the move, and the repairing of destroyed tracks took a lot of time, and it often took a long time to reach the respective deployment site. By the time they arrived, the tanks were often no longer needed. They were sent back, where they waited for new orders and new 'strolls' behind and in front of the front line. As a result, tanks were rarely deployed and often—to be honest—could do little. For an enemy that could not be panicked, and for artillery, they were quite vulnerable targets."

Nevertheless, tank units did achieve tactical successes; for example, the 4th Tank Unit of General Sergei Ulagay's II Kuban Cavalry Corps. In a precarious position, on the night of September 27, 1919, it took up position with its three tanks at the Kotluban railroad station; one tank was even hidden in a haystack. The next morning, the 1st Don Cavalry Regiment of the Reds approached the station.

A "White" Mark V captured by the Red Army

Mk. A Tank

Tank Mk. A

Only a ruse could help against this superior force. The tanks let the riders get close, started their engines, and broke out of hiding. Horses and riders were not prepared for the roar of the engines, the rattling of the tracks, and the sudden bursts of machine gun fire—the Red squadrons scattered in panic. The rest of the regiment was driven off by the arriving White cavalry.

The White Army of Southern Russia was unable to withstand the Bolshevik superiority in the long term. The offensive by the Reds' Southern, Southeastern, and Caucasian Fronts (army groups) brought about the end. The victors' booty included fifty tanks and armored vehicles.

The remains of the South Russian forces escaped to the Crimea, where they were reorganized and replenished. The reorganization of the I Tank Battalion took place in May 1920. It comprised the following units:

- 1st Tank Unit (6 Mk. Vs)
- 2nd Tank Unit (4 Mk. As)
- 3rd Tank Unit (6 Mk. Vs)
- 4th Tank Unit (4 Mk. As)

The battalion also had a Renault platoon with two tanks.

From October 14 to 16, 1920, twelve vehicles of the I Tank Battalion and eleven of the I Armored Car Battalion took part in the largest operation by armored vehicles during the entire civil war: the attack on the Kakhovsky bridgehead.

The plan called for the tanks to break through the Red defense and clear the way for infantry, cavalry, and armored cars. It should be noted that the 51st Rifle Division, one of the best divisions of the Red Army, defended the Kakhovsky bridgehead. Its shock brigade had over two hundred machine guns, flamethrowers, and guns.

The attack began at 04:25 on October 14 and was initially quite successful. The tanks broke through the first Red defense line, but the latter succeeded in separating the White infantry from the tanks. They were now on their own. Several tried to break through to the second defense line, but they were put out of action from close range by guns and hand grenades. The I Tank Battalion subsequently lost eight vehicles and was thus practically wiped out.

There were several reasons for the failure of the operation:

- The attack was made against an enemy known for his resilience and firepower without sufficient preparatory artillery fire.
- The selected timing of the attack, before sunrise, meant that the tank crews, whose visibility was restricted in any case, had to advance nearly blind. One tank, for example, broke through a dugout that was serving as a bathhouse.
- The defense succeeded in separating the infantry from the tanks, and consequently they were easily engaged with hand grenades (for example, clusters of hand grenade).

The objective of the northwestern White Army under General Nicolai Yudenich was Saint Petersburg. It received four British Mark Vs of the British Tank Battalion under Major H. Carson. The battalion landed at Reval (Tallinn), Estonia, on August 6, 1919, and a short time later received two additional Mark Vs. The vehicles had seen action in France in 1918, and their technical condition left something to be desired.

A tank Mk. A during trials

Tanks Mark A of the White Army

Following the relief of Major Carson, the Independent Tank Battalion of the Northwest Army, consisting of six Mark V tanks with British crews, was formed. The Russians recruited from technically proficient personnel. They officially joined the British military and swore an oath to the English Crown. On the basis of combat experience in France, an "armored assault battalion," which was to escort the tanks in battle, was readied for the tank battalion. As per directive no. 43 of September 9, 1919, issued by the commander in chief of the Northwest Front, in addition to a headquarters (26 persons), the battalion consisted of an infantry company (161 persons), a support company with machine guns and combat engineers, and a supply company with train; total strength was 879 men.

The tanks of the Northwest Army received their baptism of fire on September 11, 1919, during the attack by the 4th White Division on the villages of Rylovo and Polna, southeast of Gdov. Petty Officer A. Strachnov, a machine gunner in one of the tanks, recalled: "The first action at the front by our tanks resembled a parade. When we approached, the Reds hastily retreated, abandoning their trenches. Before our column appeared the division commander, General Prince Dolgoruk, in all his grandeur, wearing a gray general's coat with red lining. Next to him, with a batch of papers in his hand, was the English colonel who commanded the tank battalion."

In any event, with support from the tanks the White 4th Division drove the Reds back across the Zhelcha River. On September 28, 1919, the Northwest Army launched an offensive against Luga. There the 4th Rifle Division, with tank support, again smashed the enemy and advanced in the direction of Belaya Struga. As in the previous actions, the appearance of a few tanks did not fail to impact the enemy's morale—the Reds often fled at the sight of the steel monsters.

The following encounters, after the Reds had recovered from their first shock, were less successful for the tank crews, however. For example, on October 24, 1919, three tanks with infantry and artillery support attacked positions near a village. The Red artillery damaged two vehicles, whereupon the attack collapsed.

In principle, damaged tanks, whenever possible, were recovered from the battlefield and sent for repairs. After the failure of the Northwest Army's offensive against Petersburg, the tank battalion withdrew to Narva, where it handed its six vehicles over to the Estonian authorities.

On August 29, 1919, six more British Mark V and Mark B tanks arrived at Archangelsk, accompanied by a contingent of British volunteers under Major L. Brian, with a total of sixty NCOs and other ranks. The battalion's assignment was to cover the evacuation of the British and Allied forces from Archangelsk. It operated independently within the First Automobile Division. The tank crews also included Russian officers, NCOs, and other ranks.

During the evacuation of Archangelsk in September 1919, despite the promise to leave all the tanks for the Whites, the British left just two vehicles. Prudently—since after the fall of Archangelsk, they were captured and were given as booty to the Red Army.

The army of White general Alexander Vasilyevich Kolchak had no tanks. All of Kolchak's requests for tanks received a negative response from the British and French, who blamed delivery difficulties. The Americans, too, were less than enthusiastic when it came to supporting the Whites and provided just ten Renault tanks, which were unloaded at Vladivostok in March 1920. For reasons of secrecy, the tanks were transported on railcars covered with tarpaulins. The accompanying documents described the load as humanitarian aid from the Red Cross. Among the railway workers, however, were some who were sympathetic to the Reds. They uncoupled the cars and sent the tanks to Blagoveshchensk, which was occupied by partisans. There they were put into operational condition and assigned to the Red 1st Amur Tank Unit. It consisted of five platoons, each with two tanks and a repair section.

They took part in numerous actions from summer 1920 until the end of 1921. As on other fronts of the civil war, there too the appearance of tanks had a serious impact on the enemy's fighting morale. Often the infantry left their trenches when the rumbling, fire-spitting monsters appeared. On October 20, 1920, for example, the Red 5th Amur Brigade took the Ulrulch railway station with tank support, without loss. The Whites abandoned the field with the appearance of the tanks.

In "Directives for the Employment of Tanks in the Field," developed by N. Shamray, it states: "Tanks can inflict defeats on the enemy and leave a great morale impression on him only if they are used in concentration." Shamray and other tank commanders placed special emphasis, as cited many times, for keeping the distances traveled by the tanks under their own power as short as possible, to preserve the vehicles for their actual task of combat.

The Red Army designated captured enemy tanks on the basis of their power plants. They called the Tank Mark V the Ricardo, the Tank Mark A the Taylor, and the FT-17 the Renault. They also divided the vehicles by size: B (*bolshoi*) = large (Mk. V), and M (*malenki*) = small (Mk. A, Renault).

The Red Army's tank fleet did not consist of just captured vehicles, however. After the Renault FT captured near Odessa on March 1919 was shown at the May Day Parade in Red Square, the Soviet government decided to build tanks of this type itself. On August 10, 1919, the Krasnoye Sormovo factory in Nizhny Novgorod was named the primary manufacturer of tanks. The factory in Izhora was to provide armor steel parts, the Putilov factory the weapons, and the AMO factory the engines. The plan envisioned the completion of the first series of fifteen vehicles by the end of 1920. Despite difficult conditions, it succeeded in completing its first tank by August 31, 1920. It was given the name "Freedom Fighter Comrade Lenin." The building and testing of further vehicles were completed on December 1. In the corresponding report, the armaments industry councilor proudly stated: "All work was completed by Russian workers and technicians with their own means."

Three tanks were completed by December 1920, and another twelve by March 1921. They received the unofficial designation "Russian Renaults."

Tanks Mark A ready for action

Russian Renault Tanks

With tank output rising, the Red Army began forming tank units. In 1920, P. Vershinin, head of the tank units of the Ninth Army of the Red Caucasian front, developed an initial organization: a tank unit with a strength of one hundred men essentially consisted of three tanks and two wheeled vehicles. Courses were organized in Yekaterinodar for the training of crews; equipment captured from the White Guard was used as instruction and training material. Only trained chauffeurs were considered as tank drivers, which reduced the training time for a crew to 136 hours (driver training was the most time-consuming type).

On May 28, 1920, by order of the Revolutionary Military Council or RVSR, the official organization for tank units of the Red Army was introduced. A so-called Autotank Battalion—whose strength was in fact that of a weak company—initially consisted of a headquarters, three tanks, a radio and communications section, a workshop section, and a medical section. The 1st Autotank Battalion was established in Moscow on May 29, 1920, following this standard. Because of the limited range of the tanks, their low cruising speed, and their vulnerability to mechanical breakdown, the Autotank Battalion was assigned a special train for transporting the vehicles. In July 1920 the Autotank Battalion was reinforced by a thirty-man-strong infantry contingent with two machine guns. Order no. 1458/259 of the RVSR of August 6, 1920,

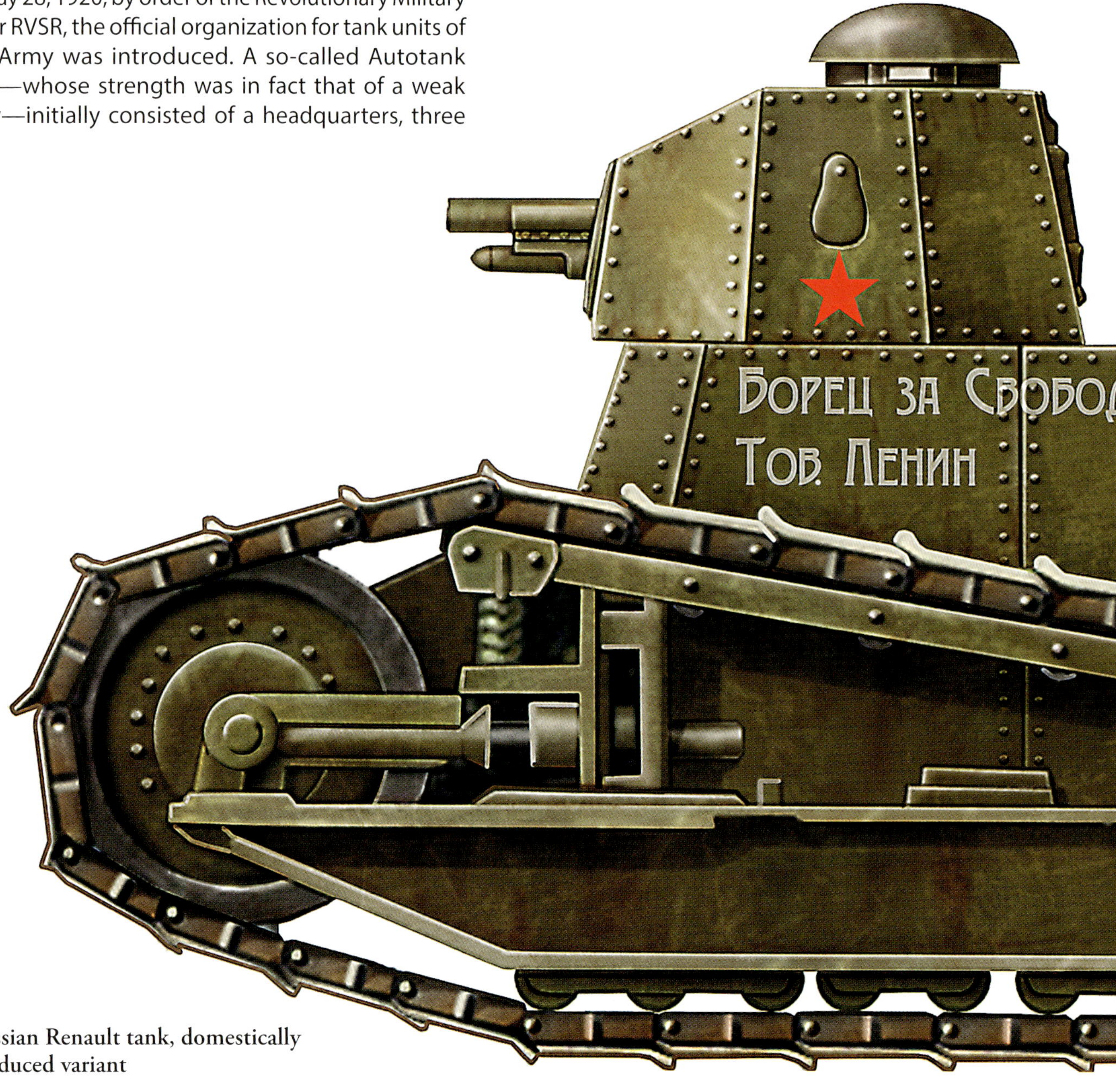

Russian Renault tank, domestically produced variant

increased the number of tanks to four, expressly stating that all tanks were to be of the same type. These changes had two main reasons:

- increased firepower and the ability to operate in two platoons each with two tanks
- simplification of servicing, training, and recovery opportunities

In its final form, the organization looked like this:

Personnel strength
Command group: 4
Two tank platoons: 34
Workshop section: 20
Headquarters and supply: 29
Infantry element: 30
Remaining elements: 18
Total strength: 135

Equipment
Tanks: 4
Trucks: 4
Cars: 5
Tanker trucks: 2
Workshop vehicles: 1
Field kitchens: 2
Motorcycles: 4
Bicycles: 6

The Red Army reached a figure of eleven Autotank Battalions organized to this standard by the summer of 1920. They saw action in the final phase of the civil war. They achieved their greatest successes in combined operations by autotank battalions and tank platoons, especially since the crews of the latter had more-comprehensive combat experience. For example, at the beginning of June 1920, the 2nd Autotank Battalion (with three Mark Vs), the 14th Armored Car Battalion, and Tank Platoon No. 8 joined the 33rd Infantry Division of the Fifteenth Army (Western Front). All the armored units were concentrated as a spear tip in front of the 293rd Infantry Division, which advanced along the important rail line and road from Polotsk to Molodechno.

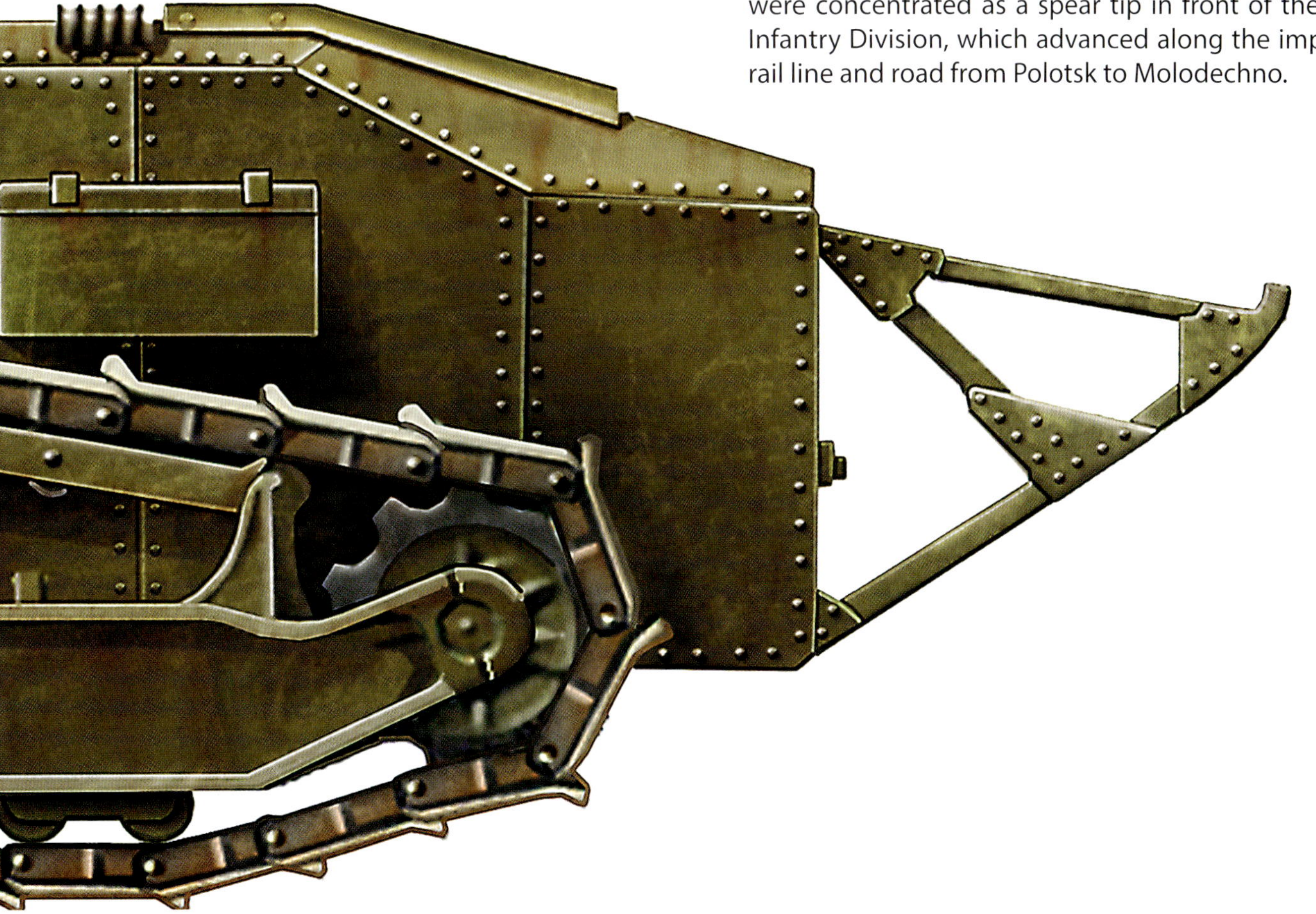

Captured Renault tank in the Krasnoye Sormovo factory

Russian Renault in service with a Red Army tank battalion

To preserve the element of surprise, the vehicles detrained on carefully camouflaged station platforms. They moved into their starting positions for the attack during the night. The 2nd Autotank Battalion was given the task of acting as a shock force, breaking through and taking the enemy positions, which were guarded by barbed wire, then targeting machine gun nests and supporting the attack by the infantry until a complete breakthrough was achieved. It would then follow the armored car battalion and expand the breakthrough together with the cavalry for an advance in depth. The Tank Platoon was given the task of providing artillery support.

The whole thing began on the morning of July 4. The attack was preceded by a fifteen-minute artillery barrage, under whose cover the tanks neared the enemy positions and took the first trenches. Their appearance sparked panic in the enemy, who began withdrawing hastily. The Armored Car Battalion completed the breakthrough with the cavalry squadrons of the 98th Infantry Brigade and took up the pursuit of the enemy with elements of the 33rd Infantry Division.

The "Directive for the Use of Tanks in Battle," which was essentially the Red Army's first tank handbook, was approved on September 6, 1920. According to the directives, tanks were numbered among the support weapons. Their primary role was to support the advancing infantry, especially when breaking through the enemy defense. Tanks assumed an important role in attacks in open terrain, which made the approach by the infantry difficult and cost heavy losses.

The tank section was regarded as a tactical subunit and the tank platoon as the basic unit, which, depending on the situation and terrain, worked together. When approaching enemy positions without preparatory artillery fire, a line with 10 m intervals was considered the suitable formation. Under artillery fire, in heavily intersected terrain, or in the face of a stubborn defense, the recommended method of attack for the platoons was either in a loose formation with intervals of 300–1,200 m (328–1,312 yds.) or in a wedge with a depth of up to 1,000 m (1,094 yds.) and width of 400–600 m (437–656 yds.). In each case, tank platoons and individual vehicles were to provide mutual fire support. The directive called for the artillery to provide supporting fire when the attack began to suppress enemy batteries and defenses. The basic objective of the attack was to break through the enemy positions, after which the tanks were to roll up the enemy defense line from the rear and take out nests of resistance and heavy weapons. Meanwhile, a second group of tanks had the task of destroying obstacles while approaching the defense position and taking out the enemy infantry in trenches with flanking fire. When this was achieved, it was to join the first group.

Command of the tanks in battle was achieved with flags and light signals and, when possible, also by using motorcycle and bicycle dispatch riders.

In the defense, tanks were to be deployed in favorable terrain for counterattacks in conjunction with infantry.

The directive in question formed the basic rules for the use of tanks and for combined arms operations on the basis of the tactical and technical possibilities of the time. It also formed the basis for the combined use of tanks, armored wheeled vehicles, and armored trains in the fighting for Tiflis in February 1921. At that time, units of the Red Army were supporting rebellious workers in the struggle against the Georgian "counterrevolution." A shock force from Kazakhstan traveled to Georgia by rail and advanced along the rail line to Tiflis. It comprised the 2nd Tank Battalion, the 55th Armored Car Battalion, and five tank platoons. The enemy had set up his defenses on the Kadschar Hills, not far from Tiflis, hoping to stop the Reds there. But they were unable to withstand the combined attack by infantry, tanks, armored cars, and armored trains on February 24 and 25, and the Red Army troops marched into Tiflis.

The tank was thus also able to celebrate successes on the Bolshevik side and take its place as a new weapon of war. The first tank units were formed, and effective tactics were developed for them.

Numerically speaking, tanks played a subordinate role during the Russian Civil War: until the end of the war, they made up just 0.41 percent of the Red Army's strength. Nevertheless, their punctual use should in no way be underestimated. Even more important was the training of its own structures, the creation of its own training system, contacts with industry, and the influence on tactics, technology, and military theory. The experiences of the civil war provided the foundation of the armored and mechanized forces of the Red Army.

A Red Renault tank in Red Square, Moscow

CHAPTER 2
DEVELOPMENT OF THE SOVIET TANK FORCES IN THE 1920S AND 1930S

The civil war ended with the victory of the Communists and the formation of the Soviet state. When the fighting was over, the Red Army land and sea forces numbered more than 5.5 million men. The personnel strength of the armored units was 28,660 persons. The armored forces consisted of 122 armored trains of various types, 49 armored-car battalions (approximately 300 wheeled vehicles), 10 tank battalions (approximately 80 vehicles), and a considerable number of support units.

The country's difficult economic situation made it impossible to maintain these troop strengths, and the Soviet government was forced to begin the gradual demobilization of the units of the Red Army. On December 18, 1922, the plenum of the Central Committee of the Communist Party of the Soviet Union decided on a minimum strength of 600,000 for the armed forces to ensure the security of the state. The armored forces were likewise reduced and reorganized. In the summer of 1923, the independent directorate of the Red Army was abolished, and its functions were transferred to the Main Artillery Directorate.

The experiences of the civil war had also revealed shortcomings in the process of organization into battalions. The distribution of armored vehicles to small units made it difficult to train personnel and maintain equipment. Therefore, in September 1923 the Revolutionary Military Council of the Republic (RVSR) decided to reorganize the tank, armored-car, and armored-train units. Armored battalions (equivalent in strength to German companies) were now concentrated into divisions (German battalion strength). A battalion consisted of five units (companies, platoons), each with two vehicles.

The number of armored trains shrank considerably; those that were eliminated became part of the reserve and went to special depots, where conversions and later new constructions were carried out. As per resolution no. 1181 of the Revolutionary War Council of the USSR, of September 28, 1924, the armored trains were also organized into divisions (equivalent to German battalions). During the civil war, armored trains had often been temporarily combined into groups. This made commanding and coordinating the individual trains difficult. The creation of divisions with a unified command was supposed to overcome this problem. Each division/battalion consisted of two light and one heavy armored train. Three such battalions were created by 1927. As of 1926, armored trains were then organized into regiments. A regiment consisted of three light armored trains (four 76 mm guns and twelve machine guns), one heavy armored train (two 107 mm guns and eight machine guns), one so-called armored platform (short train) with two 122 mm guns and four machine guns, and an armored platform with one 240 mm gun, and four machine guns. At the beginning of 1927, the Red Army had one armored-train regiment.

The changes also affected the tank units, which, following the naval example, were now concentrated in squadrons and flotillas.

The squadron consisted of heavy and light flotillas. As per RVSR order no. 1984 of September 6, 1923, "Introduction of the Organization in Independent Tank Squadrons with Heavy and Light Tank Flotillas," a heavy flotilla consisted of four heavy battalions, each with

- 4 Ricardo tanks type B (Mk. V),
- 2 trucks,
- 1 car, and
- 1 motorcycle (without sidecar).

As well, the heavy flotilla had a support battalion (company) with tractor and transport vehicles plus a workshop.

This "auxiliary battalion" had

- 1 car,
- 6 trucks,
- 5 tractors,
- 1 motorcycle,
- 1 workshop vehicle,
- 2 transport trailers,
- 1 fuel trailer, and
- 2 workshop trailers.

The personnel strength of the heavy flotilla in peacetime was 228 persons.

The light flotilla consisted of a light battalion, a hunting battalion, a small tank battalion, and a support battalion. It had

- 6 type C Taylor (Mk. A) medium tanks,
- 2 trucks,
- 1 car, and
- 1 motorcycle (without sidecar).

The so-called hunting battalion was equipped with six type M Renault (FT-17s with 37 mm guns) tanks. The so-called small-tank battalion was equipped with six type M Renaults with machine gun armament. The support forces were equivalent to a light battalion.

The auxiliary battalion consisted mainly of transport and tractor equipment and had

- 1 car,
- 4 trucks,
- 1 tanker truck,
- 5 tractors,
- 2 transport trailers,
- 1 fuel trailer,
- 2 workshop trailers, and
- 1 motorcycle.

Personnel strength of the light flotilla was 171.

The squadron was directly subordinate to the chairman of the Revolutionary Military Council and the People's Commissar for Army and Navy Matters of the USSR and was part of the strategic and technical reserve of the High Command of the Red Army. The reserve also trained the command personnel of the armored forces.

The heavy flotillas were envisaged primarily for breaking through heavily fortified enemy positions, and the light ones were for infantry support.

The creation of the squadron represented an important advance in the buildup of the Soviet armored forces. It was the Red Army's first larger tank formation with its own support units and significant personnel strengths.

It must be remembered, however, that in fact just 15 percent of the combat vehicles were with the units for training purposes. The rest were in storage in depots or were in the workshops for repairs.

In the summer of 1924, a special commission of the Moscow Military District examined the suitability of the squadron organization. Kliment Voroshilov, the commander of the military district, reported its findings to Michail Frunze, the deputy chairman of the Revolutionary Military Council of the USSR. Voroshilov found that "an independent squadron of tanks was not in keeping with the Red Army's needs in terms of materiel, structure, and strength. The training organization cannot be regarded as satisfactory."

After considering various reorganization options, in September 1924 the Revolutionary Military Council of the USSR decided on the new regimental organization. The independent tank regiment was created on the basis of the squadron and consisted of line, training, and support units. The regiment consisted of two battalions, each of two combat companies of three platoons (nine tanks per company). The battalion therefore had eighteen tanks. Personnel strength was 356 men. A third battalion was added in 1925, and each battalion was augmented by a third company. The regiment's organization was as follows:

- regimental headquarters with two platoons
- 1st Battalion (training): consisting of companies of drivers, gunners, machine gunners, and telephonists
- 2nd Battalion:
- 3 companies of type B Ricardo tanks, each made up of 3 platoons.
- 3rd Battalion:
- 1 company of type C Taylor tanks (3 platoons with 3 tanks)

and

- companies of type M Renault tanks (3 platoons each with 3 tanks).

The regiment also had support, rations, supply, medical, and workshop units.

At the time of its creation, the regiment's equipment consisted exclusively of captured tanks. In 1925 the Red Army's complement of tanks was made up of the following types (including those in storage):

- Mk. V Ricardo heavy tank: 45 vehicles
- Mk. A Taylor medium tank: 12 vehicles
- Renault light tank: 33 vehicles

As a rule, the vehicles were in a deplorable state, and mechanically they were worn out. Their condition was already assessed as critical in the early 1920s. For example, the Ricardo tanks had just ten operable 57 mm guns, and all the 37 mm guns in the Renaults were defective.

As an immediate measure, the command of the Red Army and the Main Directorate of Military Industry (GUVP) of the Supreme Council of the National Economy adopted a three-year plan for tank construction on June 2, 1926. The type and number of combat vehicles to be produced were determined on the basis of an estimate according to which they would, in combination with two rifle divisions, be able to break through a 10 km wide (6.2 mi.) defended sector and then advance to a depth of up to 30 km (18.6 mi.).

The minimum requirement was to equip one of the rifle divisions with a battalion of infantry escort tanks and others with a battalion of tankettes ("supporting machine guns," in the terminology of the time). At the same time, the number of tanks in an escort battalion of three companies was set at sixteen vehicles per company (three platoons with five tanks each, plus the company commander's vehicle). Considering the "spare" tanks, the company and battalion reserves, and the battalion commander's vehicle, this made a total of sixty-nine tanks. After the planners had calculated the possible losses on the basis of the experiences of the First World War and the Russian Civil War and recognized the need for a training company, they increased the number to 112 tanks. The same was to apply to the tankette battalion.

The maximum solution, which was to come into force a year later, provided for the creation of an additional battalion of "mobile" tanks to combat field fortifications and pockets of resistance, which would also cut or disrupt enemy lines of communication. A "mobile" battalion (i.e., fast-tank battalion) was to comprise sixty tanks, five of which were to be in a training platoon.

To implement the three-year plan for armored vehicles, the Main Directorate of the Armaments Industry (GUVP) set up the Tank Office. This central office for the design of tanks was located in Moscow and existed under various names until 1932. To develop tactical and technical requirements for armored vehicles, a Commission for Tank Construction was set up at the same time, consisting of representatives of the People's Commissariat for Military and Naval Affairs (People's Commissariat for Military Affairs) and the Main Directorate of the Armaments Industry.

At the end of 1924, the Commission for Tank Construction proposed the following basic data for the so-called escort tank: a weight of 3 tons, a speed of up to 12 kph (7.5 mph), armament of one 37 mm cannon or machine gun, a main-armor thickness of 16 mm (0.6 in.), and a crew of two. When developing the escort tank, the Tank Office used an Italian Fiat 3000 tank that had been captured during the Soviet-Polish War as a model. It was an Italian modification of the French Renault FT-17, which corresponded to the ideas of the Tank Construction Commission from a tactical and technical point of view.

The first version of the escort tank, which the Bolshevik Factory completed by March 1927, was given the designation T-16. Tests revealed considerable defects in the engine and running gear. These shortcomings were eliminated during the construction of the second version, with the designation T-18. It rolled out of the factory in May 1927 and underwent government testing from June 11 to 17. The results satisfied the military, and the Red Army adopted the vehicle under the designation Small Escort Tank Mod. 1927 (MS-1), or T-18.

MS-1 (T-18) Escort Tank of 1927

The first order for the construction of a batch of 108 T-18s was placed with the Bolshevik Factory on February 1, 1928. Production was to take place in 1928–29, and the "Bolsheviks" fulfilled their order as planned. Starting in April 1929, the Motovilikhinsky Machine-Building Plant took part in the production of the T-18, which was completed at the end of 1931 after the delivery of 962 vehicles, including prototypes. The Red Army received 959 vehicles.

The superstructure of the T-18 was very similar to that of the Renault FT-17: driver's and fighting compartments at the front, engine compartment at the rear, and rotating turret. The hull of riveted armor plates was mounted on the frame. The thickness of the vertical armor plates was 16 mm (0.6 in.), that of the horizontal plates 8 mm (0.3 in.). This was sufficient protection against small-arms bullets and shrapnel. The armament was housed in an almost hexagonal turret. A 37 mm Hotchkiss gun was first installed, later replaced by an improved Hotchkiss PS. A 6.5 mm Fedorov or a 7.62 mm Degtyaryov DT-29 machine gun served as the coaxial weapon.

The T-18 Model 1927 was powered by a four-cylinder, four-stroke carburetor engine producing 35 hp; the 1930 model was powered by an improved 40 hp engine. This enabled the tank to develop a top speed of 22 kph (13.7 mph) on well-maintained roads.

T-18s went to independent tank companies, which had been established in 1932 as per "Table of Organization 10/17." A company of sixty-eight men consisted of a staff group and three platoons with three tanks each, as well as supply and replenishment groups. In total, there were ten T-18s (including the company commander's tank). The company also had the following equipment:

- 1 car
- 3 trucks
- 2 Bolshevik tractors
- 2 cross-country vehicles
- 1 field kitchen

In the early 1930s, the independent tank company was the most important tactical tank unit of the infantry units. Later, the T-18 also went to tank battalions of the mechanized units. The tank battalion consisted of a staff platoon and a recovery platoon (command and repair), a gun platoon with two 76 mm field guns, and two or three tank companies of three platoons each (three T-18s in each platoon), plus the battalion commander's tank.

T-18, front view

T-18, rear view

Beginning in 1930, the T-18 was also assigned to the tank battalions of mechanized regiments (one battalion per regiment). They consisted of only two companies and thus numbered only twenty T-18s. From 1930 onward, the Red Army set up mechanized brigades, each with a tank regiment consisting of two T-18 battalions of three companies each. This meant that a mechanized brigade had a total of sixty T-18s.

The T-18 experienced its baptism of fire shortly after entering service in 1929, during the fighting on the Chinese Eastern Railway. The later Soviet marshal Vasily Chuikov recalled: "After the artillery fire, ten tanks moved from their starting positions. Their attack came as much as a surprise to the Chinese soldiers as it did to the Red Army fighters. We watched as Chinese soldiers and officers rose almost to their midriffs from the trenches just to see the tanks. We expected them to flee, but the surprise was apparently so great that it seemed to paralyze their will. . . . The tanks reached the Chinese positions unhindered and opened fire along the trenches. The machine gun fire disillusioned the Chinese. They fled in panic. Ten tanks broke through the enemy's defenses without loss."

The tankette, which was also included in the Three-Year Plan, was also developed by the Tank Bureau, which was given a new name in 1926: Head Design Bureau of Ordnance-Arsenal Trust (GKB OAT). Military theorists of the time regarded the light and inexpensive tankette as a promising class of weapon. As a machine gun carrier, the tankette could perform the following tasks:

- engaging living targets in the open
- destroying enemy positions in accessible terrain by fire or by running over them
- overcoming light wire entanglements
- scouting terrain and reconnaissance

T-18s during a parade in Red Square

In battle, the tankette scored points for its armor and mobility; in addition, its small size meant that it was only a small target. However, its armor protected the tankette only from non-armor-piercing rifle bullets, light shrapnel, and hand grenades at ranges of less than 400 m (437 yds.). Beyond 400 m, even steel-core small-arms bullets did not penetrate. Due to its small size and mobility, the tankette was also difficult to hit with antitank guns and heavy machine guns—at least in theory. At the time, it was assumed that the tankette was the weapon of the future and would dominate the battlefield.

The order to build a tankette with the designation T-17 (Lilliput) was placed with the Bolshevik Factory in September 1927, together with the corresponding design documents. There were two versions: with machine gun or cannon armament. An air-cooled 20 hp engine was specially developed for it. Metal-reinforced rubber belts were used for the chassis suspension.

MS-1 escort tank (T-18), 1927

In the early 1930s the Red Army frequently used the T-18 in maneuvers, against rebels, or in border hostilities in the east.

The Lilliput Tankette (T-17)

The armor of the T-17 measured from 6 to 10 mm (0.23 to 0.4 in.) in thickness. The plates were riveted to the frame. The engine was in the front, and behind it was the armored compartment for the driver, who also served as a machine gunner.

The first T-17 prototype was ready in autumn 1929. The vehicle successfully completed driving tests in the first half of the year, but the single-seater driver's cab proved to be a stumbling block. It turned out that the driver was physically unable to steer the tankette and operate the machine gun at the same time. This disadvantage was eliminated in a two-seat version of the tankette. This T-23 tankette could be used either as a machine gun carrier or as a lightly armored transport vehicle. The Red Army did not adopt either model, since the USSR had meanwhile acquired a license from Great Britain to build the more advanced Vickers-Carden-Lloyd Mk. VI tankette.

The three-year plan also provided for the creation of a so-called "mobile" tank, which was also intended to break through stronger defenses equipped with field fortifications. The GKB OAT designed the T-12 and in the fall of 1928 placed an order with the Kharkov Locomotive Plant (KhPZ, Factory No. 183), named after the Communist International (Comintern), to build a prototype. This was completed on October 15, 1929, and went into testing in the spring of 1930.

The T-12 had a classic superstructure, with the engine in the rear (180–200 hp) and the driver's compartment in the front. Unlike other Soviet tank designs, the driver sat to the right of the vehicle's longitudinal axis. The armament (one 45 mm gun, three 6.5 mm Fedorov machine guns) was housed in two turrets arranged one above the other. The disadvantage of such an arrangement was that the main turret with the gun armament inevitably interfered with target acquisition by or firing of the upper turret when it was rotated. In addition, "stacking" the turrets resulted in an overall height of 3 m (9.8 ft.), which increased the vehicle's vulnerability. The vertical armor consisted of 22 mm (0.86 in.) plates, the horizontal of 12 mm plates. Turret rotation was purely mechanical. The eight-cylinder

Hispano aeroengine produced up to 200 hp at 1,500 rpm. The engine compartment was designed with the possible replacement by a special 180 hp engine (at 1,800 rpm) in mind. The running gear was fitted with a very advanced track-tensioning mechanism. The tankette's maximum speed was 26 kph (16 mph). The choice of a planetary gearbox allowed the driving mode to be changed by 15, 7, and 2.7 kph (9.3, 4.3, and 1.7 mph), while reverse travel was possible at any speed. The track brake was also new.

Like its predecessor the T-18, the T-12 had a protruding rear end that lengthened the vehicle by 690 mm (27 in.). Thanks to its overall length of 6.5 m (21 ft., 6.9 in.), the T-12 could cross trenches 2.65 m (8.7 ft.) wide. Maximum gradient was 40°.

Shortly before work on the T-12 was completed, the Revolutionary Military Council decided on the following classification and procurement specifications for armored and other vehicles at its meeting on July 17–18, 1929 (*Note*: the original list in the Russian alphabet has been adapted here to Latin script):

A. Tankette (wheel-track drive). Purpose: reconnaissance/scouting, surprise attack. Weight: no more than 3.3 tonnes [3.6 tons]; better at 2–2.5 tonnes [2.2–2.75 tons]. Speed: at least 60 kph [37 mph] on wheels and 40 kph [25 mph] on tracks. Armor: able to withstand armor-piercing rifle-caliber bullets at 300 m [328 yds.]. Armament: one to two machine guns with a rotation range of 360 degrees; combat load of at least 2,500 rounds. Crew: two. Range: 300 km [186 mi.] on tracks, 450 km [280 mi.] on wheels. Trench-crossing ability at least 1.25 m [3.3 ft.], climbing ability 0.5 m [1.6 ft.], wading ability 0.75 m [2.5 ft.]. Able to knock over trees up to 10 cm [3.9 in.] in diameter. Change from wheels to tracks in less than five minutes without leaving the tankette. Vehicle height no more than 1.5 m [4.9 ft.]. Furthermore, on the basis of the design, a version with a 37 mm gun is to be developed for the antitank role.

B. Light tank. Purpose: Mobile support weapon for breakthrough operation by the mechanized brigades. Weight: no more than 7–7.5 tonnes [7.7–8.25 tons]. Speed: 25–30 kph [15.5–18.6 mph]. Armor: able to withstand 37 mm shells with a muzzle velocity of 700 m/sec. [2,296 ft./sec.] at 1,000 m [1,094 yds.]. Armament: 1 × 37 mm gun and two machine guns, one of them coaxial. Combat load: at least seventy-five shells and 3,500 rounds of MG ammunition. Crew: three. Range: 200 km [124 mi.]. Trench crossing ability at least 2 m [6.6 ft.], climbing ability 0.6–0.8 m [1.9–2.6 ft.], wading capability at least 1.3 m [4.25 ft.]. Able to knock over trees up to 20 cm [7.9 in.] in diameter. Furthermore, a light tank is to be designed on the same basis for test purposes with wheel-track drive, but with a weight of no more than 8 tonnes [8.8 tons], speed of 45 kph [28 mph] (on wheels), and range of 300 km [186 mi.].

C. Medium tank: Purpose: Breaking through fortified lines; capable of mobile as well as positional combat. Weight: no more than 15–16 tonnes [16.5–17.6 tons]. Speed: 25–30 kph [15.5–18.6 mph]. Armor able to withstand 37 mm shells with a muzzle velocity of 700 m/sec. [2,296 ft./sec.] at 750 m [820 yds.]. Armament: 1 × 45 mm gun and three machine guns. Combat load: at least 100 shells and 5,000 rounds of MG ammunition. Crew: four to five. Range: 200 km [124 mi.], trench crossing ability at least 2.5 m [8.2 ft.], climbing ability 1 m [3.3 ft.], wading capability at least 1.3 m [4.25 ft.]. Able to knock down trees up to 30 cm [11.8 in.] in diameter.

D. The development of a heavy tank is initially limited to design studies. Proposals are to be submitted by October 1, 1930, on the basis of which a decision will be made on the adoption of the weapon system.

E. Self-propelled gun for mechanized units (antitank artillery to accompany mechanized units). Purpose: preparation and support of the armored attack,

T-17 Lilliput tankette

engagement of tanks. Light-tank chassis. Caliber: 76 mm. Weight: not more than 7–7.5 tonnes [7.7–8.3 tons]. Cruising speed: 25–30 kph [15.5–18.6 mph]. Armor: 7 mm [0.27–0.39 in.]. Elevation range: no less than 30 degrees; traverse 12 degrees. The gun, with a crew of two, corresponds to a divisional or regimental cannon in terms of overall design and breech. Combat load: at least twenty-four shells.

F. Self-propelled antiaircraft machine gun. Purpose: protection of mechanized units against low-flying aircraft while on the move or in battle. Chassis: light or medium tank. Weight: 7–7.5 tonnes [7.7–8.3 tons]. Cruising speed: 25–30 kph [15.5–18.6 mph]. Armor: 7–10 mm [0.27–0.39 in.]. Armament: one 7.62 mm quadruple machine gun. Combat load: 4,000 rounds. Gun crew: at least two.

G. Self-propelled antiaircraft cannon. Purpose: protection of mechanized units on the move and in combat against close-support and bomber aircraft; mobile antitank defense. Chassis of a light or medium tank. Weight: 7–7.5 tonnes [7.7–8.3 tons]. Cruising speed: 25–30 kph [15.5–18.6 mph]. Side armor: 7–10 mm [0.27–0.39 in.]. Armament: one twin-barreled 37 mm antiaircraft cannon. Combat load: 100 shells. Gun crew: at least two.

H. The development of an infantry transport based on a light-tank chassis is initially limited to design studies. Proposals are to be submitted by October 1, 1930, on the basis of which a decision will be made on the inclusion of the weapon system.

I. Armored radio vehicle. Purpose: command of larger tank units. Chassis of a light or medium tank. Weight: 7–7.5 tonnes [7.7–8.3 tons]. Cruising speed: 25–30 kph [15.5–18.6 mph]. Side armor (shield): 7–10 mm [0.27–0.39 in.]. Equipment: Morse code telegraphy and voice radio; range (Morse telegraphy) 250 km [155 mi.] when stopped; at least 50 km [31 mi.] on the move.

J. Armored smoke-laying vehicle. Purpose: generation of effective artificial smoke screens. Chassis of a light or medium tank. Weight: 7–7.5 tonnes [7.7–8.3 tons]. Cruising speed: 25–30 kph [15.5–18.6 mph]. Armor: 7–10 mm [0.27–0.39 in.].

K. The development of a bridge layer is initially limited to design studies. Proposals are to be submitted by October 1, 1930, on the basis of which a decision will be made on the inclusion of the system.

L. Light tracked tractor. Purpose: tractor for divisional artillery, transport of gun crews and equipment of the motorized artillery. Weight: 3–3.5 tonnes [3.3–3.85 tons]. Maximum speed with towed load: 25–30 kph [15.5–18.6 mph].

M. Medium tracked tractor. Purpose: tractor for ARGK guns (ARGK = Artillery of the High Command Reserve) with a weight of no more than 7 tonnes [7.7 tons]. Tractor for corps artillery, transport of the goods of mechanized formations (wagon train of the 2nd Category). The chassis should correspond as far as possible to that of a light tank. Weight: ±7 tonnes. Weight of the towed load: 11–12 tonnes [12–13.2 tons]. Maximum speed with towed load: 15 kph [9.3 mph].

N. Heavy tracked tractor. Purpose: tractor for heavy ARGK guns and heavy loads. Weight: ±11 tonnes [12 tons]. Weight of the towed load: 11–12 tonnes [12–13.2 tons]. Maximum speed with towed load: 15 kph [9.3 mph].

O. The design of a new armored wheeled vehicle is deemed unnecessary. The Red Army Council is instructed to clarify with the industry the question of the possibility of converting the trucks currently in production:

Ford Model A. Ford Model AA with a Djembo rear axle or other type. The vehicles must meet the following requirements:

Light armored car (Ford Model A). Purpose: armed reconnaissance vehicle. Armament: two machine guns, one of them on an antiaircraft carriage. No armor except for machine gun shield. Installation of a third axle is desirable. Maximum speed roads: 80–100 kph [50–62 mph]. Vehicle weight: no more than 1.5 tonnes [1.6 tons]. Crew: three. Combat load: at least 2,000 rounds. Range: 250 km [155 mi.]. There is also a need to equip the same vehicle to carry a 37 mm cannon for all-round fire.

Medium armored car (Ford Model AA with a Djembo or other type of rear axle). Purpose: reconnaissance vehicle for reconnaissance battalions and mechanized formations. Armament: two machine guns, one with all-around fire capability. Armor: protection against rifle bullets from a range of 150 to 200 m [164 to 219 yds.]. Maximum speed, roads: 50 kph [31 mph]. Vehicle weight: not more than 3.8 tonnes [4.2 tons]. Crew: three. Range: 200 km [124 mi.]. Combat load: at least 3,000 rounds.

Heavy armored car. Purpose: heavy reconnaissance vehicle with antitank capability. Armament: one 37 mm cannon, one machine gun (all-around fire), one machine gun firing in the direction of travel (range of traverse, 25–30 degrees). Armor provides protection against armor-piercing small-arms bullets from 500 m [547 yds.]. Three axles with rear-wheel steering. Cruising speed, roads: at least 50 kph [31 mph]. Vehicle weight: not more than 6 tonnes [6.6 tons]. Crew: four. Range: 200 km [124 mi.]. Combat load: at least seventy-five shells and 3,000 rounds of MG ammunition. Fuel sufficient for five to six hours at average speed.

P. Motorcycles. The possibility of arming existing motorcycle types with machine guns should be examined. Purpose: as part of a reconnaissance battalion. Motorcycle and sidecar are not armored. A roughly 7 mm [0.27 in.] thick protective shield is desirable. The machine gun is mounted on the sidecar. The gun mount should enable the following: (1) firing at ground targets while on the move and air targets when stationary, (2) quick installation and removal of the weapon. Ammunition supply: at least 500 rounds.

T-17 Lilliput tankette, rear view

In addition to this guideline, the decree issued by the Revolutionary Military Council on November 3, 1929, was of great importance for the work of the People's Commissariat of Defense (NKO) in solving the problems of the technical reequipment of the Red Army, according to which the Directorate of Mechanization and Motorization (UMM) of the Red Army was created. This directorate included the Automobile Department, the Tractor Vehicle Department, the Tank Department of the Scientific and Technical Committee of the Artillery Directorate, and the Tank Forces Inspectorate. The head of the directorate was also the head of the mechanized troops of the Red Army and directly subordinate to the People's Commissar of Army and Navy Affairs of the USSR (Revolutionary Military Council of the USSR resolution no. 615, of November 18, 1929). The first head of the UMM was Innokenty Andreyevich Khalepsky.

In April 1930, a prototype T-12 was demonstrated to the Red Army staff under the direction of K. E. Voroshilov. At that time, the UMM leadership was already of the opinion that the vehicle did not fully comply with the new guidelines for armored weapons. The main points of criticism concerned its weight (instead of 16 tonnes [17.6 tons], the T-12 weighed almost 20 tons [22 tons]), which was reflected in a lower speed. The driving range also seemed inadequate, so that the T-12 was not believed to be able to operate in the depth of enemy defenses.

The decision was therefore made to eliminate the identified deficiencies in a modernized version of the T-24. The development was the responsibility of the GKB OAT with the participation of KhPZ engineers.

T-24 Medium Tank

In contrast to the T-12, the fuel tanks were moved from the rear compartment to side niches; a radio and a fourth machine gun were installed in the forward hull. The thickness of the armor plates was reduced to save weight. The roller bearings of the suspension were replaced by plain bearings.

At the end of July, the T-24 prototype arrived at Kubinka for testing. The final report by the RVZ of the USSR, dated August 13, 1930, confirmed the elimination of the criticized deficiencies and certified the suitability of the T-24 for series production at the KhPZ. The company was to produce three hundred T-24s in 1931. In fact, just twenty-five (twenty-eight chassis, twenty-five armored hulls, and twenty-six turrets) were completed, after which the type was taken out of production. The reasons were high costs, production difficulties due to the tank's complexity, and the fact that in 1931 a competitor, in the form of the TG Tank designed by the German Eduard Grote, an engineer at Rheinmetall, was available. Eduard Grote had been invited to Leningrad by the Soviet government as part of the German-Soviet cooperative effort. Together with other Germans, he played a key role in the development of a medium tank at the Bolshevik Factory in Leningrad.

In the meantime, the USSR was also negotiating with the United States for a production license for a wheeled/tracked armored vehicle based on a design by the American inventor John Walter Christie. As already mentioned,

Eduard Grote traveled to the USSR with a group of specialists at the end of 1929 at the invitation of a Soviet delegation that had visited Germany in 1929. Starting in 1930, the group worked in the design office of the AVO-5 department for aeroengines at the Bolshevik Factory and designed—who would have guessed—a promising tank for the Red Army. The development contract was awarded to the Grote group in April 1930 and envisaged a vehicle weighing 18–20 tonnes (19.8–22 tons), with approximately 20 mm (0.78 in.) of armor and a speed of 35–40 kph (22–25 mph). Armament was to consist of 76.2 and 37 mm cannon plus four to five machine guns. The prototype was unveiled in April 1931. It exhibited the classic arrangement, with the driver's compartment forward and the engine and transmission behind it. The armament was positioned on three levels. First there were two ball-mounted DT machine guns in the driver's compartment. The 76.2 mm main gun and three Maxim machine guns were mounted in a turret in the shape of a cutoff hemisphere. Finally, the 37 mm cannon was mounted in the top turret and could engage both ground and air targets. The crew of five was protected by 8–30 mm (0.3–1.2 in.) thick armor plates. The vehicle was powered by a 250 hp derated M-6 carburetor engine. The transmission worked with a multidisc main clutch with dry lubrication, a six-speed transmission, two side clutches, and two single-row axle drives.

The running gear had an independent suspension. There were five large road wheels, a rear-drive sprocket, a front idler wheel, and six return rollers on each side of the tank. The hinged track consisted of smaller punched links.

T-24s captured by German forces in 1941

A T-24 photographed during trials

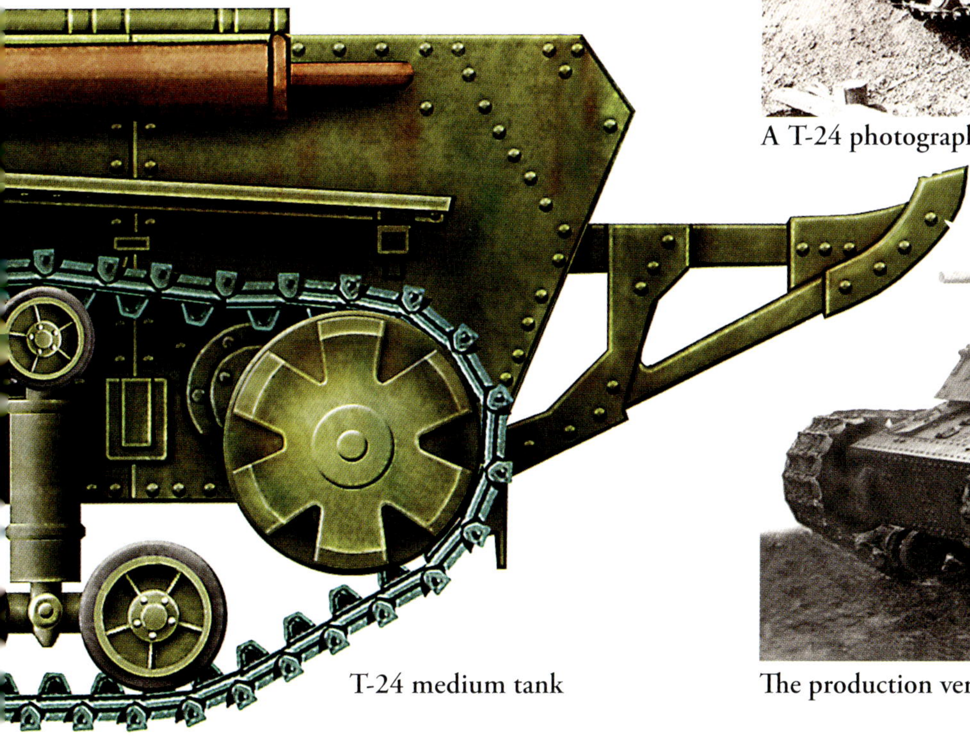

T-24 medium tank

The production version of the T-24 multiturret tank

Medium TG (Tank Grote)

Testing of the TG (Tank Grote) took place from June 27 to October 1, 1931. The TG achieved speeds of up to 35 kph (21.75 mph) on roads, and its range on unpaved roads was up to 150 km (93 mi.). The main deficiencies that came to light were difficulties with the transmission, chassis, and steering system. A commission consisting of representatives from the UMM and the All-Union Arsenal (VOAO) met in October 1931 to approve the vehicle. Although all the defects that had been identified were not fundamental and could easily be rectified, the commission decided to classify the Grote tank as an experimental vehicle for testing new technology. This was also due to the end of Grote's contract period and his decreasing willingness to be involved in Soviet armaments projects. In August 1933, Eduard Grote received permission to leave the USSR and return to Germany. The Soviets continued to work on improving his tank, in which they recognized considerable potential for expansion.

As early as the spring of 1931, a group of detainees (political prisoners) consisting of engineers Asafonov, Alexeyev, and Skvortsov began designing a medium tank based on the Grote design on behalf of the Economic Department of the United Main Political Directorate (ECOOGPU; secret police). This TA-1 tank retained the multiturret concept and housed a 76.2 mm and a 37 mm gun as well as four Maxim machine guns in two turrets. A German BMW IV engine producing 500 hp accelerated the 18.2-tonne (20 ton) vehicle to a top speed of up to 50 kph (31 mph).

The same trio of prisoners developed a wheeled/tracked version as the TA-2. The chassis was taken from the Christie tank, but with a horizontal arrangement of the springs. The TA-2 was designed to reach speeds of up to 80 kph (49.7 mph) on wheels and up to 50 kph (31 mph) on tracks. Compared to the TA-1, the TA-2 had an augmented machine gun armament with five Maxim guns. A T-3 version with improved armor and protection for the crew against toxic substances was developed at the same time. All three projects were transferred to the UMM RKKA and the experimental-design department (OKMO) of the Bolshevik Factory. The technical solutions were subsequently implemented in the T-35 heavy-armored fighting-vehicle project.

TG medium tank (Grote tank)

The Soviet military leadership's waning interest in the Grote tank was largely due to the emergence of an alternative vehicle designed by J. W. Christie. This was presented to the procurement commission under the leadership of the head of the UMM RKKA, I. A. Khalepsky, during a visit to the United States in January 1930.

The formation of the Khalepsky Commission at the beginning of 1930 was a consequence of the GUVP board's assessment that, due to the lack of experience of Soviet tank designers and the nation's underdeveloped industry, the development time and the fulfillment of tactical and technical requirements could not be met; moreover, the projects were not suitable for series production. In this context, on December 5, 1929, it was decided to study the experiences of other countries in tank design, and so the Khalepsky Commission set about selecting and purchasing samples (tanks, tractors, and other vehicles) that might be suitable for the Red Army.

One of the characteristic features of the Christie vehicle was its dual drive system. It moved on tracks in difficult terrain and on wheels over paths and roads. For wheeled travel, the tracks were removed and attached to the track shields. The American Liberty engine (the USSR produced it under license as the M-5) accelerated the tank up to 45 kph (28 mph) on tracks and 70 kph (43 mph) on wheels. These speeds impressed Khalepsky. In his report on his trip abroad, he wrote, "Considering that the Christie tank surpasses all tanks in the world in speed and that the Poles are building it, we may fall behind in terms of the tactical use of tank units. In this context, I strongly recommend that the Christie tank be built under all circumstances, with aircraft factories taking over the production of the Liberty engine and the Yaroslav Automobile Factory being set up to manufacture the other components. . . . I propose for the coming years 1930–31 to commission the industry to build at least 100 Christie tanks."

As a result, a contract was signed on April 28, 1930, according to which the United States "sold two military tanks with a total value of 60,000 US dollars to the USSR. Delivery of the vehicles will take place no later than four months after conclusion of the contract." An important clause gave the USSR "the right to manufacture, sell, and use tanks within the borders of the USSR for a period of ten years.

Prototype of the Grote tank

Grote tank, side view

Grote tank, frontal view

Grote tank on the testing grounds

The vehicles were delivered to the Soviet side at the end of December 1930. In the meantime, the question arose as to what designation the type should receive. According to the consecutive T numbering system (T = tank) adopted by the Red Army, it should have been the T-28 or T-29, but the head of the UMM decided otherwise: "Since the American Christie tank does not meet the requirements of the usual classification of the tank-tractor-automobile system and has not [yet] been introduced into service, it will not be given the usual army designation (the letter 'T'), to avoid confusion. It seems more reasonable to assign it a combination of two letters: BT (Bystrochodny Tank, or Fast Tank)."

On February 13, 1931, the Red Army adopted the Christie M.1940 as the BT-2. Initially, it was assumed that the BT-2 would be used as a "tank destroyer" to protect the T-26 from enemy tanks. The production plan envisaged the delivery of six hundred vehicles from 1932.

KhPZ acted as the official manufacturer, but first significant changes had to be made to the design. As the Soviet assessment put it: "The Christie tank, in the form in which it is currently being tested, is an extremely interesting vehicle with versatile mobility. As a combat vehicle, however, it still requires a great deal of development and the introduction of a number of design improvements and modifications."

BT-2 Wheeled/Tracked Light Tank

The KhPZ set up a special design bureau (SKB) for this purpose. By July 26, 1931, the design work for the first production version had been completed, and production began in 1933. By November 1, 1931, three prototypes had been produced, two of which took part in a military parade in Red Square in Moscow on November 7.

The BT-2 exhibited the classic arrangement of the engine compartment in the rear and the driver's compartment in the front of the hull, which was accessed by a hatch in the top armor. Behind it was the fighting compartment with the cylindrical turret. Armament consisted of a 37 mm cannon and a 7.62 mm DT machine gun. Some BT-2s had to get by without a machine gun, while others were fitted with a DA-2 twin-barreled antiaircraft machine gun. The American Liberty engine powered the first hundred vehicles. Its quality left something to be desired in the Russian continental climate, however. It refused to start in deep cold; at high temperatures it tended to overheat, and there were cases of engine fires caused by spontaneous combustion.

The running gear was optimized for either tracked or wheeled operation. It consisted of two steel caterpillar tracks, two drive sprockets, two idler wheels, and eight large road wheels for operation on roads. The changeover from wheels to tracks and vice versa took about forty minutes. When driving on wheels, the transmission powered the rear pair of wheels (drive wheels). On wheels, the BT-2 achieved the outstanding speed of 72 kph (44.7 mph), and on tracks, up to 52 kph (32.3 mph). In total, 396 BT-2s were completed in 1932 and another 224 in 1933.

The redesign of other armored vehicles that the Khalepsky Procurement Commission had purchased in England in 1930 caused much less trouble: the Vickers-Carden-Lloyd tankette (known as the "VKL" in the USSR) and the small Vickers tank.

The first five of a total of twenty tankettes arrived in the USSR in May 1930. The first demonstration before representatives of the Red Army High Command took place in August. The decision was also taken to have the tankette (or armored carette) built by Automobile Plant No. 2, for which a separate design office was set up.

The tankette was capable of operating both on wheels and tracks. Since the Soviet system already envisaged the use of armored carettes that could operate on wheels as

BT-2 light wheeled/tracked tank

One of the first production BT-2 tanks

well as on tracks, in the case of the VKL tankette they decided on a pure tracked running gear, especially since the combined wheel-track drive was technically complicated and was time consuming and expensive to produce.

The first prototype was unveiled on November 3, 1930. The vehicle had a box-shaped hull, which was made of rolled armor plates up to 10 mm (0.39 in.) thick. Positioning of the engine in the middle between the driver and machine gunners made it possible to drastically reduce the vehicle's length. In the hull roof were two entry hatches for the driver and gunner and an engine hatch. The machine gunner sat to the right of the engine and

A column of BT-2s and BT-7s on the march

BT-5 light tank

BT-7 during an attack, with infantry riding on the tank

BT-7 abandoned due to mechanical breakdown

operated a 7.62 mm DT machine gun. The four-cylinder, four-stroke engine, which was taken from the GAZ-AA truck (itself a copy of the Ford AA), produced 40 hp and gave the tankette a maximum speed of 40–42 kph (25–26 mph). The transmission also came from the GAZ-AA, which reduced production costs. For the track drive, road wheels with external damping, toothed drive sprockets, and a fine-link caterpillar track were used.

T-27 Tankette

The armored carette was adopted by the mechanized troops (as the tank forces had been called since 1930) under the designation T-27. The first forty-five production vehicles were made by the Bolshevik Factory in 1931, and Factory No. 37 (formerly Automobile Factory No. 2) and the Gorki Automobile Factory (GAZ) also joined in production. Between them, these factories had built a total of 3,295 T-27s by the time production ceased in 1934. According to more-precise information, there were 3,155 T-27 machine gun carriers and 187 XT-27 flamethrower vehicles. The following versions of the armored carette were produced:

- **T-27** (production version). Minor changes were adopted during production (the machine gun mount was changed, and the hull was welded).
- **T-27M**. Test bed for the 37 mm Hotchkiss cannon. Developed under the leadership of K. K. Sirken in 1931. Two vehicles were made: one with a 37 mm Hotchkiss cannon and one DT machine gun (which increased weight to 2,920 kg [3.2 tons]), and one with just the 37 mm cannon. A small, tracked trailer was used to transport ammunition. One vehicle was scrapped after the trials; nothing is known about the fate of the other.
- **T-27 flamethrower tankette** (experimental). Designed in 1930 at the suggestion of G. K. Kratirov. Production of the first of a total of twelve vehicles began in May 1931. Armament consisted of a DT machine gun and a so-called rucksack flamethrower with two 16-liter (4.2 gal.) tanks for flame oil. These 32 liters (8.4 gal.) sufficed for 24 to 26 jets of flame, with a range (depending on weather conditions) of 24 to 28 m (26.25–30.6 yds.).
- **OT-27/XT-27 (БХМ-4) flamethrower tankette**. An improved model with a KS-1 flamethrower (the DT machine gun was removed, and in its place the gunner was given a semiautomatic rifle). Maximum firing

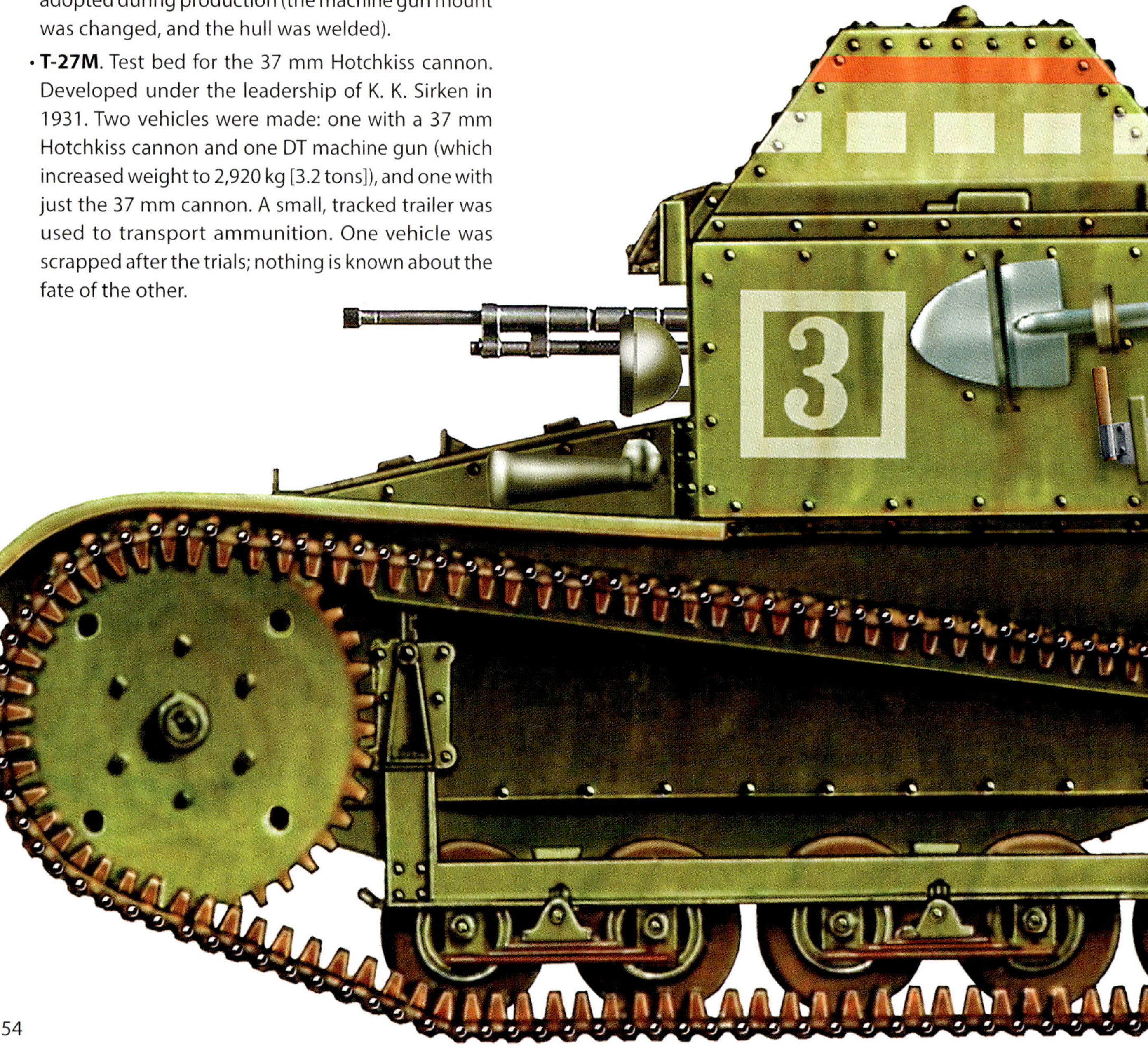

range was 25 m (27 yds.). A total of 187 examples were produced in 1932–33. They were the Red Army's first flamethrower tanks. A total of 33 OT-27 flamethrower tankettes were still in the inventory on June 1, 1941.

- **M3-27 minelayer**. Armed with a DT machine gun (with 2,500 rounds) and 170 mines in a drum weighing 480 kg (1,058 lbs.). At least five were made.
- **Ammunition transporter**. Experimental vehicle, developed between 1932 and 1933 by N. I. Kurzbeinig. On the sides of the tankette there were two carriers for 40 ammunition boxes (880 kg [1.940 lbs.]) and 24 circular pan magazines for the DT machine gun. This resulted in an increase in the vehicle's weight to 3.5 tonnes (3.85 tons), which negatively affected its mobility and speed. Following trials, in 1934 a modified 3P (Load Box) version was produced for the transport of 32 boxes of ammunition with a total weight of 680 kg (1,499 lbs.). Not adopted.

The commander of a T-27 armored carette

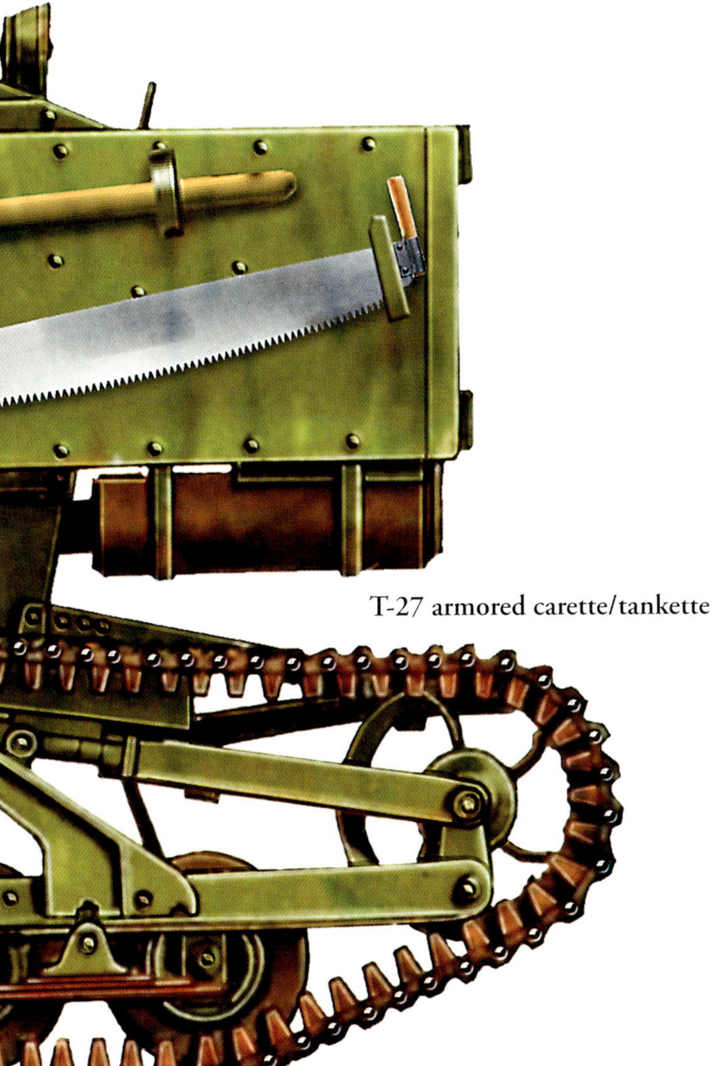

T-27 armored carette/tankette

The driver of a T-27 armored carette

T-27s taking part in a parade in Red Square

NT-27 flamethrower tankette

- **T-27 tractor**. Prime mover for towing 45 mm antitank guns. The armament remained as a rule; however, brackets (handgrips) were welded on to allow the transport of antitank gun crews. On June 1, 1941, there were 182 of these small tractors, some of which were modified during the war.
- **TT-27 with remote control**. A test series of 5 vehicles was built in 1932.
- **KT-27 self-propelled gun** (SU-76). Self-propelled artillery piece mounting a 76 mm regimental cannon to escort cavalry and motorized formations. Developed in 1933–34. Ammunition and gun crew came on a second tankette. This division was not a success. Just three prototypes were built. With the gun, the tankette was overloaded and no longer capable of off-road travel.
- **SU-3 self-propelled gun** with Kurchevsky 76 mm recoilless gun. Developed in 1933. The system did not proceed beyond testing, especially since handling the weapon proved dangerous, its ballistics were unsatisfactory, and the long-exhaust GAZ jet and debris that was thrown up gave away the vehicle's position.
- **T-27PX**. Amphibian tankette with snorkel, waterproofed body, and modified exhaust design. The tank was able to wade water obstacles up to 3 m (9.84 ft.) deep and could remain under water for 30 minutes. One prototype produced in 1934.
- **AC-T-27 airfield tractor** with KAS-2 remote starter system for starting aircraft engines. "Developed" under the leadership of A. Safronov in 1938–39. It was a conversion of the T-27 machine gun carrier.

In the early 1930s, T-27 tankettes were in service with rifle and cavalry divisions and with the newly formed airborne-landing troops. A tankette battalion consisted of one company of light tanks (ten T-26s) and two tankette companies (thirty T-27s). The instructions for tankette battalions within the rifle divisions specified their deployment as follows: "A tankette battalion, the largest administrative-tactical unit, is a powerful shock and armored weapon in the hands of the division commander (sometimes the regimental commander). It is capable of independently carrying out combat missions and tasks on the battlefield in direct cooperation with the infantry. The tankette battalion of a rifle division can be split up into regiments and battalions, especially if the terrain conditions (water, wooded, swampy) do not allow it to be deployed as a single unit or if the infantry's approach requires a dispersed deployment. The battalion may also be attached to an independently operating regiment if this is justified by the situation and the importance of the task assigned to the regiment (covering the division's retreat, bypassing the enemy, flanking operations, or operations in the enemy's rear, etc.)."

By May 1, 1933, the Red Army had formed twenty-three independent tankette battalions and twenty-seven tankette companies.

In central Asia, T-27 units were successfully deployed to combat the Basmachs, who revolted against Soviet-Bolshevik foreign rule and oppression. On the other hand, they proved to be less suitable for delaying and retreating operations.

The tankette suffered from the following shortcomings and weaknesses:

- limited effective area (range of traverse 16°)
- poor communications between tankettes and infantry because of poor field of view / observation and the difficulty of installing a radio set
- severe impairment of the crew, caused by loud engine noises and heat buildup in the fighting compartment, movements while driving (shaking), and restricted view; difficult to maintain in the field

For these reasons, in the second half of the 1930s the tankettes were gradually withdrawn from the field units and replaced by T-26 light tanks and T-37A or T-38 amphibious tanks.

Variant of the T-27 armed with a cannon

The T-37A light amphibious tank was developed in 1932 in the design office of Automobile Factory No. 2 of the All-Union Automobile Industry Association (VATO), on the basis of the previously designed T-41 and T-37 amphibious tanks and the British Vickers amphibious armored car. Even before the prototype was completed, the T-37A was adopted into the Red Army by decree of the Council of Labor and Defense on August 11, 1932. The light amphibious armored car had a riveted (or welded), sealed hull made of rolled armor plates. The transmission was located in the forward part of the hull, and the fighting compartment and driver's compartment were combined; the driver sat on the left and the commander on the right, facing in the direction of travel. The Ford AA truck engine was located at the rear of the vehicle on the longitudinal axis. Floats filled with cork were attached to the left and right above the track shields as buoyancy aids in the water. Propulsion and steering in the water were provided by a propeller screw and a rudder connected to the steering wheel. The reversible propeller blades made it possible to travel in reverse. On land, the T-37A could negotiate inclines of up to 35°, trenches up to 1.4 m (4.6 ft.) wide, and walls up to 0.6 m (1.9 ft.) high.

T-27 tankette captured by the Germans in 1941

T-27 tankette armed with a machine gun, side view

T-37A Light Amphibious Tank T-37A

The T-37A was built from 1932 to 1936, with a total of 2,677 examples being produced, of which 1,909 had cast hulls and 643 welded hulls. Seventy-five T-37As were converted into flamethrower tanks (so-called "chemical" tanks).

Until 1936, the independent tank and tankette battalions of the rifle and territorial rifle divisions were subject to different structures and numbers of tanks:

- no. 04/222: 32 T-26s, 3 T-37As
- no. 04/223: 9 T-26s, 28 T-37As
- no. 04/218: 10 T-26s, 33 T-37As
- no. 4/424: 13 T-26s, 19 T-37As
- no. 4/424: 11 T-26s, 22 T-37As

In addition, the following units of the rifle divisions were equipped with T-37As:

- tank battalions of rifle regiments of the shock divisions (no. 04/496: 34 T-37As)
- tankette companies of the rifle divisions of the territorial rifle divisions "B" (no. 5/431: 10 T-37As)
- tankette companies of the mountain division (no. 04/219: 10 T-37s)
- tankette companies of the independent territorial rifle regiments (no. 5/455: 10 T-37As)

In 1935 the T-37A underwent a modernization program to improve its driving characteristics and became the T-38. It was lower and wider, which improved its stability in the water. The improved suspension brought improved rolling and driving behavior on land and allowed higher speeds.

Instead of a differential gearbox, the T-38 was equipped with clutch steering. In addition, the hull was manufactured using mainly the welding process. In February 1936, the Red Army adopted the T-38, which remained in production until 1939. In addition to the standard model, the following modified versions were built:

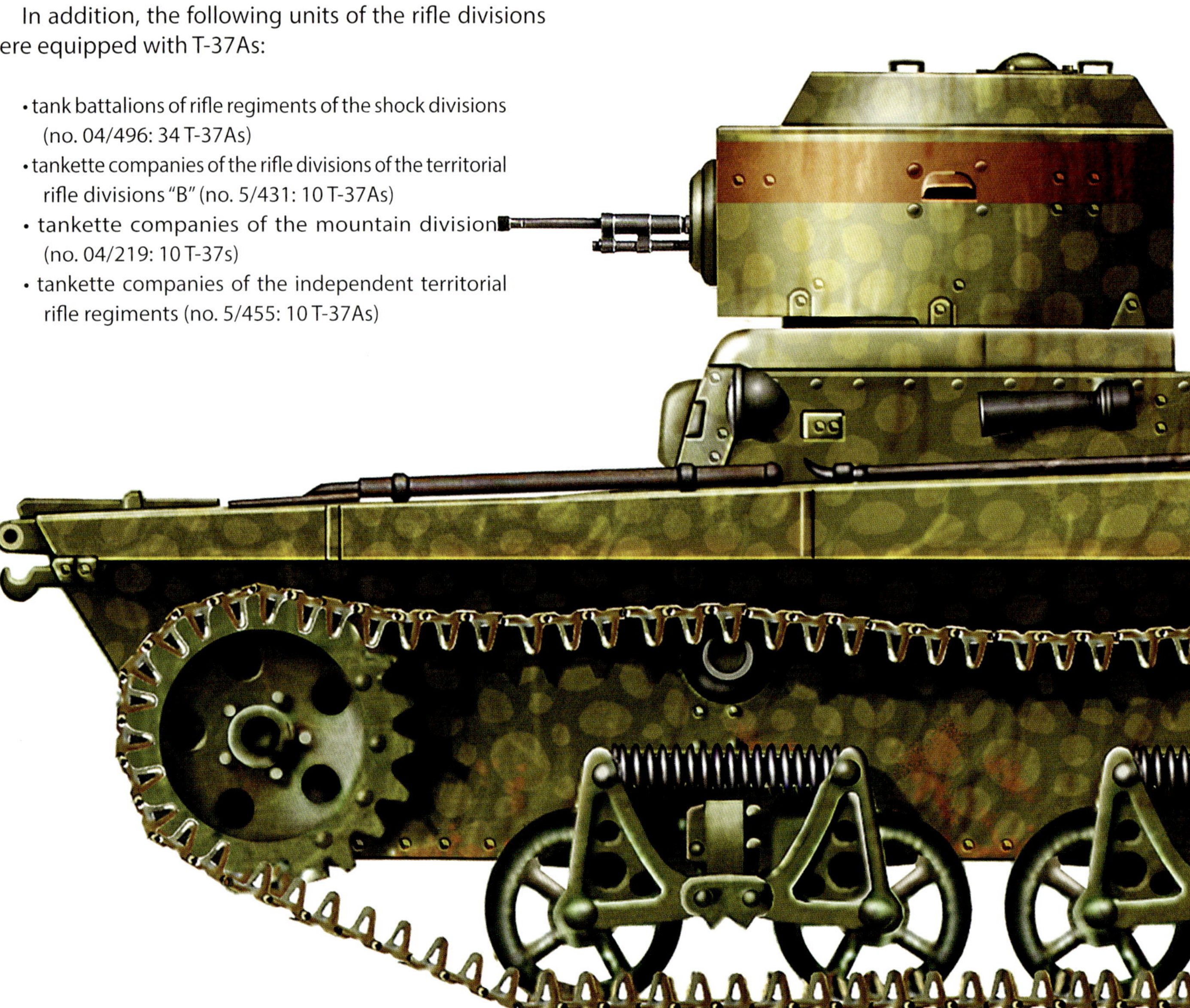

- T-38RT: radio tank with a 71-TK-1 radio set (1937), 165 vehicles
- T-38M-1: experimental vehicle (1938) with a load capacity increased by 600 kg (1,322 lbs.), a new suspension, and a new engine
- T-38M-2: experimental vehicle (1938) similar to the T-38M-1, but with a load capacity increased by just 450 kg (992 lbs.) and a different suspension
- T-38M: improved version (1938) with T-38M-1 hull, T-38M-2 suspension, and improved turret; about 15 vehicles were built
- T-38SN: experimental vehicle with a TNSh-20 20 mm cannon; 2 vehicles built

By the time production ended in 1939, 1,175 T-38s, 165 T-38RTs, and 12 T-38Ms had been built (two T-38M-1 and T-38M-2 prototypes as well as ten T-38Ms).

T-37A amphibious light tank, right side

T-37A, rear view

T-37A crossing a body of water

T-37A light amphibious tank

T-37As lined up for the parade marking the end of the maneuvers in the Kiev Military District in 1935

T-38 Light Amphibious Tank

After all three companies of the independent armored battalions of the rifle divisions were reequipped with T-26s, their T-37As and T-38s were transferred to the tank companies of the independent reconnaissance battalions. According to table of organization 04/400 of April 5, 1941, the amphibious companies were organized as follows:

- staff (company commander, deputy company commander, deputy company commander for political matters, deputy company commander for technical matters, sergeant major, leader of the maintenance platoon, T-38 with 71-TK radio set)
- 3 tank platoons each with a platoon leader, four tank commanders, 5 technical NCOs (1 of them a radio operator), 5 T-38s (1 with a 71-TK radio set)

The company was to comprise a total of thirty-six men and sixteen T-38s. In addition to an amphibious tank company, the battalion had a motorized rifle company (three rifle platoons, each with three rifle squads and one mortar squad) and a tank company (three platoons of medium tanks, each with three vehicles, plus an armored vehicle for the company commander).

As part of the reduced rifle division as per table of organization 4/120, there was an independent reconnaissance battalion No. 4/126, in which the amphibious tank company included a platoon of T-38s (T-40s) with three vehicles (one with a 71-TK radio set).

The infantry of the Red Army also included two other types of rifle units—the so-called Eastern and the Three Thousand divisions. The "Eastern" divisions belonged to Army Group Far East and had (according to table of organization 5/25) a reconnaissance battalion with a T-38 amphibious tank company. These units were largely similar to the amphibious tank companies of the tank divisions (No. 4/100) but were additionally equipped with a car and a type A repair unit on a GAZ-AAA truck (four men). Furthermore, there was no deputy company commander.

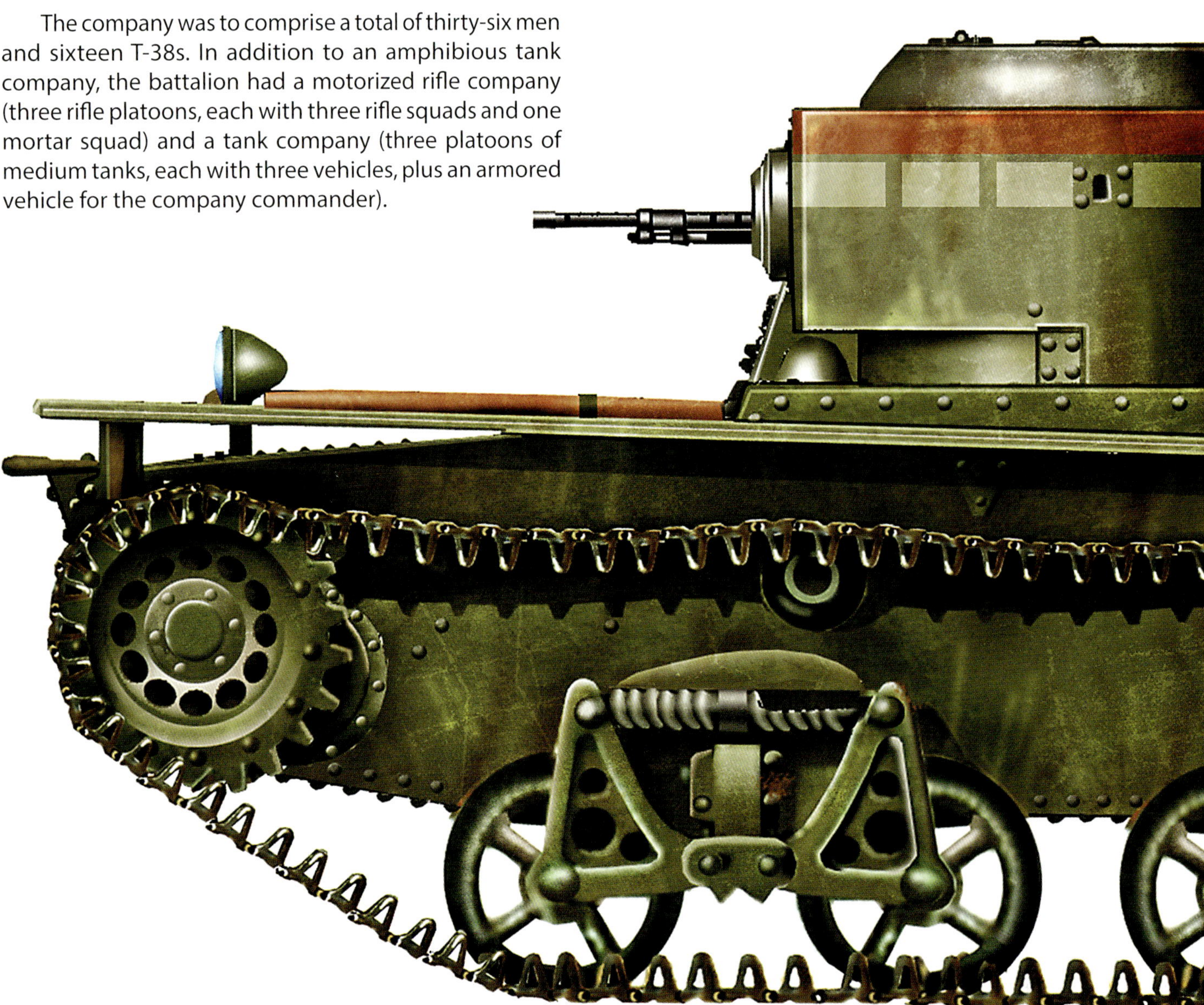

T-38, frontal view

The "Three Thousand" divisions also had their own reduced-strength (seventy-seven men) reconnaissance battalion (No. 5/56), which included an amphibious tank company (three T-38s).

The other vehicles acquired from Great Britain included the 6-tonne (6.6 ton) Vickers Mk. A (not to be confused with the Tank Mk. A; see above), which met almost all the Red Army's requirements for a light tank. The purchase was facilitated by the fact that, in addition to fifteen vehicles, Vickers also supplied the technical documentation required for their manufacture and undertook to inform the Soviet side of all design improvements within three years. In the USSR, the Vickers 6-tonner was originally designated the B-26. Three vehicles underwent trials in the Moscow region from December 24, 1930, to January

T-38, rear view showing the amphibious tank's propeller and rudder

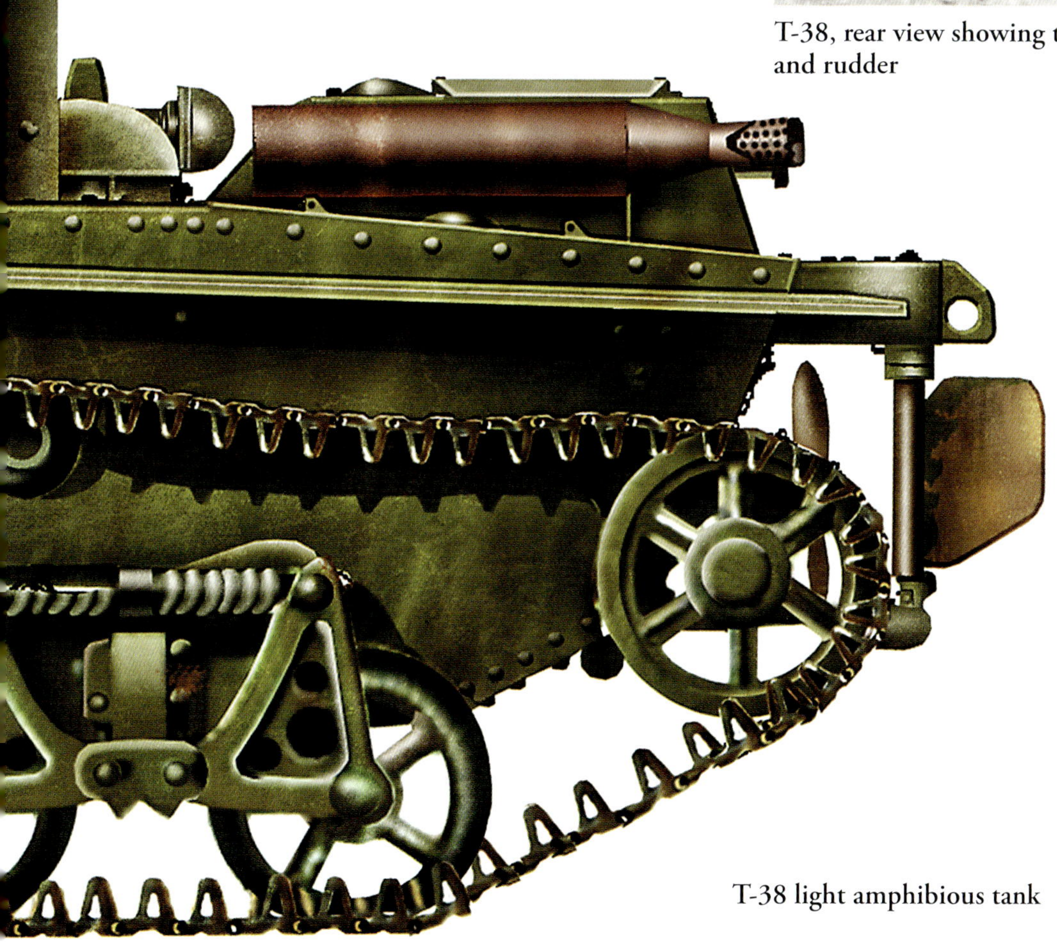

T-38 light amphibious tank

T-38 in the water

T-38 after crossing a water obstacle

T-38s prior to the start of maneuvers by the Moscow Military District in 1937

5, 1931. On January 8 and 11, the vehicles were demonstrated to the Red Army leadership, where they made a good impression. It is interesting to note the opinion of the later Marshal Mikhail Tukhachevsky, deputy people's commissar for armaments: "With regard to the British Vickers tank, which I recently inspected, I found it excellently suited to the task of accompanying infantry during attacks on enemy trenches. . . . The side-by-side arrangement of the turrets is very advantageous, so that when crossing trenches the tank can develop a strong side fire against which the trench parapet provides no protection."

The advantages of the Vickers also included the reliability and simplicity of its transmission and running gear, its relatively high cruising speed and mobility, the outstanding view from the tank, and the shape of its hull, which was easy to manufacture. Criticisms included its insufficiently powerful engine and poor access to the engine and transmission.

They also recognized the time and costs that could be saved by adopting the model, especially since it was well suited to complement other Soviet tanks. But these ideas were clouded. Soviet intelligence had learned that Poland had also acquired the Vickers tank and at the end of 1931 was given the opportunity to produce three hundred Vickers tanks with Anglo-French support, which would give the Polish armored force an advantage over the Soviet one. The Revolutionary Military Council of the USSR urged swift action and had the adoption of the B-26 in its current form examined. On February 13, 1931, the Red Army adopted the B-26 as the "main tank for escorting mixed units and formations as well as the armored and mechanized formations of the High Command Reserve" under the designation T-26.

T-26 Light Tank

The layout of the tank was the same as that of the British prototype: the driver's compartment was in the right front, the fighting compartment in the middle, the engine compartment in the rear. The hull with armored box originally consisted of armored plates with thicknesses of 6–10 mm (0.24–0.4 in.). From the second half of 1932, 13 mm (0.54 in.) plates were used. Two cylindrical turrets for DT machine guns were installed above the armored box in the fighting compartment. One of the turrets could optionally be fitted with a 37 mm gun. The engine compartment housed an air-cooled, 90 hp, four-cylinder carburetor engine. The suspension consisted of leaf springs; four return rollers on each side supported the cast steel tracks; the drive sprockets were at the front, the idler wheels at the rear. Once again, the Bolshevik Factory received the order for series production, although the Stalingrad Tractor Factory (STZ), which was still under construction, had also already been notified. It was originally planned to produce five hundred T-26s in 1931, which was later corrected downward to three hundred units, but even this number proved unattainable. Ultimately the "Bolsheviks" were able to deliver only 120 vehicles in 1931. The military was unable to accept or reject any of these, however. At the end of 1932, the Defense Committee (KO) of the Council of People's Commissars (SNK) of the USSR discussed the production of the T-26 and BT tanks. For the meeting on October 3, 1932, the head of the Military Inspectorate of the People's Commissariat (NK RKI), N. V. Kuibishev, prepared a memorandum that critically examined the output and production of these vehicles:

BT Tank ("Christie")

On September 1, the KhPZ delivered seventy-six tanks instead of nine hundred, according to the original plan of the People's Commissariat of Heavy Industry (NKTP), and 482 according to the adjusted one. Of the seventy-six

T-26 tank, view from the right front with hatches open

tanks, fifty-five were manufactured in August. The quality of the supplied BT vehicles was poor. All vehicles went to military units as training vehicles. The quality of the vehicles reflected the lack of a technological process for the heat treatment of BT parts at KhPZ. For example, in the vehicles manufactured in May, twisting of the drive shaft and chipping of the gear teeth in the transmission, as well as jamming of the splines, were noted. According to the available data from military exercises, all the abovementioned defects also occurred in the tanks manufactured in August. On the first day of the maneuvers, half the vehicles were out of action, and after the fourth day of the exercise (travel distance of 250–300 km [155–186 mi.]), only seven of twenty-eight vehicles were still serviceable.

T-26 Tank ("Vickers")

By September 1, the Voroshilov Factory produced just 362 T-26s instead of the planned 1,660 specified in the original NKTP plan, and 1,200 according to the adjusted plan. At the same time, nineteen were delivered as training vehicles and twenty-two without turrets. Of the total number of 362 vehicles, 121 units were produced in August. For September, the NKTP set a program to produce 200 vehicles instead of 450 as per the original plan. The memorandum contains the following information on the provision of construction and vehicle parts by main assemblies:

T-26 Light Tank

T-26 command tank with frame antenna

The engine of this T-26 with two turrets failed while fording a water obstacle. Here the crew is abandoning the vehicle.

Armor

On September 1, the main factories achieved the following increase in the production of armor steel: Izhora, by 38 percent of the NKTP plan (for tank hulls), Mariupol, by 25.6 percent. Only because of the major delay in tank production does the supply of armor not represent a "bottleneck" in tank construction today.

The development of tank construction initially depends primarily on the production of armor steel. Because of the serious delay in the production of steel alloys, especially nickel and molybdenum, the manufacture of alloyed armor steels (molybdenum, "Vibrak") was interrupted. The armor steel hardened and tempered with carbon did not live up to expectations, and almost 100 percent of production was rejected. Tank production therefore underwent a crisis from May to July. Lately the Izhora and Mariupol factories have completely switched to the production of new types of steel: Izhora to PI chrome-kiesel-manganese steel, and Mariupol to MI two-layer manganese steel, for which no expensive imported ferroalloys (nickel and molybdenum) and a long and expensive tempering process are required. The production of chrome silicon and manganese armor steel, which require no expensive special equipment, can be carried out by any steel mill with experience in the production of high-grade steels.

T-26s with twin turrets while on maneuvers

Ball Bearings

The 1932 tank program relied mainly on imported ball bearings. Domestic production covered no more than 10 to 15 percent of the total requirement. In terms of cost, the most-complex and -expensive ball bearings are exclusively imported. An order for 2,725,000 rubles for the tank program has not yet been completely filled.

Electrical Equipment

The requirement for electrics for the tank program was met exclusively by imports. As per resolution no. 27/SS of the NKTP, of February 10, 1932, it was resolved that as of the third quarter of this year, a program to produce electrical equipment for the tank program would begin in the Elektrozavod Factory. Elektrozavod has not yet begun the mass production of electrical equipment and devices for tanks. At present, Elektrozavod is building ten prototypes of automatic solenoid switches (type A), mass production of which has been postponed until 1933. Elektrozavod has not yet begun the construction of prototypes of the Scintilla SS solenoid switch, which is superior to the type A. Prototypes of generators and a starter for the BT tank were produced and temporarily approved for installation in the BT and T-26 vehicles. The starter for the T-26 is still in the experimental stage.

Engines

The T-26 production program is based on engines produced in the Voroshilov Factory. The 1932 production program for the fast BT tank is based on American Liberty engines and M-5 engines from aviation. The Krasny Oktyabr of the VOAO and Aviaremtest factories repaired about 500 engines by September 1. Because of the lagging production of parts necessary for recycling the engines (piston rings, pistons, crankshaft gears), the repair of engines was carried out by cannibalizing several engines, which of course is pure waste. The production of spare parts for the M-5 Liberty engine is not yet secured. At an NKTP meeting on July 4 of this year, Leningrad industry was given targets to ensure the production of spare parts for this engine, but as yet they have not been met.

Interestingly, the above document also raised the question of creating a special umbrella organization for the companies involved in tank production and a tank research institute. At the beginning of the 1930s, this idea still failed to fall on fertile ground. It did not become a reality until 1941, in the form of the People's Commissariat of the Tank Industry.

The shortcomings described above clearly show the difficulties encountered by Soviet industry during the development of the quantity production of armored vehicles. When this crisis was overcome, output rose and the quality of the vehicles improved.

A total of 11,218 T-26s were built from 1931 to 1941 in the following production variants:

- T-26 Model 1931: 2 turrets and machine gun armament
- T-26 Model 1932: 2 turrets with cannon and machine gun armament (37 mm cannon in one turret and a machine gun in the other)

- T-26 Model 1933: single cylindrical turret with 45 mm gun; the was the version built in the largest numbers
- T-26 Model 1938: conical turret and welded hull
- T-26 Model 1939: variant of the Model 1938, with thicker armor and improved conical turret; under-turret box with sloped armored plates
- T-26RT: command tank with cylindrical turret and 71-TK-1 radio set (from 1933)
- T-26TU (T-26TU-132): recovery tank; 65 vehicles produced
- T-26TT (T-26TT-131): recovery tank; 65 vehicles produced
- T-26A: artillery tank with new, more spacious T-26-4 turret and a short-barreled 76 mm tank gun; 6 prototypes built
- XT-26: flamethrower tank, with left turret removed to make room for flame oil tank, and projector in the right turret; 552 vehicles produced and 53 converted from T-26s with two turrets
- XT-130: flamethrower tank based on the Model 1933, with flamethrower instead of cannon in the cylindrical turret; 401 vehicles produced
- XT-133: flamethrower tank based on the Model 1938, with flamethrower in conical turret; 269 vehicles produced
- XT-134: flamethrower tank based on the Model 1939, armed with a 45 mm 20LK tank gun Model 1932/38, flamethrower in the hull, and 2 DT machine guns; 2 prototypes built
- T-26T ("T-26 tractor"): prime mover for artillery with canvas top, with 151 vehicles converted from tanks with two turrets; a further 50 vehicles were converted by 1941
- T-26T artillery tractor with armored top; ten single-turret tanks were converted
- The T-26s made in the late 1930s were fitted with 20 mm armor, the 45 mm Model 1938 gun, and a conical welded turret; 1,975 vehicles were produced

In his report titled "On the System of Armored Weapons for the Second Five-Year Plan" to chairman of the Defense Committee V. M. Molotov on July 16, 1933, the People's Commissar for Military Affairs Voroshilov reported on the successful implementation of the first stage of the plan to "equip the Red Army with armored vehicles":

A T-26 Model 1933 photographed after being knocked out by the Germans in 1941

T-26s with twin turrets during maneuvers

The success of socialist development guarantees the creation of our own aircraft, tractor, and tank fleets, and the first five-year plan turned the Red Army from a backward army with respect to mechanization into an advanced army, which in terms of the number and quality of combat vehicles is in no way inferior to the most powerful capitalist army.

Tank Construction in 1933

Collectively, our successes in mechanizing the Red Army up to May 1, 1933, are listed in the following table:

Number of Armored Vehicles in the Red Army up to May 1, 1933

T-27	2,430	BT	710
T-37	50	T-24	25
T-18	950	T-28	12
T-26	1,550	T-35	2
Total	**5,729**		

Assessment:

This is proof of the extraordinary success of our Soviet technology and production. On January 1, 1929, the Red Army had just ninety obsolete foreign-made tanks and several dozen T-18s. With respect to their fighting qualities, the current types of tanks in service with the Red Army can be compared only with the best foreign types. In terms of their individual characteristics, not only are they not inferior, but in some categories are even clearly superior. With regard to the actual number of fighting vehicles available, the Red Army is in first place.

As of May 1, the Red Army had 5,600 tanks, of which 4,800 are quite modern types, while the six most-important capitalist states together can muster no more than 3,000 to 4,000 modern tanks. The mobilization capabilities of Great Britain, France, and America are, however, greater than ours. This presents us with the most important task of achieving a similar level of mobilization and production, which in time of emergency can immediately provide us with the necessary quantities of vehicles.

Objectives for the Second Five-Year Plan

Our most-important strategic targets for the development and employment of mechanized forces. The rapid growth of the national economy of the USSR created the conditions for us to concentrate on the most comprehensive mechanization of the Red Army and at the same time make up for any failures of the first five-year plan. The second five-year plan will elevate mechanization to one of the most important and decisive fundamentals for future operations by the Red Army. This results in the following requirements:

The best, most powerful, and fastest tanks must be assigned to heavily mechanized units of operational and strategic importance (mechanized brigades and mechanized corps).

The high command should have a powerful reserve of tanks (quantitative and qualitative) to ensure the creation of absolute tank superiority over the enemy.

The strategic cavalry, which will retain its importance, must be equipped with mechanical means and self-propelled artillery.

Mixed units (divisions and regiments) must have their own mechanized units both for reconnaissance and combat.

On the basis of these requirements, the following main types of combat vehicles must be in mass production in the coming years:

(1) Reconnaissance tank (T-37 amphibious tank). It forms the core of the combat support troops of all mechanized formations as a means of combat reconnaissance and infantry support. Basic requirements: high speed, off-road capability (including deepwater-wading capability), mobility, small overall dimensions, low production costs, and suitability for mass production.

(2) Tank for mixed units (T-26). It forms the main type of tank of the mixed units and is also suitable for the numerical reinforcement of the High Command Reserve. The main requirements are mobility on the battlefield, armor protection against armor-piercing small-arms bullets, ability to accommodate a variety of weapons (cannon, machine guns, flamethrowers, chemical equipment), cost-effective production, and suitability for mass production.

(3) Tank for operational purposes (BT tank, hereinafter PT-1). Vehicle for independent mechanized units. Its most-important features are high speed, cross-country mobility (including wading capability), and powerful armament.

(4) Medium tank (tank for the High Command reserve; T-28). Basic requirements: powerful armament and armor as well as a speed that allows it to operate with mechanized units.

(5) Heavy tank for special purposes (the T-35 is a suitable model). Suitable for breaking through heavily fortified positions. The main requirements are powerful armament and armor that protects against small-caliber guns.

On the basis of the above, the Revolutionary Military Council of the USSR approved the following classification:

1. Tanks, five types: (a) T-37 for reconnaissance, (b) T-26 for mixed formations, (c) BT for operational purposes, hereinafter PT-1, (d) T-28 as medium tank to reinforce the Reserve of the High Command, (e) T-35 as heavy tank for special tasks
2. Special tanks for support roles, seven types (on the standard chassis of the types listed above: (a) flamethrower tank, (b) combat engineer tank, (c) self-propelled artillery, (d) radio tank
3. Armored wheeled vehicles: two types (on the Ford A and Ford AA chassis: (a) reconnaissance, (b) combat
4. Armored vehicles capable of operating on rails, two types: (a) tank, (b) armored car
5. Tractors, three types: (a) STS-2 light fast tractor, (b) Kommunar heavy fast tractor, (c) Stalinets heavy artillery tractor
6. Transporters, two types: (a) munitions transporter for the battlefield (standard chassis of the reconnaissance tank), (b) infantry transporter (on light tractor chassis)
7. Transport vehicles (in mass production as three-axle and half-track vehicles): (a) Ford A, (b) Ford AA, (c) AMO-5, (d) Ja 5

In its resolution no. 71cc/o, of August 13, 1933, the Labor and Defense Council approved the "Classification of the Red Army's Armored Weapons for the Second Five-Year Plan" submitted by Voroshilov.

The system required the development of new organizational structures for motorized and mechanized troops (in 1934 they were given the new designation "automobile and tank troops"). There were different views on this. Red Army chief of staff Boris Mikhailovich Shaposhnikov considered it most expedient to divide tanks into separate regiments and battalions to support infantry and cavalry. (This is what the French did, dividing their more than three thousand armored fighting vehicles mainly into independent battalions for infantry support). The deputy chief of staff of the Red Army, V. K. Triandafillov, and the inspector of motorized and mechanized troops, K. B. Kalinovski, objected: "To see tank units only as auxiliary weapons for cavalry or infantry means not to use their tactical and operational mobility. The combat characteristics of tanks must be fully exploited, and this is possible only in independent mechanized formations with roughly the same degree of mobility. Without abandoning tanks to support other types of weapons, it is therefore necessary to create special mechanized formations that can make full use of all the positive characteristics of the tank (speed, firepower, striking power)."

M. N. Tukhachevsky stated that tanks should not remain only a reserve force of the High Command (RGK); they must be introduced into not only the cavalry divisions, but also into the rifle divisions. Furthermore, he advocated the formation of shock divisions into three tank regiments (fifty tanks and thirty armored troop carriers each), a self-propelled or motorized artillery regiment (thirty guns) and an aviation group (thirty R-5 aircraft).

Because the Supreme Command of the Red Army could not agree on the future role and organization of tank units, the Revolutionary Military Council set up a commission headed by S. S. Kamenev, which discussed the various points of view and then came to the following disposition:

(A) Mechanized (tank) units, which could operate both independently and separately from the main forces of the army and in cooperation with them
(B) Tank units of the RGK to reinforce breakthrough operations
(C) Tank units as part of mixed formation, which play a supporting role in all types of combat

To test the theory in practice, the Revolutionary Military Council passed a resolution on June 17, 1929, with the following wording: "In view of the fact that a new type of weapon, which is the armored troops, has not been sufficiently studied both in terms of its tactical use (independently or jointly with infantry and cavalry) and in terms of the most advantageous form of organization, . . . a mechanized experimental force must take on this task in 1929–1930." A month later, the document was approved by the Central Committee of the All-Union Communist Party of Bolsheviks, which at the same time set a minimum number of 3,500 armored vehicles to be produced for the first five-year plan. As a result, a mechanized regiment was created for experimental purposes, with the following structure:

- headquarters and staff
- political section (commissars)
- 1 battalion of armored wheeled vehicles (3 platoons, each with 3 BA-27s)
- 1 battalion of tanks (command and recovery platoon, 2 tank companies of 3 platoons (10 MS-1s per company), and a motorized gun platoon with 2 cannon)
- 1 rifle and machine gun battalion (two motorized rifle companies, one machine gun company, and a mechanized gun platoon with two cannon)
- support units (supply and rations, combat engineers, medical personnel, repairs)

The BA-27 medium armored car was the first armored vehicle produced in quantity in the USSR. The design came from A. Roshkov, a permanent member of the Red Army Artillery Committee. It was based on a 1.5-tonne (1.65 ton) AMO F-15, which the AMO Factory in Moscow began producing in 1924. Design work proceeded quickly, especially since the Red Army urgently needed a replacement for its outdated fleet of wheeled armored vehicles. The design order was placed at the beginning of 1927, and tests were carried out in the summer, with the AMO F-15SP chassis modified to accommodate an armored superstructure. At the beginning of 1928, the Izhora plant delivered the superstructure to Moscow; assembly was completed in March and testing of the armored car began. After its successful completion on December 19, 1929, the vehicle was adopted by the Red Army as BA-27 (Armored Automobile Model 1927) by order no. 413/84 of the Revolutionary Military Council.

BA-27 Armored Car

The BA-27 was built in series by the Izhora factory; the chassis were supplied by the Moscow AMO Factory, which produced the F-15 truck. By the time production was discontinued in 1931, 215 vehicles had been built. In contrast to the AMO truck, the BA-27 had a second driver's seat in the rear in addition to the driver's compartment directly behind the engine. However, this was abandoned to simplify the technology and save one crew member. The fighting compartment was offset to the rear, toward the rear axle. The hexagonal turret accommodated a 37 mm Hotchkiss gun and a 7.62 mm DT machine gun. The superstructure consisted of riveted, 4–7 mm (0.16–0.28 in.) thick armor plates. The crew consisted of three men. In the mid-1930s, at least thirty-five BA-27s were made suitable for railroad use. These BA-27ShDs could be placed on rails by using a jack with a rotating device. Also, in the second half of the 1930s, Tank Repair Factory No. 2 placed BA-27 superstructures on the three-axle chassis of the GAZ-AAA truck. Designated the BA-27M, this three-axle version exhibited better off-road capability (climbing ability of 23° instead of the previous 15°) and, thanks to its more powerful GAZ engine and larger fuel tank, also had a higher cruising speed and greater range. In August 1929, a mechanized regiment equipped with MS-1s and BA-27s carried out operational exercises. It succeeded in breaking through the "enemy front" and smashed several "enemy strongpoints" in the rear. In September 1929, the regiment moved to the White Russian Military District for joint exercises with the 1st Cavalry Special Brigade. This was the first time that a mechanized cavalry group was formed as part of a cavalry brigade and a mechanized regiment. As a result, the RKKA decided to create a mechanized brigade based on a mechanized regiment. In May 1930, the experimental mechanized regiment was expanded into the 1st Mechanized Experimental Brigade. In the years 1930–32, the experimental unit developed operational-tactical procedures for the use of armored units and improved their structure. Initially, the brigade consisted of

- brigade headquarters/staff;
- political section;
- 1 armored regiment (2 battalions each of 3 companies), 10 MS-1s per company;
- 1 light (reconnaissance) regiment (rifle and machine gun battalion, armored car battalion, antiaircraft company, artillery battalion);
- 1 rifle battalion (2 rifle companies and 1 machine gun company);
- 1 artillery battalion (two batteries); and
- 1 supply and support units (maintenance, medical services, rations etc.).

BA-27 armored cars during a parade in Red Square

BA-27 armored car

The brigade's authorized strength was 2,160 officers, NCOs, and men; 60 MS-1s; 12 BA-27s; 6 76.2 mm and 6 122 mm guns; 300 vehicles; 16 tractors; and 61 motorcycles.

Maneuvers in 1930 and 1931 revealed considerable shortcomings in unit structure and armament: the brigade proved itself to be too weak to carry out independent combat assignments. The MS-1 (T-18) had insufficient mobility and firepower. The brigade was therefore reorganized in spring 1931. The restructuring was based on the demand of the Revolutionary Military Council of the USSR: "Creation of a highly mobile and efficient mechanized unit that can act as a mobile long-range combat group of an army and has the necessary means to carry out independent operational tasks in isolation from the main forces of the army."

The brigade's new organizational structure comprised four main elements:

- 1 shock group of 3 tank battalions (each with 3 companies of T-26s, 1 company of T-27s, and 1 battery of self-propelled artillery)
- 1 artillery battalion of 3 batteries
- 1 reconnaissance battalion, 1 machine gun battalion, 1 antitank battalion (3 companies of BTs), 1 combat engineer battalion, 1 chemical warfare company, and 1 antiaircraft machine gun company
- supply and repair units
- Furthermore, a political section (political commissars), an air liaison squadron, rations, and medical units were added.

With T-26s and T-27s, BT-2s, and BA-27s, the brigade received the most-modern armored vehicles then available and possessed increased striking power. It had, after all, 178 T-26s, 32 BT-2s, 91 T-27s, 48 BA-27s, 39 76.2 mm guns, 7 antiaircraft guns, 7 antiaircraft machine guns (four-barreled), and 600 soft-skinned vehicles of all types. Its authorized personnel strength was 3,752 men.

In 1932, the Red Army formed five more independent mechanized brigades following the example of the 1st Mechanized Brigade. At the same time, smaller armored units were formed, as well as four tank regiments of three battalions each to reinforce troops at breakthrough points of the main attack: the first in Smolensk, the second in Leningrad, the third in Moscow, and the fourth in Kharkov. Three independent territorial tank battalions were also formed.

To increase the striking power of the cavalry, in the early 1930s the Red Army also formed two mechanized regiments, two mechanized battalions, and two mechanized squadrons. The mechanized regiments of the cavalry divisions were structured as follows, in accordance with table of organization 06/515 approved on May 14, 1935:

1. Organization

I. Regimental headquarters

II. Units of the regimental headquarters

III. Regimental battalions

A. BT tank squadron (3 per regiment)

B. T-37 tank squadron (2 per regiment)

C. Battery of armored artillery

IV. Support units

2. Personnel

Regimental command: 44

Officers: 48

NCOs: 286

Enlisted men: 165

Total: 543

3. Equipment

BTs: 43

Armored artillery vehicles: 4

T-37s: 26

Flamethrower tanks (BKhM): 5

Lightly armored vehicles: 3

Radio sets: 5 AK 1s

Antiaircraft machine guns (four-barreled): 3

Transport vehicles:

Cars: 4

Trucks: 32

Special vehicles: 19

Workshop trucks: 9

Tractors: 7

Motorcycles: 12

Field kitchens (trailers): 4

Mobile showers: 1

Disinfection chambers: 1

At the end of 1930, independent tankette battalions and, in 1933, independent tank divisions were established in the rifle divisions to replace the motorized battalions (armored reconnaissance battalion, cavalry squadron, artillery battery, support and maintenance units) that had existed in only some divisions since 1930. Until 1935, the tank battalions in the rifle and territorial rifle divisions had varying structures and strengths:

Table of organization 04/222: thirty-two T-26s, three T-37s
Table of organization 04/223: nine T-26s, twenty-eight T-37s
Table of organization 04/218: ten T-26s, thirty-three T-37s
Table of organization 4/424: thirteen T-26s, nineteen T-37s
Table of organization 5/424: eleven T-26s, twenty-two T-37s

In 1935 the striking power of the tank battalion was increased by equipping them all with the T-26. The battalion had the following organization:

- headquarters/staff
- 2 to 3 tank companies, each with 3 platoons of 5 T-26s
- support and supply units (repair, flamethrower, and combat engineer platoons)

Personnel Breakdown of the Tank Battalion of the Rifle Division as per Organization 4/628:

headquarters: 2

officers: 24

NCOs: 125

enlisted men: 104

total: 275

T-26 (command tanks): 14

T-26: 18

T-26 (transport tanks): 2

BKhM-3 (flamethrower tanks): 3

BKhM-4 (flamethrower tanks): 2

FAI (scout cars): 3

GAZ-AAA (truck): 1

recovery/crane truck: 1

tanker trucks: 3

GAZ-AA (truck): 4

GAZ-AA (ambulance): 1

GAZ-A (car): 2

SIS-5 (cars): 5

type B workshops: 1

type A workshops: 3

ZIS-6 (tanker trucks): 3

tractors: 7

motorcycles: 4

This organization of the tank battalion of a rifle division offered the possibility, if necessary, to support the attack by the rifle battalions with a tank company. The developments in the tank forces as well as in the artillery, airborne, and engineer troops and in the Red Army's aviation caused a change in military strategies and combat tactics in the High Command. The new equipment and organization enabled not only the tactical penetration of the enemy's defenses, but also the expansion and extension of tactical successes into in-depth operational successes. This led to the development of the theory of deep battle, which made the Red Army less focused on defense and more on attack.

BA-27 armored car, view from the right front

However, the theory of a deep operation at army and front level (army groups) also encompassed the defensive. It was essentially about the cooperation of large army, navy, and air force units to defeat the enemy on a broad front and to expand tactical and operational successes as far as possible. Armies operated as part of an army group. Normally, an army was given specific operational objectives and a main direction of attack. The army group drew its striking power in the center of the offensive from well-equipped shock armies, with armies of "ordinary composition" operating on the flanks. A deep battle comprised several phases: The breakthrough through the tactical defense (positional systems) was to be achieved by the combined deployment of infantry, tanks, artillery, and airpower. This tactical success was to be extended operationally by the combined thrust with airborne units as well as motorized infantry and mechanized cavalry through the gap achieved, with bombers and airborne troops destroying the enemy's reserves in the hinterland and weakening his further resistance. In the pursuit, a complete defeat of the enemy in the respective attack area was then to be achieved, and advantageous starting positions gained for subsequent operations.

The first stage was the most important, because no deep battle could take place without first breaking through the tactical defense on a broad level. However, success on a "broad level" could be achieved only through the massive, combined use of infantry, artillery, tanks, and aircraft (several squadrons). The infantry continued to play the most important role, and all other weapons acted in its support. After the breakthrough, it was the

BA-27s and a T-27 armored carette on reconnaissance

turn of the fast troops to surround the enemy, advance in depth, capture key positions, and destroy reserves (airborne and bomber forces).

For a successful breakthrough and deep battle, the "shock group" had to include rifle divisions supported by tanks, highly mobile troops with great striking power (tanks, motorized infantry, mechanized cavalry), and airborne troops and bomber units. In the main direction of attack, so-called shock armies or corps were deployed, which had appropriate combat and sufficient command-and-control resources (radio). Of course, deep battle also required the establishment of air supremacy, sealing off the battlefield from enemy reserves, and the interdiction of enemy supplies.

The deep battle was not tied to one direction of attack. Depending on the situation and the strength/weakness of the enemy, advances in several divergent directions or an approach at various points on the enemy front with diversionary and flanking attacks were possible, or else a wide-ranging outflanking movement.

The Red Army carried out numerous maneuvers in 1931–32 to test the deep-battle theory in practice. These exercises showed that the solution to operational tasks at the army or army group level presupposed the massing of armored forces. This required the creation of forces larger than mechanized brigades.

In March 1932, the Directorate for Mechanization and Motorization (UMM) submitted a report to the Red Army staff on the organizational development of motorized troops. In particular, the report pointed out that although mechanized brigades possessed great striking power, this was not sufficient for the intended purposes. It was therefore necessary to combine mechanized brigades into mechanized corps.

The establishment of mechanized corps was intended to ensure their extensive independence from other units (i.e., they were to be able to engage in all types of combat independently and act autonomously). The corps therefore comprised all types of weaponry: tanks, motorized infantry, artillery, combat engineers, chemical-warfare troops, radio, and telecommunications units, as well as all units required for supplies, provisioning, rations, repairs, and other support.

The corps drew its main striking power from the mechanized brigades, which were capable of carrying out tactical combat missions together or independently of the corps. A rifle and machine gun brigade directly subordinate to the corps was intended to reinforce the mechanized brigades, relieving them of tasks such as mopping up and security and thus contributing to the increase in striking power.

The first mechanized corps, established between 1932 and 1934, had the following organization:

- corps headquarters
- political apparatus
- 1 mechanized brigade of T-26s (3 tank battalions, 1 rifle and machine gun battalion, 1 artillery battalion, 1 combat engineer battalion, and companies for communications (radio/signals units), reconnaissance, and antiaircraft defense (antiaircraft machine guns)
- 1 mechanized brigade with BT tanks (as above)
- 1 rifle and machine gun brigade (3 rifle battalions, 1 artillery battalion, and companies for intelligence, reconnaissance, and engineering, plus a chemical-warfare platoon)
- supply and support units (chemical-warfare battalion, combat engineer battalion, antiaircraft battalion, corps school, repair)

In autumn 1932 the 11th Mechanized Corps was created on the basis of the 11th Rifle Division in the Leningrad Military District. The 45th Rifle Division of the Ukrainian Military District then served as the basis for the formation of the 45th Mechanized Corps.

In 1934 the command of the 11th Mechanized Corps was transferred to the Transbaikal, with one mechanized brigade and subordinate units. The 7th Mechanized Corps was formed on the basis of the two remaining brigades in the Leningrad Military District, and the 5th Mechanized Corps emerged from the 1st mechanized Brigade in the Moscow Military District.

The formation of the corps was put to the test in maneuvers in the years 1932 to 1934. The experiences from these large-scale exercises showed, however, that corps were cumbersome and difficult to command. Inadequate mobility and the recovery and repair of tanks disabled on the battlefield proved to be serious weaknesses. There were too few recovery and repair units. For this reason, the mechanized corps underwent a reorganization in February 1935.

Organization of the Mechanized Corps in the Event of War

Approved by the People's Commissar of Defense of the USSR 01/25/1935.

The NKO had approved a new organization for the mechanized corps, which came into force for the mechanized units on February 20, 1935.

The organization was based on the following:

1. Reduction of size of the corps by disbanding all corps units with the exception of the intelligence section, which was made slightly larger.

Introduction of an independent tank battalion with two BT companies, an intelligence company, and a combat engineer platoon as a corps reserve to defend against flank and rear attacks.

2. The air reconnaissance section was reinforced through the addition of a liaison flight equipped with three U-2s.
3. The corps school was disbanded, and the training of cadets was transferred to the brigades.
4. To standardize the equipment of the corps brigades, the T-26 brigades were equipped with BTs. The mechanized corps thus consisted of two BT brigades and one rifle brigade. This would eliminate the difference in speed, since there was a 30–40 percent difference in speed between different brigades when moving on tracks and up to 100 percent when moving on wheels (BT). At the same time, the operational range of the mechanized corps increased significantly.
5. The structure of the mechanized brigade was standardized, and there were no longer any differences between independent and nonindependent brigades. The brigade consisted of three tank battalions, a reinforced reconnaissance company, an intelligence company, an infantry battalion, and a combat support battalion. This structure increased the brigade's mobility and command capability compared to the past. In addition, the brigade included a recovery company and, in peacetime, a fourth armored battalion for training purposes. This battalion formed the brigade school in peacetime and acted as a reserve unit in wartime to form a fourth company in the tank battalions.
6. An important aspect of the restructuring of mechanized brigades was the reduction of one tank company each. The composition of the platoon was set at three combat vehicles instead of five according to the old structure. This was due to the need to ensure better command and control of the platoons. Fourth reserve tank companies were formed to supply material and compensate for losses in combat.

This meant that the battalion would now have only forty-two armored fighting vehicles, forty of which were in the companies and two in the staff.

In addition, instead of the towed guns of the accompanying artillery, batteries of BT tanks armed with 76 mm guns were introduced, four tanks per battalion. The self-propelled batteries would remain in existence until these artillery tanks were placed in service.

7. The organization of the rifle brigades remained unchanged.

BA-27s prepare for an attack while on maneuvers.

A column of BA-27s of an armored OGPU battalion, 1932

The Total Strength of the Mechanized Corps:

Personnel: 8,200 (6,475 in peacetime)
Armored vehicles:
BT-7A: 24
BT: 310
BT tank destroyers: 8
T-37: 60
BKhM-3: 36
BKhM-4: 18
Total: 456 vehicles
Guns:
122 mm: 4
76 mm: 4
45 mm: 12
DP light machine guns: 144
Heavy machine guns: 48
Cars and trucks: 1,500.

Together with the mechanized corps, tank regiments of the High Command Reserve were also formed. They were intended to provide quantitative and qualitative reinforcement for the mechanized troops operating in the main lines of attack. The first such regiment was set up in Moscow in 1924, followed by the second in Leningrad in 1929. In the following years, four more tank regiments were established in Smolensk, Kiev, Kharkov, and Slutsk, with the delivery of new tanks. The RGK regiments were initially equipped with light tanks of the T-18, T-26, and BT types, and then medium T-28s and heavy T-35s.

The T-28 medium tank was developed by the design bureau of the Allunion Arsenal (VOAO) under S. A. Ginsburg, on the basis of the latest 16-tonne tanks from the Vickers company. The preliminary design was ready by July 23, 1931. UMM concluded an agreement with VOAO on the development of the project, the preparation of design drawings, and the construction of two prototypes of a 16-tonne T-28 tank. The first testing of prototype no. 1 took place on May 29, 1932. On the basis of the test results, the design was corrected, after which the second prototype was built, which became the standard for mass production.

T-28 Medium Tank

The T-28 entered service with the Red Army in August 1933 and was produced at the Krasny Putilovets Factory. The necessary technical documentation arrived in November 1932, and the factory delivered the first batch of twelve vehicles in April 1933. From 1933 to 1940, Krasny Putilovets built 503 T-28s. The three revolving turrets were one of the tank's outstanding features. The large main turret, which could be electrically rotated through 360° along the longitudinal axis of the vehicle, housed a 76.2 mm KT-28 (or PS-3) cannon and two DT machine guns. A PT-1 periscopic sight, a PTK commander's panoramic sight, and a TOP telescopic sight served as aiming and sighting aids. Forward of the main turret were two small turrets armed with machine guns and a traverse range of 220°. The running gear consisted of twelve road wheels arranged in pairs on each side, which in turn were combined into two frames. A shield made of armor plates partially covered the running gear. At the top, the track ran on four rubberized return rollers, and the rear drive wheel had a removable sprocket. This running-gear design gave the vehicle very smooth running and good off-road mobility, especially when the ground pressure was low. The T-28 could negotiate inclines of up to 45°, overcome trenches up to 3.5 m (11.5 ft.) wide, and climb walls up to 1 m (3.3 ft.) high. All T-28s were equipped with 71-TK-1 or 71-TK-3 radios with frame antennas and a Safar onboard intercom system for the six-man crew. The following versions were produced:

- T-28-1: Preproduction model (1932). Armament: Model 1932 37 mm main gun and three DT machine guns.
- T-28 Model 1933: First production version, built in 1933–34. Armament: 76.2 mm KT-28 main gun and 4 DT machine guns. 41 vehicles produced.
- T-28 Model 1934: Main production version, produced from 1934 until 1938. Armament: 76.2 mm KT-28 main gun and 4–5 DT machine guns. A total of 266 vehicles produced.

- T-28 Model 1938: Main production version from 1938 to 1940. Armament: 76.2 mm L-10 main gun and 5 DT machine guns. A total of 131 examples produced.
- T-28 Model 1940: With conical main turret. Armament: 76.2 mm L-10 main gun and 5 DT machine guns. Just 13 examples built.
- T-28E with strengthened armor protection. A total of 111 vehicles upgraded to this standard in 1940.
- T-28A: Fast version of the T-28. By redesigning the final drive and transmission, it was possible to increase cruising speed to 56 kph (35 mph) on roads and 46 kph (28.5 mph) on unpaved roads. Fifty-two vehicles were produced from June to December 1936. Further production was halted because of the planned introduction of the T-29 (T-28 with wheel/track running gear).

T-28 medium tank

T-28s during a parade in Red Square on May 1, 1936

Other vehicles intended for RGK units included the T-35 heavy tank. It was created by the tank design bureau founded in 1931 under N. V. Barykov, the successor to the AVO-5 bureau that had designed the Grote tank. The new design bureau was commissioned by the UMM RKKA to develop and build a new 35-tonne breakthrough tank of the TG type by August 1, 1932.

The vehicle was developed as a multiturret tank based on the earlier T-30 and T-32 heavy-tank projects. The Soviet engineers probably used the design documents of the 34-tonne (37.5 ton) A1E1 Independent tank, built by Vickers in 1929, since this was the only way they could complete the first prototype of the T-35 in record time by August 20, 1932. Some components and features were adopted from the T-28: the driver's compartment was in the front of the tank, the fighting compartment in the middle, and the engine and transmission in the rear. The armament was housed in five turrets on two levels. A 76.2 mm gun and a 7.62 mm DT machine gun were housed in the round turret with 360° of traverse, which towered over all the others. Two 45 mm Model 1932 tank guns were installed in the diagonally arranged turrets below the main turret; they fired to the front right and rear left. The two machine gun turrets were located next to the 45 mm turrets. The main turret was separated from the rest of the fighting compartment by a bulkhead. The front and rear 45 mm side turrets were connected by a corridor, and the driver's compartment was also connected to the fighting compartment via a side hatch in the bulkhead. Propulsion was provided by a liquid-cooled M-17T twelve-cylinder carburetor engine producing 500 hp. This output was clearly insufficient for a 50-tonne (55 ton) colossus.

T-28, view from the left front

T-28 put out of action with a destroyed track

This was particularly true of later versions of the T-35, whose weight rose to 55 tonnes (60.6 tons) due to thicker 30 mm front hull armor. In difficult terrain, the vehicle did not even have sufficient power to turn about its own axis.

The rather complex four-speed transmission worked with a main disk friction clutch and a sideslip clutch. The running gear comprised eight road wheels with rubber tires on each side, connected in pairs to form four sprung pairs: six return rollers with rubber tires, an idler wheel with chain tensioner, and a rear drive sprocket. The road wheels, cushioned with spiral springs, were protected by deep armor skirts. Due to its considerable length, the tank was able to negotiate trenches up to 3.5 m (11.5 ft.) wide and obstacles up to 1.2 m (3.9 ft.) high, climb gradients of up to 20°, and wade through water up to 1 m (3.3 ft.) deep. It reached a top speed of 30 kph (18.6 mph) on paved roads.

T-35 Heavy Tank

All T-35s were fitted with 71-TK-1 radios with frame antennas. The final production vehicles with conical turrets and thicker armor weighed 55 tonnes (60.6 tons); the crew was reduced from eleven to nine men.

The prototypes of the T-35 were built at Plant No. 174, which had been founded in 1933 following the example of the tank construction department of the Bolshevik Factory. The tank design office under N. V. Barykov also belonged to this factory and was given the new name: Experimental Department for Design and Mechanical Engineering (OKMO).

The Red Army accepted the T-35 on August 11, 1933, and it was put into production at the Kharkov Locomotive Factory. The first batch of ten vehicles was delivered in 1934. A total of two prototypes and fifty-nine production vehicles was built by 1939.

The T-28 medium tank and the T-35 heavy tank were put into service by various RGK tank regiments. On December 12, 1935, the 1st and 4th Regiments of the RGK and the T-28 Tank Instruction Battalion were restructured into the 1st, 4th, and 6th Tank Brigades. The training battalion in Kharkov formed the basis of the 5th Brigade of the RGK, which was equipped with the T-35.

A medium-tank brigade consisted of four battalions and, depending on its organization, had up to 117 tanks, including 80 T-28 medium tanks, while the rest were T-26 and BT light tanks. A heavy-tank brigade consisted of ninety-four tanks; these included sixty T-35 heavy tanks, with the rest being light tanks.

In 1936 the army command decided to turn the two remaining mixed tank regiments of the RGK into heavy-tank brigades, and thus the second brigade was created in the Leningrad Military District and the third in the Moscow Military District. This decision was put into words by the order of the USSR People's Commissar of Defense of May 21, 1936:

A T-35 captured fully intact by the Germans in the summer of 1941

T-35 multiturret heavy tank, produced in 1937

In order to standardize the special tactical and technical training of mixed tank units, I order that

1. Heavy- and medium-tank brigades will be assigned to the High Command Tank Reserve (TRGK) as of July 1 of this year.
2. The 2nd Independent Tank Regiment is renamed the 2nd Medium Tank Brigade RGK, and the 3rd Independent Tank Regiment is renamed 3rd Heavy Tank Brigade RGK.
3. To the High Command Tank reserve belong

    1st Medium Tank Brigade RGK: Smolensk

    2nd Medium Tank Brigade RGK: Strelna

    3rd Heavy Tank Brigade RGK: Ryazan

    4th Medium Tank Brigade RGK: Kiev

    5th Heavy Tank Brigade RGK: Kharkov

    6th Medium Tank Brigade RGK: Slutsk
4. With respect to training and operations, the High Command Tank Reserve is directly subordinate to the head of the Directorate for Motor Vehicles and Tanks (ABTU RKKA, formerly UMM) as chief of the tank forces of the High Command Reserve, whereby the TRGK units are otherwise subordinate to the commanders of the military districts.

The chief of the High Command Tank Reserve is charged with the constant monitoring of mobilization preparations and the state of readiness of the TRGK units.

The People's Commissar of Defense of the USSR
Marshal of the Soviet Union K. Voroshilov

In 1939 the brigades were renumbered: the 5th Brigade became the 14th, the 4th Brigade became the 10th, the 1st Brigade became the 21st, and the 6th Brigade became the 20th. At the same time, a new brigade organization was adopted:

Organization of a T-35 and T-28 Heavy Tank Brigade in 1939 (Personnel Strengths):

headquarters
commanding officers: seven
supply, munitions: thirty-six
technical section: six

Staff tank platoon: 21 (2 T-28s, 3 BT-7s)
Staff: 10
reconnaissance company: 90 (17 BT-7s)
intelligence company: 57
combat engineer company: 63
flamethrower company: 55
antiaircraft machine gun company: 60
political section: 10
editing and printing: 4
Red Army house: 5

Support units:
maintenance platoon: 16
music platoon: 11
supply platoon: 16
fire brigade: 12

T-35 Tank Battalion: 503
headquarters: 5
HQ platoon: 21 (2 T-35s, 3 BT-7s)
tank company: 111 (10 T-35s)

T-35, the first version with cylindrical turrets

tank company: 111 (10 T-35s)
tank company: 111 (10 T-35s)
supply units: 24
repair units: 120

T-28 Tank Battalion: 498
headquarters: 5
HQ platoon: 21 (2 T-28s, 3 BT-7s)
tank company: (10 T-28s)
tank company: (10 T-28s)
tank company: (10 T-28s)
supply units: 24
repair units: 120

T-28 Tank Battalion: 498
training unit's strength: 545
1 company for the training of drivers and T-35 turret commanders
1 company for the training of drivers and T-28 and BT mechanics
1 company for the training of T-28 turret commanders
1 company for the training of radio operators
1 company for the training of drivers and tractor drivers

Because of the limited numbers of T-35s, only a few brigades reached the strengths specified in the order. The rest were equipped with T-28s. For example, in the 10th and 21st Brigades, which took part in the "liberation campaign in the Western Ukraine" (the Polish campaign) in autumn 1939, there were 98 and 105 T-28s, respectively, and not a single T-35. In this campaign the T-28s covered a distance of 350 to 400 km (217 to 248 mi.) and demonstrated a fairly high level of reliability.

In the mid-1930s the Red Army needed fast, mobile units for actions in the western steppe region of Mongolia. From February to March 1936, a special tank brigade and a special tank regiment were created from

T-35 during the parade in Red Square on May 1, 1937

A German officer and Ukrainian boys on a knocked-out T-35 in the summer of 1941

the 20th Independent Light Mechanized Brigade of the Transbaikal Military District.

The Special Tank Brigade was organized as follows in January 1937:

- headquarters
- 1 intelligence company
- 1 reconnaissance battalion
- 1 tank battalion
- 1 rifle and machine gun battalion
- 1 combat support company
- 1 repair company
- 1 motor transport company
- 1 field bakery

The brigade numbered 1,415 officers, NCOs, and enlisted men. The tank regiment consisted of a battalion of BT tanks and two battalions of medium tanks. In the second half of 1938, the regiment was expanded into the 8th Tank Brigade. All told, three light-tank brigades equipped with BA-20 and FAI light armored cars plus BA-3, BA-6, and BA-10 medium armored cars were formed in the Transbaikal Military District.

The BA-20 light armored car was built on the chassis of the GAZ-M1 automobile, which had been in production since 1936. The welded hull consisted of rolled armor plates, the fighting compartment with rotating turret and 7.62 mm machine gun sat relatively far to the rear. The range of elevation of the machine gun in the ball mount ranged from −13°/+23°. The armored car was fitted with bulletproof tires "padded" with GK sponge rubber. Communications equipment consisted of a 71-TK-1 radio set with frame antenna, which in the 1938 modernization gave way to a long whip antenna. The Red Army often used the BA-20 for reconnaissance, communications, and security tasks.

The standard version of the BA-20 was joined by the modernized BA-20M version, with 9 mm (0.35 in.) of armor in the front and the turret, which on the BA-20M was now conical rather than cylindrical in shape. As well, the whip antenna was moved to the left side of the hull. The BA-20ZhD was produced for use on rails in cooperation with armored trains.

Off-road, the BA-20 could negotiate gradients of up to 12°, cross trenches up to 0.35 m (1.15 ft.) in width, and climb obstacles up to 0.24 m (0.8 ft.) in height—less than impressive compared to other wheeled and tracked vehicles. But after all, it was basically just a "beefed-up" civilian automobile. In total, 2,013 BA-20s were produced from 1936 to 1942.

BA-20 Light Armored Car

The BA-20 light armored car replaced the similar FAI, which was built on the chassis of the Ford A in the early 1930s. The BA-20 was given a more powerful engine than the FAI, a new transmission, and a more rigid frame.

The BA-3, BA-6, and BA-10 armored cars belonged to the same family of medium, three-axle armored vehicles. Their story went back to the FAI armored car, which had been developed by the Izhora Factory's design bureau at the beginning of 1932. It was based on the chassis of the Ford Timken, which had been shortened by 400 mm (15.75 in.). All the vehicles in the family had the same layout: the engine in front, the driver's cab behind it, and, relatively far to the rear, a rotating turret with a 37 mm Hotchkiss cannon and a DT 7.62 mm machine gun. Another DT machine gun was operated by the driver. A total of 109 vehicles were built.

Unlike the BAI, the BA-3 was armed with the 45 mm 20K Model 1932 cannon from the T-26 tank and a DT machine gun in the turret, which increased firepower considerably. A total of 221 examples of the BA-3 were produced.

The BA-6 used the chassis of the GAZ AA, was powered by a Soviet 40 hp carburetor engine, and ran on bulletproof tires. In total, 394 BA-6s were produced from 1936 to 1939.

Introduced in 1938 and built until 1941, the BA-10 was built on a modernized GAA AAA truck chassis and was in turn an improved version of the BA-6. The welded superstructure consisted of rolled armor plates. The turret armament consisted of a 45 mm Model 1934 tank gun and a coaxial machine gun plus another machine gun in a ball mount in the offset bow plate. Telescopic and periscopic sights were provided for aiming. Its armament was thus equal to that of the T-26 and BT tanks, with the BA-10 weighing just half or a third as much. For a vehicle of its class, the BA-10 had good off-road characteristics, negotiating gradients of up to 24° and wading water obstacles up to 0.6 m (2 ft.) deep. Caterpillar tracks of the "Overroll" type could be placed around the rear wheels to improve off-road capability, which turned the BA-10 into a half-track vehicle.

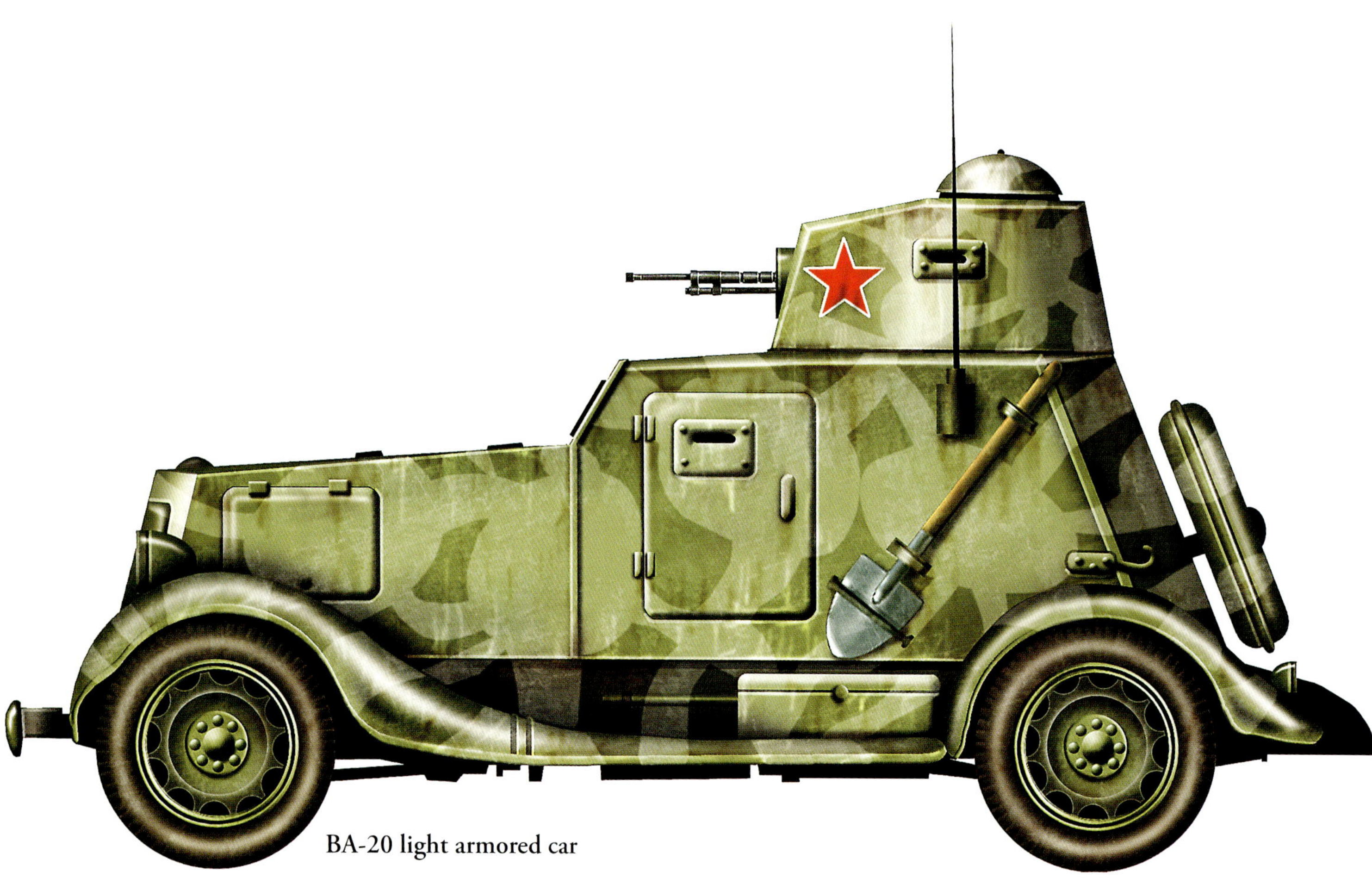

BA-20 light armored car

BA-20, view from the front right

BA-20 in winter camouflage carrying Soviet riflemen

BA-20 ZhD railroad version (ZhD = *Zheleznaya doroga*, railway)

Additional wheels were also fitted on both sides, which could rotate freely on the axles. These wheels reduced ground pressure and made it easier to negotiate ditches. In 1939, the armored car was modernized into the BA-10M, with improved steering, reinforced radiator protection, and a new 71-TK-1 radio. A BA-10SchD rail version had rail wheels and a lifting mechanism for transferring from road to rail and vice versa. From 1938 to August 1941, 3,413 BA-10s and BA-10Ms were produced. Wheeled armored vehicles of the BA family not only were used by light armored brigades but were also part of the equipment of cavalry, tank, and motorized rifle divisions, as well as the troops of the NKVD.

BA-20s taking part in a parade

BA-10 Medium Armored Car

The implementation of the "Systems of Tank-Tractor-Auto Armored Weapons of the Red Army and the Systems of Tank Armament for the Second Five-Year Plan" resulted in the creation a coordinated vehicle fleet, a reorganization, and reequipment of the Soviet armored forces. By the end of the Second Five-Year Plan (1937), the tank forces, which at that time were still called "motorized and armored troops," comprised tank battalions and mechanized regiments of rifle and cavalry divisions, heavy-tank brigades of the High Command Reserve, and mechanized brigades and corps.

In August 1938, mechanized regiments, brigades, and corps became tank regiments, brigades, and corps. While the number of units was maintained, and with minor structural changes, the number of armored vehicles increased almost 1.5 fold, especially since the platoons were now equipped with five tanks instead of three.

Until the end of 1939, the Soviet armored forces consisted of four tank corps (10th, 15th, 20th, and 25th), twenty-four independent light-tank brigades, four heavy-tank brigades, and three "chemical" (flamethrower) brigades, plus a considerable number of tank battalions and regiments of the rifle and cavalry divisions. The armored forces had blossomed into the army's main fighting force. Within three years (1936–38) they grew in numbers, more than doubling in size.

The training of crews, officers, and workshop personnel could not keep pace with this growth rate. The training of new leaders and junior officers as well as "specialist soldiers," who formed the backbone of the armored troops, proved to be a particular sticking point. Tank commanders, drivers/mechanics, and gunners were trained directly in the formations and units; exceptions were specialists such as radio operators, tank engineers, and flamethrower gunners, who attended courses in the weapons schools / training units of their respective branches of service.

In the first half of the 1930s, vehicle commanders were trained in corps schools and training units of the individual brigades. The corps school for commanders consisted of four battalions. The 1st Battalion trained commanders for the BT, the 2nd Battalion for the T-26, and the 3rd Battalion for wheeled vehicles, while the 4th Battalion acted as a sort of driving school for the drivers of transport vehicles.

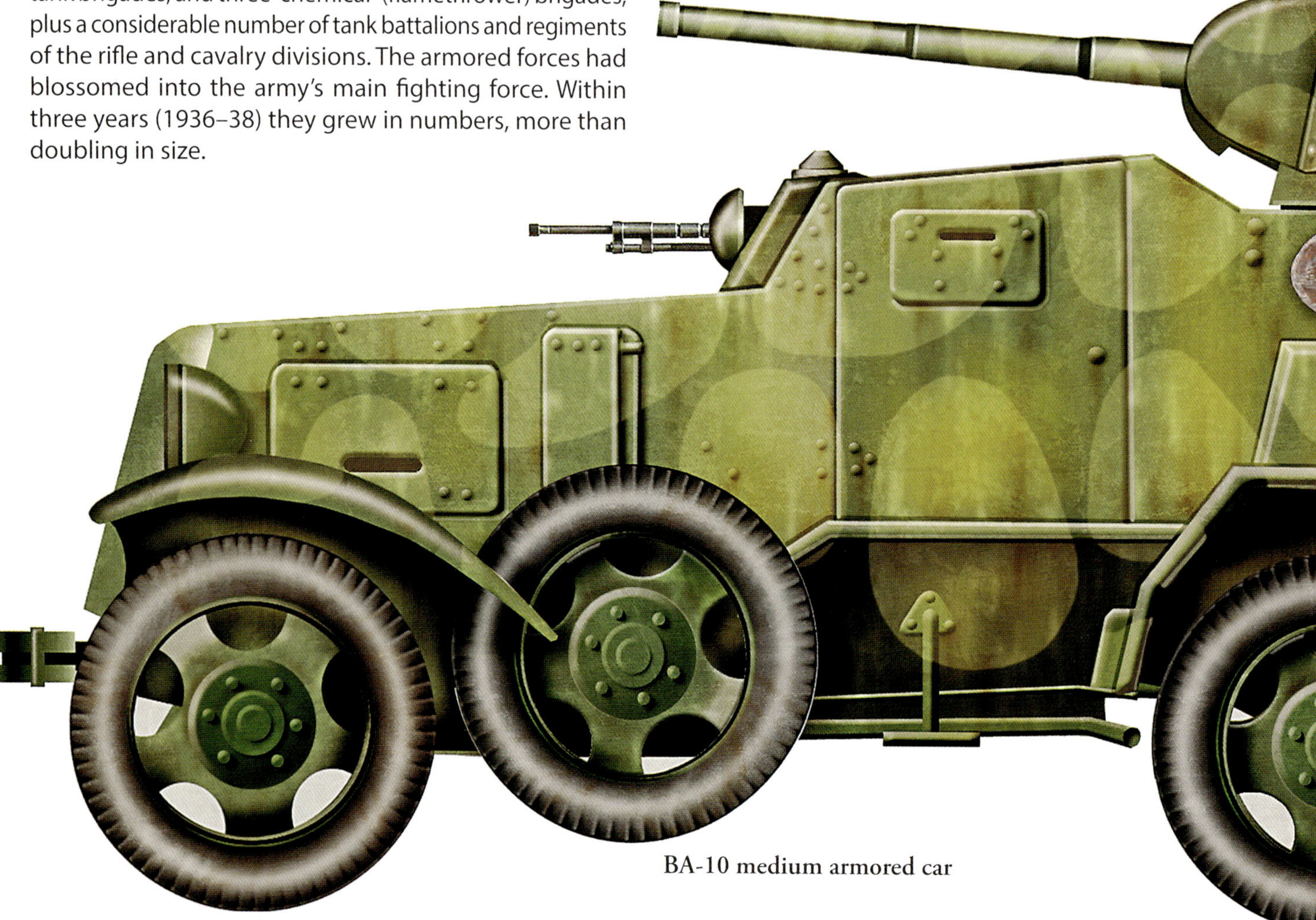

BA-10 medium armored car

In the independent mechanized brigades, the 3rd Battalion assumed responsibility for the training of vehicle commanders and other tank personnel. The training battalions had three tank-training companies, an armored-vehicle-training company, and a training company for tank drivers. The course duration for enlisted men was six to eight months, depending on their specialty. The courses were somewhat longer for tank commanders and section leaders.

At the beginning of 1935 the corps schools were disbanded, and their training responsibilities were transferred to the mechanized brigades. Each brigade established its own 4th Training Battalion. The mechanized regiments proceeded in a similar manner, setting up regimental schools, and independent tank battalions set up their own training and instruction companies.

BA-10, front view

BA-10, rear view

BA-10s taking part in a parade

This system came quite close to the requirements and needs of the respective units but could not completely solve the general training problem at a time when new formations were constantly being created. It was particularly difficult to provide commanders and tank crews for those mechanized and tank units that had emerged from rifle and cavalry units. Rapid and comprehensive retraining of all personnel was required. The existing school and training facilities could not cope with this task. Therefore, the retraining of crew and command personnel was organized directly in these formations with the help of appropriate instructors, who came from mechanized, tank, and school units. For some time, the newly established formations remained essentially training units as regiments and brigades.

A column of BA-10 medium armored cars on a forest road in the summer of 1941

To more quickly meet the needs of new formations for trained personnel, the military districts established a network of temporary training courses and schools.

For the accumulation of cadres of junior command personnel, various forms and methods of their training were used, which made it possible to successfully solve the problem of providing new formations with cadres of junior commanders and other junior specialists. The task of training the lower command level (e.g., platoon commanders) and technical personnel was also successfully solved in these years, although this was even more difficult, since this clientele required more-demanding and longer training, which in turn required instructors with a higher level of expertise and general education. Until 1930, this training took place at the so-called Leningrad tank courses, which were naturally reluctant to hand over personnel for the training of newly formed tank and mechanized units. It was therefore necessary to expand training operations considerably. The decision was made to establish tank (force) schools based on existing military schools, mainly infantry schools. In October 1930, the Orel Tank School was founded, based on the Ivanovo-Voznesensk Infantry School. The Saratov Tank School followed in 1931 as a "conversion" of the retraining facility for reserve officers that had existed since 1918. In the same way, the Gorky Tank School was created in 1932 from an infantry school that had existed since November 1918, as was the Ulyanovsk Tank School. The school for motor vehicle technicians founded in Moscow in 1930 was converted into a school

The crew of a BA-10 during a mission briefing

for tank technicians in 1933, and a second school for tank technicians was established in Leningrad in the same year.

Between 1930 and 1933, six new tank schools were established to train lower command and technical personnel. All six tank schools were able to accommodate a total of 6,700 course participants. The middle command personnel of the armored forces were trained in advanced and retraining courses in Moscow and Leningrad. In 1932–33 alone, three thousand officers from other branches of the armed forces attended the tank-retraining courses.

The training of intermediate and higher technical personnel took place in the "Courses for the advanced training of technical personnel of the armored forces of the Red Army" created in Kazan in 1934. Due to their short duration (six months), the advanced courses could not provide comprehensive operational and engineering training. For this reason, the Military Academy for Mechanization and Motorization of the Red Army was founded by order no. 039 of May 13, 1932, of the Revolutionary Military Council in Moscow. It was intended to provide command personnel of the armored forces, military, and specialist engineers with the necessary knowledge of military technology as well as the design and construction of military vehicles. The academy could accommodate up to 2,500 students.

The following ranks and positions were defined for officers in the armored forces: lieutenant, captain, major, colonel, brigade commander, division commander, and corps commander. The following ranks were assigned to military technical personnel: 2nd- and 1st-rank military technician; 3rd-, 2nd-, and 1st-rank military engineer; brigade engineer; divisional engineer; and corps engineer. In August 1937, in addition to the decree of the Soviet government of September 22, 1935, the following ranks were introduced: first lieutenant, junior military engineer, and junior political instructor. There were also new insignia based on the usual rank insignia. A decree of the Council of People's Commissars of December 2, 1935 (in addition to the decree of the Central Executive Committee and the Council of People's Commissars of September 22, 1935), introduced a new uniform with sleeve and collar insignia for officers and political commissars of the armored troops, which indicated their affiliation to the armored troops.

CHAPTER 3
THE MODERNIZATION AND EXPANSION OF THE SOVIET TANK ARM ON THE EVE OF THE SECOND WORLD WAR

The types of armored vehicles created by the Red Army during the first two five-year plans were put to the test in the Spanish Civil War (1936–39) and the conflict with the Japanese at Lake Khassan (1938).

The USSR sent a large quantity of military equipment to support Republican-Communist Spain. This included 347 light tanks (including 50 BT-5s and 281 T-26s) plus 60 armored wheeled vehicles (37 BA-6s, 3 BA-3s, and 20 BA-20s). These vehicles were often used by armored units formed by the Republican army from international volunteers. On the opposing side, Italian L3/35 tankettes and German Panzerkampfwagen I light tanks formed the backbone of the armored units that operated on the side of the Nationalist leader, General Franco.

Armed with the 45 mm gun, the Soviet types soon demonstrated a clear superiority over the opposing armored vehicles, which were armed with machine guns only. It soon proved that antitank guns were much more dangerous opponents. The shells fired by the 37 mm Rheinmetall and Bofors guns and the 25 mm and 20 mm cannon made by Scotty and Solothurn easily penetrated the armor of the BT-5 and T-26 tanks. This led to the failure of several offensive operations by the Republican army because of heavy losses in armored vehicles. The Soviet vehicles demonstrated good off-road capability in Spain and adequate technical reliability. Thanks to their effective 45 mm guns, the BA-3 and BA-6 were easily able to deal with the light tanks provided by the Germans and Italians. The armored wheeled vehicles proved equally reliable and were successfully used for reconnaissance and various secondary roles.

The main disadvantage of all the armored vehicles sent to Spain—by both sides—was the inadequacy of their armor protection. Even the armor-piercing shells fired by 13.2 mm Hotchkiss heavy machine guns easily penetrated the armor of the BA-23, BA-6, and BA-20, to say nothing of the 37 mm shells fired by German antitank guns.

The placement of a fuel tank with a capacity of more than 100 kg (220 lbs.) in the driver's cab of the BA-10 over the heads of the driver and commander / forward machine gunner proved to be a serious design error. If a bullet pierced the frontal armor and punched a hole in the tank, the crew in the front of the vehicle got a "gasoline shower"—and if the fuel ignited (as was often the case), they usually had no chance of survival. The engine performance of the tracked vehicles left much to be desired, and the suspension often broke.

Many volunteer tank soldiers criticized the inadequate armor protection of the Soviet vehicles. The greatest weight was given to the statements by General Dmitry Grigorievich Pavlov, who had commanded an international armored brigade in Spain and had returned to the USSR in June 1937. There he was appointed deputy head of the Directorate for Motor Vehicles and Tanks and in November 1937 became its head. Urton Pavlov:

> The armor protection of new tanks for the Red Army should offer the following:
>
> - for amphibious tanks: protection against armor-piercing rifle bullets and shells fired by light antitank rifles from all ranges, or have a thickness of 12–15 mm [0.47–0.59 in.]
> - for light tanks: protection against fire from heavy machine guns and small- and medium-caliber antitank rifles at all ranges, or from 37 mm antitank guns from 600 m [656 yds.] or a thickness of at least 20–25 mm [0.79–0.98 in.]
> - for medium tanks: protection against fire from 37 mm guns from all angles and from 47 mm guns from a range of 800 m [875 yds.], or a thickness of at least 40–42 mm [1.57–1.65 in.]
> - for heavy tanks: protection against fire from 47 m guns from all ranges or 76 mm guns from 800 to 1,000 m [875–1,094 yds.], or a thickness of at least 60 mm [2.36 in.]
>
> When building new tanks, it must be possible to increase the armor protection by at least one level during modernization.

There were also complaints about the armament of light tanks: Because of the weak fragmentation and explosive effect of their 45 mm guns, engaging antitank guns and the destruction of enemy field fortifications proved difficult. Pavlov: "To be able to engage modern fortified defense zones, some medium and heavy tanks must be equipped with a tank gun with a caliber of at least 76 mm to 107 mm or a howitzer with a caliber of 122–152 mm."

To eliminate the revealed shortcomings of Soviet wheeled and tracked tanks, the "System of Tank Armament of the Red Army for the Third Five-Year Plan" became the focus of attention. It was approved by decree of the Defense Committee and the Council of People's Commissars for the Five-Year Plan (1938–42):

> **Decision by the Directorate of Motor Vehicles and Tanks of the Red Army on the System of Armored Weapons in the Third Five-Year Plan**
>
> **December 15, 1938**
> **Secret**
>
> One of the main requirements that determined the work on the armored vehicles system in Five-Year Plan III was Comrade Stalin's instructions. According to his instructions, aircraft "should be simple, have been extensively tested before being introduced into service, [and] function reliably, and their operation should not make excessive demands on the pilot. The construction of our aircraft and their quality should be designed for the average and below-average pilot.

These instructions also apply without exception to armored vehicles.

The work of the third Five-Year Plan for the armored weapons system of the Red Army was to strive for the following main goals:

1. Modernization of all the Red Army's tank types, both in terms of improving their design and their quality
2. Design improvement and improvement of the quality of combat vehicles in production at the beginning of the third Five-Year Plan
3. Creation of new models of special and auxiliary vehicles for combat use
4. Solving new problems that arise relating to armored vehicles

Modernization of Combat Vehicles of the Red Army

The work on the modernization of Red Army combat vehicles is determined by the following main considerations:

1. The five tank types that were introduced into service by the Red Army during Five-Year Plans I and II were improved each year both in quality as well as in design. As a result, the tanks differ by year of production, both in terms of the individual assemblies and in terms of quality.
2. The variations in quality, depending on the year of production and in some cases also the tactical and technical layouts (equipment), causes difficulties for the troops during operational and tactical use. In addition, vehicles from different years of production cause difficulties both in terms of maintenance and the supply of spare parts.
3. As a result of the modernization of the equipment produced in the first and second five-year plans, the troops should receive combat vehicles that are homogeneous in their tactical and technical design and quality. In addition, certain types of combat vehicles must be modernized (e.g., the engine and running gear of the T-26) to improve the tactical and technical characteristics of the vehicles produced during Five-Year Plans I and II.

Design Improvement and Improvement of the Quality of Combat Vehicles in Production at the Start of the Third Five-Year Plan

Design improvement and enhancement of the quality of combat vehicles in production is determined by the following main considerations:

(a) The comprehensive introduction of automatic weapons in the armies of our potential enemies
(b) The creation of new equipment for active and passive antitank defense
(c) The trend in modern armies of being able to create heavily fortified defense zones in the shortest time

Creation of New Models of Special and Auxiliary Vehicles

Work on the creation of new designs is determined by the following main requirements:

1. The creation of larger mechanized formations up to tank armies, capable of solving all tasks both on the battle space and in the entire depth of the modern battlefield, requires functioning rear services and a reliable recovery service. This provision aims to reduce the number of combat vehicle types from which larger mechanized formations are to be formed.
2. All types of auxiliary and special vehicles for mechanized units must be tracked.
3. In addition, all provisions and instructions relating to the section on the improvement of vehicles in production and the development and construction of new models of combat, special, and auxiliary vehicles remain in force.

Main Requirements for the Modernization, Improvement, and Construction of New Types of Combat Vehicles

1. Increased firepower. The task here is to equip combat vehicles with large-caliber, fast-loading cannon and artillery pieces.
2. Increased effectiveness of fire. The task here is to equip combat vehicles with devices for fire control as well as suitable aiming and observation equipment.
3. Strengthening of passive armor protection by increasing armor thicknesses and by changing the structure (use of riveted plates, conical turrets, etc.)
4. Further introduction of diesel engines for combat vehicles, with the objective of reducing weight and size [of the tanks], lowering fuel consumption, and increasing range
5. On the basis of the demands from mechanized units, all main types used by mechanized formations must have both wheel and track drive.
6. Provision of equipment for driving in fog, in smoke, and in darkness
7. Provision of devices to ease the task of driving (automatic transmissions, remote control)
8. Development of equipment for deep wading underwater for all types of combat vehicles
9. Increasing the mobility and resilience of all combat vehicles:
   (a) Reliable crossing of obstacles at high speeds
   (b) Reliable operation for 5,000–6,000 km [3,100–3,730 mi.]. An increase in reliability is also necessitated by the need to reduce the rear-echelon services.
10. Development of sealants and waterproofing, which simultaneously solve the problem of protection against chemical-warfare agents and water ingress during deep wading
11. Equipment with [cold protection] means to ensure reliable operation at low temperatures down to minus 50°C.
12. Improvement of off-road capability under all ground conditions (mountainous and wooded terrain, swamps)
13. Comfortable accommodation of drivers and crews to ensure reliable and safe negotiation of obstacles at high speeds
14. Construction and technical requirements must be designed for the average and below-average tank soldier.

Combat Vehicle Types That Are to Be Developed in the Third Five-Year Plan

Based on the main objective of reducing the number of combat vehicle types and increasing the strength of the armored forces; while simultaneously reducing the rear services, the following types of combat vehicles were to be developed in the Third Five-Year Plan:

1. A standard, fast and amphibious reconnaissance vehicle with wheeled/tracked running gear
2. A standard tank for mechanized and mixed units:
   (a) For mechanized units with wheeled-tracked running gear and high speed
   (b) For mixed units: as for mechanized units, but with increased armor protection
   (c) A standard breakthrough tank with heavy armor and armament on tracked running gear

The developments resulting from the new "System of Armored Vehicles" were to take place simultaneously. There was a special requirement for an amphibious tank weighing 5–6 tonnes (5.5–6.6 tons) with wheeled/tracked running gear and a diesel engine producing 150–180 hp. The Main Directorate of Motor Vehicles and Tanks (GABTU RKKA, formerly ABTU) tasked the design bureau of Factory No. 37, under N. A. Astrov, with the development of this tank, the T-39. Even during preliminary design work, however, it became clear that development would take too much time, especially as the diesel had not yet been developed and the wheeled/tracked running gear would not fit the weight, size, and cost parameters. In spring 1938, GABTU agreed with the designers' objections and changed the tactical and technical requirements: the diesel was replaced by a carburetor engine, and the running gear was limited to tracked drive. By that time, the design bureau had already concluded the preliminary design of the tank, whose internal designation was Object 010, in accordance with the new specifications. After the project was approved, GABTU gave the vehicle the designation T-40.

T-40s in winter camouflage

T-40s during an attack

T-30 light tank with TNSh 20 mm cannon

T-40 Light Amphibious Tank (Object 020)

Testing of the first four prototypes began in July 1939. The identified shortcomings were rectified and on December 19, 1939, the Red Army introduced the vehicle into service in accordance with the Defense Committee's decree no. 443ss. Responsibility for production of the T-40 was given to Factory No. 37 with rather tight deadlines: Three preproduction vehicles were to be ready by March 1, 1940, and a further 15 by August 1, with series production beginning on October 1.

The design was relatively compact. The engine and transmission were in the starboard side of the front end and took up part of the fighting and driver's compartments. The two-man crew consisted of the commander and the driver. The commander was certainly overburdened with his other functions as gunner, loader, and radio operator, especially since he also had to observe, monitor the battlefield, reconnoiter targets, and coordinate cooperation with other vehicles. The armament, consisting of a 12.7 mm DShK machine gun and a 7.62 mm DT machine gun, was housed in the turret on the roof of the fighting compartment. Due to the arrangement of the engine and transmission, the turret was located to the left of the longitudinal axis. The armor, consisting of 5–20 mm (0.2–0.8 in.) thick armor plates, provided protection against rifle bullets and shrapnel. A four-stroke, six-cylinder GAZ-11 in-line engine producing 85 hp powered the vehicle. The torsion bar suspension invented by Ferdinand Porsche was used for the first time in Russian tank construction (as well as in the KV-1 heavy tank). There were four road wheels and three return rollers, one drive sprocket, and one idler wheel on each side. The width of the slender hinged track was only 260 mm (10.23 in.). In the water, a propeller took over propulsion, and a rudder the steering. The T-40 developed a speed of 5–6 kph (3.1–3.7 mph) on the water and up to 44 kph (27 mph) on roads. Production continued until December 1941, and the vehicle went to the reconnaissance battalions of the armored and motorized divisions of the western special military districts. With the beginning of the German-Soviet war, production was limited to two simplified, nonamphibious versions, which were sent to tank brigades and independent tank battalions to support the infantry:

T-40 light amphibious tank

- T-40S: without propeller, PTO shaft transmission, rudder, bilge pumps, surge shield, heat exchanger, and compass
- T-30: With reinforced armor (front and sides 15 mm [0.6 in.], turret front 20 mm [0.8 in.]), and straight tail end without cutout for the propeller. Several vehicles were fitted with a TNSh-20 (ShVAK) automatic 20 mm cannon and a coaxial DT machine gun with 750 or 1,512 rounds of ammunition.

T-40, view from the front rightw

The "standard tank type for mechanized and mixed units" as per the "System of Tank Armament of the Red Army for the Third Five-Year Plan" was designed by the design bureau of Factory No. 183 under Mikhail Ilyich Koshkin. It was based on the GABTU's tactical and technical requirements for a highly maneuverable BT-20 wheeled/tracked tank, dated October 13, 1937:

1. Type: light high-speed tank with Christie-type wheeled/tracked running gear with Christie-type six-wheel drive
2. Combat weight: 13–14 tonnes [14.3–15.4 tons]
3. Armament: One 45 mm gun with stabilizer, three DT machine guns, and one defensive flamethrower, or one 76 mm gun, three DT machine guns, and one defensive flamethrower. Every fifth vehicle was to be equipped with antiaircraft defensive weapons.

The crew of a T-40 climbs into its vehicle.

4. Combat load: 130–150 45 mm or 50 76 mm shells, 2,000–3,000 rounds of machine gun ammunition
5. Armor protection: frontal armor 25 mm [0.98 in.], conical turret 20 mm [0.78 in.], side and rear armor 16 mm [0.6 in.], roof and floor 10 mm [0.39 in.]
6. Speed: Same speeds on tracks and wheels. Maximum speed 70 kph [43.5 mph], minimum speed 7 kph [4.3 mph]
7. Engine: ShPZ diesel, 400 hp
8. Crew: three men
9. Range: 300–400 km [186–248.5 mi.] on tracks
10. Ground clearance 0.4 m [1.3 ft.] on tracks. Vehicle height 2.3 m [7.54 ft.].
11. Specific ground pressure: 0.5 kg/cm^2 [7.1 psi] on tracks

In March 1938, the product with the internal designation A-20 was approved. At that time, several senior members of the army command already doubted the necessity of a wheeled/tracked drive. Experience had shown that the wheeled drive was relatively seldom used. As well, under battle conditions a tank on wheels traveled little faster than on tracks. A further argument for the tracked running gear was the better types of steel by then available, which gave the tracks a longer life. As a result, the decision was made to develop a pure tracked vehicle, A-20G (T-32), in addition to the A-20 with wheeled/tracked drive. Dispensing with the wheeled drive on the A-32 not only simplified the design and construction but also made it possible to increase the armor protection and install more-powerful armament (76 mm gun) due to the weight savings.

At a meeting with the Supreme Military Council in August 1938, Koshkin succeeded in obtaining approval for production of metal models of both a wheeled/tracked A-20 tank and a purely tracked A-32 vehicle. By mid-1939, prototypes of the A-20 and the A-32 were available and were submitted to the state commission for examination. The commission determined that both tanks were "superior in strength and reliability to all previously produced prototypes, but neither could [yet] be given preference." The tests carried out in the fall of 1939 and, above all, the experiences of the Soviet-Finnish Winter War clearly confirmed that only tracked vehicles could guarantee mobility in rough terrain, especially in the fall and winter. At the same time, the need to further improve the combat characteristics of the A-32 and, in particular, to strengthen its armor protection was identified. By decree of the Defense Committee No. 443ss of December 19, 1939, the Red Army adopted the A-32 as the T-34:

Acceptance by the Red Army:

2. T-32 tank: tracked vehicle with V-2 diesel engine, production in Factory No. 138 of the People's Commissariat for Medium Mechanical Engineering (Narkomsredmash), with the following changes:
   (a) The thicknesses of the main armor plates are increased to 45 mm [1.8 in.].
   (b) improved exterior view
   (c) The T-32 is to be armed as follows:
      (1) One F-32 76 mm gun paired with a 7.62 mm machine gun
      (2) One hull machine gun (radio operator)
      (3) One autonomous 7.62 mm machine gun
      (4) One 7.62 mm antiaircraft machine gun
   The vehicle is given the designation T-34.

The design of this vehicle marked a quantum leap in international tank design. For the first time, a tank combined strong armor protection, an ideal shape, a high degree of mobility, and off-road capability with a powerful armament. Effective armor protection was ensured not only using thick rolled armor plates, but also by the fact that they were sloped. The effectiveness of the tank's armor protection is evidenced by the fact that during the Battle of Stalingrad in 1942–43, an average of 4.9 shells (probably from the German 50 mm tank guns in use at the time) were needed to put a T-34 completely out of action. With the introduction of more-powerful tanks and antitank guns, this ratio soon fell to between 1.5 and 1.8 rounds but remained comparatively high. The T-34 was first armed with the 76.2 mm L-11 gun, which was soon replaced by the more powerful F-32 and F-34 models. This armament was the same as that of the KV-1 heavy tank.

T-34 Model 1941 Medium Tank, Produced in the Krasnoye Sormovo Factory

A powerful diesel engine and wide tracks gave the T-34 its great mobility and off-road capabilities, and it achieved speeds up to 55 kph (34 mph), negotiated gradients up to 30°, crossed trenches up to 2.5 m (8.2 ft.) in width, and cleared obstacles 0.73 m (2.4 ft.) high. Without preparation it could wade bodies of water up to 1.3 m (4.25 ft.) deep. Its ease of production made it possible to have the T-34 built using unskilled labor, which was carried out in seven armaments factories, not all of which had experience in tank construction. Of particular importance for mass production were the assembly line and the introduction of the automatic arc-welding process for joining the armor plates.

However, the first version of the T-34 also had considerable disadvantages; its transmission and running gear in particular left much to be desired. The tank's poor reliability became apparent during the testing of the first production vehicles in November and December 1940. At that time, three vehicles achieved a total driving time of 350 hours and 47 minutes. However, this was possible only thanks to continuous repairs by a two-man team of specialists, who alone spent 414 hours tinkering with the T-34; in addition, the crews spent a further 158 hours and 9 minutes on repairs. Of the total testing period of 922 hours and 56 minutes, the tanks were mobile for only 38 percent of the time; the remaining 62 percent of the time was taken up by repairs, most of which the crews were unable to carry out themselves. The drivers were the hardest-working men, since they had to exert forces of up to 32 kp (70.5 pounds of force) when steering and shifting gears. When changing gears, the muscle power of the arm was often not enough; the driver had to use his leg to help or join forces with the radio operator to engage the gears. The four-man crew was one man too few for a medium-sized armored fighting vehicle at that time. The commander not only had to observe, spot targets, etc. but also act as a gunner. In addition, his view was severely restricted when the hatch was closed.

The Red Army leadership was well aware of these disadvantages but nevertheless decided to go ahead with series production. It did so for two main reasons: First, despite all its shortcomings, the T-34 was clearly

T-34/76 on the attack with infantrymen riding on the tank

superior to the BT-7 light tank, not to mention the T-26. Second, the vehicle was relatively easy to manufacture, and Factory No. 182 and the Stalingrad Tractor Factory (STZ) were able to get started after an appropriate preparation period as soon as the supply chain for the necessary parts was in place.

The decision was therefore made to go into series production, with an improved model being developed at the same time. This T-34M had, among other things, a cupola with improved view for the commander, five crew members, a wider turret, and a new transmission. This vehicle practically anticipated the T-34 of 1944 with its new turret, 85 mm gun (T-34/85), and other improvements. It was to go into series production as early as 1941 and replace the T-34 Model 1940 (T-34/76). However, work on the T-34M was discontinued at the beginning of the war.

The same decree no. 443ss issued by the Defense Committee that produced the T-34 also provided for the construction of a modernized BT-7M wheeled/tracked tank powered by a V-2 diesel engine for use by mechanized formations. On April 2, 1940, People's Commissar of Defense Voroshilov approved the development of the SP light tank (Project 126). It received the official designation T-50, was mainly intended for infantry support, and was to supplement the T-34.

The decision to mass-produce the T-34 was taken by the Politburo of the Central Committee of the CPSU (b) in June 1940, and production was carried out, as planned, by Factory No. 183 in Kharkov and the Stalingrad Tractor Factory (STZ). The first production vehicles went to units in the western special military districts. By June 1941, a total of 1,225 T-34s had been completed, 967 of which were located in five western military districts.

The T-50 emerged from the competition between the two Leningrad factories, Kirov, and No. 174 Voroshilov. Prototypes were tested in January 1941. The winner was the model from Factory No. 174, which the Red Army adopted in February 1941.

According to the plans of the People's Commissariat of Defense, the T-50 was to become the Red Army's most produced tank, since around 14,000 T-50s were planned for the development and expansion of the mechanized formations alone.

T-34 Model 1941 medium tank

T-34/76 in winter camouflage

A column of T-34s during a halt

T-34/76 captured by German troops

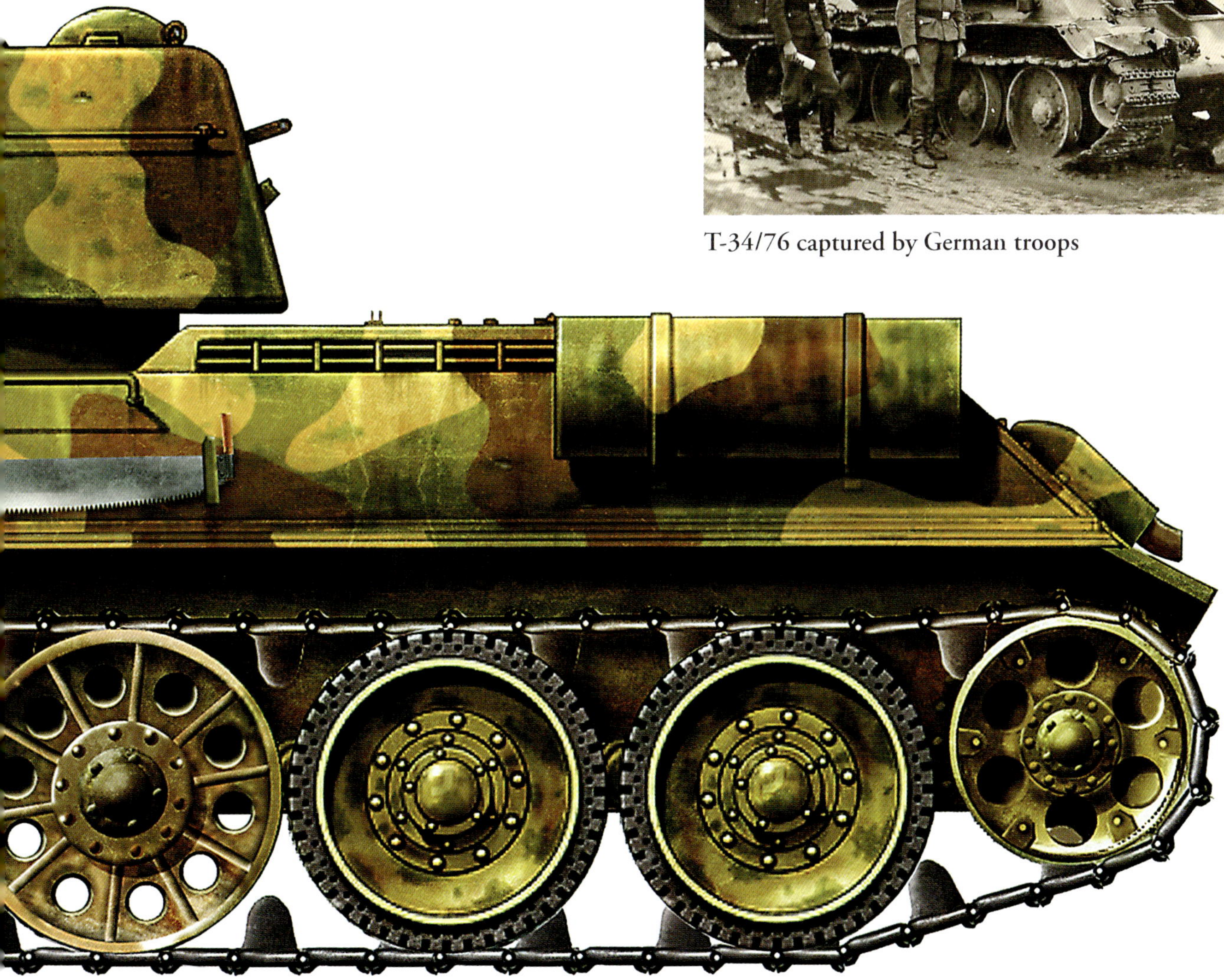

T-50 Light Tank

Like the T-34, the T-50 combined solid armor protection with capable armament and a powerful diesel engine. It had the same layout, with the driver's compartment at the front, the fighting compartment in the middle, and the engine and transmission at the rear. The 15, 20, 30, and 70 mm thick (0.6, 0.78, 1.2, and 2.75 in.) welded armor plates were also steeply sloped. The liquid-cooled V-4 six-cylinder diesel engine was started either by hand crank and inertia starter or via an electric motor. The transmission consisted of a two-disc dry clutch and a four-speed gearbox, as well as a slipping clutch and side clutch. On each side of the torsion-bar-sprung chassis there were six road wheels without rubber tires, three return rollers, the idler wheel, and the rear drive sprocket. These features gave the T-50 excellent off-road characteristics. It negotiated gradients of up to 45°, crossed trenches up to 2.2 m (7.2 ft.) wide, and climbed 0.7 m (2.3 ft.) high obstacles.

Although the T-50 was actually intended as an "infantry" tank, it was capable of a top speed of up to 50 kph (30 mph). The turret had a commander's cupola with vision slits for battlefield observation; the vehicle was also equipped with a radio and an onboard intercom system. However, the start of series production at Factory No. 174 was very slow, which was partly due to the modern design of the T-50 (which was more complex than that of the T-26), but also to the fact that the single-row, 300 hp, six-cylinder, B-4 diesel engine was intended for it. The industry had great difficulties in developing and manufacturing this engine. As a result, a small series of just sixty-three vehicles were ultimately built. To increase the armor protection against 37 mm and 47 mm antitank guns, the T-50 was fitted with additional frontal armor in 1938, with the result that combat weight increased, negatively affecting the speed and mobility.

At a meeting of the Supreme Military Council in April 1938, the decision was made to produce a new heavy breakthrough tank with powerful armament and armor that would be able to operate even in the most difficult terrain:

(a) Type: tracked vehicle
(b) Armor: 60 mm [2.35 in.], not to be penetrated by antitank guns up to and including 47 mm at all ranges
(c) Engine: M-34 considering the transition to a diesel engine
(d) Armament: one 76 mm gun with a muzzle velocity of no less than 560 m/sec. [1.837 ft./sec.], two 45 mm guns with coaxial machine gun, one antiaircraft machine gun
(e) Speed: 25–35 kph [15.5–21.7 mph]
(f) Range: 200–250 km [124–155 mi.]
(g) Combat weight: no more than 55 tonnes [60.6 tons]. Dimensions must make rail transport possible.

A T-50 light tank, designed by Leningrad Factory No. 174

The three guns naturally required three turrets, which inevitably led to an increase in the weight of the vehicle, with clearly inadequate armor protection. Two Leningrad design bureaus received development orders: the Kirov Factory design bureau (chief designer Josef Kotin) and the Kirov Machine-Building Factory (chief designer Nikolai Barykov). In October 1938, they presented their designs to the review commission: on the one hand, the SMK

T-50 light tank after fording a stream

T-50 light tank

The version of the T-50 adopted by the Red Army

Rear view of a T-50

heavy breakthrough tank (abbreviation of Sergei Mironovich Kirov, a high party functionary and follower of Stalin, who had been assassinated in 1934); on the other, the "Project 100" (later referred to as the T-100). The commission examined both designs and concluded that they met the tactical and technical requirements. On December 9, 1938, they were presented at a meeting of the Defense Committee of the Politburo of the Central Committee of the Communist Party. During the discussion, Stalin approached the wooden model of the SMK and asked, "Comrade Kotin, why do your tanks need three turrets?" Kotin: "Because of its powerful armament: one 76 mm cannon and two 45 mm cannons." Stalin: "Don't make a 'Mur & Merylise' [the name of a luxury department store in prerevolutionary Moscow] out of a tank!" Stalin often used this expression when talking about things that seemed too complicated and universal to him. Then he took off the small rear turret with the 45 mm gun and asked Kotin: "How much have I taken off now?" "Three tons," Kotin replied. "Use the weight to strengthen the armor," Stalin explained and continued: "You must strive for stronger armor and better protection for the crew. A tank does not need several turrets. It would be best to keep it to one!"

This diverted the designers to new solutions: instead of a three-turret model, they designed (a) a two-turret model and (b) a single-turret model with increased armor protection. The design office of the Kirovsky Factory immediately set about implementing the single-turret model, which was named Klim Voroshilov (KV) after Soviet Marshal and Defense Commissar Kliment Voroshilov.

The prototypes were developed and built in a very short time, and testing began at a test site near Moscow in September 1939.

SMK Heavy Tank

When the Red Army invaded Finland on November 30, 1939, its high command decided to test the new heavy tank there. A special unit was set up with the three SMK, T-100, and KV prototypes and assigned to the 20th Heavy Tank Brigade fighting on the Finnish Mannerheim Line. The KV model proved to be the most successful and was adopted by the Red Army as the "KV heavy tank" on December 19, 1939, by resolution no. 443-ss of the Defense Committee. (After the introduction of the KV-2, armed with a 152 mm howitzer, the previous KV was given the extended designation KV-1, which we are already using here to distinguish it. A KV-3 version with reinforced armor and a more powerful engine was also developed).

> Accepted into the Red Army:
>
> "KV" tank: Heavy armor, manufactured at the "Kirov" plant of the People's Commissariat of Heavy Machine-Building (Narkomtyashmash) in accordance with the tactical and technical requirements of the NKO, with all deficiencies identified during testing being eliminated. The tank must be equipped with
>
> (a) 1 × 76 mm F-32 cannon paired with a 7.62-caliber machine gun in a turret mount,
>
> (b) one 7.62 mm machine gun served by the radio operator, and
>
> (c) one 7.62 mm machine gun in the turret rear.
>
> It is necessary to provide the crew with an all-around view from the tank.

The Kirov Factory began series production of the KV in February 1940. In accordance with the decree by the Council of People's Commissars of the USSR and the Central Committee of the CPSU (b) of June 19, 1940, the Chelyabinsk Tractor Plant (ChTZ) was also integrated into series

SMK heavy tank, view from the front right

SMK heavy tank

SMK heavy tank

T-100 heavy tank

production. On December 31, 1940, it delivered the first KV, while the construction of a special building for KV production began.

An output of 1,200 KV tanks of all versions was planned for 1941; 1,000 of these at the Kirov Factory (400 KV-1, 100 KV-2, 500 KV-3) and 200 (KV-1) at ChTZ. However, only a few vehicles were completed there by the start of the war. In 1940, only 139 KV-1s and 104 KV-2s were built, to which a further 393 vehicles were added in the first half of 1941 (including 100 KV-2s). By June 1941, 636 KV heavy tanks had been produced, 508 of which were in the western military districts. The total number of KV models built in Leningrad and Chelyabinsk up to the end of production in 1942 is estimated at 3,539 vehicles.

T-100 heavy tank, view from the front

KV-1 Heavy Tank

The KV-1 heavy tank was designed as a single-turret tank with a classic superstructure. The driver sat in the front section of the welded hull, and the fighting compartment was located in the middle section; the engine and transmission were located in the rear. The engine was a twelve-cylinder V-2K diesel producing 500 hp, and the transmission was an eight-speed gearbox with multidisc clutch. Due to supply bottlenecks, some vehicles were fitted with M-17 gasoline engines. The design of the multiplate clutch was not technically mature, which led to the breakdown of many KV-1s in the first months of the German-Soviet war—the crews abandoned the vehicles and fled the scene or were taken prisoner. Nevertheless, thanks to its powerful engine, the KV-1 was able to negotiate inclines of up to 36°, trenches 2.5 m (8.2 ft.) wide, and walls 1 m (3.3 ft.) high. The wide tracks caused a ground pressure of just 0.77 kg/cm^2 (10.95 psi), which meant that the KV could also cope well in boggy terrain. There were two turret types for the KV-1: a welded turret made of 75 mm thick sheet metal or a cast turret with 95 mm (2.95 in.) thick walls. During production, the armor protection of the hull was reinforced with additional 25 mm (0.98 in.) armor plates, and the wall thickness of the cast turret was increased to 105 mm (4.1 in.).

It is therefore not surprising that the KV-1 emerged unscathed from many battles, although it was often struck by dozens of shells, none of which penetrated. The main armament initially consisted of a 76.2 mm L-11 gun, later an F-32 of the same caliber, and from 1941 it received the 76.2 mm SIS-5 gun. In addition, it had three 7.62 mm machine guns: one on the left in the glacis (30° of traverse), a coaxial machine gun next to the main gun, and one in a ball mount in the turret rear. Some tanks were fitted with a rotating turret on the commander's hatch to accommodate an antiaircraft machine gun. The machine gun combat load amounted to 3,024 rounds.

In the prewar years, the Red Army searched for optimal organizational structures, especially in the armored forces. Weak points primarily concerned the cumbersome and complex command of the mechanized tank corps. At a meeting of the Military Council of the People's Commissariat of Defense in 1934, People's Commissar of Defense Voroshilov made no secret of his negative attitude toward the corps and practically blocked their further development and modernization. As a result, no corps exercises were carried out in the years 1936–38.

To revise the organizational and personnel structure of the troops in accordance with the decree of the Main Military Council of July 22, 1939, a special commission was set up under the chairmanship of the Deputy People's Defense Commissar, Army general first-rank G. I. Kulik. The commission examined the organization and structure

T-100 heavy tank, view from the front

of rifle and cavalry divisions, the artillery, and air defense units. At one of the meetings, deputy chief of the general staff M. V. Zakharov posed the following question: "Is it advisable to include tank battalions in rifle divisions; are tank and mechanized corps needed at all?" Most of the commission members insisted on leaving the tank battalions in the rifle divisions. At a meeting of the Supreme Military Council, K. E. Voroshilov and B. M. Shaposhnikov made the following decision: "Leave the tank battalions only in the assault rifle divisions, remove them from the others, and convert them into tank brigades of the RGK." A heated discussion ensued about the fate of the tank corps. S. K. Tymoshenko proposed that the structure of the tank arm be revised and include a strong motorized division instead of the rifle and machine gun brigade. Shaposhnikov and Kulik insisted on the abolition of the tank corps as a large unit that was far too unwieldy and difficult to manage. Kulik even agreed with the point that tanks should no longer be used for independent operational tasks. On the other hand, E. A. Shchadenko and S. M. Budyonny persistently tried to convince the commission that the tank corps played a significant role in deep and breakthrough operations. D. G. Pavlov, as head of the GABTU, avoided expressing his point of view and took a neutral position.

In the end, the majority of members voted in favor of retaining the corps and forming armored brigades (four battalions each) with the following main tasks:

- independent operations: equipped with BT tanks
- reinforcement of rifle divisions and corps: tank brigades of the RGK

In addition, eight light reserve tank regiments were to be set up or deployed for the training of crews, tank commanders, and command personnel. It was also proposed that motorized rifle brigades be disbanded, and their vehicles made available to light regiments with wheeled tanks. At the same time, it was recommended that the tank corps be retained in the interests of the infantry and cavalry for attack and breakthrough operations, and that their cooperation with the artillery be intensified. It was also recognized that tank corps should be allowed to act independently, especially when the enemy had been weakened.

Despite the commission's recommendation to retain the tank corps, People's Commissar of Defense Voroshilov wrote in his report no. 80870, of August 22, 1939, to the Central Committee of the CPSU (b) and the Council of People's Commissars of the USSR: "Mechanized corps, large formations that are difficult to manage, are to be disbanded. Therefore, four mechanized corps are being disbanded."

The swan song of the Red Army's tank corps was their participation in the "liberation campaign in western Ukraine," the invasion of eastern Poland (which at the time included parts of Ukraine and Belarus). During

KV-1 heavy tank

the "liberation campaign," troops from the Belorussian and Ukrainian army groups marched into Poland on September 17, 1939. They had been established only the day before in the special military districts of Belarus and Kiev. According to the official version, the purpose of the campaign was "the liberation of the oppressed workers, peasants, and laborers of western Ukraine and western Belarus."

The 15th Tank Corps (the former 5th Mechanized Corps) belonged to the Belorussian Front (Army Group) and the 25th Tank Corps (the former 45th Mechanized Corps) to the Ukrainian Front. Interesting is the report by the commander of the 25th Armored Corps, Colonel I. O. Yarkina, to the head of the GABTU, D. G. Pavlov: "From September 16 to 23, 1939, the 25th Armored Corps marched continuously without a single day of rest. During this time, it covered approx. 450 km [280 mi.]. The corps captured the towns of Chortkiv, Buchach, Monstadiska, Halych, Burschtyn, and Bolschowice. During the capture of these points, the corps brought about 1,000 [Polish] officers, 81 gendarmes, and 12,000 soldiers as prisoners and captured about 10,000 rifles, 150 machine guns, 20 cannons, about 300 motor vehicles, and 12 airplanes. Its own losses amounted to eight killed and twenty-four wounded.

"Marches of 400–450 km [248–279 mi.], plus 200 km [124 mi.] covered on night marches to Yarmolintsy, were an unprecedented strain on the equipment. We had carried out only a corps exercise with the entire equipment section shortly before the start of the campaign. In total, all the corps' combat vehicles have covered between 700 and 800 km [435 and 497 mi.] between August 30 and today. Despite this extreme strain on the vehicles and the long daily marches, only thirty BT-7s broke down due to technical difficulties, some of which could be easily repaired. These figures speak without exaggeration for the exceptionally conscientious attitude of all corps members in fulfilling the task set by the party and the government. In addition, we consider it necessary to inform you that we have solved the problem of supplying the corps with fuel under these difficult conditions and despite carrying out combat operations. At the Podzhumlyane and Bolshovice stations we took over 120 tons of gasoline, in Shurawno 165 tons, Stanislavów 25 tons, and Galish 70 tons. Only by taking over these quantities of fuel was it possible for the corps to fulfill its assigned task. The corps was supplied at the place of accommodation and from the country. At the present time, the 25th Tank Corps has 1.5 days' supply of fuel and lubricants, 2 days' supply of ammunition, and food for 2 days (except sugar)."

The invasion by the 15th Tank Corps of the Belorussian Front was less successful. Due to a lack of fuel, almost all its tanks were immobilized on September 19. Commander M. P. Kovalev, second-rank army commander, openly admitted his inability to supply the troops. "It's a good thing nobody had to fight there," Marshal of the Soviet Union S. M. Budyonny (who organized the supply of fuel to the 15th Tank Corps by air) later commented. The image of roads clogged with armored vehicles that had not a drop of fuel left was another reason for disbanding the corps. At a meeting on November 21, 1939, the Supreme Military Council, in the presence of Stalin and Molotov, decided to disband the four tank corps and establish fifteen motorized divisions in their place as part of the rifle troops, while independent tank brigades were to form the High Command Reserve (RGK). A motorized division was to consist of two motorized rifle, tank, and artillery regiments and be equipped with 475 machine guns, 66 heavy howitzers, 74 artillery pieces, 257 tanks, and 73 armored vehicles. Its personnel were to comprise 11,600 soldiers in wartime and 9,000 in peacetime. Remarkably, the number of tanks in the motorized division continued to decrease relative to the corps, whereas the number of motorized infantry and artillery pieces increased significantly. At the same time, the Russian motorized division of 1939 approached the structure of the German panzer division of 1941, one of the most powerful units of its time. In contrast to the Soviet tank division, the German panzer division had more personnel, with around 17,000 men, but with 147 to 229, significantly fewer, tanks (which was related to the reduction to one tank regiment due to the expansion of the tank force, since German panzer divisions originally had two tank regiments). Thus, the Soviet motorized division came very close to an optimal combination of tanks, artillery, and motorized infantry.

According to the decision of the Military Council, the armored corps, rifle, and machine gun brigades, as well as the rifle and machine gun battalions of tank units, were to be disbanded. The noncombat support units in the tank brigades were reduced.

After the Soviet-Finnish war, which had cost the Red Army heavy losses in men and material, Voroshilov was replaced by S. K. Timoshenko as people's commissar of defense on May 7, 1940. The "File of Comrade Timoshenko's taking over the post of People's Commissariat of the USSR from Comrade Voroshilov" stated: "The development of mechanized and tank forces . . . falls short of modern requirements for the use of tanks in concentration. . . . The existing tank brigades are not supported by a sufficient number of motorized units. The People's Commissariat of Defense has exercised unacceptable caution in the development of tank and mechanized troops, which is why the proportion of mechanized troops is low and the number of tanks in the Red Army is insufficient. The armament of tank units . . . also lagged behind modern requirements, because of which the introduction of modern heavy tanks was extremely slow. In the last two years, the available fleet of armored vehicles has been intensively used in combat conditions (Khalkhin-Gol, the campaign in western Ukraine and western Belarus [the invasion of Poland], and in the war with the Whites [Finns]), which is why a large part of it requires major and medium repairs. However, despite the availability of sufficient repair capacities, the repair of these vehicles is delayed due to the lack of necessary spare parts."

KV-1 heavy tank on the testing grounds. Note the supplemental armor on the turret and hull front.

To be fair, it should be noted that the Red Army's armored forces grew rapidly under Voroshilov's leadership. At the end of the first five-year plan (1932), the tank fleet comprised around 5,000 vehicles, but by May 1940 it had quadrupled to 20,074 vehicles, making it by far the strongest armored force in the world. The 20,074 vehicles consisted of

- T-35 heavy tanks (60),
- T-28 medium tanks (470),
- BT light tanks (7,300),
- T-26 light tanks: 7,983,
- T-26 flamethrower tanks (1,027), and
- T-37, T-38, and T-40 amphibious tanks (3,023).

There were also 3,155 T-27 tankettes armed with machine guns and 187 XT-27 tankettes with flamethrowers.

The victorious German campaign in the west from May to June 1940 had a decisive influence on the attitude of the Soviet military leadership toward large, armored units. Fast German armored units, in cooperation with the Luftwaffe, had quickly defeated the armies of France, Great Britain, Belgium, and the Netherlands. The role of the German armored and motorized units was decisive for this magnificent victory.

At the end of May 1940, Stalin summoned the chief of the general staff, B. M. Shaposhnikov, and his deputy, I. V. Smorodinov, to the Kremlin. Stalin asked, "Why are there no mechanized and tank corps in our army? These have proven their combat value with the German-Fascist army in Poland and in the West. We must tackle this question immediately and set up several corps with 1,000–1,200 tanks."

Stalin's order marked the rebirth of the corps. The General Staff of the Red Army quickly designed a mechanized corps with a new organizational and personnel structure, which the Council of People's Commissars approved just as quickly:

Council of People's Commissars of the USSR, July 6, 1940, Moscow, Kremlin, no. 1193-464-ss

The Council of People's Commissars of the USSR decides

1. Approval of the organization of the mechanized corps, consisting of two tank divisions (TD), a motorized division (MD), a motorized rifle regiment (MRR), an air transport squadron, a corps transport battalion, and a corps intelligence section. In addition, the mechanized corps receives an air brigade consisting of two short-range bomber regiments and a fighter regiment.
2. The tank divisions of the mechanized corps and the independent tank divisions are organized into

   (a) two tank regiments, one battalion of heavy tanks, two battalions of medium tanks, and one battalion of flamethrower tanks per regiment;
   (b) one mechanized regiment, consisting of three rifle battalions and one battery with six guns regimental artillery;
   (c) one artillery regiment of two battalions: one battalion of 122 mm howitzers and one battalion of 152 mm howitzers; and
   (d) air defense battalion, reconnaissance battalion, combat engineer bridging battalion, and rear services.

A tank division has heavy tanks: 105, medium tanks: 227, flamethrower tanks: 54, total: 386; armored vehicles: 108, 152 mm howitzers: 12, 122 mm howitzers: 12, 76 mm regimental guns: 6, 37 mm antiaircraft guns: 12, 82 mm mortars: 18, 50 mm mortars: 54, heavy machine guns: 6, machine guns: ***, light machine guns: 122, submachine guns: 390, automatic rifles: 1,528.

3. A motorized division with composition and structure according to the decree by the KO of May 22, 1940, no. 215-ss.
4. Personnel Complement:

   (a) Corps command of a mechanized corps with one motorcycle regiment in peacetime: 2,662 men, and in wartime: 2,862 men
   (b) One tank division in peacetime: 10,493 men, and in wartime: 11,343 men
   (c) one mechanized division in peacetime: 11,000 men, and in wartime: 12,000 men

Knocked-out or abandoned KV-1 in the summer of 1941

5. Altogether the Red Army has nine mechanized corps and two independent tank divisions, a total of eight mechanized corps commands with motorcycle regiments and corps units, eighteen tank divisions, and eight motorized divisions.

The existing tank brigades, mainly in the border districts, were envisaged for restructuring into tank divisions. Motorized divisions were created from rifle formations. Enlisted men and the command personnel came from disbanded cavalry divisions and corps. In 1940 these were, in the Western Special Military District, the 3rd Cavalry Corps and the 7th, 11th, and 4th Cavalry Divisions; in the Kiev Special Military District, the 4th Cavalry Corps and the 16th and 34th Cavalry Divisions; in the Leningrad Military District, the 25th Cavalry Division; in the North Caucasus Military District, the 10th and 12th Cavalry Divisions; in the Far East, the 31st Cavalry Division; and in the Transbaikal Military District, the 15th and 22nd Cavalry Divisions. The 8th Mechanized Corps of the Kiev Special Military District was formed on the basis of the 8th Mechanized Corps.

The commander of the 6th Cavalry Corps, A. I. Yeryomenko, became commander of the 3rd Mechanized Corps, whose formation began in the west and ended in the Baltic Military District. Many cavalrymen became tank soldiers in 1940.

The 2nd Mechanized Corps, to which the 11th and 16th Tank and the 15th Motorized Divisions, plus the 6th Motorcycle Regiment, the 182nd Independent Signals Battalion, and the 49th Combat Engineer Battalion, belonged, was created from the 55th Rifle Corps, the 173rd Rifle Division, and the 4th Tank Brigade in the Odessa Military District. The 8th Mechanized Corps of the Kiev Military District was created from the 4th Cavalry Corps, the 7th Rifle Division, and the 14th Heavy and 23rd Light Tank Brigades.

KV-2 heavy tank with 152 mm howitzer for infantry support and engaging field positions

The following mechanized corps were established by the end of 1940:

- the 1st, in the Leningrad Military District: 1st and 3rd Tank Divisions, 163rd Motorized Division, 5th Motorcycle Regiment
- the 2nd, in the Odessa Military District: 11th and 16th Tank Divisions, 15th Motorized Division, 6th Motorcycle Regiment
- the 3rd, in the Baltic Military District: 2nd and 5th Tank Divisions, 84th Motorized Division
- the 4th, in the Kiev Special Military District: 8th and 32nd Tank Divisions, 81st Motorized Division
- the 5th, in the Transbaikal Military District: 13th and 17th Tank Divisions, 109th Motorized Division, 8th Motorcycle Regiment
- the 6th, in the Western Special Military District: 4th and 7th Tank Divisions, 29th Motorized Division, 4th Motorcycle Regiment
- the 7th, in the Moscow Military District: 14th and 18th Tank Divisions, 1st Motorized Division, 4th Motorcycle Regiment
- the 8th, in the Kiev Special Military District: 12th and 34th Tank Divisions, 7th Motorized Division, 2nd Motorcycle Regiment

The 6th Tank Division was formed in the Transcaucasian Military District, and the 9th Tank Division in the Central Asian Military District. At the end of 1940 the 9th Mechanized Corps was also formed in the Kiev Special Military District.

Besides nine mechanized corps and two independent tank divisions, the People's Commissariat for Defense also planned twenty-three independent tank brigades and units in battalion and regiment strength as elements of rifle and cavalry divisions. More than 18,000 tanks of various types were required to equip these units, including 6,354 heavy and medium tanks (KV and T-34). This would be possible by spring 1942 at the earliest.

In March 1941, at the suggestion of the chief of the general staff, G. K. Zhukov, the government approved new measures for the formation of tank units. The nine mechanized corps were to be joined by a further twenty, which were to be equipped with around 32,000 armored vehicles, including 16,600 T-34 and KV tanks. It would take at least four to five years to meet this demand with the tank industry's previous capacities (1940–41).

One of the reasons for this strangely exaggerated rearmament was probably the Soviet secret service's faulty assessment of the potential of the German tank industry. According to their estimates, the Wehrmacht and Waffen-SS had 10,000 tanks at the beginning of 1941, a number that could rise to 21,400 to 22,000 by the end of the year. This was based solely on the presumed capacities of the German tank industry, a truly blatant overestimation! And if Germany were to use all available resources, it was estimated that the number of tanks could grow to 40,000 vehicles by the beginning of 1942!

A two-stage plan was adopted so as to have a sufficient number of operational units in the near future and to ensure the implementation of the program to establish mechanized corps. In a first step, twenty-six mechanized corps were to be established in the following districts:

- Leningrad Military District (1st and 10th Mechanized Corps)
- Baltic Special Military District (3rd and 12th Mechanized Corps)
- Western Special Military District (6th, 14th, 11th, 13th, 17th, and 20th Mechanized Corps)
- Kiev Special Military Districts (22nd, 8th, 4th, 16th, 15th, 9th, 19th, and 24th Mechanized Corps)
- Odessa Military District: (2nd and 8th Mechanized Corps)
- Transcaucasian Military District (28th Mechanized Corps)
- Far Eastern Front (30th Mechanized Corps, 59th and 69th, etc.)
- Transbaikal Military District (5th and 29th Mechanized Corps)
- Moscow Military District (7th and 21st Mechanized Corps)

In a second step, the remaining four mechanized corps were to be established and stationed in the inner military districts.

Curiously, the corps to be established in the first step were differentiated into operational corps and those in the process of formation. The nineteen operational corps were given priority in equipment and personnel and the seven "in the formation process" (13th, 17th, 20th, 19th, 24th, 18th, and 21st Mechanized Corps) were supplied according to the "utilization of leftovers" principle. The last-mentioned corps were only partially equipped when the war between Germany and the Soviet Union began. They were in fact large training formations. So that they could be employed as antitank regiments and battalions in critical situations, as per the General Staff directive of May 16, 1941, fifty tank regiments of mechanized corps were armed with 76 mm and 45 mm guns and DT machine guns until they received tanks. The measures taken could play a major role in increasing their combat readiness and bolstering the antitank defenses. In the Western Special Military District, five tank regiments of the 20th, four of the 17th, and a tank regiment and a reconnaissance battalion of the 13th Mechanized Corps were to be liberally equipped with antitank guns. Each regiment received eighteen 45 mm guns, twenty-four 76 mm guns, and twenty-four (heavy) machine guns, and the reconnaissance battalion eighteen 45 mm guns. These measures were supposed to be implemented by July 1, 1941.

All four mechanized corps of the second step (25th, 23rd, 26th, and 27th) were downsized.

To reach their authorized strengths, the combined mechanized corps required more than 30,000 tanks, including 16,600 of the new T-34s and KVs, plus more than 7,000 armored vehicles. Existing stocks and production capacities were insufficient to meet these requirements. Equipping these corps with new tanks would take at least four to five years. More than 40 percent of the older main types (T-26 and BT) had been built between 1931 and 1935. These vehicles underwent a maintenance and modernization program, which had not been completed by the summer of 1941. Neither sufficient spare parts nor repair facilities were available for the required work. Soviet industry was able to deliver only 11 percent of the required spare parts by June 1, 1941. This once again showed the weaknesses of "socialist planning" in the USSR, which, while it had created a gigantic army, the largest in the world, had foolishly neglected to ensure the supply of the spare parts it required.

In a detail comparison with the authorized strengths of German panzer divisions (1941), it is striking that the Soviets had only half as many light field howitzers and one-fifth the number of medium guns. On the other hand, with a strength of 375 tanks (with 3,000 men) compared to 147 to 209 on the German side, (6,000 men; including rifle regiments) they possessed a clear numerical superiority. A Soviet motorized division had 273 tanks with a personnel strength of 6,000 men. In the motorized infantry, the numbers of antitank guns were quite similar on both sides, as well as in other areas.

As practice showed, the German organization was much better suited to modern mobile warfare than the Soviet one, even though the Soviets had significantly more tanks. Of course, the Germans had already been up against numerically superior opponents in the Western campaign of 1940. The secret of their success lay to a not inconsiderable extent in their better and more flexible leadership at all levels. Unlike the French, British, or Soviet forces, the German armed forces did not act according to command tactics, but according to mission tactics, which gave officers, NCOs, and even enlisted men leeway to fulfill their mission. And naturally, the German soldiers were among the best in the world in terms of training, fighting ability, and fighting morale.

One of the main disadvantages of the Soviet mechanized corps was the presence of at least five types of tanks, which could not operate as a unit within a formation (the Germans also had this problem but solved it better). Heavy KV-1s were suitable as breakthrough tanks, while light T-26s were designed to support the infantry. Combined in detachments as part of rifle divisions or in independent brigades/regiments, however, the T-26 was quite useful. Then there were the fast BT-7 and T-34 tanks, which were suitable not only for tactical—in contrast to the slow KV and T-26—but also for operational missions. In general, the entire range of tanks produced by the Soviet Union before the war was represented in the mechanized corps. The Red Army (in contrast to the German *Panzertruppe*) never really got to grips with the interaction of the various tank types, and so the T-26 and KV-1 often became the "mobility brakes" of the mechanized corps.

The following report by the chairman of the defense committee, Voroshilov, to Stalin reflects the situation in tank construction immediately before the start of the war:

Report by the Chairman of the Defense Committee of the Council of People's Commissars of the USSR, K. E. Voroshilov, to the Secretary of the Central Committee of the CPSU (b), I. V. Stalin

Concerning the Situation in Tank Construction, January 10, 1941

On your instructions in December 1940, employees of the Defense Committee (KO) were sent to the following factories producing tanks and tank parts for a detailed examination of tank construction: Kirov Factory, Izhora and No. 174 (Leningrad), No. 183 and No. 75 (Kharkov), Mariupol, STZ, as well as No. 264 (Stalingrad) and No. 37 (Moscow).

According to the information obtained by these employees, the qualitative condition of the new tank types and the implementation of the program are characterized by the following facts:

KV Tank (Kirov Factory, Leningrad)

The KV tank surpasses the old tank types in terms of driving performance, armor, and armament and is the best vehicle of all new models of heavy tanks produced by our tank industry in the last two to three years. The Kirov Factory met its production goals. By January 1, 1941, the plant completed 243 vehicles, with an annual target of 243 units, and handed them over for military acceptance. 238 vehicles were delivered to military units, 51 of them to Kovno, 52 to Bialystok, 41 to Stryi, 48 to Lviv, and 22 to the Kiev district. Representatives of the ABTU of the Red Army, who took part in the factory testing of the first series of U-7 and U-21 tanks to determine the strength of individual components after 3,000 km [1,864 mi.], believe that the KV tank is a fully operational combat vehicle. This is confirmed by factory test certificates and military acceptance certificates for each vehicle. As a result of the work carried out at the factory to eliminate identified design and technical defects, the latest versions of the KV tank have been significantly improved in their driving performance. For vehicles of the first series, the factory guaranteed uninterrupted operation over 200 km [124 mi.]. According to an agreement between the plant and the GABTU of the Red Army, the guarantee has already been given for 2,000 km [1,242 mi.]. However, according to the results of tests carried out at the plant together with representatives of the Red Army, it has been established that not every mass-produced KV tank achieves trouble-free operation over 2,000 km, due to insufficient strength of individual components.

The following defects in the KV tank have not yet been rectified:

1. The air filter does not do a good job of cleaning dust from the air, resulting in premature engine wear.
2. The cooling system of the KV tank does not guarantee normal operation of the engine due to the high water and oil temperatures.
3. Despite its reinforcement, the transmission still has defects—premature wear of the gearwheels for second to fourth gears and destruction of the roller bearings after 1.5 thousand km of driving.
4. The tracks must be replaced after 1.5 thousand km [932 mi.] of travel, since they wear out and lose their strength (cracks appear).
5. The V-2 diesel engine, with an output of 600 hp, is not powerful enough for KV tanks, especially the version with the 152 mm howitzer [KV-2], and does not achieve the desired speeds (20–21 kph [12.4–13 mph] on paved roads instead of 35 kph [21.75 mph], 14 kph [8.7 mph] on unpaved roads, 10–11 kph [6.2–6.8 mph] on uneven terrain). When turning in second gear, the tank stops and has no power reserve.

Factory No. 75 (Kharkov) is currently working on increasing the power of the diesel engine for KV tanks to 700 hp and the service life to up to 200 hours in accordance with the KO decree of November 19, 1940.

6. The existing openings in the roof for the air intake are not yet secured against the possible penetration of burning liquids into the interior of the tank.
7. The turret shoulder and the turret ring are exposed, which can cause the turret to jam if it is hit by a shell.
8. The hatch closures of the transmission compartment have not been improved and can be opened from the outside.
9. There is no ventilation in the fighting compartment if the engine is not running.
10. Not improved: storage of ammunition, field of view, and steerability—all of this makes the crew's work more difficult.

The aforementioned defects must be remedied by March 1, 1941, as per KO decree no. 428-s of November 19, 1940.

At the same time, it should be noted that due to the overloading of the design bureau with work on the design of new types of tanks, the elimination of the shortcomings of the KV tanks at the "Kirov" plant is still proceeding slowly (tanks with 90 mm and 100 mm armor, T-50 tanks); by December 28, 1940, the Kirov plant had produced one vehicle with 90 mm and 100 mm armor. It showed good results on a 140 km march.

Tank production capacity at the Kirov Factory has been significantly expanded. Five main facilities are engaged in tank production. Currently, the Kirov Factory can produce 55 to 60 tanks per month. The assembly plant and the subassembly plant can already produce 60 to 70 sets per month, but the mechanical workshops are still inadequate in terms of area and equipment.

The second base for production of KV tanks is the tractor plant in Chelyabinsk (ChTZ), which is gearing up for an annual output of 300 tanks. However, production preparations at ChTZ are proceeding too slowly.

T-34 Tank (Factory No. 183, Kharkov)

Factory No. 183 delivered 114 T-34s as of January 1, 1941, with an annual target of 500 units. The delay in production of the T-34 at Factory No. 183 is caused by a poor technological process and inadequate equipment, tools, and facilities.

Military tests from October to December 1940 along the Kharkov-Kubinka-Smolensk-Kiev-Kharkov route with a total length of about 3,000 km [1,864 mi.], including 1,000 km [621 mi.] on paved roads and 2,000 km [1,242 mi.] on various surfaces, including overcoming natural obstacles, showed that the performance of 2,000 km without overhaul guaranteed by the factory could not be met. Individual components of the tank are not stable enough and fail after 800–1,200 km [497–745 mi.] due to the following defects:

(a) The main clutch plates are warped and tripped.
(b) Cast track links wear quickly and break.
(c) Fan blades break.
(d) The transmission is not sufficiently robust and is structurally imperfect; it is difficult to change gears, the teeth of the gears wear out quickly, the gears jam on the shafts.

The visibility from the vehicle is unsatisfactory; the viewing devices are positioned unfavorably and have too small an observation angle (53 degrees from the turret). It is impossible to clean them of dirt without leaving the tank. Ventilation of the fighting compartment is inadequate: after 12 shots have been fired from the main gun, the CO content is 0.5 mg/l, with a permissible level of 0.1 mg/l, which can have a detrimental effect on the crew. It is cramped in the turret of the tank, [and] the ammunition holders are not well thought out, which makes the crew's work more difficult and reduces the possible rate of fire.

In a decree dated November 19, 1940, the Defense Committee ordered Factory No. 183 to eliminate the defects of the T-34 tank and to increase the overhaul intervals to 7,000 km [4,350 mi.] and those of the running gear to 3,000 km [1,864 mi.] from February 1, 1941.

The production capacity of Factory No. 183 for the T-34 is being expanded. The plant can currently produce 100–120 vehicles per month. There is enough production space at the plant, but the workshops are not yet fully equipped with equipment.

The second T-34 production base is STZ. According to the 1940 plan, the plant was to produce 100 T-34s, but by December 28, 1940, not a single tank had been delivered and only 11 vehicles had been produced. Production preparations and processes at STZ were very slow. There is enough space for tank production, but the workshops are not equipped with the necessary equipment.

T-40 Amphibious Tank (Factory No. 37, Moscow)

The T-40 amphibious tank has passed extensive military and field tests. The last tests were carried out in October of this year along the Moscow-Smolensk-Minsk-Zhitomir-Kiev-Bryansk-Moscow route, with a total length of about 3,000 km [1,864 mi.], crossing a number of rivers (Dnieper, Desna, Pripyat) and the 7 km wide [4.3 mi. wide] Knyaz' Lake.

The test results showed that the T-40 met the Red Army's tactical and technical requirements. At the same time, several serious shortcomings were identified during the tests. For example:

1. Increased wear of the engine piston group due to poor functioning of the air filter and piston ring lubrication
2. Difficulty starting the engine, especially at low ambient temperatures
3. The tracks jammed between the drive sprocket and the fender.
4. Insufficient strength of the return rollers with respect to bearings and rubber running characteristics
5. Increased wear of the track parts

According to the KO decree, Plant No. 37 is obliged to ensure that the initial overhaul interval of the T-40 is not before 8,000 km [4,970 mi.] and that the chassis has a mileage of at least 4,000 km [2,485 mi.]. The main difficulty at Factory No. 37 is the unsatisfactory supply of main assemblies, especially hulls and engines.

T-50 Light Tank

The Defense Committee approved the tactical and technical requirements for the T-50 tank with decree no. 427 of November 19, 1940, and commissioned the People's Commissariat for Medium Machine Building (NKSM) and the People's Commissariat for Heavy Machine Building (NKTM) to produce two prototypes each. In December 1940, Factory No. 174 NKSM (Leningrad) produced two T-50s, which are currently being tested at the plant. The Kirov Factory NKTM (Leningrad) stated that two T-50s could be produced only by January 20–25, 1941.

Production of Armor Steel and Tank Hulls

The following factories of the People's Commissariat of the Shipbuilding Industry (NKSP) were engaged in the production of armor plates of all thicknesses in 1940: Izhora, Mariupol, and Kulebak; factories of the People's Commissariat of Ferrous Metallurgy (NKShM): Vyksa and Taganrog. In connection with the expansion of tank production in 1941, the following plants were involved in the production of armor steel: Red October NKShM (Stalingrad) for the production of rolled plates up to 45 mm [1.77 in.]; Zaporizhzhal NKShM for the production of rolled plates up to 75 mm [3 in.]; Kirov factory NKTM (Leningrad) for the production of rolled plates up to 75 mm. The production of hulls and turrets for tanks and armored vehicles takes place in the following plants: Izhora and Mariupol, Plant No. 183 (Kharkov), Vyksa, and, since 1941, Factory No. 264 (Stalingrad), Factory No. 78 (Chelyabinsk). Factory No. 264 proved to be a significant brake on the production of armored T-34 hulls. The construction, provision of equipment, and preparation for the production of tank hulls at this plant is progressing extremely slowly. Tank production at STZ depends on the capacity of this plant. Factories producing armored hulls and turrets for tanks lack presses and mechanical equipment.

Production of Tank Engines

Diesel engines are manufactured and installed in just one factory, No. 75 NKSM, Kharkov: V-2K 600 hp for the KV, V-2 500 hp for the T-34, V-2-V 350 hp for the Voroshilovets tractor, and additionally the planned V-3 of 300 hp for the T-50.

The V-2K, V-2, and V-2-V diesel engines are difficult to manufacture and still do not offer sufficient service life before they are overhauled. The warranty period for diesel engines is 100 hours. By decree no. 428-ss, the Defense Committee obliges the NKSM Factory No. 75 to extend the warranty period for the operation of diesel engines to 150 hours from January 1, 1941, and to 200 hours from June 1, 1941.

Until recently, the following defects in the V-2 diesel engine were not rectified:

1. Fuel leakage at the connection point between the cylinder head and cylinder block
2. Development of the fuel pump drive clutch
3. Loss of compression due to premature wear of piston rings and cylinders
4. The design of the air filter is not well thought out, which significantly shortens the service life of the diesel engine.

Production capacity of Factory No. 75 NKSM was only 5.5 to 7 thousand diesel engines per year. By January 1, 1942, the demand for these diesel engines in relation to the production capacities of the tank factories will be 800–1,000 units for KV (Kirovsky factory), 500–600 units for KV (Chelyabinsk factory) and T-34 (Factory No. 183, Kharkov) 2.3–2.6 thousand units for T-34 (Stalingrad plant), 2.4–2.8 thousand units for the T-50 (Factory No. 174, Leningrad), 2–2.4 thousand units for Voroshilovets Tractor (Factory No. 183), 1–1.1 thousand units for ??? [*sic*]; a total of 9–10.5 thousand units. Since the service life of a diesel engine until the first overhaul interval is too short, the Defense Committee has decided to produce diesel engines under the following condition: For every two new tanks accepted, a replacement engine will be supplied. This increases demand by 4.5–5.25 thousand units per year. In addition, production of the M-17-T engine installed in the BT-7 was discontinued. Some of the BT-7s will therefore have to be equipped with V-2 diesel engines. Thus, the total demand for diesel engines for tanks on January 1, 1942, will be 16–18 thousand units per year.

To supply the tank-building industry with engines and spare parts, the existing capacities for the production of diesel engines must be expanded as quickly as possible. At present, there are proposals to increase the capacity of the NKSM Factory No. 75 and to create a new factory for the production of diesel engines at the Stalingrad Tractor Factory in accordance with the decision of the Council of People's Commissars of the USSR and the Central Committee of the Communist Party (b) No. 976-368 of June 7, 1940. The Defense Committee set the following tasks for our tank industry (KO decree no. 124 of May 28, 1939 [2]; no. 37 of August 29, 1940; no. 390 of October 9, 1940; and no. 428 of November 19, 1940):

1. Research into and introduction of armor with increased resistance (without increasing the thickness) and the production of cast armor steel
2. Increasing the service life of the main assemblies (engine, transmission, side clutches, tracks, etc.)
3. Development and production of an improved transmission and chassis (planetary gearbox, torsion bar suspension, road wheels with internal rubber shock absorption, rubber-coated tracks, etc.)
4. Improvement of the drive system (comfort for the crews, reduction of the effort required for shifting and steering, etc.)

signed. Voroshilov

CHAPTER 4
THE SOVIET TANK ARM IN THE GREAT PATRIOTIC WAR

In the spring and summer of 1941, two unprecedented forces were concentrated on the western borders of the USSR (including occupied territories): the Red Army on one side and the German Wehrmacht and its allies on the other. At the time of the German attack on the USSR on June 22, 1941, the balance of forces was as follows:

	Red Army	**Enemy**
Divisions:	190	166
Personnel strength:	3,289,851 (western districts)	4,306,800*
Guns and mortars:	59,787	42,601
Tanks and assault guns:	15,687	4,846*
Aircraft:	10,743	4,846*

* *Author's note*: According to official Soviet sources. The actual strength of the German armed forces at the beginning of Operation Barbarossa was approximately 3 million men, 3,580 armored vehicles, 7,184 guns, and 1,830 aircraft. The armored vehicles and aircraft of Germany's allies made little difference. Vehicles, equipment, and troops that did not take part in the attack are probably also included in these figures.

The Soviet troops were outnumbered by the enemy only in the western military districts, but this deficiency was quickly eliminated: By July 1, manpower had climbed to 5.8 million and by the end of 1941 to 7.2 million soldiers. Thus, the Red Army already had a clear material superiority at the time of the German attack but had not yet completed the process of strategic preparation for its own attack according to Stalin's plans. In the border battles, the Red Army suffered catastrophic losses in men and material. Eight mechanized corps were completely destroyed.

Lieutenant General Yakov Fedorenko, deputy people's commissar for defense, saw some of the reasons for the devastating defeat in organizational and tactical weaknesses and the fact that the mechanized corps had not yet been fully equipped:

SECRET

DEPUTY PEOPLE'S COMMISSAR FOR DEFENSE OF THE USSR

Lieutenant General of the Armored Forces FEDORENKO

REPORT ON COMBAT OPERATIONS BY THE ARMORED FORCES ON THE WESTERN FRONT FOR THE PERIOD FROM JUNE 22 TO JULY 27, 1941

I. Readiness of the Mechanized Corps at the Beginning of the War

Preparation of the 5th, 6th, 7th, 11th, 13th, 14th, 17th, and 20th Mechanized Corps with combat and auxiliary material, ammunition, fuel, and lubricants and their deployment before the fight against the fascists.

(a) Mechanized corps (with the exception of the first three) were equipped with 15–20 percent of combat and auxiliary material. Artillery units, which are part of the mechanized corps, were equipped with about 10–15 percent. The equipment based on which the mechanized corps was deployed and with which it entered the battles consisted mainly of T-26, BT-2, and BT-7 tanks with an average fuel reserve of 75–100 hours.

(b) The tactical training of the mechanized corps was carried out in accordance with the program for the armored forces, but in most cases it had to act as infantry and did not have enough suitable weapons.

(c) Before the outbreak of hostilities, the mechanized corps was not fully supplied with fuel and lubricants, although it reported a need for fuel and lubricants in good time, since there was not enough transport capacity for transport (tankers, fuel drums). The organization of the delivery was also not well thought out. Fuel and lubricants were delivered mainly during the day, [and] the transport columns were not given cover, which is why these convoys were often exposed to the enemy air force without protection, because of which fuel and lubricants did not reach the formations.

(d) The deployment of the mechanized corps did not correspond to the intentions of the Western Front command: the 13th and 14th Mechanized Corps were in the immediate vicinity of the border, and the tank division stationed in Brest was under enemy artillery fire. It took longer to move back to its starting position than it took the enemy advancing across the border.

CONCLUSION: The supplying of ammunition, fuel, and lubricants to the mechanized corps requires a radical change.

The supplying of ammunition, fuel, and lubricants calls for a tracked vehicle (capable of moving off-road) with mandatory armor that provides protection at least against armor-piercing small-arms rounds.

II. Reconnaissance

Tank divisions and units were usually not informed of the results of aerial reconnaissance, which led to blind actions. Ground reconnaissance units did not have enough trained personnel and almost no means of communication. As a result, the weak reconnaissance forces could not penetrate the enemy's reconnaissance and security veil and conducted reconnaissance only by observation.

Independent reconnaissance subunits that penetrated deep into the enemy zone and reached important reconnaissance targets were unable to transmit important messages due to a lack of radio equipment.

CONCLUSION: Armored units lacked aerial reconnaissance and suitable means for ground reconnaissance. In the future it is necessary to

provide tank units with aerial reconnaissance to a depth of 100–150 km [62–93 mi.].

The units must have capable reconnaissance units that are equipped with radios with a range of at least 50 km [31 mi.].

Reconnaissance in the main direction should be carried out by powerful forces capable of penetrating the enemy's reconnaissance and security screens. Reconnaissance in secondary directions can be carried out by motorcycle teams.

III. Cooperation by Tank Units with Infantry, Artillery, and Aviation:

The problem of the cooperation between these branches of service is relevant.

Without addressing this issue, it is unthinkable to hope to win battles or at least achieve partial successes. Nevertheless, the commanders of units and large formations did not devote the necessary attention to this issue.

(b) There was no artillery preparation before tank attacks, and where it did take place, it lasted only 10 to 15 minutes, which did not ensure the elimination of important enemy defenses, mainly antitank guns. The artillery did not provide sufficient support for the tanks. Attacking tanks encountered heavy fire from antitank guns and suffered significant casualties since there was no proper coordination between tanks and artillery.

(c) The infantry generally lagged behind the tanks and did not follow them to the lines they had reached.

(d) The question of interaction between tanks and the air force was also not thoroughly thought through: our tanks had no air identification markers, and the infantry also never marked its positions. This made it difficult for the air force to distinguish between its own and enemy units.

CONCLUSION: It is necessary to improve artillery reconnaissance and extend artillery preparation for tank attacks to disrupt the antitank system and prevent

A platoon of T-40 light amphibious tanks reaches the frontline railway station.

the enemy from engaging advancing tanks. The artillery should be supported by the air force. Tanks should go on the attack without waiting for the end of artillery preparation and cover from the air. Only when the problem of the interaction of these three types of weapons has been solved will tank attacks be successful.

IV. Deployment of Tank Units

At the beginning of the fighting on the Western Front, of all the mechanized formations only the 6th Mechanized Corps was fully equipped. The 14th Mechanized Corps had two tank divisions with 50 percent light tanks, while in the 11th Mechanized Corps, only one division was 50 percent equipped with light tanks. The remaining corps (17th and 20th) were not equipped with tanks and consisted of units of tank soldiers without vehicles. Only the training units had vehicles for training purposes. The commander of the 7th Tank Division of the 6th Mechanized Corps, Major General of Armored Troops Borzilov, wrote in his report: "At this stage, instead of a corps, it is better to rely on tank divisions and individual regiments, which are better adapted to the tactics of the German army." The last position is completely wrong; we do not have to adapt to the enemy's tactics, [but] we must force the enemy to adapt to our tactics. A fully equipped mechanized corps can solve tasks at army and even army group level. However, the actions of the 6th Mechanized Corps at the beginning of the war and the 5th and 7th Mechanized Corps did not produce significant results. The reasons for this failure were as follows:

The commander of a T-26 briefing his crew

The lack of air reconnaissance and communications aircraft led to blind actions.

The inadequate support by bomber aircraft and the weakness of our artillery led to poorly prepared attacks against strong defenses.

Inadequate defense by our fighters made it possible for enemy dive-bombers to attack tanks with incendiary and high-explosive bombs unhindered.

Improper use of the mechanized corps in difficult terrain without communications with infantry, artillery, and air force for counterattacks within the framework of the general defense of the front (see report by the commander of the 7th Tank Division).

CONCLUSION: Mechanized formations have not lost their importance and are a powerful weapon in the hands of the army and the high command, but they should not be used in isolation from other troops, but in joint cooperation and with the obligatory support of powerful air units.

signed

Head of the Western Front Tank Command Colonel Ivanin, Military Commissar of the Tank Command of the Western. Front Regimental Commissar Zinkov

Similar reports were also sent to the head of the Main Tank Directorate of the Red Army Fedorenko by the heads of tank commands on other fronts.

Heavy losses of military equipment made it necessary for the Soviet High Command to significantly change the organizational structure of the tank forces. Therefore, in accordance with the High Command's directive letter of July 15, 1941, the disbandment of the mechanized corps began and went on until September 1941. In connection with the dissolution of the corps, the associated tank divisions were subordinated to the commanders of the armies, and the motorized divisions were reorganized into rifle divisions. On July 6, the High Command ordered the formation of twelve new RGK tank divisions to increase the striking power of the armored units. Ten divisions (101st to 110th) were formed from the 26th and 27th Mechanized Corps and a number of formations from the Moscow, Orel, and Volga Military Districts. The 111th and 112th Tank Divisions, on the other hand, were formed from units from the Transbaikal Military District and the Far Eastern Front. Due to the lack of tanks, the 101st, 103rd, 106th, and 107th Tank Divisions were formed as motorized

Female Soviet officers inspecting a knocked-out German Panzerkampfwagen IV tank

rifle divisions, with just one tank battalion and two motorized rifle regiments. The armored divisions were formed according to table of organization 010/44:

- division headquarters
- 1 headquarters company
- 1 reconnaissance battalion
- 2 tank regiments
- 1 motorized rifle regiment
- 1 antitank artillery regiment
- 1 antiaircraft artillery regiment
- 1 workshop and repair company
- 1 supply section
- military prosecution office
- 1 field post office
- 1 independent rifle platoon of the NKVD
- 1 special battalion of the NKVD

The division had the following authorized equipment strengths:

- KV heavy tanks: 20
- medium tanks: 42
- light tanks: 143
- T-37A / T-38 amphibious tanks: 22
- medium wheeled armored vehicles: 22
- light wheeled armored vehicles: 17
- Komsomolets tractors: 20
- Komintern tractors: 21
- STS-3/5 tractors: 31
- cars: 24
- trucks: 565
- type A/5 workshop trucks: 37
- tanker trucks (fuel): 76
- tanker trucks (water): 8
- motorcycles: 173
- buses: 22

The remaining armament (excluding personal small arms) consisted of 15 12.7 mm machine guns, 3 M4 triple-mount machine guns, 37 Maxim heavy machine guns,

181 DP light machine guns, 27 50 mm mortars, 18 82 mm mortars, 4 76 mm regimental guns, 24 76 mm divisional guns, 12 37 mm antiaircraft guns.

Directive no. GKO-570ss, "Concerning Tank Units," was adopted by the State Defense Committee on August 23, 1941. It defined two new main types of organization of armored forces:

- the independent tank battalion of the rifle division
- the tank brigade

The creation of tank divisions was no longer planned. According to instruction no. 0063 of August 12, 1941, issued by the State Defense Committee on behalf of Stalin's People's Commissar of Defense, the formation of 120 tank brigades began and was to be completed by January 1, 1942. The brigades were organized as follows:

- brigade headquarters (as per table of organization 010/75): 54 personnel
- intelligence section (as per 010/76): 175 personnel
- reconnaissance battalion (as per 010/77): 107 personnel
- tank regiment (as per 010/78): 548 personnel
- medium- and heavy-tank battalion (1)
- light-tank battalion (2)
- motorized rifle regiment (as per 010/79): 709 personnel
- antiaircraft battalion (as per 010/80): 223 personnel
- supply company (as per 010/82): 62 personnel
- workshop and repair company (as per 010/82): 91 personnel
- medical platoon (as per 010/83): 28 personnel

The brigade's authorized personnel strength was 1,871 soldiers of all ranks; this was roughly equivalent to a German regiment. According to the table of organization, the brigade was supposed to have the following equipment:

- KV heavy tanks: 7
- T-34 or T-50 medium tanks: 22
- T-40 or T-60 light tanks: 64
- medium armored wheeled vehicles: 8
- light armored wheeled vehicles: 7
- cars and trucks: 249
- tractors: 14

Knocked-out T-34s

T-34 captured by German troops

- DP light machine guns: 41
- heavy machine guns: 6
- 45 mm and 57 mm antitank guns: 8
- flamethrowers: 16
- 50 mm mortars: 6
- 82 mm mortars: 6
- 37 mm (antiaircraft) guns: 12

Due to the lack of vehicles, many tank brigades had only a motorized rifle battalion instead of a motorized rifle regiment. Experience with the deployment of tank brigades in the aforementioned structure proved that the existence of an "intermediate body" of regimental size made it more difficult to lead the brigade. For this reason, the rifle regiments were soon abandoned and replaced by motorized rifle battalions. These brigades were established from September to December 1941 in accordance with tables of organization 010/303–010/310 and consisted of a motorized rifle battalion and just two tank battalions of mixed composition:

- one company of heavy tanks (5 KV-1s)
- one company of medium tanks (7 T-34s)
- one company of light tanks (10 T-60s or other models)

The brigade thus had just forty-six tanks, with a personnel establishment of 1,471 men:

- 19 KV-1s
- 16 T-34s (2 for the battalion staff)
- 20 T-60s

During the Red Army's counteroffensive at Moscow in December 1941, the need for light tank brigades that could work together with ski brigades and cavalry divisions became clear. At the beginning of January 1942, therefore, the formation of the "C" tank brigades began in accordance with tables of organization 010/317 and 010/318 for cavalry and infantry. They were to be absolutely "light," with a minimum number of support and maintenance units. Each brigade was to consist of 372 men and 46 tanks (roughly equivalent to a German panzer battalion). However, it was not possible to form the required number of such brigades. In February 1942, the Red Army therefore opted for tank brigades consisting of just 282 men and 27 tanks, which were incorporated into rifle divisions. In 1942, the number of T-34s in the brigades rose to between 35 percent and 87 percent; on average, T-34s made up 60 percent of the armored combat vehicles in the independent tank brigades. The brigade, according to the most-common tables of organization, 010/270–010/277, which applied to most units in the second half of 1942, was composed as follows:

- **Brigade Headquarters** (as per table of organization 010/270): 44 personnel

- **1 battalion of medium tanks** (as per 010/271): 151 men and 21 T-34s
- HQ and HQ platoon: 24 men and 1 T-34
- 2 companies of medium tanks, each with 44 men and 10 T-34s (3 tank platoons)
- 1 technical support platoon
- **1 (mixed) tank battalion** (as per 010/272), 146 men, 10 T-34s, 21 T-60s or T-70s.
- HQ and HQ platoon: 1 T-60 or T-70
- 1 company of medium tanks with 3 tank platoons
- 2 companies of light tanks, each of 3 tank platoons
- 1 repair platoon
- **1 motorized rifle battalion** (as per 010/273) with 403 men.
- HQ and HQ platoon 3 BA
- tank landing company
- 2 machine gun companies each with 112 men, 9 light machine guns
- 2 heavy machine guns, 3 antitank rifles (PTR)
- 1 antitank rifle company (PTR)
- 1 mortar battery, 63 men, 6 82 mm mortars
- 1 antitank battery (as per 010/274): 52 men, 6 76 mm guns
- **1 intelligence company** (as per 010/275): 147 men, 1 T-34
- **1 reconnaissance company**: 43 men
- **1 repair company** (as per 010/276): 101 men
- **1 medical platoon** (as per 010/310): 21 men

Authorized personnel strength was 1,354 men.

Even in the early stages of the war, when the Red Army was forced onto the defensive, tank brigades proved to be very effective in supporting rifle divisions. This was not least due to the fact that the Soviets had already gained experience with brigade-sized units before the war. Parallel to the creation of new tank brigades, independent tank battalions were set up to reinforce the rifle divisions. The first table of organization (010/85) for these "independent" tank battalions was approved by the people's commissar of defense (Stalin) on August 23, 1941. Accordingly, the 130-man battalion (the size of a company in the German military) comprised one company of medium and two companies of light tanks of nine T-34s and twenty T-40s or T-60s. By the end of 1941, the Soviets had set up sixty-two battalions of this kind. Some received British tanks from aid supplies instead of T-34s. Although the Red Army was on the defensive in 1941, the battles fought by the tank units were naturally often offensive in nature: reconnaissance advances, counterattacks with the aim of exhausting the enemy or restoring broken defensive lines. However, since the striking power of the divisions was insufficient (light tanks predominated), offensive operations usually failed miserably. "Resounding" successes required mixed divisions with heavy armored fighting vehicles. For this reason, the reinforced tank battalion was created in accordance with table of organization 010/302 from November 28, 1941:

- battalion headquarters
- 1 company of heavy tanks with two platoons
- 1 company of medium tanks with three platoons
- 2 companies of light tanks, each with three platoons

The battalion's equipment consisted of

- 5 KV-1 heavy tanks
- 11 T-34 medium tanks
- 20 T-40 or T-60 light tanks

Personnel strength: 202 men

Of course, not everything went smoothly, and there were often improvisations due to material or supply bottlenecks. Many formations/conversions took place "on the move," so to speak: new crews from training units came forward with tanks. During a rest period, the division personnel were distributed to the companies together with the "newcomers" and the equipment they had brought with them—the new reinforced battalion "stood." From January to May 1942, there followed detailed changes in the structure of independent tank battalions (tables of organization 010/321, 010/322, 010/360, 010/361, 010/362, 010/363), all of which consisted of three to four companies and differed mainly in the number of tanks—from sixteen to forty-one. Battalions equipped with the same type of vehicle (KV, British tanks, sometimes T-34s) often had a smaller number than those of mixed composition. For example, a battalion according to table of organization 010/361 included forty-one armored combat vehicles: five KVs, thirty T-34s, and sixteen T-60s. In addition, at the beginning of 1942, several separate flamethrower tank battalions were formed according to table of organization 010/366—twenty-one vehicles, including ten KV-8s, nine TO-34s, and two T-34s. In total, the Red Army formed eighty-seven independent tank battalions by January 1, 1943.

The last table of organization, 010/467, appeared in July 1943, and according to it a tank battalion consisted of thirty-one tanks: twenty-one T-34s and ten T-70s. However, only a few of these were created, since it had become clear in the meantime that (a) the independent tank battalion no longer met the requirements of the front, and (b) the industry could now supply the necessary numbers of tanks to form larger formations. As a result, the number of independent tank battalions decreased to thirty-eight by January 1, 1944; by the end of the year there were only five.

The tank regiment now proved to be a more favorable form of organization. Like tank battalions, tank regiments were to reinforce the rifle divisions in the attack, and they were also incorporated into mechanized brigades. According to table of organization 010/292, adopted in September 1942, an independent tank regiment consisted of

- regimental headquarters
- 2 companies of medium tanks
- 1 company of light tanks
- repair platoon
- reconnaissance platoon
- transport platoon
- supply platoon

With 23 T-34s and 16 T-70s plus 339 men, the regiment was roughly equivalent in strength to a German panzer battalion.

T-28 captured by German troops in the summer of 1941. The soldier is holding a 76.2 mm shell.

The vulnerability of the light T-70 to antitank fire led to the adoption of the new regimental table of organization, 010/414, in January 1943, which reduced the number of T-70s to seven and increased the number of T-34s to thirty-two. Like the previous one, this regiment could also be part of mechanized brigades or cavalry divisions.

The Red Army formed the first armored combat engineer regiment (as per table of organization 010/472), which consisted of twenty-two T-34s and eighteen PT-3 mine-clearing tanks. Its job was to clear lanes through minefields. Seven more armored combat engineer regiments were formed by the end of the war.

Tables of organization 010/463 and 010/464, for tank regiments of twenty-one vehicles, followed in February 1944. The first was equipped with T-34/76s only and the second with T-34/85s (they otherwise differed only in the number of personnel).

Table of organization 010/464, for tank regiments of mechanized brigades with thirty-five T-34/76s or T-34/85s, came into effect in February 1944. The number of tank regiments changed as follows during the war:

until January 1, 1943: 34
until January 1, 1944: 135 (84 independent, the rest in mechanized brigades)
until January 1, 1945: 112 (70 independent)
until May 1, 1945: 103 (61 independent)

In addition to tank battalions and regiments with standard equipment, the Red Army also formed flamethrower tank battalions. As per table of organization 010/366, a flamethrower tank battalion consisted of

- battalion headquarters (2 T-34s)
- 2 companies of KV-8s (5 vehicles each)
- 1 company of OT-34s (9 vehicles)
- support platoon

Five independent flamethrower tank battalions were formed in the summer of 1942, and eleven more that autumn. Broken-down or destroyed KV-8 flamethrower tanks were replaced by OT-34s (flamethrower variant of the T-34). The 512th Independent Flamethrower Tank Battalion, for example, had only OT-34s on February 1, 1942, specifically sixteen tanks. During the war, several flamethrower tank battalions were expanded into regiments. With several minor exceptions, their organization was the same as that of the other tank regiments (table of organization 010/463):

- regimental headquarters (1 T-34)
- 2 OT-34 flamethrower tank companies (each with 9 OT-34s and 1 T-34)
- reconnaissance platoon
- repair platoon
- transport platoon
- supply platoon
- medical platoon

Equipment:
- 3 T-34s
- 18 OT-34s
- 6 BA-64 armored cars
- 53 trucks and special vehicles
- 7 motorcycles

Personnel strength: 240 men

Flamethrower battalions and regiments were used mainly in attacks on fortified positions and in fighting in built-up areas, to "smoke out" bunkers and barricaded buildings. N. I. Chuikov described the use of a flamethrower tank during the fighting in Stalingrad in autumn 1942: "We recovered three damaged tanks from the battlefield: one flamethrower tank and two medium tanks. They were repaired, and I decided to surprise the enemy and launch a counterattack with three tanks and 50 riflemen on the morning of October 29. The counterattack began early in the morning, just before sunrise. It was supported by artillery from the left bank and Colonel Erokhin's rocket launcher regiment. It was not possible to make any major territorial gains, but the results were impressive: the flame tank set three enemy tanks ablaze, while the two tanks in the middle drove the enemy out of two trenches, which our infantry immediately occupied."

The 235th Independent Flamethrower Brigade, the only one in the Red Army, distinguished itself in the fighting at Stalingrad. It was formed at Lyublino near Moscow in the summer of 1942 as per tables of organization 010/235–010/239 and was organized as follows:

- brigade headquarters
- headquarters company
- 506th Flamethrower Tank Battalion
- 508th Flamethrower Tank Battalion
- 509th Flamethrower Tank Battalion
- maintenance company

In October 1942 the brigade had the following equipment:

- 5 T-34s
- 36 KV-8s
- 18 OT-34s

The T-60 light tank, which entered service in 1941, was created on the initiative of the design office of Factory No. 37 under N. A. Astrov and approved by Stalin himself. On July 17, 1941, the State Defense Committee issued resolution no. 179, "On the construction of T-60 light tanks at Factory No. 37 of the People's Commissariat of Medium Machine Building." The introduction of the T-60 was intended to make up for the losses of the Soviet armored forces as quickly as possible, using production facilities that could not manufacture other, more-complex tanks.

T-60 light tank in the parade in Red Square on November 7, 1941

T-60 Light Tank

The T-60 was developed from the T-40 light amphibious tank. The T-60 was originally produced in the T-60 (30) version, which was practically identical to the T-40 except for the armored shield in the forward part of the hull. The main variant of the T-60 was in fact based on a thorough modernization of the T-40. Compared to the latter, the T-60 had thicker armor (first 15–20 mm [0.6–0.8 in.] and then 20–35 mm [0.8–1.4 in.] on the glacis, first 15 mm and then 25 mm [1 in.] on the sides), and better armament—a 20 mm cannon instead of a large-caliber machine gun. A hatch in the 6–10 mm (0.2–0.4 in.) armored floor served as an emergency exit. The T-60 was the first series-produced tank with a heater for the engine coolant. The modernization improved the tank's basic fighting qualities and simplified its design but, at the same time, limited its operational possibilities since the amphibious capability was no longer available. Like the T-40, the T-60 had four torsion-bar-sprung road wheels with rubber tires and three return rollers, as well as a drive sprocket at the front and an idler wheel at the rear. The vehicle was powered by a GAZ-202 carburetor engine with a maximum output of 70 hp. Despite a significant increase in weight due to the armor, the speed and off-road capability of the T-60 remained almost unchanged compared to the T-40. It reached speeds of up to 45 kph (28 mph) and mastered gradients of up to 29°, trenches 1.7 m (3.3 ft.) wide, and obstacles up to 65 cm (25.5 in.) high. It was armed with an automatic 20 mm TNSh-20 cannon with a rate of fire of 754 rpm, a theoretical range of 7,000 m (7,655 yds.), and a combat range of up to 2,500 m (2,734 yds.). The weight of armor-piercing projectiles in a ten-second burst was 12.8 kg (28.2 lbs.). The belt-fed weapon fired explosive shells with tracer, as well as armor-piercing incendiary projectiles with a

T-60 light tank with 20 mm TNSh cannon

tungsten carbide core and an initial velocity of 815 m/sec. (2,673 ft./sec.), which penetrated lightly armored targets. The introduction of an armor-piercing subcaliber projectile increased the armor penetration to 35 mm (1.4 in.), and at close range it could penetrate the (side) armor of the early German Panzerkampfwagen III and IV tanks. In addition, there was a 7.62 mm DT tank machine gun with an impressive ammunition load. The TMFP-1 telescopic sight served as a means of aiming, and the driver observed through a triplex glass block. The armament was housed in a conical octagonal turret.

The first T-60 built in series rolled off the production line at Moscow Plant No. 37 on January 15, 1941. However, the evacuation of the factory on October 26, 1941, meant the end of production in Moscow after a total of 245 vehicles had been completed. Instead of it moving to Tashkent as originally planned, the Moscow plant was

T-60, view from the front right

T-60, view from the front

relocated to Sverdlovsk in the Urals, where a new Tank Factory No. 37 began production of the first two dozen T-60s on December 15. By September 1942, a total of 1,240 T-60s had been produced there, after which Tank Factory No. 37 was converted for other production. Factory No. 38, which was also founded on the basis of some evacuated factories in Kirov, produced its first T-60s in January 1942, with series production starting in February 1942. In the first quarter of 1942, 241 tanks were produced, and a further 539 by June 1942. Factory No. 264 in Krasnoarmeysk, which had previously produced armored riverboats, produced the first forty-five T-60s in December 1941. The number reached 1,186 vehicles by June 1942, of which a significant number took part in the Battle of Stalingrad. However, most T-60s were produced in the automobile factory in Gorky (Gorkovski Avtomobilny Zavod, GAZ), which delivered the first three vehicles in September 1941, 215 in October, and 471 in November. By the end of 1941, 1,124 T-60s were produced in Gorky (now Nizhny Novgorod, located about 400 km east of Moscow), and a further 1,649 in 1942. All the factories together produced a total number of 5,973 (5,920 according to other sources).

The T-60 saw its first action in the fighting near Moscow; it was present in almost all tank brigades and battalions that defended the capital on November 7. Forty-eight T-60s of the 33rd Tank Brigade took part in the parade in Red Square. These were tanks produced in Moscow, and tanks produced in Gorky first saw action near Moscow on December 13. T-60s arrived on the Leningrad front in the spring of 1942, when sixty vehicles and their crews joined the 61st Tank Brigade. The 61st Tank Brigade had its baptism of fire on January 12, 1943, when the Soviets for the first time succeeded in penetrating the German blockade ring around Leningrad (Army Group North did not lift the blockade until January 27, 1944). In addition, the brigade, like the 86th and 118th Tank Battalions, which were also equipped with the T-60, led the attack by the 67th Army and crossed the Neva over the ice. The units equipped with medium and heavy tanks could not follow until the following day, after a 2–3 km deep (1.25–1.9 mi.) bridgehead had been established and engineers had reinforced the ice.

T-60 hit by a shell and destroyed

The tank's inadequate armament and armor immediately (Red Army soldiers called it the "suicide tank") became apparent, however, and the T-60 was therefore replaced by the T-70, which entered service with the Red Army on March 6, 1942. While the T-60 was inferior in some respects to the Soviet light tanks of the 1930s, the T-70 was more or less on a par with them, except for the lack of a third crew member. The latter reduced the tank's effectiveness considerably, since in addition to his own tasks, the T-70's commander also had to perform the functions of the gunner and loader.

A T-60 carrying infantrymen, all of whom are armed with submachine guns, during an attack

T-70 Light Tank

The T-70 was put into series production at three plants simultaneously (Sverdlovsk, Kirov, and Gorky). It differed from the T-60 mainly in its stronger armor, armament, and an engine consisting of two six-cylinder carburetor engines connected in series. The hull was welded together from rolled armor plates in thicknesses of 15, 25, 35, and 45 mm (0.6, 1, 1.4, and 1.8 in.). The faceted turret, also welded, was located on the left side of the hull relative to the longitudinal axis. The 45 mm cannon and the 7.62 mm DT tank machine gun were housed in a cylindrical mount; range of elevation was –6°/+20°. Both weapons were triggered mechanically via foot pedals; they were aimed using TOP or TMF telescopic sights. The chassis was similar to that of the T-60 but used five rubber-tired road wheels on each side. The T-70 developed speeds of up to 45 kph (28 mph) on paved roads. It could climb gradients of up to 28°, cross 1.6 m (5.25 in.) wide ditches, and climb obstacles 0.6 m (2 ft.) high.

The T-70M variant, production of which began in September 1942, had a reinforced running gear with larger drive sprockets, wider road wheels, reinforced return rollers, and axle drives. Track width was increased from 260 to 300 mm (10.23 to 11.8 in.).

Prototype of the T-70

The first production T-70s were produced without radio equipment but were later fitted with 12RT or 9P radio sets (command tanks), and all vehicles were equipped with an intercom system. A total of 8,226 T-70s of various versions left the production line. They formed part of the equipment of tank brigades, tank companies of motorcycles, and SU-76 self-propelled gun regiments, where they served as command tanks.

T-70 light tank

Among the light armored vehicles that entered service with the Soviet armored forces in 1942 was the BA-64 armored car. Its development took place from July to December 1941, and it was based on the new GAZ-64 all-wheel-drive military car. The designers at the Gorky Automobile Factory (GAZ) borrowed features from prewar Soviet all-wheel-drive vehicles and the German Sd.Kfz. 221 light armored car.

T-70, view from the front left

T-70 light tank on a reconnaissance sortie

T-80 light tank, a further development of the T-70

BA-64 Light Armored Car

The BA-64 was used for reconnaissance, communications, and security purposes and was the first Soviet wheeled armored vehicle with all-wheel drive, thanks to which it could negotiate gradients of more than 30° on firm ground and 18° on slippery surfaces and ford bodies of water up to 0.9 m (2.95 ft.) in depth. The narrow hull and superstructure were produced from armored sheet metal, and with its sloping surfaces the BA-64 could not deny its origins in the German Sd.Kfz. 221 armored car. It offered considerably improved protection for the crew against small-arms fire and shell fragments. The BA-64 also had bulletproof tires with foam rubber filling. The driver sat in the forward part of the fighting compartment, and behind him the commander, who also served the DT 7.62 mm machine gun in the open-top rotating turret. Its −36°/+54° range of elevation enabled it to engage ground and air targets. While on the move, the driver could observe while protected through a replaceable block of bulletproof glass. Two of these blocks also protected the viewing openings on the turret sidewalls. Most BA-64s were equipped with 12RP radios. At the end of 1942, a modernization was carried out with a wider wheelbase, which improved the vehicle's poor lateral stability on slopes and in curves. The front suspension was fitted with two additional shock absorbers. The upgraded vehicle was now called the BA-64B. Other versions of the BA-64 included the

- BA-64W railroad armored car, produced by the Vyksa Factory;
- BA-64G railroad armored car, produced by the Gorky Factory;
- BA-64D, with DShK 12.7 mm machine gun;
- BA-64, with Goryunov 7.62 mm machine gun;
- BA-64, with PTRS-41 14.5 mm antitank rifle (self-loading);
- BA-64E transporter for up to 6 men;
- BASh-64 staff vehicle; and
- BA-64S half-track snowmobile.

The BA-64 was produced in quantity by the Gorky Automobile Factory (GAZ), which delivered 3,903 BA-64s and 5,160 BA-64Bs from April 1942 to February 1946.

Increasing the production of armored vehicles became a top priority for the party and government with the start of the war. As early as June 24, 1941, the people's commissar

BA-64 ZhD armored car for use on railroad tracks

BA-64 light armored car

for medium mechanical engineering, V. A. Malyshev, made corresponding demands on tank production at a meeting of the Politburo of the Central Committee of the Party, attended by industrial functionaries. The next day, the Politburo decided to increase the production of heavy and medium tanks. The Central Committee of the All-Union Communist Party of Bolsheviks and the Council of People's Commissars passed two joint resolutions: "On the production of armor steel and heavy tanks" and "On increasing the production of heavy T-34 and T-50 tanks, artillery tractors, and tank diesel engines in the third and fourth quarters of 1941." Behind them was the demand for the creation and pooling of a powerful tank industry. By decree of the Presidium of the Supreme Soviet on September 11, 1941, the People's Commissariat of Tank Industry (NKTP) was created under the chairmanship of V. A. Malyshev, who also remained deputy chairman of the Council of People's Commissars and chairman of the Council of Mechanical Engineering in the Council of People's Commissars of the USSR. Companies from other People's Commissariats now came under the umbrella of the NKTP. The extremely simplified transfer procedures took only one to two weeks. By September 12, 1941, the new People's Commissariat already comprised eleven former plants of the People's Commissariat for Medium Mechanical Engineering (NKSM):

- Factory No. 183, also known as the Kharkov Locomotive Factory (KhPZ). The factory had been active in the building of tanks since 1928 and had produced tanks on a large scale since 1932, including T-34s prior to the outbreak of war.

- Factory No. 75 in Kharkov: It emerged from the KhPZ engine factory in January 1939 and also produced V-2 diesel engines for T-34s before the outbreak of war.
- Factory No. 37 G. K. Ordzhonikidze in Moscow had produced tanks since 1931, including the T-40 amphibious tank on the eve of war.
- Factory No. 174 Voroshilov in Leningrad, alias Bolshevik and previously Obukhovsky, had been active in tank construction since 1928. On the eve of war, it was producing the T-26 and was preparing to build the T-50.
- Kirov Factory in Leningrad, formerly Putilovsky, which had built tanks since 1932 and, prior to the outbreak of war, the KV-1 and KV-2 types.
- Stalingrad Tractor Factory. On the eve of war, the factory had begun production of a small batch of T-34 tanks.
- Kharkov Tractor Factory, which in the 1930s had worked closely with KhPZ.
- Chelyabinsk Tractor Factory. On the eve of war, the factory was preparing to begin production of KV tanks; however. it had not yet begun quantity production.
- Communist Youth International Automobile Factory in Moscow. Since it had no experience in building tanks, it was to support Factory No. 37.
- Ural Turbine Works Sverdlovsk, under construction since 1937, began the production of turbines in May 1941. It was now to take up the production of diesel engines with facilities evacuated from Leningrad.
- Ural Factory Railroad Car Factory (UVZ) in Nizhny Tagil. An industrial giant designed to produce 42,000 cars per year. At the beginning of the war, construction was nearing completion, and production had already started. In fact, output was fewer than 16,000 cars per year, and some factory halls were empty. UVZ had its own metal production facilities and, due to its size and the empty halls, offered the best conditions for accommodating evacuated companies.

In addition, the 8th State Design Bureau was incorporated into the People's Commissariat. The Stalingrad Mechanical Institute and five technical schools (Stalingrad Tractor Construction, Nizhny Tagil, Kharkov, Chelyabinsk, Kharkov Mechanical Engineering) were added. In addition

BA-64, view from the front right

to the NKSM factories, a further seven from other commissariats were incorporated into the NKTP in the early days:

- Factory No. 112 in Gorky, also known as Krasnoye Sormovo. This factory was once a pioneer in Soviet tank construction and copied several Renault FT-17 tanks, after which its focus shifted to other areas. On the eve of the war, the plant belonged to the People's Commissariat for Shipbuilding and built submarines. On September 19, 1941, it became part of the NKTP.
- Ural Heavy Machine Production Factory (Uralmash) in Sverdlovsk. Under the People's Commissariat of Heavy Industry before the war, it was one of the largest Soviet machine factories. Transferred to the NKTP on September 19, 1941.
- Repair Factory for Steam Locomotives in Murom, also known as Factory No. 176. Placed under the People's Commissariat for Communications before the war.
- Vyksa Crushing and Grinding Equipment Factory, also known as Factory No. 177. Subordinated to the People's Commissariat for Machine Tool Construction before the war. Transferred to the NKTP on September 17, 1941.
- Ordzhonikidze Factory in Podolsk, alias Factory No. 180. Under the People's Commissariat of the Oil Industry before the war.
- Repair Factory for Steam Locomotives in Saratov. Under the People's Commissariat for Rail Transport before the war.
- Kolomna Steam Locomotive Works. Placed under the People's Commissariat of Heavy Industry before the war.

At the same time, the Third Main Directorate of the People's Commissariat of the Shipbuilding Industry became part of the NKTP and formed its Third Main Directorate. This Main Directorate had long been associated with tank building and specialized in the construction of tank parts.

BA-64 with open entry hatch

BA-64s on patrol

The Third Main Directorate joined the NKTP on September 13 and comprised four factories and a research institute:

- Illich Factory in Mariupol. Before the war it supplied tank hulls to the KhPZ.
- Izhora Factory in Kolpino, Leningrad Region. Prior to the war it produced KV hulls for the Kirov Factory.
- Metallurgical Works in Kulebaki, also known as Factory No. 178.
- Factory No. 264 in Stalingrad. Prior to the war it produced T-34 hulls for STZ.
- NII-48 in Leningrad. This research institute concerned itself with armor steel and questions relating to armor.

The administrative apparatus was also transferred from the shipbuilding plants to the NKTP. The people's commissar for shipbuilding industry, I. I. Nosenko, became one of V. A. Malyshev's deputies.

In addition, a commission was set up on September 13, 1941, to take over the repair plant for steam locomotives in Chalovsk (People's Commissariat for Railways). The plant was transferred to the NKTP on September 12, 1941, by GKO decree no. 655ss.

Therefore, as of mid-September 1941, the NKTP comprised a large group of companies. It included all factories active in tank construction before the war, several companies that switched to tank construction, and several factories that were to take over evacuated tank factories (or parts thereof). However, the process was not yet complete: from October to December 1941, further factories that had no experience in tank construction joined the NKTP.

By the end of 1941, the process of industrial redistribution in favor of tank production was essentially complete, and the NKTP had become one of the largest industrial People's Commissariats in the USSR; it included several industrial giants with more than 10,000 employees. During the war, 200,000–250,000 people worked under its wings, sometimes in catastrophic conditions. Some of the companies involved in 1941 were about to relocate beyond the Urals; others were converted into parts suppliers. At the same time, the tank industry had to solve the problem of a sharp increase in tank production. Under these unfavorable conditions, the solution was seen mainly in the simplification of production technology and design. This made it possible to save on raw materials and labor and to free up machine tools, which ultimately helped increase output. However, simplification did not always necessarily go hand in hand with a deterioration in quality. Examples include the abolition of heat treatment for armor steel, the use of steel with a reduced alloying-element content, etc.

BA-64 light armored cars frequently operated together with motorcycle troops

The introduction of new technological processes became an effective means of increasing productivity. To simplify and shorten the production of armor parts, in some cases riveting was replaced by welding, or casting by stamping. Automatic welding using flux was already widespread in the first half of 1942. In 1942–43, the Electrofusion Institute developed a whole series of automatic electric welding machines for various purposes. The use of these machines freed up sixty qualified welders at Plant No. 183 as early as 1942, which increased to 140 skilled workers by 1945. Automatic welding also brought

Assembling T-34 tank guns in the Kirov Tank Factory in Chelyabinsk

the advantage of uniform weld seams and reduced the need for reworking. In general, rationalization measures and the introduction of new production processes significantly reduced production costs. While a T-34 cost around 269,000 rubles in 1941, it was 193,000 rubles in 1942 and finally 135,000 rubles in 1945.

All NKTP tank factories were directly subordinate to the people's commissar, thus avoiding the main directorates (*glavki*) so typical of Soviet industry. This increased their efficiency considerably. The NKTP's *glavki* concerned only parts manufacturers and repair plants. The NKTP system also did not allow any external intervention by regional and municipal party functionaries, as was usually the case with Soviet companies. All applications for the manufacture of this or that additional product for local use were subject to approval by the People's Commissariat. The energetic measures taken by the Soviet leadership to increase tank production with the ruthless use of manpower, including political prisoners and forced laborers, not only compensated for the tank losses suffered at the beginning of the war, but also ensured a steady increase in output and, despite further horrendous tank losses, an increase in the tank fleet until the end of the war.

In the spring of 1942, the output of combat vehicles allowed the formation of larger formations than brigades (i.e., tank corps). The creation of tank corps was based on the brigades' lack of suitability for combined-arms combat, as had become apparent. This was because the effective deployment of armored units on the battlefield required extensive self-sufficiency with the integration of infantry and artillery under a joint command. This was the major shortcoming of the brigades.

The Red Army formed the first four tank corps in April 1942 as per the guidelines in People's Defense Commissariat No. 724218ss of March 31, 1942. Each corps consisted of a corps headquarters, two tank brigades, and a motorized rifle brigade and had the following authorized strength:

- 20 KV heavy tanks
- 40 T-34 medium tanks
- 20 T-60 light tanks
- 20 76.2 mm field guns
- 12 45 mm antitank guns
- 20 37 mm antiaircraft guns
- 66 antitank rifles
- 4 120 mm heavy mortars
- 42 medium 82 mm mortars
- 539 trucks and cars.

Personnel strength was 5,603.

The strength of a tank corps of this structure corresponded to about half that of a prewar motorized division. It had field, antiaircraft, and antitank guns as well as five battalions of motorized infantry (three battalions in the motorized rifle brigade and one battalion per tank brigade). Nevertheless, there were still weaknesses in the command structure, and there was a lack of reconnaissance, repair, and other units, such as rear services.

The first four corps were sent to the front one month after their formation. In the meantime, the process of forming new tank corps took on an "avalanche-like character."

The NKO directives no. 724485ss of April 15, 1942, and no. 724486ss of May 9, 1942, ordered the establishment of eight further tank corps: the 8th, 9th, 10th, 11th, 12th, 13th, 14th, and 15th. In addition, the individual army groups (fronts) began to establish a further seven tank corps in accordance with directives nos. UW 2/88 and UW 2/90 of April 15, 1942: the Southwestern Front, four (21st, 22nd, 23rd, and 24th); the Western Front, two (5th and 6th); and the Kalinin Front, one (7th). The High Command Reserve followed from May to June 1942 with three more tank corps (6th, 17th, and 18th).

The formation of a tank corps proceeded swiftly. For example, the formation of the first corps from the core of the 1st Tank Division and the 1st Guards Tank Brigade began

Availability, Output, and Losses of Armored Vehicles of the Red Army During World War II

	1941	1942	1943	1944	1945 (to June)	Total
Tanks and self-propelled guns from the start of the war (June 22, 1941) in thousands	22.6	7.7	20.6	24.4	35.4	110.7
Losses of tanks and self-propelled guns in thousands	20.5	15.1	23.5	23.7	13.7	96.5
Tanks and self-propelled guns delivered in thousands	5.6	28	27.3	34.7	13.5	109.1

Production of KV-1 heavy tanks in the Kirov Factory in Chelyabinsk

on March 31, 1942; however, the corps moved to the Bryansk Front at the end of April. The 24th Tank Corps, under General V. M. Badanov, laid the foundation stone in Voroshilovgrad on April 20, 1942, in accordance with orders from the Southern Front and reported readiness for transfer on May 2. However, the 17th Tank Corps, under Lieutenant General N. V. Feklenko, was the quickest to move, beginning its formation on June 19 and being placed under the command of the Bryansk Front on June 26.

From April to June 1942, a total of fourteen tank corps were formed in the High Command Reserve and eleven tank corps in the army groups (fronts). However, it soon became apparent that the number of tanks was too low. With one hundred vehicles, they had ten times fewer than the prewar mechanized corps and 2.75 times fewer than the tank regiments of the motorized divisions.

This deficiency was only partially remedied in April, when the 3rd Tank Brigade was transferred to a corps by NKO decree no. 724485ss, of April 15, 1942.

In accordance with division no. 010/369, it was given a ninety-nine-man command group to coordinate the operations of the brigades. Nevertheless, there was still a lack of artillery, engineers, reconnaissance, repair, and intelligence units as well as rear services.

Initial deployments of the corps in the spring of 1942 showed that they did not have the necessary operational and tactical independence and were also completely dependent on superior armies or fronts in terms of logistics. All of this had a negative effect on the corps' operations. Once again, reorganization was called for. According to NKO order no. 00106, of May 29, 1942, the "mixed" tank brigades of the corps were replaced by a heavy KV tank brigade with fifty-three vehicles (thirty-two KVs, twenty-one T-60s) and two medium-tank brigades with sixty-five tanks each (forty-four T-34s and twenty-one T-60s). This meant that the corps now had 183 tanks. As early as June 1, 1942, NKO directive no. 00108 changed the composition of the heavy-tank brigade again, which now received fifty-one tanks: twenty-four KVs and thirty-seven T-60s. In total, the corps had 181 tanks.

According to NKO directive no. 0484, of June 15, 1942, the corps received its own fuel supply company (according to no. 010/388-B) consisting of seventy-four soldiers for the flexible supplying of the tank corps with fuels and lubricants on the march or on the battlefield. According to NKO order no. 726059ss, of June 24, 1942, the tank corps even received their own field post offices according to no. 014/69-B, with five personnel.

According to NKO order no. 726444ss, of July 13, 1942, some tank brigades were transferred from table of organization 010/345 to 010/270-010/277, which meant a target number of 1,066 men and 53 tanks (32 T-34s and 21 T-70s). Accordingly, the corps now had 159 tanks. In addition, according to NKO order no. 726019ss, there was a guards rocket launcher section (08/83, 250 l/s) with eight BM-8 or BM-13 "Stalin Organs," a reconnaissance section (010/389) with 208 men, 20 Bren Universal Carriers (armored personnel carriers supplied by Great Britain), and twelve armored wheeled vehicles, as well as a wheeled infantry battalion (010/353) with 287 soldiers.

GKO decree no. 2791 of January 28, 1943, established the following organizational structure for the tank corps:

Unit	Personnel Strength
1. Corps Headquarters	122
2. Tank Brigade (3 per corps)	each 116, total 348
3. Motorized Rifle Brigade	215
4. Mortar Regiment	827
5. Self Propelled Gun Regiment	304
6. Guards Rocket Battalion	244
7. Reconnaissance Battalion	111
8. Motorcycle Battalion	285
9. Intelligence Section	257
10. Engineer Battalion	491
11. Fuel Supply Company	74
12. Repair Company (tracked)	72
13. Repair Company (wheeled)	70
Total	**3,430**

Motorized rifle brigades for tank corps were formed according to the tables of organization 010/370–010/380, which came into force in April 1942. They consisted of

- brigade headquarters
- 3 motorized rifle battalions
- 1 mortar battalion
- 1 artillery battalion
- 1 antiaircraft Battalion
- 1 antitank rifle company
- headquarters company
- reconnaissance company
- machine gun company
- technical services
- medical section

In total, 3,152 men

Equipment and armament:

- armored vehicles: 7
- armored personnel carriers: 10
- cars: 345
- motorcycles: 10
- 37 mm cannon: 12
- 45 mm guns: 12
- 76 mm guns: 12
- 120 mm mortars: 4
- heavy machine guns: 18
- DShK 12 antiaircraft machine guns: 12
- DP machine guns: 110
- PTR 54 antitank rifles: 54
- PPSh submachine guns: 910
- rifles: 1,050

The Soviet tank corps formed from May to June 1943 were comparable to a German panzer division in terms of the number of tanks. In May the number of tanks in the corps reached 180, while the authorized strength of a panzer division was 160–221. The German panzer division, which had just one panzer regiment but a larger number of other units, had an authorized strength of about 16,000 men, compared to 5,600–7,000 in a Soviet tank corps with two to three tank brigades.

Among the advantages of German panzer divisions were the presence of stronger field artillery, antitank, and antiaircraft forces and a large number of vehicles and troop types for various purposes. It should not be forgotten, however, that very few of the German panzer divisions on the Eastern Front at this time were still at their authorized strengths.

In the opinion of the Soviet military leadership, large units with a strong armored core were required for major offensive operations, similar to the shock armies of the prewar period. This consideration led to the formation of mixed tank armies consisting of tank corps, several rifle divisions, and cavalry corps. The formation of the first two such armies (3rd and 5th) began with the 5th Tank Army on May 25, 1942 (according to formation order no. 994021 of the High Command). It consisted of the following formations:

- 2 tank corps (2nd and 11th)
- 1 independent tank brigade
- 1 rifle division (340th)
- 1 light artillery regiment
- 1 guards rocket launcher regiment
- 1 antiaircraft battalion
- support units

The 3rd Tank Army had the same organizational structure; its formation also began on May 25, 1944, as per formation order no. 994022. The 4th Tank Army was formed on July 22, 1942, by High Command order no. 0094124. It consisted of the following units:

- 2 tank corps (22nd and 23rd)
- 3 rifle divisions
- 2 antitank regiments
- 2 antiaircraft regiments
- 1 guards rocket launcher regiment
- support units

On July 26, 1942, the High Command issued order no. 994125 for the formation of the 1st Tank Army from the following formations:

- 2 tank corps (13th and 28th)
- 1 tank brigade (158th)
- 2 rifle divisions
- 2 antitank regiments
- 2 antiaircraft regiments
- 1 guards rocket launcher regiment
- support units

The composition of the armies changed over the course of the war. For example, the 5th Tank Army, newly formed in September 1942, had two tank corps (1st and 26th), one cavalry corps, six rifle divisions, one independent tank brigade, two independent tank battalions, and an independent infantry regiment. Considering the positive experiences of the Bolsheviks with the 1st and 2nd Cavalry Armies during the Civil War, Supreme Command order no. 170687, of November 12, 1942, ordered the formation of cavalry armies based on the 4th Guards Cavalry Corps, located in the North Caucasus. The army was to include the following formations:

- 9th, 10th, 11th, and 12th Guards Cavalry Divisions
- 30th, 63rd, and 110th Cavalry Divisions
- 140th Tank Brigade
- 65th Motorized Rifle Brigade (4 motorized rifle battalions, two of them with armored personnel carriers, light tank battalions, and motorcycle battalions)
- 134th, 221st, and 225th Tank Regiments
- 13th, 14th, and 29th Antitank Regiments
- 68th Artillery Regiment
- 10th Guard Rocket Launcher Regiment
- 255th, 285th, and 591st Antiaircraft Regiment (armed with 12.7 mm machine guns)
- 585th Antiaircraft Regiment
- 4 independent battalions of light tanks and motorcycles

In addition, there was the 216th Mixed Aviation Division (two fighter regiments with Yak-7s and two close-support regiments).

According to the table of organization, the army was supposed to have 178 tanks, 94 armored vehicles, 129 armored personnel carriers, 497 motorcycles, 74 guns (18 122 mm and 152 mm, 32 76 mm, and 24 45 mm), 36 mortars, and 328 antitank guns. Although such an army could operate quite successfully in the mountainous terrain of the North Caucasus, High Command directive no. 170692, of November 19, 1942, nevertheless provided for the formation of two corps from the available cavalry divisions rather than a cavalry army. Nevertheless, the desire for a cavalry army persisted. In the 1944 offensives in Belarus, Ukraine (Lviv-Sandomierz), and Bessarabia (Jassy-Kishinev), temporarily formed large formations of tank and cavalry corps played an important role. Normally, these formations disbanded after the end of operations, but the formation formed in October 1944 on the 2nd Ukrainian Front did not disband until January 1945. It was given guard status and consisted of the 4th and 6th Cavalry Corps and the mechanized 4th Guards Corps.

The experiences with tank armies in the summer of 1942 in defensive and offensive operations at Voronezh (5th Tank Army), at Kozelsk (3rd Tank Army), and especially during the counteroffensive in the Stalingrad area (5th Tank Army) led to important insights regarding deployment and organization. The presence of rifle divisions and tank and cavalry corps of varying mobility in the tank armies had a negative effect on the command, deployment, and supply of the formations. They proved to be cumbersome to lead and unwieldy. However, weaknesses in the organization should not be blamed for everything. After all, the Soviets were facing the German Wehrmacht, which was a master of its trade, especially in mobile and armored warfare, and was able to overcome many a seemingly hopeless situation or turn it into a defensive or offensive success. Stalingrad may be cited as a counterexample, but it should not be forgotten that the Red Army did not break through German formations, but weaker Italian and Romanian ones, and was thus able to form the encirclement ring. Incidentally, by then nine-tenths of the city was already in German hands.

At a special meeting at the end of January 1943, the GKO dealt with the reorganization of the tank armies. The decision was made to exclude nonmotorized rifle divisions and to use mechanized corps instead, which could also follow the tank units and better secure captured territory. On January 28, 1943, the State Defense Committee passed decree no. GKO-2791ss, "On the Formation of Ten Tank Armies." From March to June 1943, ten tank armies were to be formed according to the new structure, with two tank corps, one mechanized corps, and the necessary support troops. For this purpose, it seemed necessary to withdraw ten tank corps from the front as the basis of the new tank armies, as well as ten mechanized corps. The situation was very reminiscent of 1940, when, in addition to the nine already formed, a further twenty mechanized corps were to be created overnight. As is well known, the Red Army ultimately formed six tank armies during the war, which significantly increased its operational effectiveness. As for the mechanized corps, nine were established by the end of 1942 and thirteen by the end of 1943. The first two mechanized corps were given guard status right from the start.

Order No. 00220 for the Formation of Mechanized Corps, October 22, 1942

I order:

1. The formation

(a) of the 1st Mechanized Guard Corps, based on the 1st Guard Rifle Division released by Army Group Bryansk

(b) of the 2nd Mechanized Guard Corps, based on the 22nd Guard Rifle Division released by Army Group Northwest

A train carrying T-34s produced in the Stalingrad Tractor Works heads for the front.

Operational Readiness by the Corps:

1st Mechanized Guard Corps on November 10 of this year in the Atkarsk-Tatishchevo area

2nd Mechanized Guard Corps on November 25 of this year in the Morchansk area

The 1st and 2nd Mechanized Guard Corps shall be organized as per appendix no. 1 and shall each comprise 17,347 men.

Mechanized brigades are to be formed on the basis of the guards rifle regiments of the 1st and 22nd Guards Rifle Divisions.

The head of the Main Directorate (Glavupraform), comrade Shchadenko, is responsible for the formation of the mechanized corps.

The chief of the GABTU of the Red Army receives the order to set up the tank regiments and the independent supply and repair sections.

The artillery commander of the Red Army will

form two antiaircraft artillery regiments from the available antiaircraft units of the division and bring artillery and antitank units of the brigades up to their full strength.

The commander of the guards rocket launcher units shall form two M-13 guards rocket launcher divisions.

The formation of the units mentioned in paragraphs 5, 6, and 7 must be completed by November 5 for the 1st Mechanized Corps and by November 20 for the 2nd Mechanized Corps.

The head of the Main Personnel Directorate and the heads of the Main Directorates of the NKO shall ensure the assignment of command personnel for the 1st and 2nd Mechanized Guard Corps by November 1 of this year. The command personnel shall be specially selected.

The chief of the Main Directorate for the Organization of the Red Army shall supplement the mechanized guard corps with officers and men from guard units, including cadets from regimental and military schools.

The People's Defense Commissar

I. Stalin

Appendix No. 1 to NKO Order No. 00220

List of Units and Personnel for the 1st and 2nd Mechanized Guard Corps		
№	Unit	Strength
1	Corps Headquarters	145
2	Mechanized Guard Brigades (3 per corps)	3,997
3	Independent Guard Tank Regiments (5 per corps, 3 per brigade)	357
4	Guard Artillery Regiment	989
5	Independent Guard Antitank Battalion	298
6	Independent Guard Antiaircraft Artillery Regiment	420
7	Independent Guard M-13 Rocket Launcher Battalion	250
8	Staff of the Artillery Commander	63
9	Independent Guard Machine Gun Battalion	246
10	Guard Training Battalion	623
11	Independent Guard Engineer Battalion	491
12	Independent Guard Intelligence Section	293
13	Independent Guard Chemical-Warfare Defense Company	52
14	Independent Guard Reconnaissance Company	169
15	Independent Guard Corps Supply Section	294
16	Independent Guard Corps Repair Section	214
17	Independent Guard Medical Section	103
18	Guard Corps Field Bakery	70
19	Field Workshop	12
	Total	**17,437**

As can be seen from the table above, experience with the formation of tank corps was considered when developing the organizational and personnel structure of the mechanized corps. The mechanized corps received the necessary combat and combat support troops. However, the individual corps differed in some respects due to different guidelines for formation. For example, the 1st and 2nd Mechanized Corps each had three mechanized brigades and one tank brigade, an antitank regiment, an antiaircraft regiment, a guards rocket launcher battalion, a reconnaissance battalion, a repair section, a combat engineer company, an intelligence company, and a fuel supply company. The 3rd and 5th Mechanized Corps had two tank brigades instead of just one, and the 4th and 6th Corps each received two tank regiments instead of tank brigades. Thus, the six mechanized corps established by the beginning of 1943 had three different structures and strengths. This influenced their numerical composition. The 1st and 2nd Mechanized Corps each had 175 tanks; the 3rd and 5th, 224 each; and the 4th and 6th, 204 each. However, the basic organization was that of the first two corps, and all corps established according to a different table of organization as well as newly established corps were either created according to the original table of organization or gradually converted to it.

The mechanized brigades, which formed the basis of the mechanized corps, were formed in accordance with table of organization 010/370-010/380, approved in September 1942, and had the following structure and personnel:

- brigade headquarters, 83
- administrative company, 104
- reconnaissance company, 148
- 3 mechanized rifle battalions, 707 men, each of which had a
- staff platoon
- machine gun platoon
- supply platoon
- 3 mechanized rifle companies
- PTR antitank rifle company
- antitank battery
- 82 mm mortar battery
- tank regiment, 339
- reconnaissance platoon
- machine gun platoon
- supply platoon
- 2 companies of medium tanks
- company of light tanks
- maintenance company
- company armed with submachine guns, 102
- PTR antitank rifle company, 76
- mortar section, 210
- artillery battalion, 256
- antiaircraft battalion, 186
- motor transport company, 80
- medical platoon, 33

Total 3,726 (authorized strength)

Weapons and Equipment:

- 23 T-34 tanks
- 16 T-70 tanks
- 10 armored wheeled vehicles
- 10 armored personnel carriers
- 492 trucks and cars
- 503 rifles
- 887 carbines
- 1,158 submachine guns
- 400 automatic rifles
- 113 light machine guns
- 45 heavy machine guns
- 12 DShK 12.7 mm antiaircraft machine guns
- 81 antitank guns
- 30 82 mm mortars
- 6 120 mm mortars
- 12 45 mm antitank guns
- 8 37 mm antiaircraft guns
- 12 76.2 mm field guns

For a long time, the Red Army tank corps was inferior to the German panzer division in terms of equipment, but the mechanized corps had been superior to its German counterpart, the motorized infantry division (later: Panzer Grenadier Division), in this respect since its foundation. With a few exceptions, the German motorized infantry division still had no tanks in 1942.

On October 8, 1942, the Main Tank Directorate (GABTU) received the following directive from People's Commissar of Defense Stalin: "Equipped with the KV and Churchill tanks, independent breakthrough regiments of 21 tanks each will be set up, which belong to the High Command Reserve and have Guard status." This instruction was subsequently formalized in the form of NKO directive no. 1104913ss. The planned regiments of 214 men were organized as follows as per table of organization 010/267:

- regimental headquarters
- 1st Tank Company (5 tanks)
  - 1st Platoon: 2 tanks
  - 2nd Platoon: 2 tanks
- 2nd Tank Company (5 tanks)
  - 1st Platoon: 2 tanks
  - 2nd Platoon: 2 tanks
- 3rd Tank Company (5 tanks)
  - 1st Platoon: 2 tanks
  - 2nd Platoon: 2 tanks
- 4th Tank Company (5 tanks)

Ceremonial field parade by a Red Army tank brigade

1st Platoon: 2 tanks
2nd Platoon: 2 tanks
- maintenance squad
- medical squad

Equipment and Armament:
- 21 KV or Churchill tanks
- 3 BA-64 armored cars
- 26 trucks
- 2 cars
- 2 other four-wheeled vehicles
- 4 tanker trucks
- 2 workshop trucks
- 4 motorcycles

T-34/85s on the advance with infantry riding on the tanks

The crew of a T-34/85 after a successful action

The breakthrough regiments were intended for breakthrough operations at focal points of the front, in cooperation with infantry and artillery. They received heavy tanks from mixed tank divisions or from the disbanded heavy-tank brigades that had been created in small numbers in the summer of 1942. In February 1944, the existing heavy-tank regiments were reorganized and supplemented by others. Organization of a heavy-tank regiment of 375 men:

- regimental headquarters
- 4 tank companies (2 platoons each with 2 vehicles plus the company commander's tank)
- 1 company armed with submachine guns
- engineer platoon
- supply platoon
- medical platoon

At the end of 1944, the Red Army concentrated heavy tanks on the main lines of attack by the armies and fronts, where they were to break through "heavily fortified defense lines and fortified areas" with artillery and infantry support. In December 1944, independent heavy guard tank brigades of 1,666 men were formed with the following structure:

- brigade headquarters
- administrative company
- reconnaissance company
- 3 heavy regiments (4 tank companies of 5 heavy tanks plus the regimental commander's vehicle)
- mechanized rifle battalion (submachine guns)
- maintenance company
- antiaircraft machine gun company
- medical platoon

Equipment and Armament:
- 65 IS-2 tanks
- 3 SU-76 self-propelled guns
- 2 BA-64 armored cars
- 19 armored personnel carriers
- 205 trucks and cars
- 28 motorcycles

Heavy breakthrough regiments received both the KV-1 and its lighter version the KV-1S (S stood for "fast"), which according to GKO resolution no. 1878ss, of June 5, 1942, had been ordered for the following reasons:

> Combat experience has revealed the following shortcomings of the Kliment Voroshilov tank:
>
> - The tank's great weight (45.7 tonnes) reduces its mobility and complicates its use.
> - insufficient reliability of the transmission due to low strength of the first-gear pinion and the crankcase
> - The engine cooling system is not powerful enough. As a result, it is often necessary to downshift to lower gears, which reduces the average speed of the tank and severely restricts the use of maximum engine power.

Tankers and motorized infantry during a break in the fighting on an M4A3 Sherman supplied to the Soviets by the Americans

British Valentine light tanks in Soviet service, seen here during an attack with infantry support

- The all-around view is inadequate due to the lack of a commander's cupola and the unfavorable arrangement of the optical devices.

In addition to the complaints from the ranks of the troops, there were also complaints about many defects in components and the manufacturing process. This was particularly true of the diesel engines, the production of which displayed poor workmanship and quality control. This was also true of the entire assembly process.

The same resolution directed the Kirovsky Factory in Chelyabinsk to produce tanks of the KV series with a maximum weight of 42.5 tonnes (46.8 tons) starting on August 1, 1942. To reduce the weight of the tanks, decree no. 200 of the People's Commissariat for Tank Construction permitted a reduction in the thickness of the plates:

- The thickness of the forward, bottom, and side plates as well as those of the welded turret is to be reduced from 75 to 60 mm [2.95 to 2.4 in.].
- Proposal: Removal of the armored inner bulkhead in the driver's compartment . . . the deadline for completion of this work is June 15, 1942.
- The thickness of the floor plates is to be reduced to 30 mm [1.2 in.].
- The thickness of the gun mantlet is to be reduced to 80–85 mm [3.15–3.35 in.]. The dimensions of the main gun are also to be reduced while retaining the current range of elevation.
- The width of the track links is to be reduced to 650 mm [25.6 in.] (the deadline for completion of this work is July 1, 1942).

During these modernization measures, the tank hull was made lighter and flatter overall, the weight of the drive units and chassis was reduced (e.g., by using narrower tracks), and the cast mantlet was made smaller. Due to an acute shortage of aluminum, an iron radiator was used instead of an aluminum one. New fans and a new eight-speed transmission were also fitted. The KV-1S (42.3 tonnes, or 46.6 tons) thus replaced the KV-1 (47.5 tonnes, or 52.4 tons) in production.

Red Army troops of a reconnaissance unit equipped with British universal carriers receive mission orders.

KV-1S Heavy Tank

Apart from its lower weight, the KV-1S had the following main differences from the KV-1:

- a smaller turret with a commander's cupola affording an all-around view
- In addition to the new transmission with silumin (aluminum-silicon alloy) crankshaft housing and axle drives, a new main clutch was installed.
- new engine-cooling system
- lighter road wheels and narrower tracks
- greater use of cast parts

Testing of the KV-1S took place between July 28 and August 26, 1942. The Red Army accepted the tank on August 20 and quantity production began at the beginning of August. A first batch of 180 KV-1S tanks was completed in September 1942. A total of 626 were produced in 1942 and another 464 in 1943. Total production of the KV-1S was 1,090 examples (1,106 according to other sources). Also produced were 25 KV-8S flamethrower tanks with the KV-8 flamethrower turret and ten more vehicles with an ATO-42 flamethrower in the standard KV-1S turret.

Even at the time of its development, the KV-1S no longer met the requirements of a modern heavy tank because of the fact that the designers had retained the armament of the KV-1 (76.2 mm SIS-5 gun) and considerably reduced the thickness of its armor to roughly that of the T-34 medium tank with significantly higher production costs. For this reason, production of the KV-1S was gradually reduced in favor of greater production of T-34s and stopped entirely in August 1943.

The heavy-tank regiments of 1943 also received a relatively small number of KV-85 tanks. The KV-85 with its more powerful 85 mm gun was the Soviet response to the appearance of the German Panzerkampfwagen VI Tiger, which was heavily armored and armed with an 88 mm gun. No Soviet, British or American tank could compete with the Tiger in terms of combat power. The State Defense Committee responded to its appearance with resolution no. 3289ss of May 5, 1943, "On Improving the Cannon Armament of Assault Guns and Tanks." It instructed Soviet designers to convert the 85 mm 52-K antiaircraft gun (derived from the German 88 mm antiaircraft gun) into a tank gun, which was to penetrate the frontal armor of a Tiger at 1,000 m (1,094 yds.) / angle of impact 90° with armor-piercing projectiles. The design office of Plant No. 9, headed by F. R. Petrov, thus created the D-5T-85 85 mm gun. Engineers from KhKZ and Factory No. 100 under the direction of Josef Kotin installed them in the turret of the projected Iosif Stalin (IS-1) heavy tank. As the hull and chassis of the IS-1 were not yet ready, the turret was placed on a KV-1S hull, which required a slight enlargement of the opening for the turret ring. In addition, the radio operator's position was omitted, and his hull-mounted machine gun was

KV-1S heavy tank

KV-1S, view from the right front

KV-1S during trials

KV-1 crews preparing for action

moved to the driver's side. On August 8, 1943, even before testing was completed, the Red Army accepted the KV-85 in accordance with GKO decree no. 3891. As preparations for series production took place as testing was being carried out, the first production KV-85s left the halls of Factory No. 100 just a few days after the official introduction of the prototype and were sent to the front. A further 147 units were produced at the Chelyabinsk Kirov Factory. That was it, because three months later KhKZ was already building the first IS-1 tanks.

In 1943, not only the turret armament of the heavy KV-1, but also that of the medium T-34 was modernized. The need for this was emphasized by the People's Commissar for Tank Construction V. A. Malyshev and the inspector of the tank and mechanized troops of the Red Army Y. N. Fedorenko at a meeting at the end of August 1943 at the Krasnoye Sormov factory complex (Factory No. 112). In his speech, the People's Commissar explained that the "victory in the Battle of Kursk" had cost the Red Army heavy losses. German Tigers and Panthers had fought Soviet tanks from 1,500 m (1,640 yds.), while the Soviet 76 mm tank guns had only been able to pose a threat to Tigers and Panthers at ranges of less than 600 m (656 yds.). "In a figurative sense," said the People's Commissar, "the enemy has arms one and a half kilometers long and we have arms only half a kilometer long. We must immediately install a more powerful gun in the T-34."

Knocked-out and burned-out KV-1

KV-85 Heavy Tank

When the extremely powerful, well-armored German PzKpfw VI Tiger appeared at the front at the end of 1942, the Soviet KV-1 and KV-1S heavy tanks became obsolete overnight, so to speak. The armor of the KV types, which the previous German tank guns could penetrate only under favorable conditions, posed no problem for the 88 mm tank gun of the Tiger, even at longer ranges. Conversely, the Soviet 76.2 mm SIS-5 cannon could penetrate the armor of the Tiger only at ranges of less than 200 m (218 yds.), mainly on the sides and rear. Between April 25 and 30, 1943, various Soviet guns took a captured Tiger under fire. The results showed that parts of the frontal armor of the Tiger could be penetrated only by the Soviet 85 mm M1939 (52-K) antiaircraft gun (the counterpart to the German 88 mm antiaircraft gun and developed on its basis; see above) at ranges of up to 1,000 m (1,094 yds.). On May 5, 1943, the State Defense Committee adopted resolution no. 3289, on "Reinforcing the gun armament of assault guns and tanks." This resolution set Soviet gun and tank designers the task of developing 85 mm guns for self-propelled guns and tanks with the performance of the same antiaircraft guns. The guns were to be used both in the standard turret of the KV-1S and that of the new Iosif Stalin (IS) tank. The Main Artillery Design Bureau, under Vasily Grabin, proposed the S-31 85 mm tank gun, developed on the basis of the SIS-5 76.2 mm gun. The design office of Artillery Plant No. 9, under Fyodor Petrov, on the other hand, developed the D-5T 85 mm tank gun. It soon became apparent that the 85 mm gun did not fit into the turret of the KV-1S. The situation was all the more dramatic since development of the new heavy Iosif Stalin tank was rather delayed. The problem was solved by a proposal from the designers of the Kirovsky Factory in Chelyabinsk and Factory No. 100, under Josef Kotin. The plan was to install the D-5T in the larger turret of the IS tank, which had not yet been fully developed. Since the hull of the IS had not yet been fully designed, it was proposed to mount its turret on the chassis of the KV-1S. The prototype of this hybrid was presented on July 20, 1943.

KV-85 heavy tank on the testing grounds

KV-85 heavy tank

KV-85 seen from the front

KV-85 seen from the left front

On August 8, 1943, even before testing was completed, the Red Army accepted it as the KV-85 in accordance with State Defense Committee resolution no. 3891. The first vehicles left the assembly halls of the Kirovsky Factory just a few days later.

The KV-85 was the last model in the KV series and represented the next step on the way to a vehicle that was clearly superior to all previous Soviet tanks in terms of armor and armament. The D-5T cannon, with a barrel length of 42 caliber, gave the 9.2 kg (20.3 lb.) armor-piercing round an initial velocity of 792 m/sec. (2,598 ft./sec.), enabling it to penetrate the armor of the Tiger at an impact angle of 90° at a range of 500–1,000 m (547–1,094 yds.). The gun was mounted with trunnions in the turret front and was fitted with a powerful mantlet. The numerous small parts and the high demands on workmanship and quality were a disadvantage. These slowed down the production of the D-5T considerably, so that it was soon replaced by the simpler and technologically less complex 85 mm SIS-S-53 gun. The installation also required changes to the ammunition storage, and the combat load had to be limited to seventy shells. Instead of a movable hull machine gun in a ball mount, a fixed machine gun was installed, which was aimed via the movement of the tank and was therefore suitable only for coarse scattering fire. However, this change made it possible to dispense with the radio operator's position in the hull and thus a fifth crew member. The 10 R radio was now operated by the commander. Since the KV-85 was essentially a transitional model, it was built for only a relatively short time. In August 1943, twenty-two KV-85s were produced, and sixty-three each in September and October.

KV-85, rear view

German troops inspecting a knocked-out KV-85

T-34/85 Medium Tank

The T-34, with the more powerful 85 mm gun, was developed in a short time and adopted by the Red Army by GKO decree no. 5021ss, of January 23, 1944. In February, Factory No. 112 began quantity production, followed shortly afterward by Factory No. 183, and in June by Factory No. 174. The first tanks were armed with the D-5T 85 mm gun and later with the S-53 ZIS gun of the same caliber, which was distinguished by its simple design, compactness, and lower manufacturing costs. However, the 85 mm gun required a larger turret (which accommodated a third man, thus freeing the commander from having to load the gun). This, together with heavier armor, increased the weight of the T-34. Thanks to the tank's powerful diesel engine, however, this had little effect on speed and maneuverability. A total of 15,690 T-34/85s were built during the war, and from March 1944 onward the model was used to equip the guards tank brigades. With the expansion of production, the T-34/85 also gradually replaced the T-34/76 in the other units. Despite this, the design office of the Ural Wagon Works (Uralvagonzavod, UVZ) was already working on the development of a medium armored fighting vehicle to replace the T-34/85 in 1943. This T-44 model, which was adopted by the Red Army in 1944, represented a new generation of Soviet tanks.

While retaining the classic superstructure (engine and transmission at the rear), the designers under A. A. Morozov installed the diesel engine at right angles to the longitudinal axis of the tank and reduced the size of the drivetrain. All in all, the overall height of the hull could be reduced by 300 mm (11.8 in.) compared to the T-34, and the turret, with 85 mm gun, could still be placed in the middle of the hull. Furthermore, it was possible to increase the frontal armor thickness to 120 mm (4.7 in.) without overloading the forward suspension. The installation of a one-piece glacis plate required the driver's hatch to be relocated to the hull roof, and a bow machine gun to be dispensed with. The five-speed transmission consisted of the "guitar," which consisted of a differential with three spur gears, a multidisc main clutch, a side

T-34/85s in a Berlin suburb, 1945

T-34/85 medium tank

A column of T-34/85s during a pause in the advance

clutch, and a side drive. The running gear consisted of five running wheels with rubber tires on each side, the drive sprocket in the rear, and the idler wheel at the front. The torsion suspension of the road wheels increased the reliability of the running gear and driving comfort. On roads, the T-44 reached a top speed of 45–50 kph (28–31 mph). It mastered gradients of up to 30°, crossed ditches up to 2.5 m (8.2 ft.) wide, and climbed over obstacles up to 0.73 m (2.4 ft.) high.

Production of the T-44 began in 1944 at Factory No. 75, which had returned to Kharkov after the evacuation. By the end of the war, a total of 205 T-44s had been produced; the "total production run" amounted to 1,823 units. After the war, the T-44 was replaced by the T-54, which formed the backbone of the Soviet armored forces for many years.

T-34/85s advancing with supporting infantry

IS-1 HEAVY TANK

The "Iosif Stalin 1" or IS-1 was the first vehicle of a new family of Soviet tanks that differed from the KV types in having improved armor protection, a new 520 hp engine and power train, and heavier armament. The latter consisted of three 7.62 mm DT machine guns and an 85 mm D-ST-85 gun with fifty-nine rounds of ammunition. Because of its 85 mm gun, the IS-1 was also sometimes called the IS-85. The 44-tonne (48.5 ton) vehicle reached speeds of up to 40 kph (25 mph) and had a range of 150 km (93 mi.).

On September 4, 1943, the vehicle was accepted by the Red Army in accordance with GKO decree no. 91 3891ss. With the same resolution, ChKZ received the order to develop a version with a 122 mm gun and, based on this, an ISU-152 self-propelled gun. The increase in caliber was not least due to the desire to fire powerful explosive ammunition against fortifications, for which the 85 mm gun was not equipped or did not have suitable ammunition. In addition, the armor protection of enemy tanks also increased, which the 85 mm cannon would most likely not be able to penetrate from all distances in the near future, even at close range. As early as 1943, the IS-1 could penetrate the armor of the Tiger from 500 to 1,000 m (547 to 1,094 yds.) only in certain places and with an ideal angle of impact. The IS-85/IS-1 was therefore only a transitional model to a vehicle with more-powerful armament. Series production began in October 1943 and ended in January 1944 with the introduction of the IS-122 (IS-2). In total, just 107 IS-1s were produced.

IS-2 viewed from the front

IS-2 from the front left

Iosif Stalin 1 heavy tank (Object 237)

IS-2 Heavy Tank

The IS-2 (IS-122) formed the backbone of the Soviet heavy-tank formations for a long time. It was designed on the basis of GKO decree no. 4043ss, of September 4, 1943, which instructed Factory No. 100 to present and test a prototype with a 122 mm gun by October 15, 1943. In accordance with GKO decree no. 4479, of October 31, 1943, the Red Army accepted the vehicle as the IS-2. It was not a new design, but a further development of the IS-1 with improved armor and armament.

The desire of the ChKZ designers to achieve maximum armor protection with relatively low weight and dimensions led both to positive and negative results. One of the positives was the relatively low overall material consumption of the IS-2—with the same combat weight as the German Panther medium tank (46 tonnes, or 50.7 tons), the IS-2 was much better protected and even outperformed the 56-tonne (61 ton) Tiger I; it fell only slightly behind the 68-tonne (75 ton) Tiger II. The disadvantages were a logical consequence of the demand for increased armor protection and compactness: a driver's hatch was dispensed with, which in the event of a hit meant the almost certain death of the driver, who could get out only via the fighting compartment; the same applied to the three-man turret crew, since some of the fuel was stored in tanks in the fighting compartment.

The main armament of the IS-2 consisted of the 122 mm D-25T gun, a modification of the A-19 corps cannon, which was available in large numbers. This was fitted with a two-chamber muzzle brake, which reduced recoil and allowed a more compact design of the other recoil brake device. In addition, the aiming system and individual controls for the gunner were placed on its side. At the time, the D-25T was the heaviest gun in series production and installed in a tank. Its muzzle energy was 820 tm, while that of the 8.8 cm KwK 43 of the PzKpfw VI Ausf B Tiger II heavy tank was 520 tm, while the KwK 36 and KwK 42 of the Tiger I and the Panther medium tank were capable of 368 tm and 205 tm, respectively. In a way, however, this is a milkmaid's calculation, as we shall see in a moment. For one thing, armor penetration is determined not only by the muzzle energy, but also by the muzzle velocity (excluding shaped charges) and the ammunition used.

The quality of German armor-piercing ammunition was considerably better than that of the Soviets, and their range of armor-piercing ammunition also included subcaliber ammunition with very high penetration. The BR-471 armor-piercing shell produced for the D-25T of

IS-2 heavy tank (Object 240)

the IS-2 came nowhere near it and penetrated only 122 mm (4.8 in.) of armor steel at an impact angle of 60° at 500 m (547 yds.) or 155 mm (6.1 in.) at 90°, which hardly ever happened under operational conditions. In contrast, the D-25T could fire only 1.35 rounds per minute, even with a well-coordinated crew, due to its two-part ammunition, whereas the Tiger and Panther could fire up to 7.0. In addition, the IS-2 had a low combat ammunition load of only twenty-eight rounds of shells and propellant charges. The secondary armament consisted of three 7.62 mm DT machine guns and a 12.7 mm DShK antiaircraft machine gun mounted on the turret.

Armor thicknesses were 120 mm (4.7 in.) of frontal armor and 100 mm (3.9 in.) on the turret front. During the war, the "stepped frontal armor" was replaced by a uniformly "blended" upper part, which considerably improved its protective qualities. In 1945, tests were carried out at the Kubinka proving ground in which an IS-2 with a "blended" upper front was fired at with the powerful 88 mm 43/1 L/71 tank destroyer gun from a captured German Hornisse (Hornet, also Nashorn, or Rhinoceros) tank destroyer. Like the shorter 88 mm KwK 36 gun of the Tiger I, it was also unable to penetrate the IS-2's upper frontal armor.

Quantity production of the IS-2 began at ChKZ in November 1943. A total of 3,225 IS-2s were produced at Chelyabinsk from December 1943 to June 1945. A further ten vehicles were built by the Kirov Factory in Leningrad toward the end of the war.

The IS-2 saw service in the guards tank regiments, which had been formed as per table of organization 010/460, approved in February 1944. According to the table of organization, the regiment consisted of 374 men and the following units (selection):

- regimental headquarters (1 tank)
- political section
- engineer platoon
- maintenance platoon
- medical platoon ("regimental medical center" [PMP])
- 1st Tank Company (5 tanks)
  - 1st Platoon: 2 tanks
  - 2nd Platoon: 2 tanks
- 2nd Tank Company (5 tanks)
  - 1st Platoon: 2 tanks
  - 2nd Platoon: 2 tanks
- 3rd Tank Company (5 tanks)
  - 1st Platoon: 2 tanks
  - 2nd Platoon: 2 tanks
- 4th Tank Company (5 tanks)
  - 1st Platoon: 2 tanks
  - 2nd Platoon: 2 tanks

rifle company (submachine guns; 94 men)

IS-2, view from the right front

IS-2, rear view

Armament and Equipment:

- 21 IS-1s or IS-2s
- 3 armored personnel carriers (universal carriers)
- 1 BA-64 armored car

In the attack, IS-2s were used mainly as flank cover and fought off counterattacks by German tanks. They normally marched either in separate companies or in regimental columns behind the attacking tank units. Due to their heavy armament, IS-2s were also used in combat in built-up areas and against fortified positions. For these purposes, an IS platoon or an IS company was usually assigned to a tank brigade to support the first attack wave. The heavy IS tanks moved in line approximately 200–300 m (218–328 yds.) behind the T-34s. In defense, IS-2 heavy tanks were used to defend against enemy tanks or to combat identified artillery positions. In the suspected area of attack, the IS tanks normally deployed in a checkerboard pattern 1.5–2 km (1–1.25 mi.) wide and up to 3 km (1.9 mi.) deep, forming a kind of "in-depth defense" position that could act in all directions, while a few IS tanks positioned themselves as "corset stays" with the medium T-34s in front.

IS-2, overhead view

Column of IS-2s driving down a military road

IS-2s in readiness position

Knocked-out IS-2. The tank's ammunition exploded, blowing off the turret.

The IS-2 was used by some of the heavy guards tank brigades set up in December 1944 (see above), which were intended to act as assault brigades at the focal points of attacks by fronts or armies. It was also proposed that the brigades be used to combat enemy armored groups.

Let us now turn to the Soviet self-propelled guns. The successful use of self-propelled German assault artillery (Sturmgeschütze) in the offensive and defensive roles forced the Soviets to reconsider their initial opinion of self-propelled guns as "spoiled tanks." Previous experience in the use of "self-propelled artillery" in comparison with tank units had shown that they could not keep up with the latter in terms of speed and mobility and, left to their own devices, were often quite vulnerable. Nevertheless, there was now a need for armored weapon carriers to accompany infantry and tanks in attack and defense. This proved all the more advantageous as self-propelled guns could be equipped with even more powerful armament and armor than standard tanks.

IS-2s in the streets of Berlin

IS-2 during a victory parade

By decree no. 2429ss, the NKTP ordered the Ural Heavy Machinery Factory (Uralmashzavod [UZTM]) and Factory No. 592 to develop an armored, self-propelled 122 mm howitzer on a T-34 chassis as quickly as possible. In NKTP order no. 721, UZTM brought together a group of designers under L. I. Gorlizki for this order. The first factory tests with the U-35 prototype took place on November 30, 1942, followed by state trials from December 5 to 19. On December 2, 1942, the Red Army accepted the vehicle as the SU-122 on the basis of the factory tests in accordance with GKO decree no. 4559. Quantity production was carried out by UZTM.

An IS-2 with supporting infantry engaging the enemy

An IS-2 advancing in open terrain. The logs fastened to the hull sides helped the tank cross muddy patches.

SU-122 Assault Gun

As previously mentioned, the SU-122 was built on the chassis of the T-34, on which was mounted an enclosed superstructure for the M-30 field howitzer. The gun had a 20° range of traverse, and the range of elevation was –3°/+25°. A projecting gun shield protected the recoil brakes. The aiming system enabled both direct and indirect fire, as was usual with artillery. The ammunition consisted of fragmentation/high-explosive and shaped-charge shells. The latter could penetrate up to 100 mm (3.9 in.) of armor plate. The SU-122 was in no way inferior to the T-34 in terms of mobility and cross-country mobility. It could climb slopes up to 35°, cross trenches 2.5 m (8.2 ft.) wide, overcome obstacles 0.73 m (2.4 ft.) high, and ford water up to 1.3 m (4.3 ft.) deep. The SU-122 had quite satisfactory characteristics, and only its rate of fire left something to be desired, due to the use of two-part ammunition. In 1942–43, Uralmashzavod built a total of 638 vehicles. The design of the SU-122 served as the pattern for all medium and heavy Soviet self-propelled guns of the Second World War.

The equipping of the first self-propelled gun units with SU-122s began at the end of December 1942 in accordance with resolutions 112467ss and 112470ss. The first two regiments (1433rd and 1434th), each with an authorized strength of 307 men, were created according to table of organization 08/158, and had SU-76 self-propelled guns:

Assembling SU-122 self-propelled guns

SU-122 self-propelled gun

Regimental headquarters

headquarters platoon: 1 SU-76 (regimental commander)

1st SU 76 Battery (4 SU-76)

- 1st Platoon: 2 SU-76
- 2nd Platoon: 2 SU 76

2nd SU 76 Battery (4 SU-76)

- 1st Platoon: 2 SU-76
- 2nd Platoon: 2 SU 76

3rd SU 76 Battery (4 SU-76)

- 1st Platoon: 2 SU-76
- 2nd Platoon: 2 SU 76

SU-122 Battery (4 SU-122)

- 1st Platoon: 2 SU-122
- 2nd Platoon: 2 SU 122

SU-122 Battery (4 SU-122)

- 1st Platoon: 2 SU-122
- 2nd Platoon: 2 SU 122

ammunition platoon

supply platoon

repair platoon

medical platoon

artillery repair workshop

In total, the regiment had eight SU-122s and seventeen SU-76s.

SU-122 self-propelled gun during trials

Originally, thirty self-propelled gun regiments were to be formed on the basis of this table of organization; however, since the industry was unable to produce sufficient numbers of vehicles that quickly, table of organization 08/191 reduced the authorized strength of the regiments to two SU-76 and three SU-122 batteries and 289 personnel. Each regiment had twenty self-propelled guns, eight SU-76s, and twelve SU-122s.

A train carrying self-propelled guns prior to leaving for the front

An SU-122 with infantrymen riding on the self-propelled gun

SU-76 Self-Propelled Gun

In contrast to the SU-122, the SU-76 was built on the chassis of the T-70 light tank, and the improved SU-70M on that of the T-70M. The driver sat in the front left of the hull, with the engine situated on the right. The fighting compartment, with the built-in 76.2 mm ZIS-3 gun, was at the rear. Initially it was armored all-around but, during modernization measures, was connected with the transition to the T-70M tank chassis; the roof was done away with. The drive was suboptimal. It consisted of two parallel-mounted GAZ-202 gasoline engines with an output of 70 hp. The vehicle was difficult to steer, and strong vibrations led to the rapid failure of transmission parts. These defects became apparent during the type's first combat deployment on the Volkhov front. They were so serious that series production was discontinued after 698 SU-76s had been manufactured, and it was to be resumed only once the defects had been rectified. However, the front's great need for self-propelled guns led to a half-hearted decision: the "parallel" engine was to be retained, but individual engine components were to be replaced or reinforced to extend its service life. The modernized model (without the armored fighting-compartment roof) was called the SU-76M and went into series production in the summer of 1943. The overall result was disappointing—the reliability of the propulsion system had not improved at all: the engines failed one after the other, which largely prevented the SU-76M from being used in combat. Those responsible were severely punished. On June 7, 1943, the State Defense Committee passed resolution no. 3530, "On SU-76 assault guns," according to which the chief designer of the SU-76 was sent to the 32nd Tank Brigade for frontline probation. While serving as its deputy chief of maintenance, he was killed in action on August 3, 1943. The people's commissar for tank construction, Isaak Saltzman, was relieved of his post and demoted to director of the Kirov Factory in Chelyabinsk. The head of the Main Artillery Directorate, Nikolai Yakovlev, was reprimanded and instructed to pay particular attention to the future composition of the test and trial commissions. The SU-76M underwent another revision, this time with success. The GAZ 203 engines were arranged one behind the other and together drove just one shaft. The modernized model proved to be significantly more durable and had good off-road mobility. It could negotiate inclines of up to 28°, trenches up to 1.6 m (5.25 ft.) wide, and vertical obstacles up to 60 cm (2 ft.)

SU-76 self-propelled gun

high. Without special precautions, it could wade through water up to 90 cm (2.95 ft.) deep. The SU-76M was generally equipped with 12RT-3 or 9R radios and a TPU-3 onboard intercom system. Trials with the revised self-propelled gun took place in August 1943, after which it was adopted by the Red Army under the designation SU-76M. Series production was carried out at Factories No. 38 and No. 40 as well as at the Gorky Automobile Plant. When the production of armored vehicles reached its maximum in 1944, the SU-76M accounted for about 25 percent of total production. A total of 360 SU-76s and 13,932 SU-76Ms were produced.

As on the German side, the Soviet assault artillery was also part of the artillery, and its units were subordinate to the Main Artillery Directorate. In NKO order no. 0972, of December 21, 1942, it set up the Department for Mechanical Traction and Self-Propelled Artillery. The first operational experience with self-propelled gun regiments showed its potential in supporting infantry and tanks. At the same time, it turned out that their subordination to the artillery was ill considered, especially since they drove on tank chassis and the artillery had no experience in the tanklike training of self-propelled-gun crews. In addition, there were maintenance, repair, and spare-parts problems, since the artillery lacked the appropriate facilities for self-propelled guns. However, the "artillery

SU-76 self-propelled gun, view from the front

SU-76 self-propelled gun, view from the rear

component" of indirect fire proved its worth, which benefited infantry and tanks in attack and defense. All in all, it seemed only logical to assign the assault guns to the tank forces in organizational terms. On April 23, 1943, NKO order no. 0291 was issued with the following content (excerpt):

> 1. The self-propelled artillery is transferred to the authority of the Commander of the Tank and Mechanized Forces of the Red Army.
>
> 2. The commander of the artillery of the Red Army transfers his authority to the commander of the Tank and Mechanized Forces of the Red Army.
>
> This applies to
>
> self-propelled-gun regiments of the army groups and the High Command Reserve.
>
> A training center for the assault artillery is to be established that will train all personnel and establish and maintain all training materials, depots, and artillery regiments.
>
> The 18th, 19th, and 21st Self-Propelled Gun Training Regiments are to be provided with all necessary personnel, equipment, and materiel.
>
> The same applies to the assault artillery schools in Kiev and Rostov.
>
> and to the following personnel of the Assault Gun Section of the Artillery Instruction Battalion and the 3rd Training Battalion, which is responsible for the training of assault gun crews.

When the assault artillery was transferred to the tank arm, there was a desire to equip the divisions, regiments, and brigades with the same type of assault gun. It was recognized that the availability of different types would only lead to difficulties in command and control; in the supply of ammunition, fuel, and spare parts; and in the training of the crews. For this reason, in April 1943 the existing and nascent assault gun regiments were moved to the new table of organization, 010/456:

> Regiment headquarters with headquarters platoon
> (1 SU-76 regimental commander)
> 1st Battery (4 SU-76)
> 2nd Battery (4 SU-76)
> 3rd Battery (4 SU-76)
> 4th Battery (4 SU-76
> 5th Battery (4 SU-76)
> ammunition supply platoon
> repair platoon
> motor transport platoon
> supply company
> medical platoon
> Strength: 253 soldiers and 21 assault guns

The crew of an SU-76 climb aboard their self-propelled gun.

Position of the crew in the SU-76

Refueling an SU-76

As of October 1943, table of organization 010/484 applied to those regiments with the reduced personnel strength of 225 men.

Toward the end of the war, the large number of SU-76 light self-propelled guns made it possible to form independent self-propelled-gun battalions, which were to replace the towed 45 mm, 57 mm, and 76 mm guns in the antitank battalions of the rifle divisions. Table of organization 04/434 took effect in May 1944. According to it, the battalion had three batteries of SU-76s (four self-propelled guns per battery) and one SU-76 or T-70 tank in the headquarters platoon.

Operational experience with these battalions proved their effectiveness in the infantry support role. If there was no threat from enemy tanks, the batteries could be used as artillery. Closed deployment was recommended for antitank defense.

In the last phase of the war, several self-propelled-gun regiments were assigned to the advancing armies and fronts. At the same time, certain difficulties arose in coordinating their deployment and in providing material and technical support. For this reason, it was decided in January 1944 to set up self-propelled-gun brigades. According to table of organization 010/508, the following structure applied to SU-76 brigades:

Brigade command:
- brigade headquarters
- headquarters company (2 T-70, 3 armored personnel carriers)

1st, 2nd, and 3rd Battalions, each with:
- headquarters platoon (1 T-70)
- 1st Battery (5 SU-76)
- 2nd Battery (5 SU-76
- 3rd Battery (5 SU-76)
- 4th Battery (5 SU-76)
- motor transport platoon
- supply platoon
- medical platoon

motorized rifle battalion armed with submachine guns
antiaircraft machine gun company
repair company
medical company

An SU-76 self-propelled gun crossing a body of water with the aid of a ferry operated by the combat engineers

Four brigades (the 6th, 8th, 12th, and 14th) were formed according to this table of organization, each with 1,122 men and the following equipment:

- 5 T-70 light tanks
- 3 M3A1 Scout armored cars
- 60 SU-76 assault guns

Three more light self-propelled-gun brigades were formed, using vehicles supplied by the Anglo-Americans, including two (the 16th and 22nd) equipped with American T-48 half-tracks armed with a 57 mm gun (Soviet designation: SU 57). According to table of organization 010/408, they consisted of battalions of three batteries with a total of fifty-seven SU-57s and five British Valentine IX tanks. In the third brigade—the 18th—SU-57s replaced the Valentines as per table of organization 010/508.

Soviet infantry advancing with supporting SU-76s

An SU-76 self-propelled gun regiment moving to the front

The SU-122 regiments were formed in accordance with the table of organization approved in April 1943:

- regimental headquarters
- headquarters platoon (1 T-34 regimental commander's vehicle, 1 BA-64)
- 1st Battery (4 SU-122)
- 2nd Battery (4 SU-122)
- 3rd Battery (4 SU 122)
- 4th Battery (4 SU-122)
- ammunition platoon
- repair platoon
- motor transport platoon
- supply platoon
- medical platoon

Strength: 255 men, 16 SU-122 assault guns, 1 T-34 tank, and 1 BA-64 armored car

It was assumed that the SU-122 regiments would be suitable not only for directly supporting the infantry but also for fighting the dreaded PzKpfw VI Tiger. These hopes were based above all on the BP-460A hollow-charge projectile developed for the 122 mm M-30 howitzer, which could penetrate up to 140 mm (5.5 in.) of armor steel. However, the practical firing of an M-30 field howitzer in April 1943 at a stationary tank target at a distance of 500–600 m (547–656 yds.) produced discouraging results: out of fifteen shots, not one hit the target. The second factor that outclassed the SU-122 was its low rate of fire due to its two-part ammunition: two to three rounds per minute at most.

Reason enough for the GKO to issue decree no. 3187, of April 15, 1943, urging the People's Commissariat for Armaments to develop a new self-propelled gun with a gun that could still penetrate 150 mm (5.9 in.) of armor steel at an impact angle of 30° at 750–1,000 m (820–1,094 yds.). GKO decree no. 3289ss, issued on May 5, 1943, provided for the creation of a self-propelled gun that was to mount a gun derived from the 85 mm Flak 52-K on a T-34 chassis. The 52-K became the 85 mm gun D-5S, which provided the Red Army with the SU-85 assault gun in the summer of 1943. It had the same design as the SU-122:

The engine and transmission were located in the rear, the gun with superstructure in the center and forward hull section.

SU-85 Assault Gun

The 85 mm gun D-5S was produced in two versions: the D-5S-85 and D-5S-85A. They differed in the manufacturing method used to make the barrel, the breech construction, and weight: 1,230 kg (2,711 lbs.) for the D-5S-85 and 1,370 kg (3,020 lbs.) for the D-5S-85A. The barrel length L/48.8 (i.e., 48.8-caliber lengths) allowed firing with direct aiming at 3.8 km (2.4 mi.), with a maximum firing range of 13.6 km (8.5 mi.). Range of elevation was −5°/+25°, and the weapon could be traversed ±10°. The SU-85 could fire with a chance of success only if it fired while stationary. The combat load consisted of forty-eight rounds of ammunition, most of which were stored in racks on the left side of the hull. The rate of fire was six or seven rounds per minute. The following ammunition types were available:

- the 53-BR-365 blunt-tipped armor-piercing round, with a weight of 16 kg (35.3 lbs.) (projectile 9.2 kg (20.3 lbs.), explosive charge 164 g (5.8 oz.) of TNT) and a 4-G-365 propellant charge (2.48–2.6 kg [5.5–5.7 lbs.]); initial velocity 792 m/sec. (2,598 ft./sec.)
- the 53-BR-365K sharp-tipped armor-piercing round, with a weight of 16 kg (35.3 lbs.) (projectile 9.2 kg [20.3 lbs.], explosive charge 48 g (1.7 oz.) of TNT or A-IX-2) and a G-365 propellant charge (2.48–2.6 kg [5.5–5.7 lbs.]); initial velocity 792 m/sec. (2,598 ft./sec.)
- the armor-piercing subcaliber 53-BR-365P round, with a weight of 11.42 kg (25.2 lbs.) (projectile 5.0 kg [11 lbs.] with 54-G-365 core) and a propellant charge of 2.5–2.85 kg (5.5–6.3 lbs.); initial velocity 1,050 m/sec. (3,445 ft./sec.)
- the 53-O-365 high-explosive/fragmentation round, with a weight of 14.95 kg (33 lbs.) (projectile 9.54 kg [21 lbs.], explosive mass 761 g (26.8 oz.) of TNT or amatol, and a 54-G-365 propellant charge (2.6 kg [5.7 lbs.]); initial velocity 785 m/sec. (2,575 ft./sec.)

There were different variants of the 53-O-365 with different fuses for different detonation points.

A captured SU-85 self-propelled gun in service with the Wehrmacht

SU-85 self-propelled gun

The BR-365 armor-piercing round normally penetrated 111 mm (4.4 in.) of armor plate at 500 m (547 yds.) and 102 mm (4 in.) at a range of 1,000 m (1,094 yds.). The BR-365P subcaliber round was capable of penetrating 140 mm (5.5 in.) of armor steel at 500 m (impact angle of 90°) and 83–88 mm (3.25–3.45 in.) of armor steel at 600–1,000 m (656–1,094 yds.), plus 98 mm (3.85 in.) at close range with an impact angle of 30°.

SU-85 self-propelled gun, view from the front

SU-85 assault guns were issued to regiments formed in accordance with table of organization 010/483 of October 1943:

Regimental headquarters with headquarters platoon (1 T-34 regimental commander's vehicle, 1 BA-64)

- 1st Battery (4 SU-85)
- 2nd Battery (4 SU-85)
- 3rd Battery (4 SU-85)
- 4th Battery (4 SU-85)
- ammunition platoon
- repair platoon
- motor transport platoon
- supply platoon
- medical platoon

Strength: 230 crew, 16 SU-85s, 1 T-34, and 1 BA-64

In 1944, these regiments were organized in accordance with table of organization 010/462. Their reinforced batteries consisted of two platoons, each with two SU-85s plus the battery commander's vehicle. The regiment thus had a total of twenty-one SU-85 assault guns. It also had a company of infantry armed with submachine guns and a platoon of engineers and, all in all, numbered 318 men.

Gorlizki therefore suggested that for the time being, only the hull of the SU-100 be produced with a cradle in which both the D-5S 85 mm gun and the D-10S 100 mm gun could be inserted. This resulted in the SU-85M transitional model, and it was later possible to switch production smoothly to the SU-100. The SU-85 thus enjoyed various advantages of the SU-100, such as stronger frontal armor and improved observation and aiming devices. It could also carry 60–85 mm shells instead of the previous 48 mm. UZTM completed the first SU-85M in July 1944; it completely replaced the SU-85 in production from August onward. Production of the SU-85M continued until November 1944, when the People's Commissariat for Ammunition announced the start of production of 100 mm BR-412B armor-piercing shells for the D-10S gun. A total of 315 SU-85Ms were produced. Series production of the SU-100 began in September 1944, and output reached 1,350 units by the end of the war.

The troops appreciated the SU-85. The commander of the 7th Mechanized Corps, Major General Katkov: "The SU-85 self-propelled gun is currently a fairly effective means of countering the Wehrmacht's heavy tanks. It is not inferior to the T-34 in terms of driving range and mobility, and the new 85 mm gun proved itself quite well in combat. However, with their well-armored and armed Tiger, Panther, and the Ferdinand tank-destroyer, the Germans tried to open the battle at long distances—1,500 to 2,000 m (1,640–2,187 yds.). Under such conditions, the power of the 85 mm gun and the frontal armor of the SU-85 are insufficient. It is necessary to strengthen the armor and, above all, to equip the self-propelled gun with a new gun with increased armor penetration, so that it can effectively fight the Tigers at a distance of 1,500 m."

Such a self-propelled gun was available in the form of the SU-100, developed by Factory No. 9 from the SU-85 and armed with a 100 mm D-10S cannon. With a barrel length of L/56 (5,608 mm, or 18.4 ft.), the D-10S accelerated an armor-piercing projectile to 897 m/sec. (2,942 ft./sec.) with a maximum muzzle energy of 648 tf.m. There was only one problem: at the time of the weapon's adoption by GKO decree no. 6131, of July 3, 1944, no armor-piercing shells were (yet) available; their industrial production did not start until the second half of 1944. UZTM chief designer L. I.

A train loaded with SU-85 self-propelled guns before leaving for the front

The crew of an SU-85 self-propelled gun

SU-100 Assault Gun

The same table of organization, 010/462, applied to SU-100 units as well as to regiments equipped with the SU-85. The formation of assault gun brigades began in late 1944, three of which (the 207th, 208th, and 209th) were equipped with SU-100s. The fourth brigade (the 231st) was formed from March to May 1945; however, it did not take part in the European hostilities.

SU-100 self-propelled gun, view from the front

The brigades had the following organizational structure:

- brigade headquarters with headquarters company (2 SU-100) and reconnaissance company (3 SU-76s)
- 3 SU-100 regiments as per table of organization 010/462
- antiaircraft machine gun company
- repair company
- SMERSH counterintelligence section

Strength: 1,492 men, 65 medium and light assault guns

The SU-100 regiments experienced their baptism of fire in the fighting for Budapest in January 1945. The first SU-100 assault gun brigades were sent to the front in February 1945. SU-100s were committed in large numbers during the fighting on Lake Balaton in response to the counteroffensive by the Sixth SS Army (which was an "army" only on paper). In the costly fighting, the SU-100 proved an effective weapon against the German heavy tanks. The SU-152 heavy assault gun, which was armed with the powerful 152.4 mm ML-20 Model 1937 heavy howitzer, proved to be an even more dangerous foe for the Tigers and Panthers.

SU-100 self-propelled gun

An SU-100 self-propelled gun regiment has moved into its starting position for an attack.

An SU-100 self-propelled gun fording a stream

SU-100 self-propelled gun, view from the side

SU-152 Heavy Assault Gun

The development order was issued to the design office of Factory No. 100 by GKO decree no. 2692, of January 4, 1943, when the Soviets realized that the new German Tiger could be fought successfully at realistic combat distances only with armor-piercing shells from the 152 mm ML-20 howitzer and the 122 mm A-19 cannon. Thanks to the preparatory work carried out, the "100s" were able to present a prototype in a very short time—within twenty-five days—which the Red Army promptly adopted after brief testing by decree no. 2859 of the State Defense Committee on February 9, 1943, under the designation SU-152.

Its superstructure was like those of the other Soviet assault guns with the exception of the SU-76. The chassis was supplied by the KV-1S tank and now mounted the 152 mm howitzer in a protected superstructure. The gun, with its two-part ammunition, was carried in the forward section with the driving and fighting compartments; the engine and transmission were located in the rear. The crew consisted of five men. To the left of the gun were the seats for the driver, gunner, and loader. The commander and another gunner were located to the right of the gun. One of the two fuel tanks was also situated in the fighting compartment, which significantly reduced the crew's chances of getting out of a SU-152 alive if it was hit. The hull and superstructure were welded together from rolled steel plates. The slightly sloped armor had a thickness of 20–75 mm (0.8–2.95 in.). In terms of off-road capability, the SU-152 was similar to the KV-1S tank, with a top speed of 43 kph (26.7 mph) on roads.

The 152 mm ML-20S M1937 howitzer shells, weighing over 48 kg (105 lbs.), were lethal to all types of enemy tanks and penetrated the frontal armor of all types from up to 800 m (875 yds.) at an impact angle of 90°. The armor-piercing round could literally shatter medium tanks, and the armor of the Tiger and Panther also offered no reliable protection. If there was a lack of armor-piercing shells, the crew loaded concrete or fragmentation rounds. Although the latter did not penetrate the armor of enemy combat vehicles, they did shatter weapons, sights, running gear, and other equipment, depending on where they struck. The impact force of the projectiles was so great that even turrets were lifted out of their hulls. In the Battle of Kursk, in the summer of 1943, the SU-152 was the only Soviet combat vehicle that could compete with the German Ferdinand tank destroyer in terms of weapon effectiveness. However, due to its size, low speed in the field, slow rate of fire, and a combat load of only twenty rounds of ammunition, it remained tactically and factually inferior to the Ferdinand, Tiger, and Panther.

The Kirov Factory in Chelyabinsk was commissioned with the series production of the SU-152, which was later equipped with a large-caliber antiaircraft machine gun.

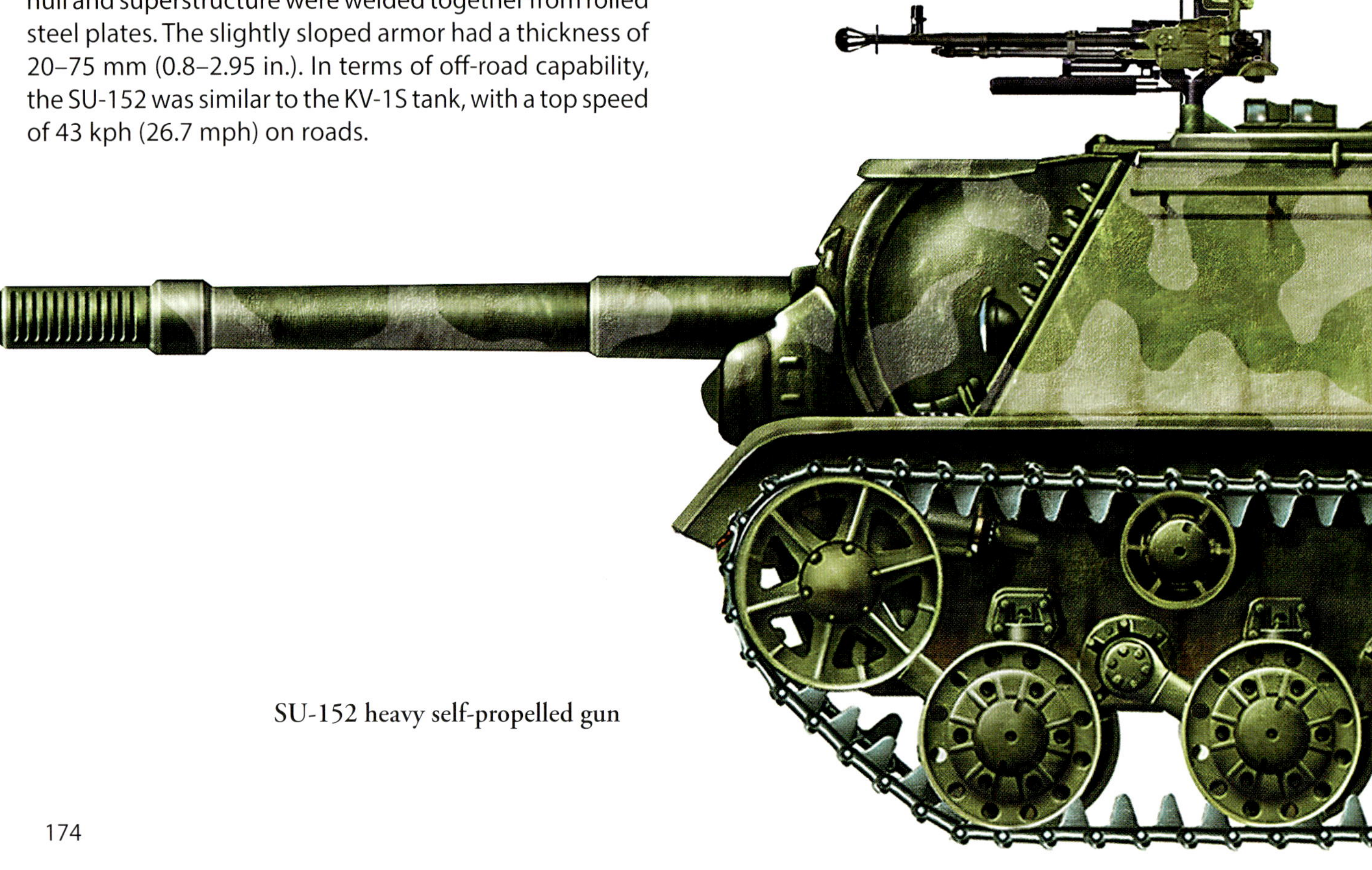

SU-152 heavy self-propelled gun

After production of the KV-1S was terminated, the February switched to the chassis of the IS-1 tank, and the assault gun was then called the ISU-152. In total, 671 SU-152s were built by December 1943.

As for the ISU-152, Factory No. 100 was to present a prototype by December 1, 1943. All work was completed ahead of schedule, and in accordance with GKO decree no. 4043, of September 4, 1943, series production began in December, reaching an output of 1,827 ISU-152s by the end of the war.

The ISU-152 went to the heavy-assault-gun regiments of the RWGK. According to the table of organization 010/454, adopted in April 1943, they consisted of

- regimental headquarters with headquarters platoon (1 KV-1S regimental commander's vehicle, 1 BA-64),
- 1st Battery (2 ISU-152),
- 2nd Battery (2 ISU-152),
- 3rd Battery (2 ISU-152),
- 4th Battery (2 ISU-152),
- 5th Battery (2 ISU-152),
- 6th Battery (2 ISU-152),
- ammunition platoon,
- repair platoon,
- motor transport platoon,
- supply platoon, and
- medical platoon.

Equipment:
- 1 KV-1S tank
- 12 ISU-152 assault guns
- 1 BA-64 armored car

In October 1943 the number of batteries was reduced to four in accordance with the new table of organization, 010/482, while the number of vehicles per battery was raised to three. The regiment thus retained its twelve ISU-152s, but it became easier to lead the units.

SU-152 heavy self-propelled, view from the front

SU-152 on the move

SU-152 heavy self-propelled gun, view from the side

An SU-152 moving into firing position

ISU-152 Heavy Assault Gun

In 1944 the growing output of ISU-152s made it possible to strengthen the heavy regiments in accordance with table of organization 010/461:

- regimental headquarters with headquarters platoon (1 ISU-152 regimental commander's vehicle)
- 1st Battery (5 ISU-152)
- 2nd Battery (5 ISU-152)
- 3rd Battery (5 ISU-152)
- 4th Battery (5 ISU-152)
- rifle company (submachine guns)
- ammunition platoon
- repair platoon
- motor transport platoon
- engineer platoon
- supply platoon
- medical platoon

With 420 personnel, the regiment's authorized strength was

- 21 ISU-152 assault guns,
- 4 armored personnel carriers,
- 2 cars,
- 5 special vehicles,
- 3 tanker trucks,
- 43 trucks, and
- 6 motorcycles.

At the beginning of 1944, it turned out that the People's Commissariat for Armaments could not supply the required number of 152 mm ML-20 guns, because of which a surplus of finished ISU-152 hulls accumulated at ChKZ.

In order not to weaken the dynamics of the formation of heavy-self-propelled-gun regiments, the People's Commissariat of Armored Industry decided to arm the

ISU-152 self-propelled gun taking part in a parade

ISU-152 with a 122 mm A-19 corps gun. The modified armored vehicle received the designation ISU-122 and was put into service with heavy-self-propelled-gun regiments, which had been established according to table of organization 010/461. The same regiments also received the ISU-122S, equipped with a 122 mm D-25S gun. The D-25S had a semiautomatic wedge breech and electric ignition, which simplified operation. The regiments formed according to table of organization 010/461 were given guard rank.

On March 1, 1945, the 66th Heavy Guards Assault Gun Brigade was formed in the White Russian–Lithuanian Military District in accordance with table of organization 010/516, the only one in the Red Army. Its composition was similar to that of the SU-100 brigades, and with 1,804 men it had sixty-five ISU-122s and three SU-76s.

Altogether, by May 9, 1945, the Red Army formed the following self-propelled-gun units:

- 12 assault gun brigades (7 light, 4 medium, and 1 heavy)
- 256 assault gun regiments (119 light, 81 medium, and 56 heavy)
- 70 independent assault gun battalions as part of rifle divisions
- 21 assault gun battalions as part of light assault gun brigades

The main regulation governing the combat use of the first assault gun regiments was the "Provisional instruction for the combat use of self-propelled artillery," approved by the commander of the Red Army Artillery on January 5, 1943. The "General Provisions" section describes the use of the assault guns:

> 1. Self-propelled artillery combines high mobility with powerful armament and good armor protection, whereby it contributes decisively to the destruction of close targets through constant operational readiness, speed, and surprise and ensures close cooperation with the infantry (tanks, cavalry).
>
> 2. The self-propelled artillery is used as support artillery and as a mobile reserve for the commander of the mixed formations (tanks) and is deployed in the main assault sectors at a decisive moment for close support of the infantry (tanks, cavalry).
>
> 3. The external similarity of self-propelled guns and tanks, as well as a certain similarity in their manner of fighting, should in no way equate these two modern means of combat in their application.

ISU-152 heavy self-propelled gun

4. In the attack, self-propelled artillery destroys fortified enemy positions and pockets of resistance that prevent our infantry (tanks, cavalry) from advancing. In defense, it fights enemy infantry and tanks that have broken through the defenses. Self-propelled artillery works mainly by targeted fire (direct fire), depending on the position of individual guns or groups of guns as part of a battery or regiment.

5. Single guns or batteries are characterized by their excellent mobility when accompanying infantry units (tanks, cavalry). They take up positions that provide them with cover and good opportunities for action and carry out the support mission by means of targeted fire, after which they quickly take up new firing positions without interrupting the interaction with the infantry (tanks, cavalry).

6. Reliable communications between the regimental commander and the combined arms staff (tanks), as well as from gun to gun within the batteries, ensure the rapid deployment of the regiment and its disengagement from combat.

7. The officers of all ranks of the self-propelled artillery regiment maintain constant operational readiness and contact with infantry, tanks, and cavalry in any form.

After the self-propelled artillery was placed under the Main Tank Directorate, the officers of the self-propelled-gun units naturally also had to carry out the orders of the officers of the armored and mechanized troops to which they were subordinate.

An example is given in the following order to the tank and mechanized troops of the 3rd Belorussian Front of January 6, 1944 (analogous translation):

ORDER FOR THE TANK AND MECHANIZED FORCES OF THE 3RD WHITE RUSSIAN FRONT

January 6, 1944

Subject: Combat deployment of self-propelled artillery

Until now, commanders of tank and mixed formations have misused self-propelled artillery without paying attention to its fire effectiveness and its interaction with tanks, infantry, and artillery, or recognizing that the self-propelled guns are being used as tanks.

As a result, the enemy, recognizing the limited effectiveness and low mobility of self-propelled guns, quickly eliminates them.

For example, the commander of the 397th Rifle Division ordered the commander of the 26th Guards Assault Tank Regiment to support the infantry attack in the front line with 152 mm self-propelled guns of the following regiment on December 5, 1943, during the battle for the village of Vysokoe and Hill 139.4. In the course of a 30-minute battle, four SU-152s were lost without taking effect.

The practice of using self-propelled-gun regiments also showed that the leaders and crews of the self-propelled-gun units themselves did not have a good grasp of the tactics of using these weapons.

ISU-152, view from the front right

A battery of ISU-152s in firing position

On 11/21/43, the commander of the 397th Rifle Division ordered the commander of the 1901st Light Self-Propelled Gun Regiment to accompany the infantry attack. The commander of the 1901st Light Assault Gun Regiment himself violated all the basic regulations governing the use of self-propelled artillery. Instead of organizing the battle properly, he ordered the battery commanders to be the first to break into the village of Prisno. The attack was defeated and five SU-76s were lost.

Leadership on the battlefield is inadequate, and the self-propelled-gun crews essentially act on their own, which is why there is hardly any concentrated fire on an important target.

A major disadvantage that weakens the firepower of the self-propelled-artillery regiment is its fragmentation into individual guns, which makes it difficult to direct and concentrate fire, and also to resupply ammunition, fuel, and lubricants in time.

For example, on 12/14/43, parts of the 1901st Light Self-Propelled Gun Regiment, which was deployed with the 348th Rifle Division, as well as a unit with SU-152s of the 26th Guards Tank Regiment, were assigned to the 41st Rifle Division, while it would have been advisable to deploy the 1901st Light Self-Propelled Gun Regiment as a single unit.

Before you pick up the Red Army's assault artillery deployment regulations, be guided by the following instructions:

MAIN TASKS OF THE SELF-PROPELLED ARTILLERY

Self-propelled-artillery regiments are assigned to infantry, cavalry, and tank formations and carry out missions in all types of combat with their full strength. The regiment usually fights as a unit.

(A) In attack, . . . self-propelled-artillery regiments accompany and support tanks, infantry, and cavalry with direct fire and also cover the flanks.
(B) In defense, they fight enemy tanks and infantry from positions in front of the front line as well as enemies who have broken through the defense.

The use of self-propelled artillery should be preceded by a thorough reconnaissance of the enemy's strength, weaponry, and terrain, using all types of reconnaissance.

As a rule, self-propelled guns fire directly from partially covered positions and with brief firing halts without exposing their sides and rear to the enemy's antitank fire.

4. To assist self-propelled guns in overcoming natural and man-made obstacles and to protect them from enemy tank-killing squads, the commanding officer to whom the self-propelled-artillery regiment is subordinate deploys combat engineers and machine gunners to accompany them.

TASKS OF THE SELF-PROPELLED ARTILLERY IN THE ATTACK

1. The main task of self-propelled artillery in the center of the attack is to destroy enemy guns and tanks that are holding down the advancing units with surprise fire.
2. Depending on the strength and nature of the enemy's defenses, a self-propelled-artillery regiment may be deployed as a single unit to accompany rifle, tank, and mechanized formations, as a mobile reserve for the commander, or to split into mobile groups to support a breakthrough.
3. The self-propelled artillery must be given its orders clearly, stating:

(A) Missions and deployment of the formations and the artillery that supports them
(B) Targets to be destroyed
(C) The timing of the capture of the initial position
(D) Orientation and demarcation points
(E) The location of the command post of the commanding officer of the units involved
(F) The procedure for supplying ammunition and fuel on the battlefield

5. During attacks on heavily fortified positions, the assault groups are assigned individual self-propelled guns (preferably large caliber) whose task is to destroy machine gun nests and bunkers.
6. In retreat, the self-propelled artillery provides cover for the troops retreating from the battlefield.
7. If enemy tanks appear, the self-propelled artillery fights them together with other types of artillery and gives its own tanks and infantry room to move.
8. In battle, the commander of the self-propelled-artillery regiment leads personally, follows the regiment's fighting units, observes the battlefield, and maintains close contact with the commander of the unit to be supported. During the attack, he ensures that 2/3 of the batteries fire while 1/3 change positions.
9. During the attack, the batteries generally proceed "in line," with distances of 50–75 m [54–82 yds.] between the heavy guns and 40–50 m [43–54 yds.] between the medium and light guns. The regiment itself advances in one line or staggered in two lines. When staggered, the distance between the lines is 100–200 m [109–218 yds.\.

The self-propelled artillery regiment moves (depending on the terrain and caliber of the guns) behind the tank, rifle, or cavalry units.

10. The combat distance against enemy tanks is up to 1,500 m]1,640 yds.\ for heavy and medium guns and up to 1,000 m]1,093 yds.\ for light guns.

TASKS OF THE SELF-PROPELLED ARTILLERY IN THE DEFENSE

In a defensive role, self-propelled artillery is used

(a) as an armored antitank gun . . . from ambush and as a means of antitank defense in the most likely main lines of attack for enemy tanks. To this end, the self-propelled artillery regiment occupies the line of defense, prepares it, and takes camouflage measures to avoid being taken by surprise. Particular attention must be paid to the scouting of approach routes.
(b) for fire support during counterattacks by our own tanks and infantry from the depths of the defense;
(c) as a mobile antitank reserve. In this case, the self-propelled-artillery regiment is located at a distance of 2–3 km [1.24–1.9 mi.] from the forward edge of the defense. The regiment is assigned 2–3 routes for possible forward movements. All routes are to be reconnoitered in advance as indicated in point A.

2. During withdrawal movements, self-propelled artillery can be deployed as a rearguard. It sets up defensive lines and ensures that at least two batteries can fire simultaneously during retreat movements.

This order is to be communicated to all personnel of the self-propelled-artillery regiments, including the commander and the leadership of tank units up to and including the company commanders.

The commander of the armored and mechanized troops of the White Russian Front (*signature*)

The deputy chief of staff of the armored and mechanized troops (*signature*)"

The formation of units and formations with trained personnel was no less important during the war years than equipping them with vehicles. Before the war, command cadres were trained at the military academy for armored and mechanized troops. There were sixteen war schools for training lower-level command personnel with the following profiles:

- platoon leaders of tank, armored reconnaissance, and motorcycle units
- technical leadership personnel of motorized combat and motorcycle units (vehicle technicians)
- technical leadership personnel of motorized support units (tractor technicians)

The duration of training at the schools was set at two years. Personnel further down the hierarchy received their training directly from the troops or in the training units of the individual units.

With the outbreak of war in 1941, the demand for command personnel rose sharply. For this reason, the military academy for tank and mechanized troops released around four hundred officers after their third year and technical officers after their fifth year in July 1941. The

ISU-122 self-propelled gun

academy repeated this in October 1941 after shortened courses for command personnel with 100 troop officers in the third year and 234 technical officers in the fourth year. In the same month, 104 former commanders completed their studies and left the academy, which switched to "war courses" from October 1941 onward, putting more command personnel through shortened courses. Course duration was now one year for regular officers and three years for technical officers.

The establishment of four additional military schools with six-month courses for regular officers and eight-month courses for technical officers was to ensure the training of the middle and lower levels. Tactical and weapons training were given priority in the curricula.

In his order no. 0832, of October 17, 1942, the people's commissar of defense (Stalin) stipulated that those frontline soldiers who had attended at least seven classes should also be admitted to training at the tank schools.

In May 1943 the training period for cadets from all military schools was extended to one year, and the training program was divided into two parts: In the first part (eight months), training to become tank commanders and platoon leaders took place. In the second part (four months), their knowledge was deepened by repeating those sections of the training program that the cadets had not mastered well. Successful "model boys" were able to leave the course after completing the first part. In any case, the quality of the training increased significantly with the introduction of the one-year courses.

By September 15, 1944, three guard tank schools had been established for commanders and platoon leaders of the units to be equipped with the new T-44:

- Kharkov Guards Tank School (for the 33rd Guards Tank Brigade)
- Syvash Guards Tank School (for the 6th Guards Tank Brigade)
- Taman Guards Tank School (for the 63rd Guards Tank Brigade)

Each school could accommodate up to one thousand cadets.

By May 9, 1945, thirty-two military schools had trained lower officer ranks for the armored troops, including four military schools that trained specialists for foreign military vehicles (i.e., the material from Anglo-American aid deliveries).

The People's Defense Commissariat attached great importance to the actual use of the tank soldiers in their respective fields. For example, the people's commissar of defense issued order no. 0953 on December 13:

> So far, there have been many cases in the fronts and military districts where mid- and lower-level officers and ordinary tankers have been deployed outside their specialties, including tank drivers, gunners, artillerymen, technicians, et al. as gunners, machine gunners, [and] mortar crews, and in other types of troops and rear services.
>
> I ORDER THAT
>
> 1. by December 30, 1942, the soldiers' councils of the fronts and military districts shall withdraw all personnel of the middle and lower command levels as well as tank crews who are being used for purposes other than those for which they were assigned, from units, formations, and facilities of the rear services and transfer them:
>
> (a) the midlevel command and technical personnel in the fronts (army groups)
> - to the replacement units of the armored and mechanized troops, the lower ranks, and enlisted men
> - to tank training regiments and reserve tank battalions of the fronts
>
> (b) in military districts
> - to replacement units and tank training regiments stationed within the district
>
> (c) After recovery from wounds and illnesses, tank soldiers may be released from the hospitals only to their own units or formations, training regiments, and reserve tank battalions (points "a" and "b").
>
> The use of personnel of all the abovementioned categories for other purposes is strictly prohibited as of today.

The people's commissar of defense also cracked down on the disbandment of tank units that had lost their equipment at the beginning of the war. The following order is of interest in this context:

ORDER FOR THE DISBANDMENT AND HANDOVER OF MATERIAL BY TANK UNITS

Recently, a number of cases have become known in which commanders of fronts and armies disbanded tank formations and units that had lost their tanks in the course of fighting. As a result, the personnel of these units are not used for their intended purpose, and transport and special vehicles, of which there is an acute shortage, are wasted. In this way, units that have lost valuable personnel and expensive equipment in combat are eliminated at the stroke of a pen. Such behavior not only is unacceptable but is also to be regarded as criminal.

I ORDER THAT

1. no tank units and formations may be disbanded without my permission. The removal of transport and special vehicles from tank units is prohibited.
2. all command personnel of disbanded tank units and formations are to be reported to the head of the personnel directorate of the tank forces of the Red Army. The lower command and crews shall be sent to reserve tank regiments on the instructions of the Chief of the Main Armored Directorate of the Red Army.
3. in the future, tank units and formations that lose their vehicles in combat will be transferred to the rear in full strength to be available to the head of the Main Armored Directorate of the Red Army for restaffing.

People's Defense Commissar J. STALIN

ISU-122 self-propelled gun

During the war, Soviet tank troops carried out both offensive and defensive operations. Depending on the situation, strength, leadership, terrain, orders, and available means, a fixed or mobile defense was used. The purpose of the fixed defense was to pin the enemy down and prevent him from advancing. The main purpose of the mobile defense (delay) was to gain time, inflict losses on the enemy, and maintain the striking power of one's own troops. In this case, temporary territorial losses were permissible in the eyes of the Red Army.

At the beginning of the war, the mechanized corps of the border military districts were forced onto the defensive, if they were still capable of counterattacking at all. It was often a matter of holding important lines, areas, or objects. Tank units and formations were assigned the task of counterattacks and counterattacks.

The battered mechanized corps were disbanded at the end of summer 1941, and tank brigades, independent regiments, and battalions became the most-important tactical units. During this phase of the war, tank units were often transferred to rifle divisions as reinforcements. There they served as fire support during attacks and counterattacks and in defense.

In the first period of the war, tank units were often deployed in ambushes due to the enemy's overwhelming numerical superiority in armored vehicles. (This was not actually the case; only the German tank units were deployed in closed formations, unlike the Soviet ones.) For example, the 4th Tank Brigade, under M. E. Katukov, fought off attacks by up to a hundred tanks with motorized infantry in the Battle of Mtsensk in the autumn of 1941 with fire attacks in just one day (October 6). The battle lasted the whole day. The brigade knocked out forty-three tanks, destroyed sixteen guns, and lost just six tanks itself. (At Mtsensk, the German 4th Panzer Division, which was equipped with the Pz.Kpfw. III and IV, encountered larger numbers of the superior T-34 for the first time.)

The Battle of Kursk (July–August 1943) should rightly be regarded as the high point of the skillful combination of defensive and offensive actions by tank forces. In this battle, the opposing sides had a total of around 8,000 tanks and self-propelled guns at their disposal. (At the beginning of July 1943, the German armed forces had a total of about 7,000 armored combat vehicles, including about 5,850 Panzerkampfwagen, in all theaters of war, including the replacement units in Germany.) The use of Russian tanks in defense was characterized by their concentration on decisive lines of attack in combination with deep echelons, antitank fronts, minefields, and strong artillery concentrations. Each echelon had a specific purpose. Let us limit ourselves here to the use of tanks: individual tank regiments and brigades as well as assault gun regiments formed the first echelon and were located within the defense zones of rifle divisions and corps, whose tank reserves they partly formed. Some tank units (companies, platoons) were deployed as part of antitank fronts in defensive strongpoints and, together with antitank guns, formed their core.

Tank corps and some of the tank brigades were assigned to the second echelon and reserve and were located 30–50 km (19–31 mi.) behind the forward edge of the defense. They were the most-important mobile means of reacting to sudden changes in the situation with regard to the direction of attack by German armored formations. For example, from July 5 to 12 in the area of the so-called Voronezh Front, a Soviet tank army, three tank brigades, and two tank regiments advanced in the direction of Oboyan; a tank army and four tank corps marched on Prokhorovka to achieve a breakthrough there (which failed with heavy losses). In total, twenty armored brigades of the Voronezh Front and eighteen brigades of other army groups carried out daily marches of 40–60 km (25–37 mi.).

Great maneuverability and striking power made the armored troops the main weapon of the Soviet ground forces, which ensured the achievement of the main objectives of the Red Army's main offensive operations.

In offensive operations, Soviet tank units were used mainly for two specific operational and tactical purposes—direct support of infantry and as a "battering ram" in operations by large mixed formations.

Independent tank divisions, regiments, and brigades were formed to support the infantry. Starting in 1943, self-propelled-gun units were added. Depending on the terrain conditions and the strength of the enemy, these tank and self-propelled-gun units moved differently. If the attack took place in open terrain and defense was expected to be rather weak, the tank units moved about 200–400 m (218–436 yds.) ahead of the infantry. If the attack took place in more-difficult terrain and a strong defense was to be expected, it was usually the other way around, and the armored units moved about 200 m behind the infantry.

The density of direct infantry tank support increased steadily during the war: initially there were only five to ten vehicles per kilometer, but after 1941 the number increased to thirty to forty tanks and self-propelled guns, and from 1943, up to sixty to seventy units. The increase in density can be explained in part by the increase in Soviet tank production and the increase in tanks from

T-34/85s advancing with infantry support

Knocked-out T-40 amphibious tanks

American and British aid supplies, and in part by the fact that the German troops increasingly went on the defensive from the second half of 1943 and therefore relied more on deeply echeloned defensive positions and trench systems. Breaking through such a defense required a massing of attacking forces, a high artillery density, and a deep echelon of attack formations. Therefore, compared to previous operations, the quantitative composition of the infantry close-support armored groups increased two or three times; the majority consisted of heavy armored fighting vehicles and self-propelled guns, whose large-caliber armament dramatically increased their firepower.

From 1943 onward, groups were formed from the tank and self-propelled-gun units of the rifle divisions, which were directly commanded by the division commander.

These groups operated on two levels. The first usually consisted of two waves. In the first, tanks advanced at a distance of 200–400 m (218–436 yds.) from the infantry. They suppressed enemy fire that had survived the preceding artillery strike. The second wave consisted of assault guns, which moved 100–200 m (109–218 yds.) behind the tanks and sometimes in the midst of the infantry. The self-propelled guns gave fire support to the attacking tanks of the first wave; they were usually followed by (further) rifle lines.

Later, this tactic was extended by mine-clearing tanks (in pairs or threes) taking the lead, followed by tanks of the first echelon (one or two battle lines of heavy and medium tanks). The second echelon of the brigade (a regiment of heavy tanks) moved 200–300 m behind, followed again at a distance of 200–300 m by infantry units. For example, the 31st Guards Rifle Division formed up in the Orel arc during the counteroffensive at the end of July 1943. During the destruction of Army Group Center in June 1944, the divisions of the 11th Guards Army were forced to launch even more waves of attacks at reduced distances. In this operation, minesweeping tanks, heavy tanks and assault guns, flamethrower tanks, and assault gun batteries of rifle battalions formed six waves with intervals of between 100 and 200 m. The lateral distances were only about 50 m (54 yds.).

The attack by tanks and infantry took place under a barrage of fire, preceded by a powerful artillery strike, and accompanied by IL-2 close-support aircraft. During counterattacks by enemy tanks, the main task of the infantry support vehicles was to defend against them, usually from cover.

Gradually, tanks and assault guns were transformed from infantry support weapons into the core of assault units, around which other weapons and troop types were grouped. After successful breakthroughs, armored units that had functioned as infantry support units were given the task of acting as advance units of rifle divisions and corps. The aim was to keep the enemy on the move, pursue them, encircle them if possible, and gain key positions for further operations, including important bridges for crossing water obstacles.

Great importance was always attached to close cooperation with infantry, artillery, and close-support aircraft. This extended down to battalion and company level: sometimes rifle battalions were assigned individual armored platoons, and rifle companies were assigned individual armored fighting vehicles or assault guns—depending on the mission.

In the third phase of the war, the armored troops focused on gaining more independence by increasing firepower, mobility, and technical support. If you like, they came closer and closer to the German model, to which higher Soviet commanders grudgingly paid respect.

The use of combined arms reached a high point in the establishment of tank armies as well as tank and mechanized corps. According to NKO directive no. 325, of October 16, 1942, tank and mechanized corps were defined as means of the army groups and armies:

> The tank corps is subordinate to the commander of the front or the army and is deployed in echelons in the main direction of attack. . . . In an attack operation, a tank corps has the task of carrying out a massive thrust to fragment the enemy's main forces, encircle them, and destroy them in cooperation with the air and ground forces of the army group. The corps should not get involved in battles with enemy tanks unless it has a clear superiority over the enemy. In the event of an encounter with strong enemy tank formations, the corps deploys antitank artillery and some of its tanks against enemy tanks, while the infantry, for its part, prefers its antitank artillery. The corps shielded with all these means bypasses the enemy tanks with its main forces and separates the enemy infantry from their tanks. The main task of the tank corps is to destroy the enemy infantry.
>
> During defensive operations by an army group or army, tank corps are not given their own defensive sectors and are used for counterattacks from depth. They are located at the intersection points of the armies outside the range of enemy artillery fire (20–25 km).
>
> Mechanized corps are deployed at the head of army groups or armies in the main lines of attack. They ensure the success of the attack and pursue the enemy. The mechanized corps is not divided into brigades, and the mechanized brigades are not subordinate to the commanders of the rifle units. Once the attack has been successful, the mechanized corps, which has sufficient motorized infantry, tanks, and support weapons, can conduct further attacks alone against an enemy that has not yet regained its footing. The deployment of the mechanized corps in breakthrough operations takes place only after the main defensive line has been overcome by the mixed formations and after the attacking infantry has eliminated the enemy artillery. In special cases, the mechanized corps can

Tanks advance with infantry riding on the vehicles.

> independently break through the enemy's front and advance in depth if the enemy's defenses are weak. This requires reinforcement and support of the mechanized corps by howitzer artillery, close-support aircraft, and, if possible, heavy breakthrough tanks.

Tank armies formed the mobile shock groups of the army groups. According to the relevant theories of the time, they were deployed only after a successful breakthrough. In other words, only after the mixed formations had broken through the main battle line and sometimes the enemy's second line. In practice, however, tank armies were usually deployed together with mixed formations for breakthrough operations, whereby they had to perform certain (special) tasks. In the case of the originally created tank armies of mixed composition, their rifle divisions were to tactically effect the actual breakthrough, and the tank corps were to develop it into a strategic success.

Experience with the deployment of armies of mixed composition in 1942 showed that they were lacked the mobility for such tasks and were difficult and cumbersome to lead. The tank armies of uniform composition created in 1943, which comprised only tank and mechanized corps, were highly mobile and powerful. They were "a powerful tool of the high command" and were deployed with army groups at frontline focal points. Their most-important operational tasks were

- advances in depth to fragment the enemy,
- encirclement of the strongest enemy forces,
- destruction of operational and sometimes strategic enemy reserves, and
- to capture, secure, and hold important objects and lines until the main body arrives.

A characteristic feature of the conditions under which tank armies and corps operated was their separation from the main forces of the army group. In many operations, tank armies and individual corps were separated from the main body by up to 30–40 km and sometimes over 100 km after completing their mission. This realization also influenced the organizational structure (combat strength). During the war, structural improvements were made to the armored and mechanized formations to ensure their independence. At the end of the war, apart from its armored units, a tank army usually consisted of

- 1 antiaircraft division,
- 1 guards rocket launcher regiment,
- 1 howitzer regiment,
- 1 or 2 antitank regiments, and
- 1 motorcycle regiment.

Acting as support units were
- 1 air liaison regiment (Po-2 aircraft),
- 1 transport regiment,
- 1 combat engineer battalion, and
- 1 to 2 repair battalions.

There were also the necessary rear-echelon services.

At the end of the war, a tank army consisted of 3 corps (2 tank and 1 mechanized corps) with more than 50,000 troops, 850–920 tanks and assault guns, more than 800 cannon and heavy howitzers, and more than 5,000 wheeled vehicles. It was a powerful and mobile large force that could turn the tactical success of a breakthrough into a strategic one. The tank armies contributed to the successful completion of a series of encirclement operations of large enemy groups.

During the war, the equipment and organizational structure of the Soviet tank forces were qualitatively changed, which contributed to the strengthening of their striking power and firepower. The proportion of tank units in the Soviet ground forces rose from 4.4 percent in December 1941 to 11.5 percent at the beginning of 1945.

The Soviet Union not only was the largest country in the world in terms of area but also had the most powerful tank arm in the world at the end of the war. This included six tank armies, twenty-four tank and fourteen mechanized corps, twenty-seven independent tank brigades, and seven assault gun brigades, and dozens of tank regiments and battalions with a total of over 25,200 tanks and 10,100 assault guns. However, the armored troops had also suffered heavy losses, and those soldiers who survived had gone through a tough school of war. On a tactical-operational level, the Soviet armored weaponry played a significant role in the victory over an enemy that was always outnumbered but difficult to defeat. People in Russia still do not like to hear that it took the Germans just under six months to reach Moscow, whereas it took the Soviets over three years to capture Berlin—and only thanks to massive American and British support and the opening of a second front in the west (landing in Normandy). A mixture of traditional patriotism, hidden inferiority complexes, and a number of domestic political reasons keep glorified memories of the victory alive even after more than three-quarters of a century.

CHAPTER 5
DEVELOPMENT OF THE SOVIET TANK ARM AFTER 1945

The tank arm (including self-propelled guns) formed the main weapon of the Soviet land forces during the war. After the war ended, it was re-formed and further expanded. In the process, attention was paid to the conversion processes of 1940–41, when mechanized corps sprouted from disbanded tank brigades and battalions. In 1945 the tank arm was re-formed in another way. In decree no. 301, of June 10, 1945, Marshall of the Soviet Union I. Stalin, people's defense commissar, listed the most-important directions the reform was to take:

1. To create a standard (unified) organization of fighting troops, including tank troops, the following reorganizations are to take place:

- tank and mechanized corps into tank and mechanized divisions
- tank, mechanized, and motorized rifle brigades into tank, mechanized, and motorized rifle regiments
- Tank regiments into tank battalions (each with 21 tanks), tank battalions of mechanized regiments into mechanized battalions. Tank battalions of the rifle corps each have 35 tanks and are designated independent tank battalions. The reorganization of the tank and mechanized units is to be completed by June 30 of this year.

2. The following applies:

(a) Organization of a tank division: three T-34 tank regiments each with 65 tanks, heavy IS guards tank regiment (65 tanks), motorized rifle regiment, howitzer artillery regiment (224 122 mm howitzers), mortar regiment (36 120 mm mortars), antiaircraft artillery regiment (16 37 mm guns and 16 DShK machine guns), guards rocket launcher battalion (8 M-13 rocket launchers), supply elements, and rear-echelon services. The personnel complement of the tank division in wartime is 11,964 men.

(b) Organization of a mechanized division: three mechanized regiments, one tank regiment of 65 T-34s, heavy IS guards tank regiment (65 tanks), howitzer artillery regiment (24 122 mm howitzers), mortar regiment (36 120 mm mortars), antiaircraft artillery regiment (16 37 mm guns and 16 DShK machine guns), guards rocket launcher battalion (8 M-13 rocket launchers), supply elements, and rear echelon services. The personnel complement of a mechanized division is 14,000 men.

3. The reorganized tank and mechanized formations and units retain their assigned numbers, names, and flags.

4. Generals and officers of the reorganized tank and mechanized units retain their ranks, rights, and salaries.

5. The chief of the general staff, together with the commanders of the tank and mechanized troops of the Red Army, is responsible for the implementation of this order by June 20.

In the first phase the tank arm therefore essentially limited itself to structural changes. The reorganizations introduced by order no. 0013 on behalf of the people's commissar of defense led to an increase in the number of tanks and thus the striking power of the units. The new tank divisions consisted of

- 3 tank regiments,
- 1 guards self-propelled-gun regiment,
- 1 motorized rifle regiment,
- 1 mortar regiment,
- 1 antiaircraft artillery regiment,
- 1 howitzer battalion,
- 1 guards M-31 rocket launcher battalion,
- 1 combat engineer battalion,
- 1 signals battalion / telecommunications battalion,
- 1 motor transport battalion, and
- 1 medical battalion.
- In addition, there was also an air liaison squadron, one tracked repair company, one wheeled repair company, and a field bakery.

Personnel strength of 8,749 men, made up of 1 general, 1,224 officers, 2,156 NCOs, and 5,368 enlisted men.

Weapons and equipment: 314 tanks; 24 assault guns; 110 armored personnel carriers; 4 self-propelled ZSU-27 antiaircraft guns; 4 57 mm guns; 4 76 mm guns; 37 122 mm howitzers; 4 120 mm mortars; 8 M-31-12 and 1 M-13 multiple rocket launchers; 6 DShK machine guns; 6 ZPU-4; 2 25 mm, 29 37 mm, and 6 85 mm antiaircraft guns; 1,224 wheeled vehicles; and 167 radio sets.

While the tank corps had 228 tanks and 42 self-propelled guns, on the basis of the table of organization valid at the end of the war, the new tank division had 86 more tanks, whereas the number of self-propelled guns had been reduced by 18. The tank division numbered just 8,640 men, compared to the tank corps' authorized strength of 11,788 men.

The BTR-50P amphibious armored personnel carrier entered service with the Soviet armed forces in 1954. *Ralf Weinreich*

The organization and personnel structure of the mechanized division were largely similar to that of the tank division:

- 3 mechanized regiments
- 1 tank regiment
- 1 heavy-self-propelled-gun regiment
- 1 artillery regiment
- 1 mortar regiment
- 1 antiaircraft artillery regiment
- 1 guards M-31 rocket launcher battalion
- 1 combat engineer battalion
- 1 signals/telecommunications battalion
- 1 motor transport battalion
- 1 medical battalion

Personnel strength of 9,676 men, made up of 1 general, 1,312 officers, 2,131 NCOs, 6,232 enlisted men.

Weapons and equipment: 245 tanks; 24 self-propelled guns; 195 armored personnel carriers; 8 self-propelled ZSU-37 antiaircraft guns; 13 57 mm, 10 76 mm, and 13 85 mm guns; 37 122 mm howitzers; 2 recoilless rifles; 13 120 mm and 13 160 mm mortars; 6 DShK heavy machine guns; 4 ZPU-1 antiaircraft machine guns; 3 ZPU-4, 8 25 mm, 25 37 mm, and 9 85 mm antiaircraft guns; 1,238 wheeled vehicles; 201 radio sets.

By comparison: the mechanized corps of 1945 numbered 246 tanks and 63 self-propelled guns, with an authorized strength of 16,318 men.

The significant decline in the number of self-propelled guns in the tank and mechanized divisions compared to the tank and mechanized corps can be explained by the fact that many vehicles were transferred to the self-propelled-gun battalions of the rifle divisions.

The mechanized divisions owed their increase in firepower in large part to the considerable increase in the number of armored personnel carriers and antiaircraft guns.

The reductions in the armed forces undertaken from 1946 to 1948 affected the armored forces only to a small degree. Although three tank and eight mechanized divisions were officially disbanded, their tank regiments joined the remaining rifle and mechanized divisions. As for the tank armies, they were not disbanded but instead only changed into mechanized armies. Furthermore, in Poland the USSR formed the 7th Mechanized Army from the 65th Army, and in the Ukraine the 8th Mechanized Army from the 13th and 52nd Armies; the Independent Mechanized Army was created in Romania.

The highly mobile mechanized armies were envisaged primarily for deep operations in which they were to break through the enemy's defenses, encircle larger formations, and destroy reserves in conjunction with close-support aircraft and mixed ground units.

The 5th Mechanized Guards Army, which emerged from the 5th Guards Tank Army, can serve as an example of the organizational structure of a mechanized army. In 1955 it comprised the following formations:

- 8th Guards Tank Division
- 29th Tank Division
- 12th Mechanized Division
- 22nd Mechanized Division
- 51st Independent Guards Reconnaissance Battalion
- 110th Air Defense Brigade
- 296th Artillery Regiment
- 40th Independent Telecommunications Regiment
- 544th Independent Pontoon Bridge Battalion
- 101st Independent Radio Company for Aerial Surveillance
- 2470th Army Depot for Armored Equipment
- 548th Tank Repair Battalion
- 770th Wheeled Vehicle Repair Battalion
- 449th Military Police Platoon
- 24th Independent Motor Transport Platoon
- 42nd Independent Rifle Platoon of the Special Section of the KGB

Personnel strength: 41,056 men, made up of 18 generals, 5,761 officers, 9,224 NCOs, and 25,053 enlisted men.

Weapons and equipment:

- 1,145 tanks / main battle tanks (16 T-34 medium tanks, 893 T-54 medium tanks, 161 IS-4 heavy tanks, 75 PT-76 amphibious tanks)
- 74 ISU-122 self-propelled guns
- 24 ZSU-37 armored antitank guns
- 704 wheeled armored personnel carriers (161 BTR-40, 9 BTR-40-A, 460 BTR-152, 74 BTR-152-A)
- artillery: 34 57 mm, 39 76 mm and 34 85 mm guns; 148 122 mm and 5 152 mm howitzers; 21 100 mm cannon; 2 85 mm and 1 107 mm recoilless guns; 38 120 mm and 26 160 mm mortars
- antiaircraft weapons: 44 12.7 mm DShK machine guns; 14 ZPU-1 and 12 ZPU-4 antiaircraft machine guns; 20 25 mm, 132 37 mm, 73 85 mm, and 8 100 mm antiaircraft guns
- 757 radio sets, 26 radio receivers
- 7 radar systems, 1 P-8, 3 Most-2, 2 SON-4, 1 SON-9

After the end of the war, rifle divisions continued to be equipped with self-propelled-gun battalions. According to table of organization 04/434, adopted at the beginning of 1944, such an self-propelled-gun battalion consisted of three batteries of four guns each (twelve SU-76s) and numbered 184 men. By May 1945, around thirty rifle divisions had been given self-propelled-gun battalions. According to table of organization 04/568, adopted shortly afterward, these divisions received five guns per battery and had 16 SU-76 guns and 152 men. Starting in 1946, each of the rifle divisions received a mixed self-propelled-gun/tank regiment, consisting of two T-34/85 battalions and one SU-100 or SU-76 battalion. It had a total of fifty-two T-34/85s, sixteen assault guns, and six ZSU-37 armored antiaircraft guns. Each rifle regiment also received a battery of SU-76 self-propelled guns.

In the first years after the war, newly established tank units received material from wartime production as well as new equipment that was developed shortly before the end of the war and then put into mass production. The new models included the T-44 medium tank, the IS-3 heavy tank, and the ZSU-37 armored antiaircraft gun.

T-44 tank brigade during an exercise

T-44 Medium Tank

We have already presented the T-44 earlier in this book. The T-44 operations manual published in 1944 described the T-44 as a "heavily armored, maneuverable, and fast tank of a fundamentally new type with powerful gun armament." This assessment seemed entirely justified, since it had the mass of only a medium tank but the armament of a heavy tank.

T-44 of the first production series

T-44, side view

In order to avoid disrupting mass production of the T-34/85, production of the T-44 was transferred to the relocated Charkov Steam Locomotive Factory, which was given the new designation of Factory No. 75. The T-44 was built from 1944 to 1947 in a specified number of 1,823 units. It did not see service during the war.

The short production run of the T-44 is explained by the appearance of the improved T-44V, later better known as the T-54. Developed by a group of engineers under A. A. Morozov, two prototypes were available at the end of December 1944, which were tested in the first quarter of 1945 and improved until the beginning of 1946.

T-44 medium tank

Improved T-44 medium tank

T-54 Medium Tank

With the appearance of the T-54, it was time to stop talking about tanks and start talking about main battle tanks. Series production began in 1947 at Ural Factory No. 183 and in 1948 at Kharkov Factory No. 75 and ended only in 1958 after 16,775 T-54s in various versions had been produced. In addition to the Soviet army, the USSR equipped the Warsaw Pact countries with the T-54 and supplied it to many countries around the world, where it is still in use today.

The hull of the T-54 had a sharply angled glacis made of two armor plates, the upper one 120 mm (4.72 in.) thick. The side armor measured 80 mm (3.1 in.) in thickness, the rear 45 mm (1.8 in.), and the hull roof and floor 30 and 20 mm (1.2 and 0.8 in.), respectively. The frontal armor on the cast turret was 200 mm (7.9 in.). (These thicknesses were strikingly like those of the German Tiger II or King Tiger.) Because the turret protruded too much at the sides, the hull sides had to be reinforced. The turret housed the commander, gunner, and loader; armament consisted of a 100 mm D-10T cannon and a 7.62 mm SG-43 machine gun. The D-10T was originally a naval antiaircraft gun and was installed as the D-10S in the SU-100 self-propelled gun during the Second World War. It had an exceptional firing performance by Soviet standards and could penetrate up to 160 mm (6.3 in.) of armor steel at 1,000 m (1,094 yds.), using armor-piercing ammunition. The D-10T installed in the T-54 had a length of 5.61 m (18.4 ft.) and weighed 1,948 kg (4,294 lbs.). Its

Initial version of the T-54

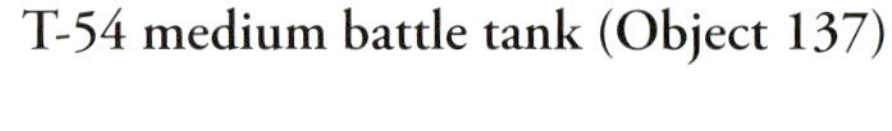

T-54 medium battle tank (Object 137)

T-54s during maneuvers

Column of T-54s on the move

maximum firing range was 14.6 km (9 mi.); however, realistic combat range was 1.5–2 km (1,640–2,187 yds.).

Turret traverse was carried out via an electric turret drive operated by the commander and gunner. The elevation in the range −4°/+17° was done manually and mechanically. A TSh-20 telescopic articulated sight served as the aiming device, and an MK-4 periscope for all-around observation. The gunner could also look outward via an all-around swivel mirror.

PT-76B Light Amphibious Battle Tank (Object 740B)

In 1951, one company each of the tank regiments of the tank and mechanized divisions was equipped with the PT-76 light amphibious tank, which the Institute of Transport Engineering (VNII-100) had developed under the direction of Josef Kotin in accordance with order no. 3472, of August 15, 1949, of the USSR Council of Ministers.

State trials took place in the summer of 1951, and in August the Soviet army adopted it as the PT-76. The PT-76 fulfilled the tasks both of a scout tank and a light battle tank for supporting motorized rifle units when crossing water obstacles. The driver's compartment was located at the front, followed by the fighting compartment with the turret, and the engine compartment in the rear. The amphibious vehicle's pontoon-shaped, welded, and sealed hull was made of thin sheet steel to maximize displacement volume and reduce weight: The upper hull front plate, inclined at an angle of 80.5° to the vertical, measured just 10 mm (0.4 in.) in thickness, the lower one 13 mm (0.5 in.). The truncated-cone-shaped, welded turret was made of 10–20 mm (0.4–0.8 in.) thick armored steel. The driver's hatch, with angled mirrors, was located in the middle of the hull roof of the upper bow plate. When immersed in water, the trim vane with motor in the driver's compartment prevented the hull roof from "flooding." The fighting compartment, with a two-seat rotating turret, had a 76.2 mm gun with a coaxial 7.62 mm SGMT machine gun. The first production vehicles carried the D-56T gun, which was then replaced by the improved D-56TM and finally, starting in 1959, the weapon-stabilized D-56TS. The STP-P Zaria system enabled partially aimed firing while on the move. A 12.7 mm DShKM machine gun on the turret served as an antiaircraft weapon (not all PT-76s were so equipped). A six-cylinder V-6 diesel engine installed longitudinally in the engine compartment provided a maximum output of 240 hp at 1,800 rpm. The engine was equipped with an ejector cooling system, protection against water ingress, and a nozzle heater (to make it easier to start the engine in cold weather). The PT-76 reached a top speed of 44 kph (27 mph) on roads and 10 kph (6.2 mph) in the water, thanks to two hydrojets.

PT-76 amphibious tank (Object 740B)

PT-76s of the Soviet naval infantry crossing a water obstacle

PT-76, view from the front right

Not least due to its low weight of 14 tonnes, it was able to climb inclines of up to 38°, overcome vertical obstacles up to 1.1 m (3.6 ft.) high, and cross trenches up to 2.8 m (9.2 ft.) wide. Thanks to independently closeable rear outlet lids and forward-facing outlets, the tank could maneuver well in water and even travel backward.

PT-76 during a combat exercise

PT-76 in the water

IS-3 Heavy Tank and the Kirovets-1

The IS-3 heavy tank, assigned to heavy-tank and self-propelled-gun regiments, was one of the wartime developments of the Chelyabinsk Kirovsky Factory and Experimental Factory 100. While retaining the armament of the IS-2 tank, the welded hull and cast turret were redesigned, a driver's hatch was (re)introduced in the hull roof, and the viewing slits in the upper glacis plate were eliminated. Because the most-frequent and most-dangerous hits on a tank are on the front of the turret, the thickness of the turret's frontal armor was increased to 250 mm (9.8 in.), and the front end was designed as a three-sided, extremely shot-resistant "pike nose"—the result of the impact of German weapons. The 122 mm D-25 cannon and the ammunition load were the same as those of the IS-2. The turret traverse mechanism had manual and electric drives, whereby the commander was able to override the gunner with the electric drive—a first for Soviet tanks. To do this, he kept the target in the field of vision of his periscope and pressed a button. If the line of sight and the axis of the gun barrel coincided, the traverse movement stopped automatically.

The gunner took aim by means of the TSh-17 turret telescopic sight. The IS-3 was equipped with a coaxial 7.62 mm DTM machine gun and a 12.7 mm DShK antiaircraft machine gun near the commander's hatch as secondary armament. Series production was taken over by the Chelyabinsk Kirovsky Factory, which produced 29 vehicles by May 24, 1945, and a total of 2,311 by the time production was discontinued in mid-1946.

This relatively low number by Soviet standards can be explained by the fact that the IS-3, despite its ideal shot-deflecting shape and many technical innovations, also had considerable disadvantages. In addition to the low rate of fire due to its two-part ammunition, these included an engine that was too vulnerable, a transmission with weaknesses, and inadequate fighting-compartment ventilation. And in the flat turret, with its many sloping surfaces, it was quite cramped for the three-man crew—an expert on the vehicle once remarked sarcastically that it would have been best to use only pygmies or leg amputees as turret crews.

The Soviet leadership did not take such a narrow view—it did not consider the shortcomings of the IS-3, which it regarded as a "product of its time," to be critical. The service life of Soviet combat vehicles in frontline operations was usually not particularly long, a fact that was ensured by German tanks, assault guns, tank destroyers, and close-support aircraft. Stuka colonel Hans-Ulrich Rudel knocked out 519 Soviet tanks with his Ju 87G Kanonenvogel (cannon bird) from summer 1943 to May 1945 alone, which was equivalent to the destruction of an entire tank corps. In peacetime, however, the shortcomings of the IS-3 were no longer acceptable. For this reason, the IS-3 was modernized and refined to eliminate design flaws (UKN program). The list of major works included

- an increase in engine life to (at least) 250 hours;
- protection of the engine compartment (hull floor) against obstacles and the effects of mines;
- increasing the distance between overhauls to 2,000 km (1,242 mi.);
- prevention of oil leaks from swivel mechanisms, axle drives, and road wheels;

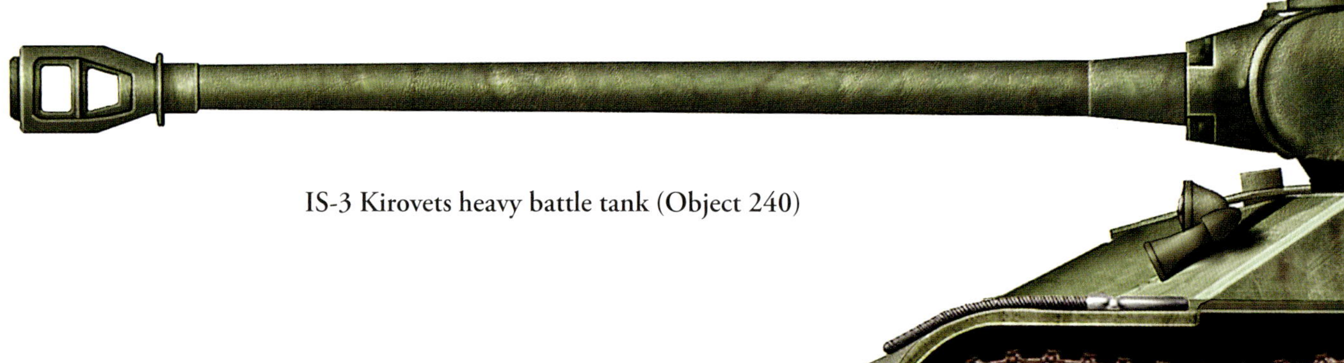

IS-3 Kirovets heavy battle tank (Object 240)

- improved fighting-compartment ventilation through a pipe blow-out device and installation of a fan with filter;
- introduction of an auxiliary loading device to facilitate loading while on the move; and
- improvement of the commander's optics.

The defects found in the IS-3 were, in one form or another, typical of almost all Soviet tanks developed during the war and in the early postwar years. Therefore, almost every type of Soviet tank was modernized as part of the UKN program from 1947 to 1953. Most of the work was carried out by tank workshops.

Further Soviet heavy-tank development was represented by the IS-4 of 1946. Unlike the IS-3, it was not an "upgrade" of the IS-2; rather, it was a new development that retained the 122 mm D-25T gun. Conceived as a breakthrough weapon, the IS-4 was intended to break through heavily defended positions and engage enemy heavy tanks and gun positions. The IS-4 was produced by ChKZ from 1947 to 1949, and during production it was upgraded to the IS-4M. A small batch of IS-4M tanks were built in 1951. That same year, ChKZ modernized all previously produced vehicle types according to changed requirements.

The crew of an IS-3 man their vehicle.

IS-3 tank, view from the front right

T-10 Heavy Tank

The T-10 heavy battle tank entered service with the Red Army in 1953. Like the following T-10A, T-10B, and T-10M, it was a further development of the IS-3. The tank was produced by the Chelyabinsk Kirovsky Factory (from May 15, 1958, the Chelyabinsk Tractor Factory) from 1953 until 1965 and from 1958 to 1963 in the Kirov Factory in Leningrad (T-10M).

The T-10 was the most advanced vehicle of its class, and with a weight of 50 tonnes (55 tons) it was the heaviest Soviet main battle tank produced in quantity. Its development took place in the design bureau of the Kirov Factory in Chelyabinsk under the direction of Josef Kotin. The prototypes were originally designated the IS-8, -9, or -10, but after Stalin's death and Khrushchev's reckoning with his tyranny, the vehicle went into production as the T-10 at the end of 1953. The hull, with its sloping surfaces and the characteristic "pike nose," made it impossible to deny its IS-3 parentage. The tank also had a streamlined cast turret with variable angles of inclination of the walls and variable armor thicknesses. Armament consisted of a 122 mm D-25A tank gun with a dual-chamber muzzle brake plus a coaxial 12.7 mm DShKM machine gun and an antiaircraft machine gun of the same caliber with collimator sight. The gunner was provided with a TSh2-27 telescopic sight, and combat range was up to 5,000 m (5,468 yds.). The T-10 was powered by a V12-5 twelve-cylinder diesel engine with centrifugal blower and an output of 700 hp. The running gear consisted of seven road wheels suspended on torsion bars on each side, three return rollers per side, the idler wheels forward and drive sprockets at the rear. In 1956 the tank was modified into the T-10A. The most important innovation concerned the D-25TS gun, which was given a fume extractor and a PUOT-1 Uragan single-axis stabilization system (vertical).

T-10, rear view

T-10 heavy battle tank (Object 730)

T-10, view from the front left

The TSh2-27 telescopic sight was replaced by a TPS-1 periscopic sight and the TTL double telescopic sight. The driver was given a TVN-1 night vision device and a hydraulic GPK-48 compass. The T-10B, which entered service in 1957, differed from its predecessor in having the PUOT-2 two-axis stabilization system and the T2S-29-4 telescopic sight. The last production version, the T-10M, mounted the new 122 mm M-62-T2 gun with 2E12 Liven two-axis stabilization

T-10M heavy battle tanks taking part in a parade in Red Square

T-10s while on maneuvers

Column of T-10s in Czechoslovakia

system and two KPVT 14.5 mm machine guns (antiaircraft and coaxial). The output of the V-12-6 engine was boosted to 750 hp, and a six-speed transmission was installed.

Thanks to series production of the IS-4 and the T-10, plus the modernization of the IS-2 and IS-3, the Soviets were able to create especially powerful divisions that were completely equipped with heavy tanks. Eight heavy-tank divisions were formed in the 1955–58 period. They differed from the usual tank divisions in not having the motorized rifle regiment and the equipping of all three tank regiments with a total of 293 heavy battle tanks and self-propelled guns, 54 antiaircraft guns, 138 armored personnel carriers, and other equipment. The division's authorized strength was about seven thousand men. At that time, no other army in the world had an armored force with the same striking power.

During the war, the Red Army had become convinced of the necessity of armored personnel carriers to accompany tank units, comparable to the Schützenpanzerwagen half-tracks employed by the Wehrmacht. The Russians had no armored personnel carriers of their own; however, they did receive various armored half-tracks from the Americans—the M2, M3, M5, and M9—and the twin-axle MZA1 Scout Car with all-wheel drive. They also received universal carriers from British and Canadian factories. Not only were they used to transport men and supplies, but also as reconnaissance vehicles and light artillery tractors. They were also armed with light antiaircraft and antitank guns. It is therefore no wonder that the Soviets began building similar vehicles shortly after the war. The first armored personnel carrier was developed by a group of engineers of the OKB for Special Vehicles in the Gorki Automobile Factory under V. K. Rubtzov in 1947. It was based on the new twin-axle GAZ-63 all-wheel-drive truck. Designated the GAZ-40, the vehicle underwent testing in 1948, and in 1950 it entered service with the Soviet army as the BTR-40.

BTR-40 Wheeled Armored Personnel Carrier

In addition to the lightly armored BTR-40, the motorized rifle divisions were also issued the BTR-152 medium six-wheeled armored personnel carrier, which had been developed by the special section of the Stalin Factory in Moscow under the leadership of B. M. Fitterman starting in November 1946.

BTR-40, view from the front right

BTR-40 in action with the Soviet invasion forces in Afghanistan

BTR-40A (ZhD) for operation on railroad tracks

BTR-40 of the East German National People's Army

BTR-40 armored personnel carrier (Object 141)

BTR-152 Wheeled Armored Personnel Carrier

A series of ten vehicles were built for test purposes in 1947. On March 24, 1950, the vehicle was accepted by the Red Army as the BTR-152. Production ran from 1950 to 1955 in the Stalin Factory and the Bryansk Automobile Factory, with a total output of 12,421 BTR-152s. Among the most-serious shortcomings of the BTR-40 and BTR-152 was their lack of amphibious capability. The BTR-50P amphibious transport vehicle, which was developed on the basis of the PT-76, had such capability and was accepted by the Soviet military by decree no. 175-89cc, of January 30, 1954, of the USSR Council of Ministers. In principle, the BTR-50P was a PT-76 without turret and open at the rear, offering space for up to twenty soldiers.

BTR-152 wheeled armored personnel carrier

BTR-152 with armored roof

BTR-152s taking part in a parade in Red Square

BTR-152, view from the right

BTR-152 of the Soviet forces in Afghanistan

Motorized infantry in BTR-152s during a parade

BTR-152E with ZTPU-2 antiaircraft machine gun

BTR-50P Amphibious Troop Transport

As well as an armored amphibious troop carrier, the BTR-50P could also be used as a transport vehicle. For this purpose, folding ramps were installed on the roof of the engine compartment for lashing down guns or vehicles. A 1,500 kg (3,306 lb.) winch was used to load and unload such pieces of equipment. Typical loads for the BTR-50P included a 76 mm gun with twenty to twenty-five rounds of ammunition and a crew of five, an 85 mm gun plus two persons, a UAZ-469 light utility vehicle plus seven persons, three 82 mm recoilless rifles with twenty-four rounds of ammunition plus twelve persons, or a 120 mm mortar with thirty-two mortar rounds plus six persons. Goods weighing up to 2,000 kg (4,409 lbs.) could also be transported on the roof of the engine-gearbox compartment. Incidentally, guns loaded on the vehicle could still be fired.

The BTR-50P entered service with the motorized rifle battalions of tank regiments of the tank and mechanized divisions. The tank regiments thus received a powerful "amphibious fist" for establishing bridgeheads or carrying troops across bodies of water.

The development of new and the modernization of existing types of armored vehicles was accompanied by an improvement in the organizational structure. Experience from wars and exercises, maneuvers, and everyday service, as well as from military science conferences, was incorporated into this. Everything served only to sharpen the role of the tank arm in attack and defense. These activities gave rise to various regulations, including these:

- Field Manual of the Armed Forces of the USSR (corps, division), 1948
- Combat Regulations for Armored and Mechanized Troops of the Soviet Army (division, corps, battalion), 1953
- Field Manual of the Soviet Army (regiment, battalion), 1953

According to these manuals, the offensive was still the most important task of the tank arm; it was intended to bring about the complete defeat of the foe or class enemy. The offensive was divided into two main phases: (a) breaking through the enemy's defenses and (b) transition to the actual offensive (deep penetration). The breakthrough was considered the most important phase, since only it could create the conditions for successful

BTR-50 amphibious armored personnel carrier (Object 750)

further development. Soviet doctrine distinguished between breakthroughs through well-defended and well-prepared zones and places that the enemy had hastily occupied and were probably only weakly defended. Breakthroughs through prepared defenses were logically considered the "supreme discipline," which is why manuals, regulations, training, and exercises paid the greatest attention to them. Heavy-tank regiments with self-propelled guns and heavy battle tanks were to reinforce the medium-tank and infantry units. As a rule, the regiment was "attached" to rifle units, which it was to support alongside the artillery in gaining key positions in the fight against particularly stubborn targets.

Once the enemy's tactical defenses had been breached across the board, the heavy-tank/self-propelled-gun regiment was transferred to the corps or army commander's reserve and subsequently served to combat enemy tanks and self-propelled guns.

In defense, tank and mechanized units were to be deployed mainly in the second echelon to conduct counterattacks from the depths. At the same time, military theory permitted the independent deployment of tank and mechanized divisions and armies as powerful reserves

BTR-50PK, view from the front

BTR-50PU command vehicle

in the main lines of attack. At divisional level, parts of the heavy regiment could be attached to the first echelon of the defense of rifle regiments. Most of the subunits and sometimes the entire regiment were to serve as a reserve for the commander of the rifle division in case the enemy broke through the main line of defense. At corps and army level, the heavy-tank/self-propelled-gun regiment (IS-2, IS-3, and SU-100) similarly served as a tank reserve for the commander of the army or corps.

In the event of an enemy breakthrough into the depths of the defense (i.e., a penetration of the first line), counterattacks by the tank reserves were considered impractical. Under these conditions, the second line was to seal off the front, with mechanized divisions encircling and destroying the enemy forces that had broken through.

Unlike counterattacks during World War II, which were usually carried out only after the initial position had been temporarily occupied, the mechanized division usually counterattacked from on the move, relying mainly on

tank regiments with T-34/85 medium tanks, which in turn were supported by IS-2, IS-3, and SU-100 heavy tanks / self-propelled guns.

At the army group level, the mechanized army usually formed the second echelon or reserve of the army group (front), which undertook powerful counterattacks and then went on the offensive.

Should the enemy succeed in breaking in with strong armored forces, heavy regiments were to help build up the defense in depth and strengthen the antitank defense of the rifle units of the first line.

To reinforce the antitank defenses of rifle corps and divisions at frontline focal points, the plan was to call up heavy regiments from the reserves of armies or the high command anyway.

However, heavy-tank units were not only to operate "from the second line" in the defense. The Soviet military leadership also envisaged their use in the "front line." On the basis of analyses of World War II operations and major postwar maneuvers, it reached the conclusion that the offensive strength of the armies needed to be significantly increased. In 1954, it therefore began to set up heavy-tank divisions that had three heavy-tank regiments with a total of 195 IS-2 and IS-3 heavy tanks. Other characteristic features were a low proportion of infantry (only one motorized rifle company per regiment), the abandonment of field artillery, and the streamlining of combat support units and rear services.

It is noteworthy that the Soviet military envisaged the use of tactical nuclear weapons in breakthrough operations alongside the heavy-tank divisions. In this context, a major maneuver, which was known as Snowball, was planned under the motto "Breakthrough of the enemy's prepared tactical defense with nuclear weapons" in autumn 1954 at the Totsk military training area. The attacking force

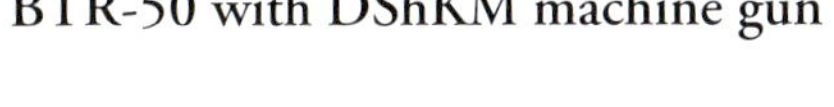

BTR-50 with DShKM machine gun

was given the task of breaking through the prepared tactical defense of the maneuvering enemy by using real nuclear weapons, while the defending force had to organize and carry out the defense under conditions of the real use of nuclear weapons. The focus was on the attacking side, whose troops dealt with live nuclear shells and tactical nuclear bombs to be dropped from the air, and while the actual targets were not manned by soldiers, the attackers had to pass through and adapt to nuclear-contaminated territory.

A total of about 45,000 men took part (among the most-important units were the 12th Mechanized Guards Division and the 50th Guards Rifle Division as part of the 128th Rifle Corps), plus six hundred battle tanks and self-propelled guns.

Three atomic bombs were supposed to ensure the success of the rifle corps' offensive. The first atomic bomb was to explode over the positions of the regimental reserves and the main artillery groupings of the "western" forces. At the same time, a combined air-artillery strike was to be carried out on the forward positions. The offensive by the "eastern" forces was to be accompanied by a second nuclear strike against the most important fortress in the rear of the "western" forces. This strike and the subsequent breakthrough were intended to destroy the defenses of

BTR-50PUs and BDRM-2 armored cars during maneuvers

the first line. A third nuclear explosion was to eliminate the enemy defense in the reserve zone and, if possible, ensure the subsequent breakthrough.

In fact, only one RDS-2 medium-yield atomic bomb, dropped from a Tu-4, was detonated. The other two "atomic" explosions were simulated by using large quantities of TNT and drums of gasoline.

BTR-50 during a parade in Red Square

At 09:34 on September 14, 1954, the Tu-4 dropped its atomic bomb from 8,000 m (26,250 ft.), and it exploded forty-eight seconds later at a height of 350 m (1,148 ft.) above the ground. Five minutes after the explosion, artillery preparation began, with subsequent ground attacks by fighter planes. At the end of the artillery/air strike, the attacking party sent radiation reconnaissance patrols toward the epicenter of the nuclear explosion. They arrived there forty minutes after the explosion and detected a radiation level of 50 U/h, which dropped to 25 U/h at a radius of 300 m, 0.5 U/h at 500 m, and 0.1 U/h at 850 m.

At 10:10, the "Eastern Party" launched its attack and passed through the radiation zone in battle formation, with reconnaissance units reinforced by radiation detection units taking the lead. The second wave of attacks followed at 11:00.

The analysis of the Totsk maneuver reinforced the Soviet leadership's conviction that a "limited" nuclear war was possible, in which conventional armed forces reinforced by tactical nuclear weapons would take control. Without questioning this thesis, Soviet military doctrine nevertheless declared the main battle tank to be the main weapon for defeating the enemy. An essay by a former chief of the general staff, Marshal V. D. Sokolovsky, in the magazine

Military Strategy stated: "In the ground forces, the proportion of tank forces will continue to increase. In terms of their combat characteristics, tanks are more resistant to the effects of nuclear weapons, have high mobility and speed in the terrain, and can maneuver quickly and cover great distances. They can quickly overcome the enemy's radioactive contamination zones and utilize the effects of their own nuclear attacks to the greatest effect. . . . With the proper organization, they can not only effectively utilize the results of nuclear attacks but also sweep away the remnants of enemy resistance with the fire from their numerous guns in the tank attack, deal swift blows to it in the flanks and rear, and advance into deep space without interruption. Of all the branches of the armed forces, the tank forces are best suited to the nature of nuclear missile warfare."

However, the Totsk maneuver also showed that not all tank types used were suitable for operations under nuclear conditions and first had to be equipped for this.

The first Soviet main battle tank to be equipped with a fully fledged NBC protection system was the T-55. Developed on the basis of the T-54B by the design bureau of Plant No. 183, under L. N. Kartsev, it was adopted by the Soviet armed forces on May 8, 1958, by decree no. 493-230 of the Council of Ministers.

Tank units of the Soviet army after taking part in Exercise Zapad-81

T-55 medium battle tanks during a combat exercise

T-55A with infantry riding on the tank

T-55 Main Battle Tank

The NBC protection system included a filter unit that supplied the crew with purified air, pumps to generate overpressure (back pressure), and components to protect against neutron radiation and other risks. In the event of a nuclear explosion, an x-ray counter immediately registered the gamma radiation and sent electrical signals to the ignition circuit of the pyrotechnic charges to seal the hull and turret and to switch off the main electrical circuit. As a result, the engine stopped, which was intended to prevent damage to equipment caused by the electromagnetic pulse from the nuclear explosion.

The strength and rigidity of the hull and turret ensured that the crew was protected from the shock wave of a nuclear explosion. After the shock wave had passed, a filter/ventilation unit (separator fan) switched on, continuously supplying the interior with purified air and creating an overpressure that prevented the penetration of radioactive particles. To protect against neutron radiation, the interior of the armor was coated with radiation-inhibiting synthetic materials that slow down and absorb neutrons. The T-55 also received the following improvements:

- The more powerful V-55 diesel engine, which produced 580 hp, was installed in place of the V-45.
- The ammunition load was increased from 34 to 43 rounds, and the capacity of the fuel tanks was increased.
- Installation of thermo-smoke devices that produced artificial smoke by injecting fuel into the exhaust manifold.
- Installation of a compressor for reliable engine starting, which extended battery life and replaced the compressed air cylinders that had to be charged externally.
- Installation of the Rosa fire-suppression system.
- Hydropneumatic cleaning of the driver's periscope.

T-55 medium battle tank

T-55, view from the right

T-55A with a DShKM antiaircraft machine gun

Upgraded T-55AMV

Production of the T-55 began in June 1958 at Factory No. 183 in Nizhny Tagil, and it was soon joined by Factory No. 75 in Kharkov and No. 134 in Omsk. By the time production ended in 1969, 13,290 T-55s had been completed (more than 20,000 according to other sources) in various versions. The T-55 was also built under license in Czechoslovakia, Poland, and Romania.

The T-55's successor, the T-62, entered service with the Red Army in 1961, and it was fitted with a very similar NBC protection system. Its development can be traced back to the latest NATO medium battle tanks, which were armed with the British 105 mm L7 A1 gun or its American counterpart the M 68. It was superior to the 100 mm gun of the T-54/T-55, while the Soviet tank offered less protection as the probability of a lethal first hit rose.

Loading ammunition into a T-55

T-62 Main Battle Tank

The T-62 countered this with thicker armor and a new streamlined three-man cast turret. It was slightly larger than the turret of the T-55 and had thicker walls: 242 mm (9.5 in.) on the front and 153 mm (6 in.) on the sides. It was armed with the U5-TS (2A20) 115 mm smoothbore gun with a 7.62 mm coaxial PKT machine gun. It was the world's first series-produced main battle tank with a smoothbore gun. It fired three types of fin-stabilized projectiles: HE-18 explosive shells, BK-4 and BK-4M shaped-charge shells, and BM-6 subcaliber hard-core projectiles. The latter reached a muzzle velocity of 1,615 m/sec. (5,298 ft./sec.) and exceeded the penetration power of the corresponding 105 mm projectiles fired by the British L7 A1 gun. The NBC protection systems introduced on the T-55 and T-62 were now also fitted to other models of armored vehicles, first and foremost infantry fighting vehicles with completely "sealed" interiors.

Exercises involving the real or simulated use of nuclear weapons showed that the organizational structures also needed to be adapted. The tank and mechanized divisions formed from the experiences of the Second World War proved to be cumbersome to lead and too immobile. Rifle divisions lacked the armored thrust to break through the enemy's tactical zone and were not sufficiently protected against the effects of the use of nuclear weapons. On the basis of an assessment of the 1957 maneuvers, the tank divisions had to dispense with one tank regiment (three instead of four). The rifle regiments of the tank divisions, restructured as mechanized regiments in 1953, became motorized rifle regiments again. Independent companies of tank destroyers were added.

At the same time, the leadership of the Ministry of Defense concluded that it should create unified motorized rifle divisions instead of mechanized and rifle divisions. In the opinion of the Ministry of Defense, motorized rifle divisions consisting of three motorized rifle regiments (each with a tank battalion) as well as tank and artillery regiments plus support units were very well able to break through the enemy's defenses and carry out operations in depth.

While the Soviet land forces still had 65 mechanized, 30 tank, and about 120 rifle divisions in 1955, by 1957 there were 47 tank and about 180 motorized rifle divisions. In the early 1960s, the striking power both of the tank and motorized rifle divisions was drastically increased

T-62, view from the front right

through the integration of independent missile units with nuclear warheads.

At the end of the 1970s, a motorized rifle division was organized as follows:

- 3 motorized rifle regiments each of 3 battalions plus 1 tank battalion (40 main battle tanks)
- 1 battalion of armored artillery (18 2S1 Gvozdika self-propelled guns), 1 battalion of armored mortars (18 2S12 Sani mortars), and 5 independent companies (reconnaissance, combat engineers, communications, repair, supply, medical services)
- 1 tank regiment of 3 tank battalions (each with 31 tanks) and 1 motorized rifle battalion, 1 battalion of armored artillery, and the same independent companies as motorized rifle regiments
- 1 self-propelled-artillery regiment (armored artillery) of 3 battalions (54 ACS 2S3 Akatsiya) and 1 rocket launcher battalion (18 BM-21 Grad)
  (some divisions had an artillery regiment that was equipped with towed D-30 152 mm howitzers instead of self-propelled guns)
- 1 independent rocket battalion (3–4 9K79 Tochka surface-to-surface missiles)
- 1 independent antitank battalion of 3 batteries (each with 6 Konkurs or Phalanx antitank missile launchers and a fire control platoon
- 1 independent tank battalion of 3 tank companies (each of 3 platoons with 4 main battle tanks), 1 medical platoon, and telecommunications, repair, and supply platoons
- 1 independent battalion for reconnaissance and electronic warfare (or 1 reconnaissance battalion) consisting of 4 companies: 1 armored reconnaissance, 1 reconnaissance and airborne company (or 2 reconnaissance and airborne companies)
  1 BRDM company, 1 telecommunications and radio intelligence company
- 1 combat engineer battalion, consisting of 4 companies plus two separate platoons
- 1 independent telecommunications battalion
- 1 repair battalion of 5 repair companies and 3 independent platoons
- 1 supply battalion of 5 supply companies, 1 workshop platoon, 1 telecommunications platoon, 1 field bakery, 1 medical platoon, etc.
- 1 medical battalion of 1 medical company and 3 independent platoons (medicine, hygiene, disease prevention) plus 3 sections (evacuation and transport, medical supply, communications)

This organization was similar to that of a tank division, except for a different number of tank and motorized rifle regiments. The tank division had three tank, one motorized rifle, one self-propelled-artillery, and one surface-to-air missile regiments, but no independent tank and antitank battalions. The tank division, with an authorized strength of 11,382 men, had the following equipment: 326 main

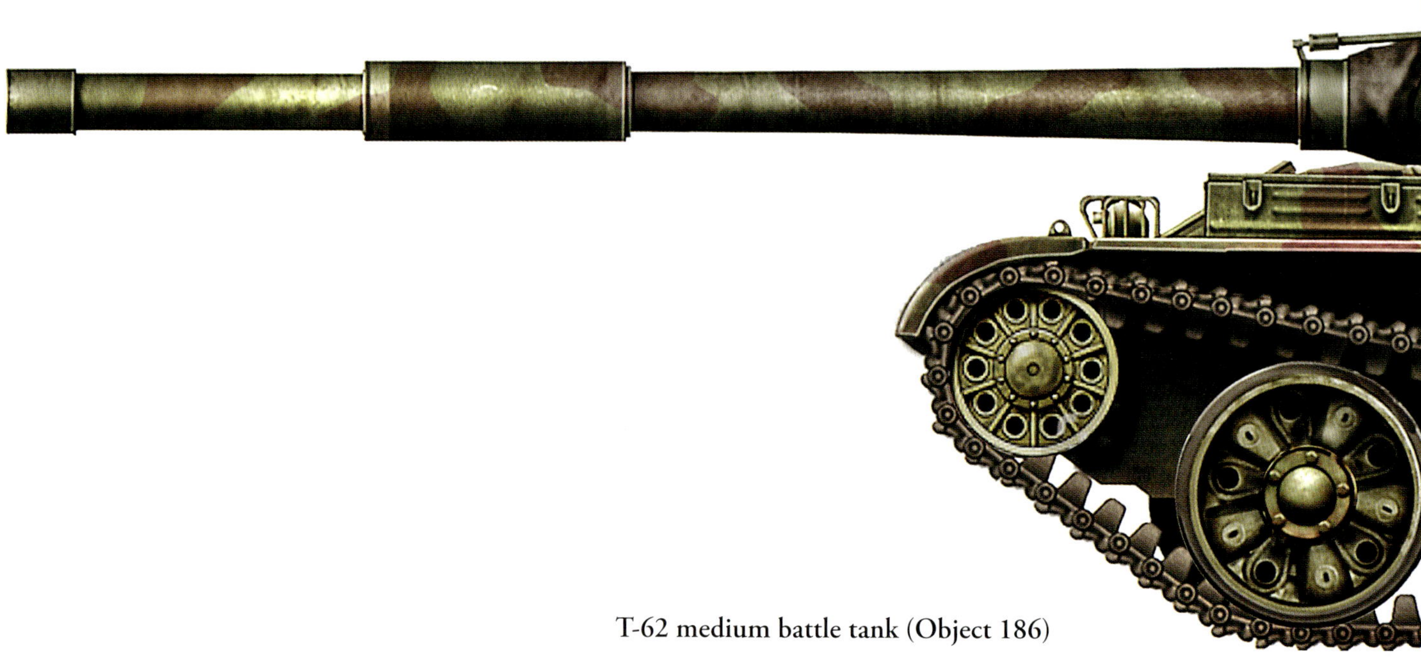

T-62 medium battle tank (Object 186)

battle tanks, 228 armored personnel carriers, 19 BRM-1K reconnaissance tanks, 29 BDRM armored cars, 142 armored howitzers (48 Akatsiya 152 mm and 96 Gvozdika 122 mm), 24 BM-21 Grad rocket launchers, 4 Tochka tactical ballistic missiles, and 9 9P148 Konkurs guided antitank missiles, plus 20 2P25 Kub (SA-6) or Kreis surface-to-air missiles, 16 9A34 (9A35) Strela-10 short-range surface-to-air missiles, and 16 ZSU-23-4 Shilka self-propelled antiaircraft weapons systems.

Interestingly, the quantitative equipment of tank divisions did not change significantly from 1945 until the end of the 1960s. In 1945 a division had 314 medium tanks, 24 assault guns, 110 armored personnel carriers, 49 guns (37 122 mm and 4 each of 57, 76, and 85 mm), 4 120 mm mortars, 8 rocket launchers, and 56 antiaircraft weapons (4 ZSU-37, 3 ZPU-4, 2 25 mm, 29 37 mm, 6 12.7 mm DShK ZPU-2, and 85 mm antiaircraft guns). In the late 1960s it was 314 main battle tanks, 19 PT-76 amphibious tanks, 24 D-30 122 mm howitzers, 133 armored personnel carriers (including 19 tracked mortars), 15 120 mm mortars, 6 Grad multiple rocket launchers, and 36 antiaircraft systems (12 ZSU-23-4 Shilka and 24 57 mm guns).

Column of T-62s in the exercise area

Of interest are the so-called "independent tank regiments for the protection of the state border" established in the early 1960s from tank brigades in the Group of Soviet Armed Forces in Germany (GSWG) and in the Far East. Six regiments were stationed on the border between central and western Germany (221st Guards, 115th, 119th,

T-62s crossing a pontoon bridge over a water obstacle

T-62s on the attack with accompanying infantry

T-62s practicing a joint advance with BMP-1 armored personnel carriers

138th, 145th, and 147th) and three in the Far East (49th, 54th, and 85th); a further regiment (the 10th) was located in the Odessa military district. In the event of a NATO attack, the "tank regiments for the protection of the state border" were to intercept the initial thrust and give the main group of the armed forces the necessary time. The regiments consisted of three tank battalions, artillery, and support units. Until the early 1980s, however, the regiments were equipped only with outdated vehicle models (IS-3M, T-10, T-55, SU-100, ISU-152, BTR-152, etc.), probably because their survivability was considered to be low anyway. Later, however, they received the latest types, including the T-64 and T-80.

From the beginning of the 1960s, the motorized rifle regiments of tank and rifle divisions received an amphibious wheeled armored personnel carrier or infantry fighting vehicle (the Russian name for such vehicles is *bronetransportyor* = armored carrier) of a fundamentally new type. The BTR-60 P was developed in 1957–58, when it became clear that the possibilities for further development of the BTR-152 had been exhausted. The new wheeled infantry fighting vehicle was to be as suitable for off-road use as a tracked vehicle and be able to cross trenches 2 m (6.6 ft.) wide and swim through water obstacles. The requirement for armor protection (weight) resulted in the need for at least three axles evenly distributed over the length of the hull. At the same time, the requirement for amphibious capability severely limited the thickness of the armor. The BTR-60P was the result of competition between the design offices of the leading automobile factories. The design office of ZIL (Zavod Imeni Likhachova; Likhachov Plant) presented the promising three-axle ZIL-153 with a completely closed, welded armored body and steerable front and rear axles.

T-62s on maneuvers

Upgraded T-62MV medium battle tank

BTR-60P Amphibious Wheeled Armored Personnel Carrier

The GAZ-49, developed by the design bureau of the Gorki Automobile Factory (GAZ) under chief designer V. A. Dedkov, proved to be the winner, and it was accepted by the Soviet army on December 13, 1959, as the BTR-60P (P = *plavat* [*плавать*]: amphibious). GAZ delivered the first batch in 1960. The BTR-60P and its derivatives were produced until 1976 and are still in service in more than thirty countries worldwide.

The BTR-70 was chosen as the successor to the BTR-60, and it entered service with the Soviet armed forces on August 21, 1972.

BTR-60P, view from the front left

BTR-60P (GAZ-49) amphibious wheeled armored personnel carrier

BTR-60Ps on the advance, carrying infantry

BTR-60PA with armored roof

Motorized infantry engaging an aerial target from a moving BTR-60P

BTR-70 Amphibious Wheeled Armored Personnel Carrier

It replaced the BTR-60P/60PA/60PB in the motorized rifle regiments. The BTR-70 was based on the BRT-50 and the GAZ-50, developed by the GAZ design bureau. Important new elements of the hull were two small side exit hatches between the second and third pair of wheels on both sides of the hull. Additional hatches were located in the roof of the transport compartment, which offered space for six fully equipped troops. They sat with their backs to each other so that they could fire their weapons through the side openings. The firing hatches could be closed with armored covers. A TNP-B device on each side provided protected observation from the interior. Another motorized rifleman sat in the front of the hull; on the other side was a machine gunner.

The fighting in Afghanistan revealed serious shortcomings in the BTR-70: In hot weather, the engines overheated, and at elevations above 2,000 m (6,500 ft.) they did not provide the required power. The elevation angle of the machine guns mounted in the turret was not sufficient to fight mujahideen on steep slopes.

The BTR-80, which was also developed at GAZ in the first half of the 1980s, was able to iron out these shortcomings. The Soviet armed forces introduced it into service in 1986. Vehicles from the first series experienced their baptism of fire in Afghanistan and became the main combat vehicle for many motorized rifle battalions. Each of the battalion's three rifle companies had eleven BTR-70s; the battalion had a total of forty-nine.

BTR-70 (GAZ-4905) amphibious wheeled armored personnel carrier

The BTR-70 wheeled armored personnel carrier saw action in Afghanistan and the Northern Caucasus, among other places.

Infantrymen climbing out through the hatches in the roof of the BTR-70

BTR-70, view from the right

Naval infantry coming ashore from a BTR-70

BTR-80 Amphibious Wheeled Armored Personnel Carrier

The design of the BTR-80 was similar to that of the BTR-60P and the BTR-70: driver's compartment in front, fighting compartment in the middle, and engine compartment in the rear. The sealed, fully enclosed body with numerous slopes was welded together from rolled armor plates. The occupants were protected from 7.62 mm small-arms projectiles by the side armor and from 12.7 mm projectiles by the frontal armor.

BTR-80, view from the front right

The BTR-80 had outstanding excellent off-road capabilities.

Motorized infantry climbing out through the side hatches

BTR-80 amphibious wheeled armored personnel carrier

Schützenpanzer BMP-1

In the 1960s the Soviet army introduced a new class of infantry fighting vehicle (Boyevaya Mashina Pyekhoty, or BMP). In contrast to armored personnel carriers (APCs), they were equipped not only with a tracked chassis, but also a powerful turret armament in the form of a 73 mm gun with a coaxial machine gun and a launcher for guided antitank missiles. This meant not only that the BMP could increase the firepower of motorized rifle units and offer the crew better protection (including against NBC weapons) than a wheeled infantry fighting vehicle, but that it could also follow the tank forces wherever they went, thanks to its tracked running gear. It was also amphibious. The BMP-1, developed by the design office of the Chelyabinsk Tractor Works under chief designer P. P. Isakov, was also the first infantry fighting vehicle in the world whose crew could fight with all small arms under full protection without having to leave the vehicle.

The Soviet land forces introduced the BMP-1 in 1966, and it remained in production until 1983. The basic principle of the BMP-1, continued by other BMP offshoots, served as an inspiration and model for many infantry fighting-vehicle developments by other armies. In contrast to the BTR models, the engine is located to the right of the driver's compartment at the front of the hull. The fighting compartment, with the turret, occupies the center section, and the troop compartment is in the rear. The welded hull consists of rolled armored steel plates. The upper bow plate is sloped at an angle of 80°, and the lower one 57°. A flat, truncated-cone-shaped turret towers above the fighting compartment, carrying the 2A28 Grom unstabilized 73 mm smoothbore gun and a 7.62 mm coaxial MG PKT. The turret rotates, and the range of elevation of the weapons is −4°/+33°, controlled by electric drives. The low-pressure smoothbore gun has a theoretical rate of fire of eight to ten rounds per minute. Its realistic combat range is 1,300 m (1,421 yds.), and the range of a direct shot with a target height of 2 m (6.6 ft.) is 765 m (836 yds.) (i.e., without allowing for ballistic drop). The PG-3 shaped-charge projectile penetrates up to 300 mm (11.8 in.) of armor steel. The gunner aims both weapons by using the 1PN22M1 combined periscope sight, which is suitable for night combat. The same sight

BMP-1, side view

BMP-1, rear view

is also used for the 9M14 Malyutka wire-guided, antitank missile, whose launching rack is located on the right above the gun. The combat range of the Malyutka (Little One) is 500–3,000 m (547–3,280 yds.), and its shaped-charge warhead melts through up to 550 mm (21.6 in.) of armor steel. The BMP-1 can carry four of these "Little Ones." To engage aerial targets, the BMP-1 was equipped with the 9K32 Strela-2 man-portable surface-to-air missile, which can be fired both from a hatch in the roof and from outside the vehicle. Weighing 9.15 kg (20 lbs.), with a length of 1,423 mm (4.7 ft.), the surface-to-air missiles can detect and engage air targets at a speed of up to 220 m/sec. (722 ft./sec.). Let us not forget the eight motorized riflemen in the rear fighting compartment, who can stick the barrels of their assault rifles into the nine ball mounts (four per side and one in the left rear door) and engage the enemy with armor protection.

The engine compartment houses a UTD-20 liquid-cooled, six-cylinder diesel engine, which develops a maximum output of 300 hp at 2,000 rpm. The tracked running gear, with torsion bar suspension, operates with spring and rubber stops as well as hydraulic telescopic shock absorbers for the six road wheels with rubber tires on each side, which are supplemented by three return rollers. The drive sprockets are at the front, the idler wheels at the rear. The hinged steel track has rubber pads. Its upper part is covered by a "hydrodynamic" housing, which allows the track drive unit to be used more efficiently in the water. Yes, the drive and steering in the water are provided by the tracks, whereby the BMP-1 reaches a maximum speed of 7–8 kph (4.3–5 mph), crawling, as it were. The vehicle's maximum road speed is 65 kph (40 mph). Due to its low specific ground pressure (0.6 kg/cm^2, 8.5 psi), the vehicle can easily negotiate swampy and snow-covered terrain, gradients of up to 35°, vertical obstacles of up to 0.7 m (2.3 ft.), and trenches up to 2.5 m (8.2 ft.) in width.

The BMP-1 fully met the expectations of the Soviet High Command regarding the combined use of motorized rifle and tank forces under nuclear combat conditions. In 1967, the General Staff informed the Council of Ministers and the State Planning Committee of the USSR that 70,000 BMP-1s were required to equip the rifle units. The comrades with the bushy eyebrows in the Council of Ministers had to swallow hard at first but issued a decree

BMP-1 amphibious tracked armored personnel carrier (Object 765)

on September 3, 1968, ordering the creation of suitable production facilities in Kurgan and Rubtsovsk. Within ten years, these plants produced around 20,000 BMP-1s; in addition, there were also deliveries from Czechoslovakia (500 units per year).

The troops of the "glorious Soviet army" that invaded Afghanistan in December 1979 included motorized rifle regiments with BMP-1 battalions. There was a rude awakening in the gloomy shadows of the Hindu Kush. Officers and soldiers were dismayed to discover that the BMP-1 did not even offer protection against small-arms fire: even 7.62 mm hard-core bullets penetrated the side, rear, and roof, which many soldiers paid for with death or injury. It also turned out that the infantry fighting vehicle, armed to the teeth, was clearly out of its depth when engaging typical "infantry" targets (enemy in trenches and positions, behind rocks, etc.), and the same applied to low-flying aircraft and helicopters (elsewhere, because the mujahideen, as far as is known, at best "flew" only carrier pigeons). The 73 mm gun also proved to be completely overrated when it came to fighting armored vehicles, because of insufficient accuracy, too short an effective range, and inadequate impact.

The USSR Ministry of Defense responded immediately to demands by the command of the Soviet troops in Afghanistan to remedy these shortcomings as quickly as possible. And so, the BMP-2 tried its luck in Afghanistan.

A column of BMP-1s on the move

This vehicle was developed in the design office of the Kurgan Machine-Building Plant and was based on the BMP-1. A small series was produced starting in 1977, and the vehicles were sent to the reconnaissance battalion and the motorized rifle battalion of the 29th Tank Division (Slutsk) for service trials. In the event of a conflict with China (there had already been skirmishes and exchanges of fire with several fatalities on the Ussuri border river in 1969), the plan was to start mass production.

Dismounted motorized infantry advancing with support from their BMP-1s

BMP-2 Infantry Fighting Vehicle

As early as April 1980, the first BMP-2s were withdrawn from the 29th Tank Division and deployed to Afghanistan. Around the same time, it was decided to begin quantity production. The improvement in firepower and effectiveness was made possible mainly by the installation of the 30 mm 2A42 automatic cannon in a new two-man round turret with electric traverse and elevation mechanism (range of elevation –5°/+74°). The gun can fire single shots or alternatively bursts with low (200–300 rounds per minute) or high (550 rounds per minute) rates of fire. Ammunition is fed from two separate feed belts: one for armor-piercing ammunition, the other for explosive/fragmentation shells, each with tracer. This makes it easy to engage armored targets at ranges of up to 1,500 m (1,640 yds.), soft-skinned vehicles and soft targets up to 4,000 m (4,374 yds.), and air targets flying at low altitudes (up to 2,000–2,500 m [6,560–8,200 ft.]) and at subsonic speeds. The turret-mounted 9M113M Konkurs antitank missile launcher is used to engage armored targets in the 75–4,000 m (250 ft.–4,375 yd.) range. To engage targets at close range, some BMP-2 variants were fitted with the AG-17 automatic grenade launcher on the left side of the turret.

At the end of 1980, the design bureau of the Kurgan Machine-Building Plant under chief designer A. A. Blagonravov presented a new BMP version (Object 688), the turret of which had the same armament as the BMP-2. The new model generally met the requirements of the military, but the then minister of defense industry, S. A. Zverev, categorically opposed the "new vehicle with old armament."

A BMP-2 during a field exercise

BMP-2 amphibious armored personnel carrier (Object 675)

BMP-2, view from the front right

BMP-2K, view from the rear

A BMP-2 crossing a water obstacle

BMP-3 Infantry Fighting Vehicle

The designers had to work out several new options before the famous *troishatka* was created—a "tetrarchy" consisting of a 100 mm gun, a 7A70 antitank missile launcher, a 2A72 automatic 30 mm cannon, and a 7.62 mm PKT machine gun with a common automated fire control system. The *troishatka* gave the BMP-3 an unprecedented combination of weapons and firepower that set it apart from all infantry fighting vehicles internationally. Ammunition includes the 100 mm 30F32 high-explosive/fragmentation round, with a range of 7,000 m (7,665 yds.), and the 9M117 Arkan laser-guided antitank missile, with an operational range of 100–5,500 m (110–6,015 yds.) and up to 650 mm (25 in.) of armor penetration (according to other sources, 750 mm [29.5 in.]), against which there is hardly any protection. The combat load is forty 100 mm grenade cartridges, which are fed from a kind of rotating-floor magazine. The automatic loading system allows a rate of fire of up to ten rounds per minute. The cadence of the 30 mm 3A72 gun is at least 330 rounds per minute. It is used mainly to engage infantry and "tank-threatening persons" at ranges up to 2,000 m (2,187 yds.) and helicopters up to 4,000 m (4,374 yds.).

The BMP-3 was accepted by the Soviet army in May 1987; the Kurgan Machine-Building Plant delivered the first batch of twelve vehicles at the end of 1987. In contrast to earlier infantry fighting vehicles, the BMP-3 has a "battle tank" layout with the engine in the rear, driver's compartment at the front, and fighting compartment behind. It is powered by a liquid-cooled UTD-29 V-diesel engine with ten cylinders and a maximum output of 500 hp. Soundproof partitions separate the engine/transmission compartment from the fighting compartment. The BMP-3 was the first Soviet armored vehicle to be equipped with a hydromechanical transmission with a power takeoff for the water jet drive. This drivetrain ensures reasonably comfortable handling on the road and off-road. It enables the vehicle to negotiate inclines of up to 30° and trenches 2.5 m (8.2 ft.) wide, and to climb obstacles with a height of up to 0.8 m (2.6 ft.). In water, the BMP-3 travels at up to 10 kph (6.2 mph).

BMP-3 armored personnel carrier (Object 888)

In the second half of the 1960s, the Soviet military leadership reconsidered the use of tactical nuclear missiles and came to the realization that they could not completely replace conventional weapons on the battlefield. It was recognized that even nuclear strikes could not completely eliminate enemy resistance, and that advancing troops would still be dependent on artillery support. With and without nuclear weapons, artillery is of great importance.

An important role in the further development of Soviet field artillery was played by resolution no. 609-201 of the USSR Council of Ministers, of July 4, 1967, which provided for the development of a series of self-propelled artillery pieces, which later went under the unofficial name "flower series." In accordance with the resolution, the artillery divisions and regiments of the tank and motorized rifle divisions converted from towed to self-propelled guns. The artillery battalions of the tank and motorized rifle regiments received the 2S1 Gvozdika

BMP-3, view from the right front

BMP-3, rear view

BMP-3, with a view of the surge shield

A BMP-3 during maneuvers

(carnation) self-propelled 122 mm howitzer, and the divisional artillery regiments the 2S3 Akatsiya (acacia) self-propelled 152 mm howitzer. In contrast to the earlier self-propelled artillery—the self-propelled guns—the armored artillery no longer had the main task of engaging enemy tanks with direct fire and assisting the infantry directly on the battlefield. The howitzer-armed 2S1 and 2S3, on the other hand, once again took on the classic tasks of field artillery in indirect aiming (i.e., engaging all types of targets beyond the usual engagement distance of the assault guns).

BMP-3, view from the front left

2S1 Gvozdika 122 mm Self-Propelled Howitzer

The 2S1 Gvozdika 122 mm self-propelled howitzer was based on the chassis of the MT-LB armored amphibious troop transport. The first examples began field trials in August 1967. The Soviet army accepted the "carnation," which had been designed on the principles of modern self-propelled artillery, on September 14, 1970. The driver's compartment (left) and the engine-transmission compartment (right) were at the front of the vehicle, while the fighting compartment with turret was in the middle and rear section. The crew consisted of four men: the driver in the front of the hull and the commander, gunner, and loader in the turret. The armor of welded 20 mm (0.8 in.) steel plates provides protection against rifle-caliber projectiles and shell fragments. Armament consists of a 122 mm D-32 howitzer (2A31), a modification of the towed D-30 medium field howitzer. Thanks to the 360° rotating turret, the weapon can fire in any direction. Its range of elevation is –3°/+70°. During "closed" firing with the power-assisted loader and the ammunition stored in the hull, the rate of fire is four to five rounds per minute, otherwise one and a half to two rounds per minute (with ammunition fed from outside through the opened hatches in the rear). Maximum range is 15.2 km (9.4 mi.). The 2S1 self-propelled howitzer was placed in service with the armored artillery battalions of the tank and motorized rifle regiments. A battalion of 228 men (including 22 officers) and 18 self-propelled howitzers was basically organized into a battalion headquarters, three batteries (each with a command platoon with battery squad and two firing platoons), a support platoon, and a medical squad.

In the early 1970s, artillery regiments of tank and motorized rifle divisions were issued the 2S3 152 mm Akatsiya 152 mm self-propelled howitzer.

Gvozdika 122 mm self-propelled howitzer

Gvozdika self-propelled howitzer during a winter exercise

Gvozdika self-propelled howitzer, view from the right front

Gvozdika self-propelled howitzer in firing position

2S3 Akatsiya 152 mm Self-Propelled Howitzer

Uraltransmash (the Ural Transport Engineering Plant) emerged as the main developer and delivered the first prototypes at the end of 1968. The self-propelled howitzer officially entered service with the Soviet army in 1973. Its design is similar in principle to that of the 2S1 Gvozdika, as is the distribution of its four-man crew. The hull and turret are welded from rolled armored steel plates (hull 20 mm, turret 15 mm [0.8 and 0.6 in.]). As with the 2S1, the armor provides protection only against small-arms fire and shrapnel as well as light antitank mines. The D-22 (2A33) 152 mm howitzer, with a barrel length of L/27 and semiautomatic wedge breech, mounted in the turret, is a modification of the D-20 152 mm gun howitzer but was fitted with a fume extractor to remove powder gases that would otherwise affect the turret crew. The ballistics and ammunition of the D-22 are otherwise the same as those of the D-20, with a maximum firing range of 17.3 km (10.7 mi.). When using the ammunition carried inside the vehicle, rate of fire is 4.0 rounds per minute, otherwise 3.5 or 2.6 rounds per minute with "external feed." The entire 152 mm range of the D-20 howitzer's ammunition is available: high explosive, illumination, smoke, and hollow-charge shells, plus laser-guided Krasnopol projectiles, and shells with chemical warfare agents or nuclear warheads.

Since the Akatsiya is based the tracked chassis of the Krug surface-to-air missile system, it can reach speeds of up to 60 kph (37 mph) on roads and, thanks to its good off-road mobility, can master inclines of up to 30°, vertical obstacles up to 0.7 m (2.3 ft.) in height, and trenches up to 3 m (9.8 ft.) wide. As mentioned, the 2S3 was assigned to the tank artillery regiments of the tank and motorized rifle divisions. A 2S3 division usually consisted of three batteries of six guns each (eighteen guns in total), but some divisions had four batteries (twenty-four guns).

In 1963, the NATO countries agreed on the 155 mm caliber for new howitzers they were developing, which were to achieve a maximum firing range of 30 km (18.6 mi.). This firing range was almost double that of Soviet self-propelled artillery, which is why there was pressure in Moscow to develop a long-range howitzer. This was the 152 mm 2S19 Msta-S howitzer, which was accepted in 1989.

2S3 Akatsiya 152 mm self-propelled howitzer

Akatsiya self-propelled howitzer, rear view

Akatsiya self-propelled howitzer, view from the front

Akatsiya self-propelled howitzer in firing position

2S3 Msta-S 152 mm Self-Propelled Howitzer

The importance that the USSR Ministry of Defense attached to this gun is demonstrated by the fact that it had its own factory built for its series production in Sterlitamak (the first batches were still manufactured at Uraltransmash in Sverdlovsk). The Msta-S was not named after a flower but was instead after the name of a river in western Russia. Its design corresponded to its predecessors, whereby great importance was attached to the use of parts and assemblies of already-established military technology, which shortened the development and construction times. The 152 mm 2A64 howitzer installed in the turret was essentially the same as the towed 2A65 Msta-B field howitzer and differed mainly in its fume extractor. In addition to the gun, the turret, which is capable of rotating 360° (elevation range, −3°/+65°), housed a 2E46 fire control system, an autoloader, a generator, and communications equipment. The fire control system consists of a ballistic computer, devices for topographical measurement and orientation, and a satellite navigation system. Thanks to the automatic ammunition feed, the Msta-S achieves a rate of fire of up to eight rounds per minute when using the standby ammunition and up to seven rounds per minute when using external rounds. Up to fifty standard rounds can be carried in the turret and hull. The range of projectiles includes the OF-45 high-explosive/fragmentation shell (43.56 kg [96 lbs.]), the OF-61 rocket projectile (42.86 kg [94.5 lbs.]), the 3023 cluster grenade with forty-two shaped charges (42.80 kg [94.35 lbs.]), the 3NSO radar-jamming projectile, and the 3WDC8 special ammunition. The howitzer also fires 3OF39 Krasnopol (50 kg [110 lbs.]) and Krasnopol-M laser-guided projectiles, as well as the entire 152 mm range of the D-20 and 2S3 howitzers. The maximum firing range with the OF-45 explosive shell is 24,700 m (15.3 mi.), and 28,900 m (18 mi.) with the OF-61 rocket projectile. During a firing demonstration in Abu Dhabi, a laser-guided Krasnopol projectile even hit its target, a moving tank, from a range of 12,000 m (7.5 mi.).

The secondary armament consists of a 12.7 mm NSVT machine gun next to the commander's cupola.

The drivetrain of the Msta-S was adopted from the T-72 and T-80 main battle tanks with minor modifications. In the rear engine-transmission compartment, a liquid-cooled twelve-cylinder V-84A multifuel engine, which is usually fueled with diesel, provides an output of 840 hp (some vehicles received the V-46-6 at 780 hp). This gave the

Msta-S 152 mm self-propelled howitzer

Msta-S 152 mm self-propelled howitzer, view from the front right

A battery of Msta-S self-propelled howitzers on the move in the maneuver area

A Msta-S 152 mm self-propelled howitzer photograph during firing

howitzer a top speed of 60 kph (37 mph) on roads. In terms of cross-country mobility, it is practically no different from the T-72 and T-80 main battle tanks and can cope with gradients of up to 30°, vertical obstacles up to 0.85 m (2.8 ft.) in height, and trenches up to 2.8 m (9.2 ft.) wide. Without preparation, it can ford water up to 1.2 m (3.9 ft.) deep.

The 2S19 Msta-S self-propelled howitzer was put into service with the tank artillery regiments of the tank divisions, some of which transferred their 2S3 Akatsiya self-propelled howitzers to the artillery divisions of other regiments, where they replaced the 122 mm 2S1 Gvozdika. This significantly increased the firepower both of the entire division and the tank regiments.

An increase in the firepower and mobility of the tank forces was also brought about by the introduction of fundamentally new types of main battle tanks. These "standard" main battle tanks are characterized by their combination of the firepower and heavy armor of heavy tanks and the mobility of light and medium tanks.

The first Soviet standard main battle tank design (Object 432) was presented by the Kharkov Design Bureau for Mechanical Engineering (KhKBM) under A. A. Morozov as early as 1961.

T-64 Standard Main Battle Tank

After brief factory trials, this T-64 went into equally brief service trials, and the first production vehicles rolled off the production line of the Kharkov Machine-Building Factory (KhZTM) in October 1963. However, the official entry into service was delayed until 1967—in the meantime, numerous design faults had become apparent that had not been discovered during the all-too-short testing period and had to be rectified.

The main innovation of the T-64 was its multilayer or composite armor. The T-64's upper glacis plate was made up of an 80 mm (3.1 in.) steel plate, two 52 mm (2 in.) glass-reinforced plastic plates, and a 20 mm (0.8 in.) steel plate arranged from top to bottom according to the "cake principle." A slope of 68° considerably increased the passage distance for projectiles and practically doubled the effectiveness of the armor.

The use of glass-reinforced plastic can be explained by the fact that this material weighs much less than armored steel while offering approximately the same resistance to shaped charges. This allowed the armor protection of the T-64 to be significantly improved without increasing the weight of the tank. Advancements in armor technology were applied not only in the hull front, but also in the turret front. Recesses were created in the frontal armor in which fillers with high resistance to hollow-charge and subcaliber projectiles were inserted: first an aluminum alloy, then layers of porcelain spheres. This increased the maximum thickness of the turret front to 600 mm (23.6 in.).

The Soviet designers were no less innovative when it came to the main armament: the T-64 was fitted with the 115 mm 2A21 smoothbore gun (a modification of the gun mounted in the T-62 tank), which for the first time in the history of tank construction was fitted with an autoloader as standard. This made it possible not only to dispense with the loader, but also to reduce the size of the turret while at the same time strengthening the armor protection. The T-64 also received a telescopic sight with an independently stabilizing sighting line and a stereoscopic rangefinder. Thanks to these innovations, the T-64 outclassed the T-62 not only in terms of rate of fire, but also in terms of accuracy. The T-64A version also received the even more powerful 125 mm gun.

But that was not all. Other innovations of the T-64 included the new chassis and a never-before-used compact opposed-piston diesel engine (five-cylinder, two-stroke), producing 700 hp. (From around 1955, the Kharkov engine plant was involved in the development of two-stroke, opposed-piston engines based on German diesel aircraft engines made by Junkers.) The tracked running gear had six lightweight road wheels with internal shock absorption

T-64A standard main battle tank

T-64BV fitted with mine-clearing equipment

and four return rollers on each side, a rear drive sprocket, and a front idler wheel. The individually suspended wheels of the lightweight camber roller running gear had coaxial torsion shafts with hydromechanical end stops. The steel hinged track was fitted with rubberized bearings.

However, the big "but" was not long in coming: the compact 5TDF diesel engine turned out to be not only very susceptible to faults and maintenance intensive, but also complicated and expensive to manufacture—the manufacturing price was more than double that of the T-55M and T-62M engines (20,000 rubles instead of 9,600 rubles).

The torsion bars on the running gear broke frequently, and on sandy ground the track slipped even on a slight incline.

The USSR Ministry of Defense was already aware of the T-64's weaknesses when it went into series production. However, its resistance to NATO's 105 mm gun (the most important tank gun in the West) and its ability to destroy the main battle tanks of all potential opponents provided the stronger arguments. As a result, three factories were awarded contracts for quantity production of the T-64: the Kharkov Plant for Vehicle Construction (KhZTM), the Leningrad Kirov Plant (LKS), and the Uralvagonzavod Plant (UVZ) in Nizhny Tagil.

In view of the limited production capacities of the 5TDF engines, UVS was to develop a "mobilization version" of the T-64 for wartime with the more powerful and reliable V-45 diesel engine. However, the hull and chassis had to be modified for this, which is why UVS reverted to designs from 1962 and opted for a different solution. This resulted in Object 439, prototypes of which were available and successfully tested in 1967.

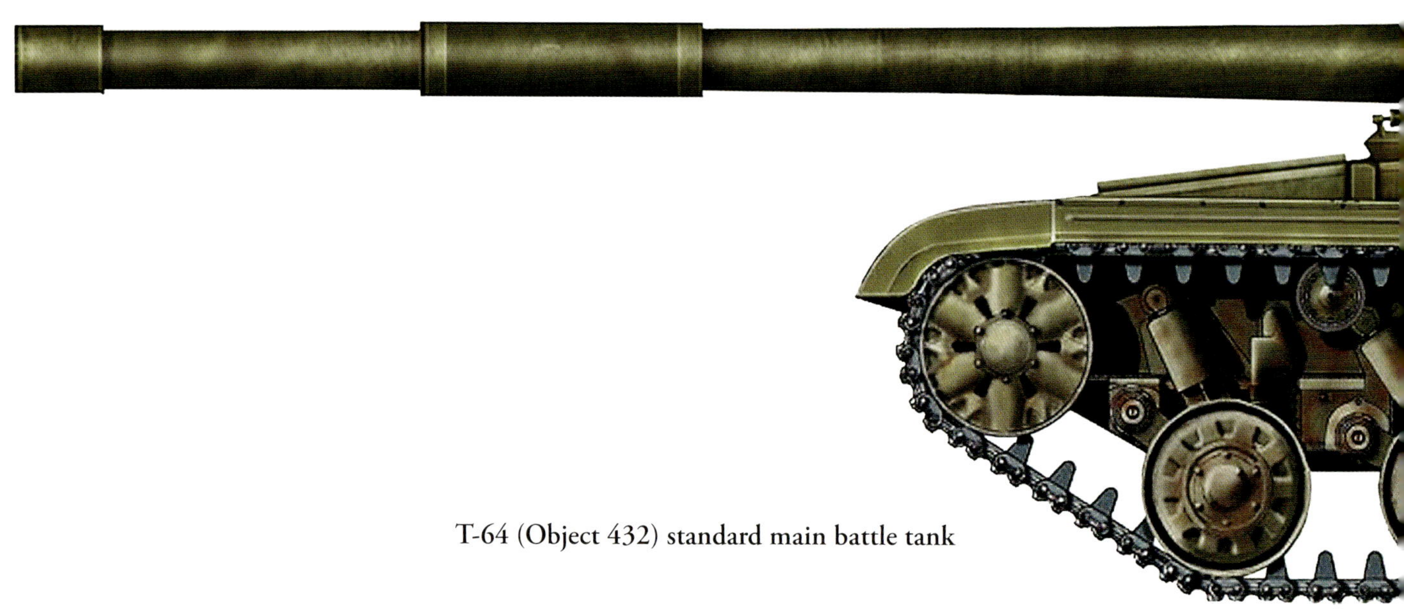
T-64 (Object 432) standard main battle tank

T-64BV standard main battle tank

T-72 Standard Main Battle Tank

More precisely, in the early 1960s the UVZ design bureau responsible for tanks, under L. N. Kartsev, had developed an automatic loader for an experimental version of the T-62 with a 115 mm gun and then with a 125 mm gun. The designers proposed installing this automatic loader in the T-64. Kartsev and his team also advocated a more reliable chassis with rubber-tired road wheels and steel tracks, which had proved their worth on the T-55 and T-62.

All this and more led to the design and construction of the Object 172, with a new engine, new autoloader, and new running gear. After successful trials, the Soviet army introduced it into service on August 7, 1973, under the designation T-72. Formally, it was a "mobilization model," intended for mass production in wartime. In fact, it became something more: the first preseries tanks rolled off the production line in 1972, and quantity production began soon afterward. The T-72 was built in greater numbers than any other main battle tank of the last quarter of the twentieth century.

As mentioned, the Kirov Factory in Leningrad was also supposed to produce the T-64. However, according to the decision by the Council of Ministers on April 16, 1968, it was to equip a version with a GAZ turbine engine (GTE), which the Leningrad plant had been working on for almost two decades. As early as 1948, the turbine production design office at Kirov had begun work on a 700 hp GAZ turbine, but this was rejected as unpromising. In fact, the documents refer to enormous fuel consumption and high operating costs. Shortly afterward, several attempts were made to design other engines of a similar class, but they also came to nothing. However, the experience gained was used by the Kirov designers in the development of the GTD-1000T tank engine in spring 1968.

This 1,000 hp unit operated according to a three-shaft scheme, with two independent turbochargers and a free turbine. The main problem was to protect it from dust, especially since 5–6 m^3 (176–211 $ft.^3$) of air passes through a GAZ turbine engine of this each second. If you consider

T-72 Ural (Object 172M) standard main battle tank

T-72 standard main battle tank, here the T-72B version, photographed during a parade

T-72, view from the front right

the amount of dust generated by a tank column on unpaved roads on a hot summer's day—or watch newsreels depicting Rommel's advances in Africa—you can imagine what tank air filters have to (and had to) do.

Equipped with an effective air purification system, the GTD-1000T otherwise lasted for hundreds of kilometers under the most-difficult conditions. It impressed with its compactness, its high performance, its ability to start without preheating in Arctic temperatures as low as –40°C, and no requirement for a liquid cooling system. However, it also had its disadvantages: high fuel consumption, high maintenance requirements, and production costs ten times higher than a diesel engine of the same power.

In the spring of 1969, a revised GAZ turbine power plant was installed in prototypes of the T-64A. A total of twenty vehicles were to receive it and undergo factory and service trials. The GTD-1000T engines proved their suitability for practical use in tests lasting several months under a wide variety of conditions. However, another problem arose: The 1,000 hp power plant was one size too big for the existing chassis and transmission. All twenty vehicles had problems with their transmissions and suspensions. This meant that there was no way around the development of a new running gear and transmission that could withstand the increased dynamic loads of the GAZ turbine engine. The newly designed torsion bar

T-72 standard main battle tank, T-72A version

suspension, with six road wheels and five return rollers, was equipped with hydraulic telescopic shock absorbers, with the two-part road wheels consisting of forged steel and aluminum parts with rubber tires. The distance between the second and third as well as the fourth and fifth road wheels is a characteristic feature. The vehicle also received newly developed connector tracks, even wider than those on the T-64, which could be fitted with rubber pads to dampen noise on paved roads. Compared to the "soles" of the T-64, these tracks offered a 25 percent larger ground contact surface, which reduced the specific ground pressure, even though the vehicle weighed almost 4 tons more. Its off-road mobility was excellent, and it could negotiate gradients of up to 30°, vertical obstacles 1 m (3.3 ft.) high, and trenches 2.85 m (9.35 ft.) wide. Without any preparations it could ford bodies of water up to 1.2 m (3.9 ft.) deep, and with OPVT deepwater-wading equipment it can move underwater at depths of up to 5 m (16 ft.). Thanks to its powerful engine, the main battle tank reaches an astonishing top speed of 70 kph (43.5 mph).

T-80 Standard Main Battle Tank

The Soviet army accepted the vehicle, equipped with the R-123M (R-123) radio system, in July 1976 under the designation T-80. At that time, it had three main battle tank types—the T-64, T-72, and T-80—all with the same weapons and very similar characteristics, although the main assemblies were not interchangeable. This led to increased manufacturing, operating, and maintenance costs. The army command therefore decided to standardize the divisions of certain army groups and military districts with tanks of the same type. The "first strategic level" in the western theater of operations (western and northern forces) received the T-80. In NATO, it was also unofficially called the "English Channel tank," since Western analysts calculated that the T-80 units could reach the English Channel in five days in the event of war. The divisions of the Central Group of the Armed Forces and eighty of the second strategic level (the Baltic and Belarusian military districts) were equipped mainly with the T-72. The T-64 was used by the divisions of the southern forces stationed in Hungary and by units in the Carpathian, Kiev, and Odessa military districts. These locations offered, among other things, the shortest distances to the manufacturers (delivery of spare parts) and specialized repair workshops. The obsolete T-54 and T-55 and the even older, repeatedly upgraded T-44 and T-34/85 were found in the tank and motorized rifle divisions of the internal military districts.

From 1960 to 1980, there were about fifteen types of use and specializations for personnel of tank divisions, and up to twenty-five for motorized rifle divisions, which was related to various factors: changes in formations and operational scenarios, different weapons and equipment, supplies and spare parts, communications, etc.

T-80 standard main battle tank (Object 219SP2)

T-80U(M), view from the front

The tank and motorized rifle divisions were divided into four levels according to their degree of mobilization (in peacetime) (listed according to the Russian alphabet):

Level A (divisions at permanent readiness) degree of mobilization: personnel 90–100 percent and equipment 100 percent

Level Б (B) (divisions requiring 1 to 3 days to achieve operational readiness), degree of mobilization: personnel 60–80 percent, weapons and equipment 75–90 percent

Level В (W) (divisions requiring 4 to 10 days to achieve operational readiness), degree of mobilization: personnel 25–50 percent, weapons and equipment 50–75 percent

Level Г (G) (divisions requiring 11 to 30 days to achieve operational readiness), degree of mobilization: personnel 1–10 percent, weapons and equipment 40–50 percent

T-80BV, view from the side

Preparing a T-80U for deep wading

The divisions of levels A and Б were regarded as immediately ready for combat. Those of levels B and Г were designated cadre divisions and made up to 70 percent of the total number.

The difference in strength between motorized rifle regiments of the Б- and B-type divisions could be up to 1,000 men (1,300–1,500 versus 200–300 men).

Divisions of the Г type existed practically only in mobilization plans (i.e., on paper). The reason for the creation of these divisions was the need to reduce multilayered "operating costs," be it for pay, food, housing, supplies, and all other types of maintenance of personnel, stores, and equipment. In divisions of the Г type, officers and ensigns made up 10–15 percent of the personnel; the number of noncommissioned officers and enlisted men depended on the minimum number required for the maintenance and care of equipment and gear in the depots.

Several operational army corps were formed in the early 1980s, with the following organization:

- 2 tank brigades
- 2 mechanized brigades
- 1 artillery regiment
- 1 air assault regiment
- 1 antiaircraft regiment
- 1 reconnaissance battalion
- 1 combat engineer battalion
- 1 BM-21 Grad rocket launcher battalion

A tank brigade consisted of three tank battalions, one mechanized battalion, one battalion of self-propelled artillery, and one air defense battalion. A mechanized brigade consisted of three mechanized battalions, one tank battalion, and artillery and air defense battalions. Each brigade also had a reconnaissance company plus combat support and repair units.

The mechanized battalion consisted of three motorized rifle companies and one tank company, and the tank battalion of four tank companies and one motorized rifle company. A motorized rifle company consisted of three motorized rifle platoons and one mortar platoon; a tank company of three tank platoons, each with four tanks. Including the company commander's tank, that made a total of thirteen main battle tanks.

The organization of the brigades and corps ensured that the formations were highly mobile and enabled them to operate in isolation from the main forces.

CHAPTER 6
THE ARMED FORCES OF THE USSR DURING PERESTROIKA

In the mid-1980s, signs of an acute economic and political crisis were clearly visible in the USSR, the main causes of which were

- stagnation of the economy, and science and technology increasingly lagging behind the Western countries;
- excessive defense spending;
- insoluble social problems;
- disintegration of the economic and political leadership and an inability to ensure economic growth; and
- mental apathy and negative phenomena among large sections of society.

In March 1985, the general secretary of the CPSU Central Committee, M. S. Gorbachev, proposed "new political thinking" to overcome the homemade crisis, which included the following:

- rejection of violent methods to solve international problems
- rejection of the principles of proletarian internationalism
- rethinking the world and pursuing a policy based on universal human values

Three main directions in foreign policy were identified as part of the "new political thinking"

1. overcoming the confrontation between East and West and reducing international tensions
2. peaceful settlement of regional conflicts
3. implementation of close contacts with all countries of the world, regardless of ideological preferences

Russian tanks advancing with air support

These points of the new military doctrine meant that following an act of aggression against the USSR, the Soviet side would not retaliate against the aggressor's territory and bases for several weeks(!). Instead of a retaliatory strike, Akhromeyev suggested looking for a "political solution." In other words, the United States could have bombed the USSR without having to expect immediate retaliation. That was the theory.

Looking at the main provisions of the 1986 Military Doctrine, it seems that the generals under Soviet marshal S. F. Akhromeyev really believed that the USSR and the United States could live in peace until 2000 and would eliminate all nuclear weapons.

All this proved to be utopian: the United States and NATO did not engage in comparable disarmament and did not make any far-reaching concessions.

From the Soviet-Russian perspective, the United States had been the aggressor since the beginning of the Cold War, while the "peace-loving Soviet Union" had merely defended itself and struck back. And now, after 1986, according to the new doctrine, the USSR would even refrain from an immediate counterattack. In accordance with the defensive character of the new Soviet military doctrine, the organizational and personnel structure of the tank and motorized rifle divisions was changed. In 1989, some type A tank divisions were reorganized into groups of Soviet forces abroad (i.e., the number of tank regiments in the divisions was reduced from three to two. At the same time, however, the number of motorized rifle regiments increased to two. In motorized rifle divisions, the tank regiment was converted into a motorized rifle regiment with a subordinate tank battalion. The independent missile battalions were withdrawn from the divisions and assigned to the independent missile brigades of the armies. The tank divisions therefore no longer had tactical nuclear weapons. In 1989, the army corps "of the rapid-reaction forces" were also given up and reorganized into motorized rifle divisions, from which they had once emerged. According to the reference book *Military Balance*, the Soviet Union had thirty-two tank divisions and more than a hundred motorized rifle divisions at the beginning of 1991.

These units had a total of 54,400 main battle tanks, of which 38,400 were stationed in the European part of the Soviet Union and Warsaw Pact countries; 16,000 were stationed beyond the Urals. These were 10,600 T-54/55s, 8,500 T-62s, 4,900 T-64s, 9,000 T-72s, and 5,400 T-80s. In the European part of the USSR and in eastern Europe, there were 5,186 self-propelled howitzers (2,331 122 mm 2S1 Gvozdika, 2,044 152 mm 2S3 Akatsiya, 494 152 mm 2S5 Giatsint, 13 of the latest 152 mm 2S19 Msta, and 304 203 mm 2S7 Pion).

During the preparations for the signing of the Treaty on Conventional Armed Forces in Europe (CFE), which among other things provided for a drastic reduction in conventional armed forces in the European part of the USSR, the Soviet Ministry of Defense nevertheless took a number of measures to ensure that the effectiveness of the Soviet armed forces was not diminished too much. Gaps in the treaty were exploited, according to which the civilian and military police forces of Western states were not covered by the treaty. Consequently, the Soviet Ministry of Defense subordinated twenty-nine of its divisions to the forces under the USSR Ministry of the Interior, each of whose units now had a tank battalion. Since the CFE Treaty applied only to the land forces, the Ministry of Defense adroitly placed a further four coastal-defense divisions under the navy.

The CFE Treaty was signed on November 19, 1990. It set an upper limit of 20,000 main battle tanks, 30,000 armored vehicles, and 20,000 artillery pieces each for the Warsaw Pact and NATO. Within these limits, individual quotas were set for the signatory states. The Soviet Union promised to reduce its conventional weapons on European territory to 13,150 main battle tanks, 20,000 armored combat vehicles, and 13,700 artillery pieces. For the first time since the beginning of the Cold War, there was massive conventional disarmament in Europe. The CFE states also undertook to allow inspections on their territory and to submit annual reports on the structure and armaments of their armed forces.

T-62s moving through a typical Russian birch forest

Main battle tanks advancing in open country

While on maneuvers, a T-55 crosses a pontoon bridge spanning a water obstacle. In the background can be seen the snorkels of deepwater-wading battle tanks.

T-62s and motorized infantry during a combat exercise

T-55s during a combat exercise with naval infantry

Battle tanks taking part in the closing parade of Exercise West 81

Remarkably, the Warsaw Pact countries accounted for nine-tenths of the cuts. Since the Soviets had already planned to withdraw the "groups of Soviet armed forces" in eastern Europe in 1991, and the collapse of the Warsaw Pact was only a matter of time anyway, the establishment of collective ceilings by the military blocs was shortsighted, to say the least.

Tanks advancing in cooperation with attack helicopters

T-72A tanks during the parade marking the end of Exercise West 81

Troop Withdrawal and Disengagement

The decree by the Presidium of the Supreme Soviet on the reduction of the armed forces and defense spending in 1989–90, which was adopted in 1989, had an extremely negative impact on the Soviet army, reducing troop strength by 500,000 men and defense spending by 14.2 percent. In compliance with this decree, the Ministry of Defense ordered all Г-type divisions and some B-type divisions to be converted into depots for weapons and equipment or to mothball their equipment. This also affected some divisions withdrawn from European countries.

With our bag and baggage—and off we go . . .

A train loaded with Soviet armored vehicles shortly before its departure toward the east

Soviet tank units withdrawing from Czechoslovakia. "Ilona" is probably waving more for the camera.

Tanks that were hastily withdrawn from the European states and the European part of the USSR before the signing of the CFE Treaty ended up in the Central Tank Reserve Depots. At these locations, 80 percent of the equipment was stored in open areas and 20 percent in unheated buildings.

While the former were listed as parts of the respective armies and are regarded as replacement units for existing formations, the central depots were essentially tank-parking areas with unfavorable storage conditions.

Studies carried out at the Central Tank Reserve Depot of the Republic of Kazakhstan in 1995 showed a steady increase in vehicles with technical failures and malfunctions. Their share in the total number of T-80Bs and T-72Bs examined was over 75 percent.

On December 8, 1991, the presidents of Russia and Ukraine and the chairman of the Supreme Soviet of Belarus signed the so-called Belovezhskaya Agreements on the dissolution of the USSR and the establishment of the Commonwealth of Independent States (CIS). On December 21, 1991, the leaders of the eleven CIS republics signed a protocol on the transfer of command of the USSR armed forces "prior to their reform" to the USSR minister of defense, Air Marshal Yevgeny Ivanovich Shaposhnikov. Gorbachev resigned on December 25, 1991. The next day, the Council of Republics of the Supreme Soviet of the USSR, which was not provided for in the USSR Constitution, dissolved itself and announced the official dissolution of the Soviet Union. Over the next year and a half, attempts were made to keep a unified CIS force alive, but in the end it was divided among the Union republics.

Soviet tank units withdrawing from East Germany

Self-propelled howitzers in the central tank depot in the city of Arsenyev

T-72s in a tank depot

Self-propelled howitzers in a depot

CHAPTER 7
THE MOTORIZED RIFLE AND TANK UNITS OF THE RUSSIAN FEDERATION

On May 7, 1992, Boris Yeltsin, as president of the Russian Federation (RF), signed the decree establishing the Armed Forces of the Russian Federation and assumed the functions of commander in chief. On May 15, the agreement on the distribution of the CIS armed forces among the individual republics came into force. Accordingly, Russia received 6,400 battle tanks, 11,480 armored vehicles, 6,415 guns, 3,450 aircraft, and 890 helicopters. The armed forces of the Russian Federation initially included all units stationed on the territory of the country as well as troops under Russian jurisdiction, with a total strength of 2.88 million men. The question of reforming the armed forces arose almost immediately. The 1990s were a difficult time for them. Chronic underfunding led to many of the best officers and soldiers leaving for the private sector, the purchase of new weapon types and systems practically ceased, many armaments factories were closed, and many a promising project was abandoned or put on hold. Immediately after the establishment of the Russian armed forces, they still appeared to be developing in accordance with the treaty, but the lack of funding put the brakes on this for some time.

In 1995, the First Chechen War demonstrated the catastrophic state of the Russian army. The units were understaffed, and the fighting revealed serious shortcomings in leadership and other areas. In the Second Chechen War (1999–2006), mainly elite units, airborne troops, and so-called contract servicemen (professional and temporary soldiers) were deployed. In 2003, their share of the forces in Chechnya reached 35 percent.

In the 1990s, it was decided to divide all units of the Russian Federation armed forces into four categories:

T-62s in the First Chechen War in 1995

T-64BVs deployed in the Transnistrian conflict

- units with permanent readiness, 95–100 percent, manned according to wartime organization
- units of reduced strength (approx. 70 percent)
- depots for military equipment and weapons (5–10 percent)
- cadre units (approx. 5 percent)

At the beginning of the 2000s, this reform was continued with the decision to fully staff the units at permanent readiness with "contract servicemen" and to fill the remaining units with conscripts.

In 2008, the RF armed forces took part in the conflict in South Ossetia (the Five-Day War). It once again revealed numerous shortcomings in the modern Russian army. The most serious of these were poor troop mobility and shortcomings in tactical leadership.

Shortly after the end of the conflict, which lasted from September to October 2008, the Ministry of Defense of the Russian Federation, under A. Serdyukov, developed plans to eliminate the main problems in the armed forces. An assessment of the international military-political situation served as the fundamental starting point for the reform concept. It envisaged a realignment of the Russian armed forces, which were to be equally capable of dealing with both a major war with several opponents in the CIS alliance and regional conflicts (border conflicts, conflicts in neighboring republics; see Chechnya).

A further reform aimed at giving the armed forces of the Russian Federation a "new image" was announced at the end of 2008. This reform was primarily intended to improve the mobility, coordination, and commandability of the armed forces, which amounted to a reduction in military districts (four instead of six), a simplification of the command hierarchy of the land forces, and a significant increase in the military budget.

Among the innovations was the abolition of divisions in favor of brigades. A. Serdyukov, who was appointed minister of defense in 2007, put it this way: "Today we have a four-tier command structure: military district, army, division, regiment. We are moving toward a three-tier structure: a military district, an operational command, and a brigade. This means that the division level is no longer required, and the regiments are now subordinate to the brigades. At the same time, all units that are not fully manned are disbanded, and only units with permanent combat readiness remain. In accordance with the provisions of the military reform, by 2012 all formations of the Russian cadre army will be fully manned and will become permanent readiness forces."

In December 2008, the tables of organization for the separate tank and motorized rifle brigades were approved. According to table of organization 10/020, an armored brigade in peacetime consists of the following:

Headquarters and staff

Core units:
motorized rifle battalion
rifle platoon (snipers)
tank battalion (3)
self-propelled-artillery battalion (howitzers)
rocket artillery battalion
air defense battalion

Support units:
reconnaissance company
combat engineer company
NBC company
telecommunications battalion
electronic-warfare company
fire control platoon (commander of the artillery)
radar platoon (commander of the air defense)
surveillance platoon (commander of reconnaissance)
repair-and-recovery battalion
supply battalion
military police company
medical company (with 50 beds)
propaganda platoon
band
Personnel strength: 2,901 men (248 officers, 730 NCOs, 1,928 enlisted men), civilian personnel: 133, trainees: 10

Weapons and equipment:
90 medium main battle tanks
4 T-72BKs
49 BMP-3 armored personnel carriers
6 armored personnel carriers (wheeled)
3 BRM-3K combat reconnaissance vehicles
12 Tor surface-to-air missile systems
6 Tunguska-M1 self-propelled antiaircraft guns
6 Strela-10M3 short-range surface-to-air missiles
36 Igla short-range surface-to-air missile systems
1 9S18M1 Kynon radar system
1 PU-12M-1 command vehicle
1 PPRU-1M-1 mobile command center
8 9S912 fire control vehicles
18 BM-21-1 rocket launchers
18 2S19 Msta-S 152 mm self-propelled howitzers
8 2S12 120 mm mortars
6 AGS-17 automatic grenade launchers

Small arms:
1,183 5.45 mm AK-74M assault rifles
1,178 5.45 mm AKS-74U assault rifles
6 7.62 mm AKM assault rifles
54 9 mm AS submachine guns
432 9 mm PYa pistols
31 7.62 mm PSS pistols
33 7.62 mm SVD-S sniper rifles
8 9 mm VSS sniper rifles
3 5.45 mm 6P39 (RPK-74M) machine guns
81 7.62 mm PKP-35 machine guns
81 RPG-7V2-81 antitank rocket launchers
180 RPO-A rocket launchers

Russian T-72As in southeastern Ukraine

Unlike the tank brigades, as per table of organization 5/06900 motorized rifle brigades consisted of three motorized rifle battalions and a tank battalion plus two artillery battalions with a total of 4,393 troops and 128 civilians.

Before the transition to the "new image," the Russian Federation ground forces (excluding airborne troops) comprised twenty-four divisions (three tank, sixteen motorized rifles, five rocket artillery) and twelve independent rifle and motorized rifle brigades. In addition, there were two divisional military bases (in Armenia and Tajikistan). Of these twenty-four divisions and two military bases, only five motorized rifle divisions and one base in Tajikistan were actually present or occupied. Of these, only 13 percent belonged to the units at a permanent state of operational readiness.

In 2009, twenty-three divisions were disbanded, and forty brigades and brigade bases were set up in their place (by December 1, 2009):

4 tank brigades
35 motorized rifle brigades
1 reserve-and-replacement brigade

The disbandment of the 2nd Motorized Taman Guards Rifle Division and the 4th Kantemirovskaya Guards Tank Division, both famous guards divisions, caused an outcry in the military. The motorized 5th Guards Rifle Brigade and the 4th Guards Tank Brigade were created from them.

During maneuvers and simulations by the 74th Motorized Rifle Brigade in January 2009, it turned out that the brigade did not achieve the combat strength of the former Soviet motorized rifle regiments. Not once during the maneuver did the brigade come together for a coordinated action. While the initial phase of the maneuver was still somewhat successful in terms of leadership, the main phase ended in chaos. As soon as the tactics became a little more complicated, there was no longer any question of a unified "brigade leadership"; each unit acted as it saw fit. One hand did not know what the other was doing. After the disastrous end of the exercise, an analysis and investigation into the causes took place, with the following results:

- The number of officers in the brigades fell sharply in comparison to the regiments. While the regiment with 2,000 men had 250 officers and 150 ensigns, the brigade with 4,000 men had only 327 officers.
- The leadership, especially at brigade staff level, completely lacked an overview; command was chaotic. The size of the unit overwhelmed the command posts.
- The brigades were "blind" due to the failure of their reconnaissance units, which was largely due to their completely inadequate equipment. The reconnaissance platoons of the battalions were not able to provide the battalion command with a complete picture of the "enemy situation" in the unit's area of operation. At the same time, received reconnaissance reports could not be processed and forwarded to the brigade command in time. In addition, the brigade command had no evaluation center for reconnaissance results and intelligence on the enemy. The only specialists available were a sergeant major and a civilian linguist.

In this respect, the brigade command was constantly in the dark and never had a complete picture of the "enemy situation," which is of crucial importance for decision-making, operational planning, and the issuing of orders.

In addition to a lack of operational capability, another, no less acute problem, came to light: logistical support. The fact is that with the dissolution of the divisions, all rear services were "pinned to" the brigades. In short, the vice president of the College of Military Experts, Major General A. Vladimirov, described the new brigade structure as follows: "Instead of combat brigades, we got ugly bloated formations that had completely lost the mobility and uniformity of the regiments but never achieved the striking power of the divisions."

To remedy the deficiencies that had been identified, additions and changes were made to the organization of the brigades. In particular, instead of reconnaissance companies, they were (again) given reconnaissance battalions with the following structure:

- battalion headquarters
- 1 armored reconnaissance company
- 1 company with technical reconnaissance equipment
- 1 electronic-reconnaissance company
- 1 telecommunications platoon
- 1 support platoon
- 1 medical platoon

It was also decided in 2010 to merge the brigades' logistics and repair units. As a result, the brigades were given seven-company logistics battalions that were difficult to lead. In autumn 2010, a new reform phase of the tank and motorized rifle units began; namely, the division into heavy, medium, and light brigades.

Heavy brigades are to be equipped with the latest Armata main battle tanks, infantry fighting vehicles, armored personnel carriers, and other vehicles on standard chassis. All tank brigades became heavy brigades.

The T-14 Armata main battle tank developed for them differed considerably from all previous Russian tank types, which in principle were often just modernized versions of their respective predecessors. The Armata, on the other hand, was a completely new design with innovative technical solutions, and its chassis served as the basis for a number of other combat vehicles.

T-14 Armata Standard Main Battle Tank

With the T-14 main battle tank developed at Uralvagonzavod, the Russians abandoned the classic pattern that had defined international tank design since the appearance of the French Renault FT tank in the First World War. Among the most-striking features are its unmanned remote-controlled turret and the accommodation of the three-man crew consisting of commander, gunner/loader, and driver in an "encapsulated" compartment in the front. The relocation of the fighting compartment from the turret to the hull ensures the survivability of the crew, which should be guaranteed even in the event of direct turret hits with detonation of the onboard ammunition.

The gun turret, installed in the center of the hull, is a robot module with a 125 mm 2A82-1M smoothbore gun, a further development of the previous 2A46 tank gun, with increased accuracy and without a fume extractor, since there is no turret crew. It fires all the 125 mm tank ammunition of its predecessors as well as long-range guided missiles against ground and air targets. Loading is carried out by an automatic loader; the combat ammunition load is forty rounds, thirty-two of which are held in the loader as ready ammunition. A modern fire control system is used for aiming. The absence of a turret crew allowed for a very compact design of the turret, which reduces the probability of hits.

Hull protection and crew protection in the compact compartment are provided by modular armor consisting of a "universal dynamic," an "active" protection complex (composite/reactive armor plus the Afganit active protection system), an electromagnetic protection system, and a fire-extinguishing system (spark suppression).

The tank is powered by an X-shaped multifuel engine with a 2V-12-3A turbocharger that produces 1,200–1,500 hp, giving the 48-tonne (53 ton) vehicle a top speed of 75–80 kph (46.5–50 mph) on roads and 45–50 kph (28–31 mph) off-road. (The German company Porsche

T-14 Armata standard main battle tank

pioneered the X configuration for tank engines. During the war, it developed a compact air-cooled diesel engine, which was supposed to replace the Maybach HL 230 in the Tiger and Panther tanks, among others. In 1945, the type 212 was installed in a Königstiger [King Tiger]. It is likely that the documents concerning the engine fell into Soviet hands after the end of the war, and the Chelyabinsk engine plant took them up again). In terms of cross-country mobility, the T-14 is on a par with or superior to other modern Soviet main battle tanks because of its hydropneumatic running gear and additional pair of road wheels (lengthened hull compared to the T-72 and T-80; seven road wheels and four return rollers per side). The tracks are equipped with rubber pads.

The Armata hull and chassis were designed as a universal platform, which serves or will serve as the basis of a vehicle family of twenty-eight types for various purposes. To date, these include the T-15 heavy infantry fighting vehicle and the T-16 recovery vehicle, which like the T-14 Armata were placed in service with heavy-tank brigades.

T-14 Armata standard main battle tank during a parade in Red Square in 2020.
Press Service of the Russian Federation Defense Ministry

T-15 Heavy Infantry Fighting Vehicle

More precisely, motorized rifle battalions of heavy-tank brigades are to receive the T-15. The highly mobile infantry fighting vehicle will accompany tank units in battle, even if nuclear and other weapons of mass destruction are used. A special feature of the T-15 is that, for the first time, it offers its crew and motorized riflemen the protection of a main battle tank. The design of the T-15 is largely based on the Armata platform, but unlike on the T-14 its engine compartment is located forward and the "encapsulated" driver's and riflemen sections are in the middle and rear parts of the vehicle. Its remotely controlled armament is housed in the rotating turret above the passenger compartment as the Epokha combat module together with ammunition, although the two are isolated from one another. In this respect a hit on the turret is the same as one on the T-14.

The Epokha combat module consists of a 30 mm 2A42 automatic cannon with selective ammunition feed, a 7.62 mm PKTM machine gun, and twin launchers for 9M133 Kornet guided antitank missiles. The ammunition combat load consists of five hundred rounds for the cannon, two thousand rounds for the machine gun, and four missiles.

The driver and gunner/commander are provided with a computer system and two multifunctional sights (one for the gunner, the other for the vehicle commander), a radar station, a two-axis weapon stabilizer, and an advanced

BMP T-15 Armata infantry fighting vehicle. *Press Service of the Russian Federation Defense Ministry*

BMP T-15 Armata infantry fighting vehicle. *Press Service of the Russian Federation Defense Ministry*

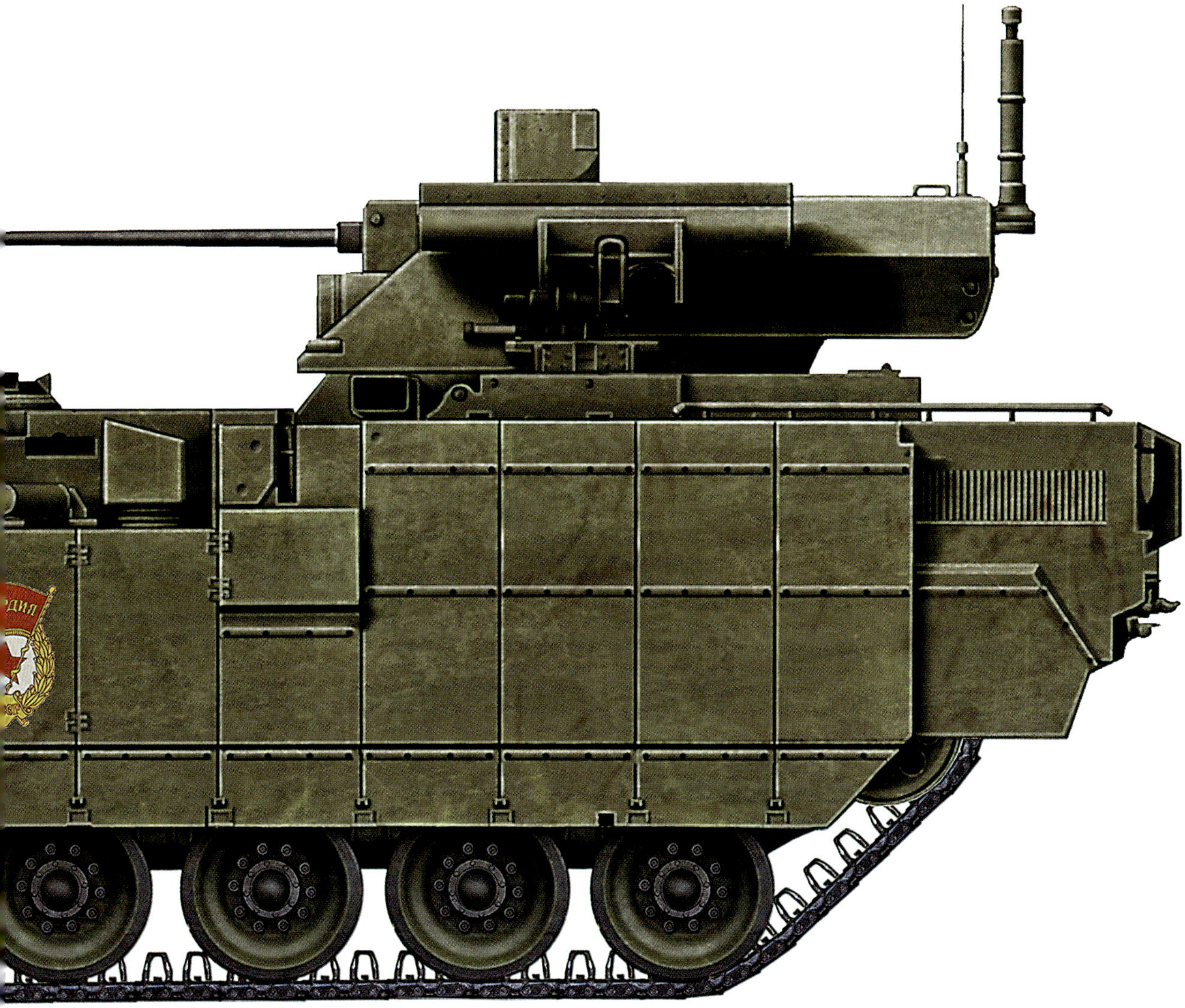

The BMP T-15 infantry fighting vehicle also uses the Armata standard chassis.

sensor system. A target-tracking system makes it possible to engage targets while stationary and on the move with great accuracy. The T-15 also has a monitoring and control system that watches over the technical status of all components, diagnoses malfunctions, and controls the onboard systems. The multifuel power plant (or A-85-3A X-configuration twelve-cylinder diesel engine) installed in the engine-transmission compartment produces up to 1,500 hp and makes possible road speeds of up to 80 kph (30 mph). The running gear consists of seven road wheels with torsion bar suspension and four return rollers on each side; the drive sprockets are in front, the idler wheels at the rear. The tracks consist of ninety-three links per side. Unlike the earlier BMP and BTR, the T-15 is not amphibious.

The T-15 infantry fighting vehicle's weapons module

Kurganets-25 Infantry Fighting Vehicle

The Kurganets-25 is a vehicle platform that serves as the basis for both a (planned) armored personnel carrier for motorized rifle brigades and an infantry fighting vehicle. Both vehicles have the engine compartment in front, and behind it a protected compartment for the driver and commander, and in the central area and the no-less-well-protected compartment for the riflemen, with a remote-control turret on the roof. The riflemen enter and exit the vehicle through double doors and a ramp in the rear, while the driver and commander use roof hatches.

The crew consists of three persons, and the vehicle can carry up to eight fully equipped motorized riflemen.

The remotely controlled turret module houses the Epokha complex, with a 2A42 30 mm automatic cannon, PKTM 7.62 mm machine gun, and two Kornet guided antitank missiles. A Baikal remote weapon station with an automatic 57 mm cannon and coaxial 7.62 mm machine gun can be mounted in place of the Epokha.

Like the T-15, the Kurganets infantry fighting vehicle has a digital computer system to automate weapon and vehicle control and to integrate the vehicle into a tactical composite combat system. Thermal-imaging sighting systems ensure day and night combat capability. Software and hardware enable the transmission of information about detected or damaged targets to other vehicles or command posts, as well as the reception of (reconnaissance) reports from other units in real time.

The remotely controlled combat module of the armored personnel carrier based on the Kurganets-25 is armed only with a 12.7 mm Kord machine gun. Although this weapon is sufficient for the vehicle's principal purpose (transport of personnel and materiel), it is clearly inferior to the proven armament of previous Russian armored personnel carriers with the KPVT 14.5 mm heavy machine gun plus the PKT 7.62 mm machine gun. All the vehicles based on the Kurganets-25 platform have a diesel engine with a maximum output of 800 hp. The running gear has seven road wheels per side, with the drive sprockets in front. The Kurganets-25 has outstanding off-road capabilities and achieves road speeds of up to 80 kph (50 mph). In contrast to the T-15, it is amphibious; propulsion in the water is provided by two water jet propellers.

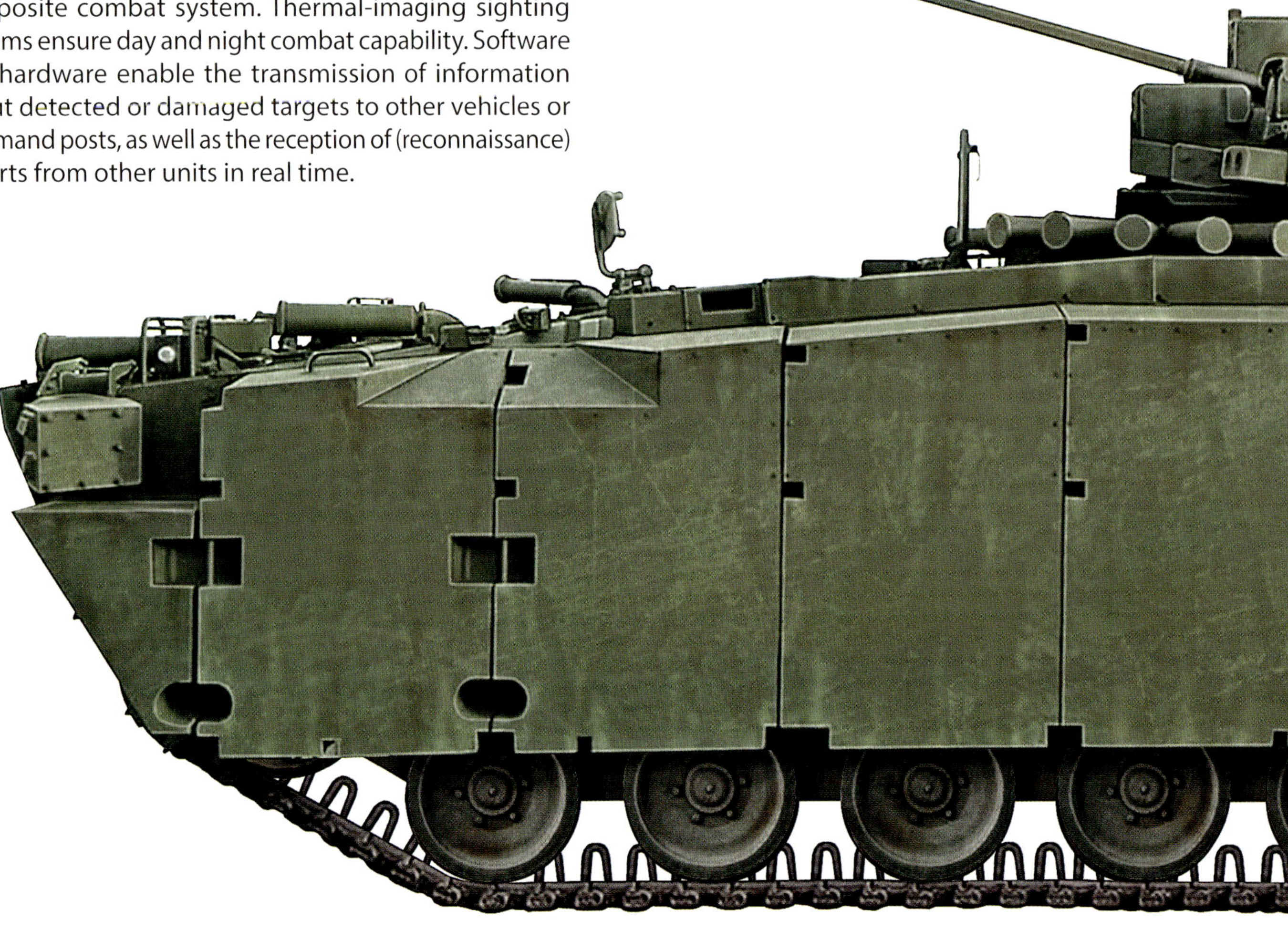

Back to the formation of the motorized rifle and tank units.

Medium (motorized rifle) brigades are conceived for use in combat under special conditions, which excludes or does not allow the use of heavy brigades. Medium brigades were formed on the basis of the old, motorized rifle brigades and were equipped with upgraded tanks of the current generation—for example, T-72B3s, T-80BVMs, and T-90Ms, as well as wheeled and tracked armored personnel carriers, depending on whether they are type A or Б brigades.

Kurganets-25 infantry fighting vehicle

The type Б brigade consists of the following units:

- brigade headquarters
- 2 motorized rifle battalion, each with
3 motorized rifle companies (each with 15 APCs)
  1 self-propelled howitzer battery (6 2S34 howitzers)
  1 antitank platoon (6 men armed with 9P162 guided antitank missiles)
  1 repair platoon (8 repair and recovery vehicles)
  1 telecommunications platoon
- 4 tank companies (each with 10 main battle tanks)
  1 repair company (5 recovery vehicles)
  1 telecommunications platoon
- 2 self-propelled howitzer battalions (each with 18 2S19 howitzers)
- 1 battery of rocket artillery (6 BM-21-1 rocket launchers)
- 1 antitank battery (12 9P162 systems)
- 1 surface-to-air missile battalion
- 1 reconnaissance battalion consisting of
  1 reconnaissance company (Iveco-class vehicles)
  1 reconnaissance company (BMP/BRM)
  1 reconnaissance company for support of the motorized rifle and tank battalions
  1 electronic-intelligence company
  1 drone reconnaissance platoon (long range)
  1 air reconnaissance squadron (short-range aircraft)
  1 telecommunications platoon
- 1 telecommunications battalion
- 1 combat engineer battalion
- 1 supply battalion
- 1 electronic-warfare company
- 1 NBC company
- 1 medical company

Authorized strength: 4,618

In contrast to the type B motorized rifle brigade, the type A brigade has three instead of two motorized rifle battalions and one tank battalion.

Circa 2012, deliveries to the motorized rifle brigades of the new BTR-80A wheeled infantry fighting vehicle, manufactured by the Arzamas Machine-Building Plant, began. The contract was concluded by the Ministry of Defense, with the company provided for the delivery of several hundred BTR-80As in 2012–14.

Armored fighting vehicle on the Kurganets-25 chassis.
armee-news.ru

The A version is a modernized version of the standard production BTR-80. Lightly armored and amphibious, this infantry fighting vehicle is used to transport motorized rifle units and provide them with fire support on the battlefield, and the riflemen are capable of fighting both on foot and from the vehicle. In terms of design, performance, and off-road capability, the BTR-80A is similar to the BTR-80 and differs mainly in the installation of a 2A72 30 mm automatic cannon with coaxial PKT 7.62 mm machine gun in the rotating turret above the fighting compartment. The distance between the weapons installations and the interior of the vehicle made it possible to increase the size of the fighting compartment, providing more space for the riflemen, and simultaneously solving the problems caused by noise and powder gas during firing.

The turret rotates 360°, and the range of elevation of −5°/+70° also makes it possible to engage low-speed aerial targets. Both the cannon and machine gun are belt-fed from the magazines, with the cannon being fed a choice of HE-incendiary or armor-piercing tracer ammunition. A mechanism allows the operator to quickly switch from soft to armored targets and vice versa. The gunner can also cock the weapons by remote control and set the rate of fire: single shot, 200 rounds per minute, or 330 rounds per minute.

Armored personnel carrier on the Kurganets-25 chassis; also see the photos on the facing page.
Press Service of the Russian Federation Defense Ministry

The combat ammunition load is three hundred rounds of 30 mm and two thousand rounds of 7.62 mm. The 1P3-9 daylight sight and the TPN-3 night sight are available for aiming. Combat range by day is approximately 3,000 m (3,280 yds.); in darkness, approximately 800 m (875 yds.).

Installation of the powerful 30 mm cannon provides a considerable increase in the wheeled armored personnel carrier's fighting capability. According to the manufacturer, its effectiveness against ground targets increased by a factor of 2.1 to 2.4 over the BTR-80, and the potential loss rate to attack helicopters is reduced by half. The BTR-80A's fighting power is also enhanced by the small arms of the riflemen, an automatic mortar, and a man-portable surface-to-air missile system.

The Arzamas Machine-Building Plant did not stop at the BTR-80A but carried out further combat upgrades to the BTR-82 and BTR-82A. According to experts, equipping motorized rifle battalions with these types will at least ensure parity with similar formations from the NATO countries.

BTR-82 Wheeled Armored Personnel Carrier

The goal of the modernization program was to comprehensively improve the vehicle's tactical, technical, and operational characteristics; firepower; mobility; protection; and radio equipment while increasing reliability and ease of maintenance and reducing operating costs. Firepower and aiming accuracy were increased by installing a remote-controlled combat module with electric drives and a digital weapon stabilizer for elevation and azimuth.

The BTR-82 wheeled infantry fighting vehicle is equipped with a 14.5 mm KPVT machine gun and 7.62 mm PKTM machine gun, whereas the BTR-82A has a 30 mm 2A72 automatic cannon and coaxial 7.62 mm PKTM machine gun. All weapons are belt-fed. The ammunition combat load comprises three hundred rounds for the cannon, five hundred for the 14.5 mm machine gun, and two thousand for the 7.62 mm machine gun.

Both versions are powered by the Kamas 740.14-300 turbo-diesel engine, which delivers 300 hp at 2,600 rpm and enables road speeds of up to 80 kph (50 mph). The vehicles offer excellent off-road mobility and can negotiate vertical obstacles up to 0.5 m (1.6 ft.) high, cross ditches up to 2 m (6.6 ft.) wide, and negotiate gradients of up to 30°. They are also able to cross water obstacles at speeds of up to 10 kph (6.2 mph).

BTR-82A wheeled armored personnel carrier.
AMZ Press Service, topwar.ru

BTR-82A. *AMZ Press Service, topwar.ru*

BTR-82A, looking toward the double doors. *topwar.ru*

BTR-82A. *AMZ Press Service*

T-72B3 Standard Main Battle Tank

In 2011, the program to reequip tank battalions of medium motorized rifle brigades with the T-72B3 main battle tank began, and it was regarded as a budget modernization of the existing T-72B fleet. The overhaul and modernization program includes the installation of a new Sosna-U multichannel tank gunner's sight in the production T-72B. This enables the gunner to detect targets by using optical and thermal imaging. In addition, Sosna-U has a laser rangefinder and can also control guided antitank missiles. This means that several tasks can be performed with just one device. The sight can be used to engage tank targets up to 5 km (3.1 mi.) away during the day and up to 3.5 km (2.2 mi.) away at night. The commander has a TKN-3MK day/night sight with an infrared channel with which he can conduct the firefight. The 125 mm 2A46M5 smoothbore gun was equipped with an automatic loader for the use of new ammunition. However, the T-72B3 retained the old V-84-1 diesel engine, with an output of 840 hp. The running gear and tracks also underwent some changes. New universal twin-pin tracks were fitted, which probably increased service life and were also easier and cheaper to maintain. The automatic Rime system, which quickly detects and extinguishes fires in the fighting compartment and engine compartment, is intended to increase survivability on the battlefield.

The "T-72B3 with improved combat characteristics" version (unofficially referred to as the T-72B3M or T-72B4), with a further increase in combat capabilities, was equipped with a TKN-4SR day/night vision sight and an A40-4 fire control computer in addition to the Sosna-U multichannel tank gunner's sight. This configuration radically improved the fire control system by introducing a target-tracking device. A more accurate gun with a new stabilized gun mount and improved Relikt reactive armor with lattice screens were also added. The new V-92S2F diesel engine delivers 1,130 hp.

T-72B3 standard main battle tank

T-72B3 standard main battle tank with added protective equipment for urban warfare. *NPK Uralvagonzavod*

T-72B3 at a display of weapons and equipment.
NPK Uralvagonzavod

T-80BVM upgraded standard main battle tank

T-80BVM Standard Main Battle Tank

The T-80BVM main battle tank, modernized by Omsktransmash, was intended to equip medium motorized rifle brigades. The combat upgrade included the installation of a multichannel Sosna-U tank gunner's sight (see above), the 125 mm 2A46M-4 cannon, a 2E58 weapon stabilization system, reinforced reactive and composite armor, a TVN-5 driver's sight, and a modified GTD-1250 GAZ turbine engine. The R-168-25U-2 Aqueduct ultra-short-wave radio was used to improve command transmission. Measures were also taken to reduce fuel consumption and increase NBC protection. There were two new types of shell for the 125 mm smoothbore gun: the 3BM59 Svinets-1, with a tungsten carbide core, and 3BM60 Svinets-2, with a uranium alloy core. Svinets-1 penetrates about 740 mm (29 in.) of armor at distances of up to 2 km (1.24 mi.), and Svinets-2 up to 830 mm (32.6 in.) from the same distance. The alloy of depleted uranium with tungsten is known to experts as Material B. The use of depleted uranium shells does not violate international agreements, and this ammunition is stored away from the other ammunition and is classified as special ammunition. To protect against enemy fire, the vehicle is equipped with anti-hollow-charge lattice screens and Relikt ERA. Like the T-72B3, the T-80BVM was given improved running gear and new tracks. The installation of the Arena-M active antitank guided-missile defense system has been planned since 2018. The vehicle has a combat weight of 46 tonnes (50.7 tons).

T-80BVM during a combat exercise. *Omsktransmash Press Service*

T-90M Standard Main Battle Tank

In 1992, the Russian armed forces introduced the T-90 Vladimir main battle tank, developed by Uralvagonzavod, which has since undergone several combat upgrades. Tank battalions of some medium motorized rifle brigades have since received the T-90M, which is also intended to bridge the gap in heavy brigades until the introduction of the T-14 Armata.

This modernized T-90 basically combines the best technical solutions of the standard T-72B and T-80U main battle tanks. The T-72B scores with a sophisticated chassis, and the T-80U with a composite armored turret and reactive armor as well as a sophisticated fire control system. At the same time, many parts and assemblies were revised, on the basis of the experience gained from combat operations and the reorientation of production toward Russian-made components. The modernization of the T-90 was aimed at improving the main combat value indicators of protection, firepower, and mobility, as well as reducing maintenance and repair costs.

An increase in the level of protection was achieved through a number of different measures, including the installation of modular Relikt reactive armor on the hull, turret, and sidewalls. The rear and lower part of the turret as well as the rear area of the hull and the rear armor plate are covered with grids against hollow charges (cage armor). The driver's compartment and fighting compartment have an internal splinter protection lining made of aramid threads (Kevlar mats). All this to withstand hits from modern NATO antitank munitions. The automatic release of aerosol smoke grenades also makes it more difficult for (mostly laser-guided) antitank guided missiles to hit the tank. And that is not all: laser-warning devices also enable the crew to align themselves with the frontal armor facing incoming projectiles (if they still manage to do so). The T-90M's built-in dynamic protection is fully modular and offers the possibility of quickly replacing modules with different levels of protection, depending on operational conditions and mission.

The less reflective surface in combination with a layer of radio-absorbing materials reduces the radar signature of the T-90M many times over compared to the parent model the T-90.

To increase survivability, the storage of fuel and ammunition in the hull was optimized (ammunition bunker with blowout openings). The T-90M was equipped with an automatic NBC overpressure system to protect the crew from chemical-warfare agents and radioactive particles, which the previous modifications of the T-72 and T-90 did not have.

The striking power of the T-90M has been increased by the installation of a new 125 mm gun, an automatic fire control system (FCS), a remotely controlled machine gun, an autoloader, and the use of ammunition with increased target impact. The new 125 mm smoothbore gun offers a 25 to 30 percent improvement in accuracy, a 15 percent increase in effective range, and longer barrel life.

T-90M upgraded standard main battle tank

T-90A standard main battle tank. *NPK Uralvagonzavod*

T-90S standard main battle tank. *vpk.name*

The fully automatic Kalina fire control system differs fundamentally from all systems previously used by Soviet main battle tanks. For the first time, Russian tank commanders are able to enjoy a panoramic sight with a thermal-imaging device and the option of automatically assigning targets to the gunner.

Propulsion is provided by the new V-92S2F diesel engine, with an output of 1,130 hp. To counteract driver fatigue on long drives or when constantly turning on the battlefield, an automatic gear change system and a steering wheel were introduced to replace the notorious "operation of levers." In addition, the T-90M tank received an integrated monitoring system, which helps prevent mechanical breakdowns and accidents and prolong the technical life by diagnosing all systems and assemblies and blocking possible incorrect actions of the driver (but does not yet detect vodka fumes). Remarkably, the Russian T-90M costs only about half as much as its main American competitor, the M1A2 Abrams, but surpasses it in combat value by one and a half times.

The T-90AM is a modernized T-90S. *NPK Uralvagonzavod*

UPGRADED BMP-2 AND BMP-3

The motorized rifle battalions of the medium brigades were also included in the modernization program by equipping them with BMP-2, BMP-3, and BTR-80 infantry fighting vehicles and modernized MT-LB amphibious tanks. At one of its meetings in the summer of 2012, the Russian Federation Military-Industrial Commission also decided to create a series of new wheeled vehicles that could be used not only as armored infantry fighting vehicles, but also as carriers of air defense systems, electronic-warfare systems, and "radio cases." Wheeled armored vehicles with more-powerful armament (both tank and artillery guns) were also being considered.

The main arguments in favor of wheeled armored vehicles are their great mobility, their speed, and the absence of a complicated and heavy tracked running gear. Added to this are their relatively low combat weight and the (generally) lower maintenance and repair costs, not to mention their more economical fuel consumption. These are all factors that play an increasingly important role in modern ("asymmetric") conflicts. On the other hand, wheeled armored vehicles with a maximum weight of 30 tonnes (33 tons) can never achieve the level of protection of a tracked vehicle—just think of the capabilities of armor. The air-filled tires of the wheeled chassis are also susceptible to "flats," shell fragments, and enemy fire. Of course, there are also "bulletproof" tires, but these cannot make up for the generally lower survivability of wheeled vehicles. Wheeled chassis simply come with a greater overall height, which is anything but advantageous on the battlefield.

But even for the Military-Industrial Commission, the advantages outweighed the disadvantages, and it ultimately gave the green light for a new universal wheeled vehicle platform called Boomerang.

BMP-2M infantry fighting vehicle, view from the front. *Kurganmashzavod Press Service*

BMP-2M upgraded infantry fighting vehicle

BMP-3 upgraded infantry fighting vehicle

Module unit for the upgraded BMP-3

BMP-2M on the training grounds.
Kurganmashzavod Press Service

K-16 Boomerang Wheeled Infantry Fighting Vehicle

From it were developed the K-16 BTR (BTR-K) and the K-17 BMP (BMP-K). At the notorious Victory Parade on May 9, 2015, preproduction samples of the K-16 (also known as VPK-7829) were demonstrated for the first time. This wheeled infantry fighting vehicle differs considerably from all other Soviet four-axle vehicles in its layout. The engine/transmission compartment is located on the right side of the nose and the driver's compartment on the left, followed by the fighting/transport compartment. The hull consists of welded armored steel plates, with a high degree of slope at the front and vertical on the sides. A folding ramp at the rear ensures that the infantry can exit and enter the vehicle quickly and safely—a major change compared to other Soviet wheeled infantry fighting vehicles, where the riflemen had to climb in and out via side hatches. A seal prevents the ingress of water, and a hinged surge shield prevents the front end from flooding when the vehicle enters the water, especially since most banks have a more or less large angle of inclination. Two water jet propellers at the stern are used to propel the vehicle in the water.

The fighting and troop compartments in the middle and rear part of the hull have a relatively large volume. The troop compartment offers space for eight to ten motorized riflemen, whose seats are suspended from the ceiling for protection against mines. An "active protection complex" is intended to protect the occupants from grenades and antitank missiles.

The BPK-7829 has a remotely controlled turret combat module with a 12.7 mm machine gun. The K-17 model of the Boomerang family will probably be equipped with the Epokha combat module, developed by the Instrument Engineering Design Bureau in Tula, with a 30 mm automatic cannon (five hundred rounds) and 7.62 mm PKTM machine gun (two thousand rounds) as well as an automatic grenade launcher and Kornet antitank guided missiles. Alternatively, a modified Epokha/Boomerang BM module with a more powerful 57 mm cannon can be installed.

Boomerang will also be equipped with an integrated communication, navigation, and fire control system that fully complies with the concept of networked combat management. The commanders or operators can receive all important information in real time and interact with other vehicles or units.

According to media reports, in addition to an armored personnel carrier and an infantry fighting vehicle, the Boomerang family includes a command vehicle and a reconnaissance vehicle with the Boomerang-Infauna electronic reconnaissance and suppression complex.

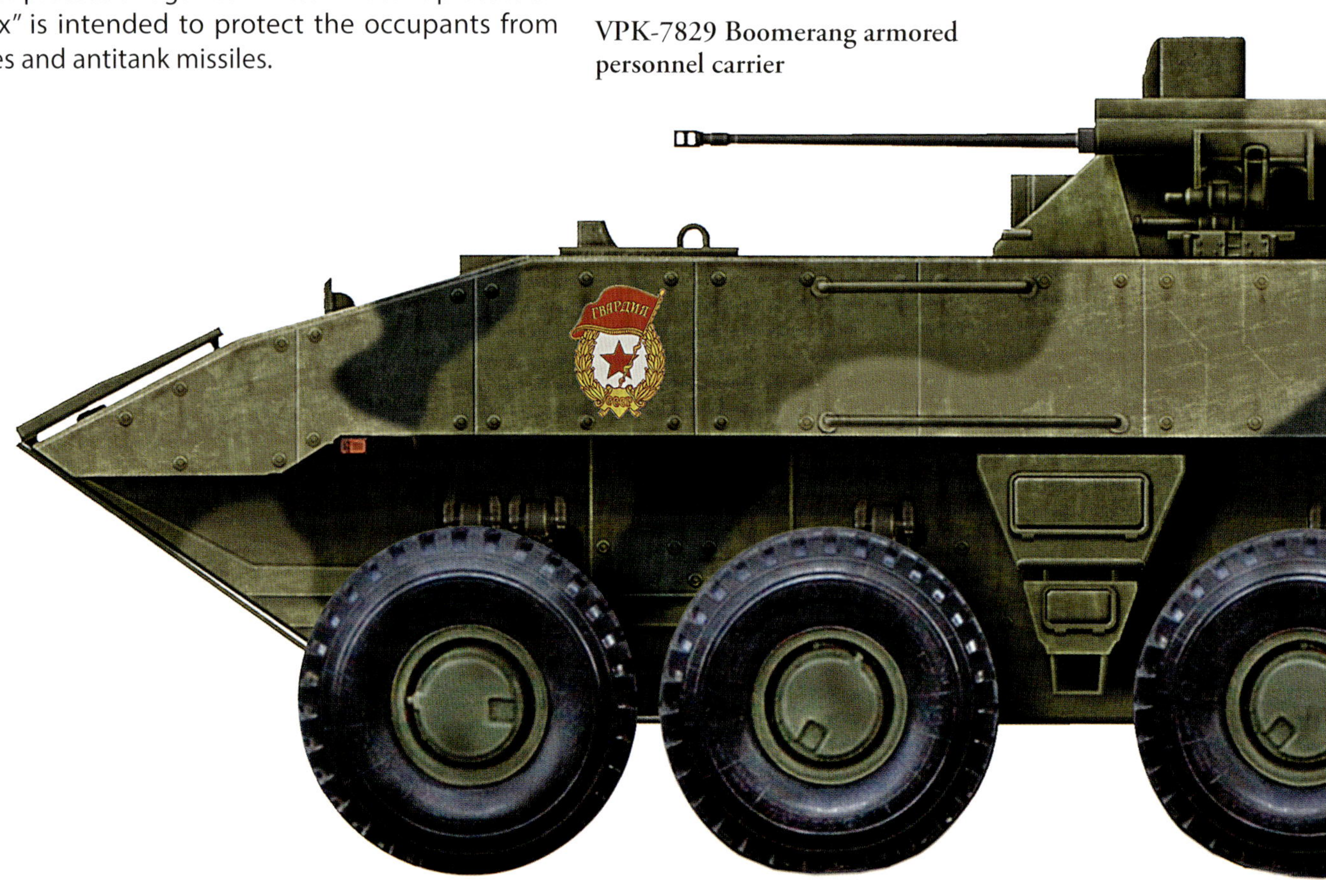

VPK-7829 Boomerang armored personnel carrier

VPK-7829 Boomerang, view from the right rear. *fastpik.ru*

Let us now turn to the light brigades, the most mobile and fastest of their kind. They are primarily intended for operations in built-up areas and in zones that are not suitable for the deployment of heavy units. Not only are light brigades highly mobile and fast, but they also protect (public) roads and march routes and require less maintenance than heavy brigades.

The Russian light brigades are equipped (or are to be equipped) with wheeled vehicles of the types Тигр (Tigr/Tiger), Рысь (Rys/Lynx), Медведь (Medved/Bear), and Воллк (Volk/Wolf), with different equipment and armament. The Russians thus adopted the German custom of giving armored vehicles the names of predatory animals, which perhaps took some effort, especially in the case of the Tigr/Tiger, due to memories of experiences during the Second World War. However, many Russians were even more surprised by the involvement of the Italian manufacturer Iveco, which not only supplied parts but was even responsible for the design in the case of the Rys.

VPK-7829 Boomerang armored personnel carrier, view from the front right. *sarov.info*

Tigr (Tiger) Armored Vehicle

By December 2011, more than 500 Tigr vehicles in various versions had been delivered to the armed forces, the troops of the Ministry of the Interior, and police units, with the army operating around 170 Tigr. They are used for reconnaissance, surveillance, transportation, and escort tasks, such as escorting convoys, patrolling areas of tension, or monitoring important facilities.

The Tigr was developed by the Military Development Center of the vehicle manufacturer GAZ, which presented the first prototypes at the international arms exhibitions IDEX-2001 and MIMS-2002. In 2002, two vehicles under the designation GAZ-233034 Tigr were operated by the Moscow police on a trial basis. In March 2007, the armed forces adopted the Tigr, which they officially operated as GAZ-233014 Tigr or STS Tigr (STS = special vehicle). The first production vehicles went to special units of the military intelligence service.

The Tigr is an armored 4×4 wheeled vehicle of chassis frame construction. The frame supports the body and most of the add-on parts. In addition to the hull, the following are mounted on the frame: the independent double wishbone suspension with torsion bar, the engine, two axles with differentials, and the reduction gear. The STS Tigr is designed to carry six to nine people. The welded hull is made of heat-treated 5 mm (0.2 in.) armor plates, which corresponds to the Russian protection class III according to GOST R 50963 (some vehicles are built to protection class V). The body has three doors and side and rear hatches with openings for firing small arms. A double-wing hatch with a swivel mount for a 30 mm

GAZ-233014 Tigr (Tiger) armored vehicle

GAZ-233014 Tigr-M armored vehicle, armed with an automatic grenade launcher and a machine gun.
Russian Federation Defense Ministry

automatic grenade launcher and a 12.7 mm machine gun is installed on the roof. The size of the hatch allows two soldiers to fire in different directions at the same time. The interior features a universal mount for communication devices with power connections. The corresponding antenna mount is located on the outside of the roof. An internal splinter shield protects the occupants from secondary fragments that have penetrated the armor. An American Cummins B205 six-cylinder diesel engine with turbocharger (205 hp) is installed in the engine/transmission compartment in the front. On roads, the Tigr can reach speeds of up to 140 kph (87 mph). It can ford water obstacles up to 1.2 m (3.9 ft.) deep without preparation.

Hopes for procurement of the Tigr received a bitter blow in December 2001, when the Ministry of Defense announced that it would not be purchasing any more vehicles as of 2014. The Tigr did not offer the crew sufficient protection (although the manufacturer had equipped the vehicle with the required protection class specified in the contract), and it also had an imported American engine. A late realization, which suggests that the Russian Ministry of Defense has also slowly come into line with the level of knowledge and decision-making of its Western counterparts.

GAZ-233014 Tigr-M armored vehicle in a training area.
AMZ Press Service

In 2013, however, there was a glimmer of hope: according to reports, modernized Tigr-M vehicles were undergoing service trials. The Tigr-M differs from its predecessor by, among other things, having the Russian YM3 5347-10 diesel engine, a new armored nose plate, a filter ventilation unit, and a square weapon station roof hatch with a hinged cover (instead of the double-winged one). It also received class V protection at the front and class III protection on the sides and rear. The only downside: although the Tigr was manufactured in Russia, it was built using imported components from the Italian company Iveco for cost and other reasons. Series deliveries of the Tigr-M to special units and individual light brigades began in 2013. The latter have received around 1,500 Tigr-M vehicles, which they use for reconnaissance purposes, as fire control vehicles, and as classic armored personnel carriers.

GAZ-233014 Tigr-M armored vehicle.
AMZ Press Service

Rys (Lynx) Armored Vehicle

The Rys (Lynx) armored vehicle was developed starting in 2001 by the Italian company Iveco Defense Vehicles (a subsidiary of Iveco). Two prototypes were sent to Russia for testing purposes in 2009. At the end of 2010, the Ministry of Defense of the Russian Federation announced the adoption of the Iveco LMV (Light Multirole Vehicle) M65 as the Rys by the armed forces and the provision of funds for the procurement of 1,775 vehicles in the period 2010–16. In 2012, production examples of the Rys appeared in public for the first time at the Victory Parade in Red Square. The design of the 4×4 Rys basically follows that of its cousin the Tigr, with the engine/transmission compartment at the front, followed by the driver's, crew, and cargo compartments.

There is room for two persons in the driver's compartment, and three in the crew compartment. The seats are arranged transversely to the vehicle's longitudinal axis. One feature of the Rys is its high level of protection for its crew. The driver's and crew compartments are separate and isolated from the engine and cargo compartments, and while the shock wave from a mine detonation may destroy the front and rear of the vehicle (engine and cargo compartments), the center section is largely unaffected thanks to its U profile, which dissipates the pressure wave and deflects fragments. In addition, its suspended seats absorb shocks. The frame consists of high-strength steel tubes to which hinged armor plates are attached. This is relatively light composite armor with steel content, which means that the Rys has a total weight that does not exceed 6,500 kg (14,330 lbs.). According to available information, the composite armor is capable of withstanding fire from 7.62 × 54 mm armor-piercing bullets. During a test, Russian ballistics experts fired a total of 210 rounds at the vehicle from various angles, without achieving a single penetration. This means that the protection offered by the Rys corresponds to the third NATO protection level according to STANAG 4569 (which corresponds to class VIa of the Russian standard GOST R 50963-96). Light support weapons—an automatic grenade launcher or a machine gun—can be installed on the roof. However, the vehicle does not have any firing hatches for small arms.

An Iveco turbo-diesel producing 185 hp and containing an automatic transmission gives the Rys a maximum speed of up to 130 kph (80 mph). It can negotiate walls up to 0.5 m (1.6 ft.) in height and ford bodies of water up to 0.85 m (2.8 ft.) in depth (up to 1.5 m [4.9 ft.] with wading preparations). Range is 500 km (310 mi.).

Iveco M65 Rys, view from the front right

Iveco M65 Rys with guards emblem. *topwar.ru*

A Rys negotiating an obstacle. *armee.lv*

In January 2013, the Russian Federation Ministry of Defense announced that the contract for procurement of the Rys would not be extended. The then commander in chief of the ground forces, Colonel General V. V. Chirkin, said, "Of course we will find a use for them. In general, they are not bad, but in terms of their combat characteristics they are clearly inferior to the Tigr vehicle."

If the procurement contract had been extended, the arms embargo imposed on the Russian Federation by NATO countries in 2014 would have prevented further deliveries of the Rys anyway. There are difficulties with the supply of spare parts for the existing vehicles.

Iveco M65 Rys (Lynx) armored vehicle

Volk (Wolf) Armored Vehicle

The next vehicles have little to do with the combat vehicle equipment of the Russian armored forces but should be presented for the sake of completeness. The Volk (Wolf) armored 4×4 vehicle was developed by the Military Engineering Center. Three prototypes appeared in public for the first time in 2010 at the Technologies in Mechanical Engineering 2010 exhibition in Zhukovsky. Tests of the basic model VPK-3927 Volk took place in 2013–14. It serves as the basis for other armored vehicles that are intended to perform various tasks in counterterrorism operations. They can be used as armored personnel carriers, escort vehicles for convoys, and patrol vehicles in tension zones and can be equipped with grenade launchers, antitank and antiaircraft missiles, and machine guns. The "Wolfpack" comprises the following versions:

- VPK 3927 Volk: the basic model with 4×4 chassis and two options: with open-top or enclosed hull for the transport of personnel
- VPK-39271 Volk-1: equipped with a one-piece armored function module
- VPK-39272 Volk-2: equipped with an open freight module with the capability of installing armored modules
- VPK-39273 Volk-3: with 6×6 chassis with module for transport of personnel
- VPK-39274 Volk-4: with mine-resistant 6×6 chassis

Development of the Volk took into consideration current requirements for crew protection and versatility, with the highest possible degree of standardization between the vehicles in the family, on the basis of a modular design principle.

This is essentially achieved by a standard chassis with rigid frame construction and drive module in the front. A protected driver's cab and a functional rear module are installed behind the drivetrain. These two-part modules can optionally be replaced by a one-part module. Particular emphasis was placed on ballistic protection against gunfire and mines. The frame concept enables additional armor to be fitted without the use of special tools. The protection area covers 85 percent of the total area with standard VIa protection, according to GOST R 50963-96 (protection class 3, according to NATO-STANAG 4569). For mine resistance, the vehicle floor has been shaped in such a way that it attenuates or deflects the blast wave. For the same reason, the floor of the modules consists of two layers, and the seats—attached to the sides or ceiling—are equipped with additional shock absorption. The crew of

VPK-39273 Volk (Wolf) armored vehicle

the fighting compartment watches through armor glass blocks. The latest Russian YaMZ-5347 four-cylinder, in-line diesel engine with Euro emission standard 4, which has a considerable modernization reserve, was installed as the drive system. Performance can be increased, according to vehicle weight, up to 300 hp. In addition, there is a five-speed manual transmission and a two-speed transfer case. Thanks to an adjustable suspension, ground clearance can be changed from 250 to 550 mm (9.8 to 21.6 in.), and a speed of 55–60 kph (34–37 mph) can be achieved even off-road. The fording depth is 1.5 m (4.9 ft.). On roads, the Volk reaches speeds of 120–130 kph (75–81 mph). The Volk is equipped with an electronic control and monitoring system that monitors fifteen engine and twenty-four suspension parameters.

VPK-3927 Volk armored vehicle, view from the front right. *militärrussia.ru*

VPK-3927 Volk, side view. *livejournal.com*

Medved (Bear) Armored Vehicle

The VPK-3924 Medved (Bear) armored vehicle was developed by the Department of Wheeled Vehicles at Moscow State University on behalf of the Ministry of the Interior. In the design phase it was given the designation SPM-3 (SPM stands for police use). The Medved is designed to serve as an armored personnel carrier and a reconnaissance and patrol vehicle in crisis zones, for escorting convoys and providing fire support for police troops. Command and medical vehicles are to follow. The driver and troop compartments are designed as sealed, protected modules, reinforced at the bottom for mine resistance; additional panels can be fitted inside. The level of ballistic and mine protection depends on the plates and panels installed. The armored capsule takes up the middle and rear of the vehicle as part of the body. The driver and commander sit in the driver's compartment, with side doors for getting in and out. The troop compartment at the rear offers space for up to ten people. Entry and exit are through double doors at the rear. Viewing windows made of bulletproof glass facilitate observation.

The armor itself consists of two layers: the outer layer is made of high-strength, relatively brittle steel, while the inner layer is made of highly ductile and crack-resistant steel. Mine resistance is provided by a V-shaped base made of several layers of steel. The V shape deflects the blast wave to the sides so that it can cause only minimal damage to the vehicle (here, the South African Casspir and Wolf Turbo wheeled infantry fighting vehicles, which have proven themselves in bush warfare, were the inspiration). A relatively high positioning of the driver and troop compartments contributes to the protection of the crew. According to available information, the ballistic protection corresponds to class VIa GOST R 50963-96, or class 3 according to NATO STANAG 4569; the mine resistance corresponds to class 2a STANAG 4569. All in all, the Bear's floor can withstand a detonation of 6 kg (13 lbs.) of TNT. The vehicle has no standard armament but is equipped for the installation of remote-controlled weapons on the roof of the troop compartment (optional machine gun, automatic grenade launcher, or antitank missiles). Television

SPM-3 Medved (Bear) armored vehicle

cameras, a laser rangefinder, an onboard computer, and a liquid crystal color monitor can be installed for observation and firefighting. The prototypes were powered by the 300 hp YaMZ-7601 diesel engine or the YaMZ 536, which produces 312 hp. The engine, transmission, and cooling systems are simple to replace and service since they are mounted on a separate frame. The running gear consists of individually mounted wheels with torsion bar suspension, optionally with hydraulic telescopic shock absorbers. The Medved reaches a top speed of 110 kph (68 mph) on roads and 45 kph (28 mph) off-road—pretty fast for a bear. Two fuel tanks with a capacity of 300 liters (79 gal.) ensure a driving range of 1,000 km (621 mi.) on roads. The Medved can negotiate vertical obstacles and trenches with a height/width of up to 0.5 m (1.6 ft.).

SPM-3 Medved on the testing grounds. *topwar.ru*

SPM-3 Medved, seen from the front left. *ser-sarajkin.narod2.ru*

Let us move on to another family of armored transport vehicles / armored personnel carriers developed for the Russian armed forces. In a radio broadcast by Echo of Moscow on May 27, 2018, the head of the Main Armored Directorate of the Ministry of Defense, A. Shevchenko, said, "We are on the verge of introducing a new, promising, and advanced generation of vehicles into the Armed Forces of the Russian Federation, which will replace the famous Kamas and Urals. The general staff has already decided to equip tactical units with these vehicles of the Tornado family." These are designs by the Ural Automobile Works, which unveiled the unprotected version Ural-63704-0010 of the Tornado-U family at the Army Forum 2015.

SPM-3 Medved, rear view. *ser-sarajkin.narod2.ru*

Ural-63095 Tornado-U Armored Truck

The 6×6 chassis of the Tornado-U was supplied by the Ural-6370 truck, already used by the armed forces. Unlike it, the Tornado-U is mine resistant. The Tornado-U's cab is surrounded by a frame that is suitable both for an unarmored and an armored body. The installation of elements with dynamic protection is planned. The three-seater cab is equipped with air-conditioning, heating, and ventilation systems. Armored protection for the cargo area is not planned, but rain protection in the form of a waterproof awning is. The six-cylinder, in-line, multifuel diesel engine delivers 440 hp; the transmission comprises a manual gearbox and a two-stage transfer case. The drive axles are equipped with center and reduction gears, the center and rear axles with differential locks. The suspension consists of tried-and-tested leaf springs; braking is via a pneumatic dual-circuit brake system. The vehicle achieves a maximum speed of 100 kph (62 mph) on roads. Off-road, it is capable of negotiating trenches approximately 0.6 m (2 ft.) wide and fording bodies of water up to 1.8 m (5.9 ft.) deep. The armored version of the *T*ornado-U displayed at the Russia Arms Expo 2015 in Nizhny Tagil was built on the same chassis; however, it had an armored cab, which is protected against small-arms fire and shell fragments.

It is similar in size and shape to the unarmored model. The most noticeable difference concerns the doors and windows, which have firing hatches, and the presence of a cover for the windshield. There is also a round hatch on the roof of the cab. Armor plates of protection class 2 protect the crew from small-arms fire and explosions. According to the manufacturer, there will be further modules available for retrofitting in the near future that will raise the Tornado-U to protection class IV. Like the unarmored version, the armored version can also be equipped with various types of superstructures or flatbeds,

Ural-63095 Tornado-U armored truck

depending on customer requirements. Two new Tornado-U models are designed for use by the armed forces to transport supplies or personnel. They differ slightly. An unprotected truck can, of course, be operated only with a high risk of damage in combat zones. The vehicle with an armored cab, on the other hand, has far-greater chances of escape and survival in the face of ambushes and booby traps.

This also includes the Typhoon armored trucks, which the truck manufacturer Kamas and the Ural Automobile Plant developed for the Russian armed forces on behalf of the Russian Federation Ministry of Defense.

Ural-63095 Tornado-U armored truck, view from the front left. *Ural Automobile Factory Press Service*

Typhoon-K Armored Truck

The Kamas company designed the Typhoon-K armored truck by using the chassis and parts of the Kamas-63969 and Kamas-63968 trucks. In 2013, it presented two prototypes, and on May 9, 2014, the Typhoon-K rolled onto Moscow's Red Square for the first time. In December 2014, a first batch of thirty vehicles were delivered to units of the Southern Military District, followed by a second batch of twenty Typhoon-Ks in January 2015. By May 2017, the fleet already numbered 260 units.

The Typhoon-K is envisaged for the transport of personnel and freight in combat and crisis zones. With the necessary equipment, it can also be used as a command and staff vehicle, as a radio vehicle, and as a carrier of artillery pieces and surface-to-air missiles. The basic version, the Kamas-63968 Typhoon-K, is designed according to the Kamas scheme, with the driver's cab and engine compartment at the front and the functional module (loading module) in the rear. The Kamas-63969 Typhoon-K, with load-bearing body, combines driver and function modules. The vehicles are characterized by high ballistic protection and mine resistance. This is provided by steel armor in combination with ceramic panels of great hardness and density. Ceramic elements effectively destroy projectile cores and distribute the impact energy over the entire module body. According to available information, the ballistic protection corresponds to NATO protection class 3 in accordance with STANAG 4569, which means that it can withstand

Kamas-63968 Typhoon-K, view from the front right.
zr.ru

Kamas-63968 Typhoon-K, view from the rear.
ru.autowp.ru

Kamas-63968 Typhoon-K armored truck

Kamas Typhoon-K in a parade. *Russian Federation Defense Ministry*

7.62 mm steel-core projectiles. Special folding mats were developed to protect against the shaped-charge warheads of antitank missiles, which (should) prevent the formation of the classic hollow-charge jet. The V-shaped floor design of the Kamas-63968 deflects the pressure wave from mines away from the superstructure. Removable antimine pallets are to be added. Mine resistance is also planned for the Kamas-63969. As described above, the seats are suspended from the sides and roof and also have additional elements such as safety belts and headrests to protect the occupants from the effects of a mine detonation. According to reports, the Typhoon-K can withstand ground detonations of up to 8 kg (17.6 lbs.) of TNT.

The Kamas-63968 has two side doors in the driver's cab and a folding ramp in the rear for entry and exit. Emergency hatches are located in the roof of the function module. The Kamas-63969 has a door on the starboard side, a rear ramp, and emergency hatches in the roof. The roof also provides for the installation of a remote-controlled combat module from Elektromaschina, which accommodates machine guns of various calibers or an automatic grenade launcher. Both types are powered by a Kamas-740.354-450 diesel engine, which delivers 450 hp. The 6×6 chassis uses large-diameter wheels (10.00-20) with 16.00 R 20 tread tires. The hydropneumatic suspension contributes to a high level of driving comfort and can be adapted to the terrain conditions. The armored trucks are also equipped with GALS-D1M onboard monitoring systems, which report engine malfunctions, for example. Finally, the vehicles demonstrate outstanding off-road capability; they can cope with gradients of up to 30° and ford bodies of water up to 1.75 m (5.7 ft.) deep. The maximum speed on road is 105 kph (65 mph).

Typhoon-U Armored Truck

Production of the Typhoon-U began at the Ural Automobile Factory in 2014, and in 2015 it entered service with the Russian army. By July 2015 there were thirty vehicles in the complement of the southern military district. Like the Typhoon-K, the Typhoon-U was intended to take on a variety of tactical missions, transport people and freight, and tow guns and trailers on all kinds of roads and off-road. It was intended that several dozen derivatives of the basic type would be created for motorized rifle, airborne, and other units. At present, the Typhoon-U series consists of two armored vehicles: the Ural-63095, with a three-man armored cab and a separate module for twelve persons, and the Ural-63099, with an armored standard module.

Access to the cab and the function module is by way of two side doors and a hinged tail ramp (or an installed ramp door). There are two hatches in the roof.

The designers of the Typhoon-U placed great emphasis on maximum protection against mines and gunfire. Between the engine compartment and the driver's and function modules, there are armor steel and ceramic plates with the protection level of combat vehicles. According to reports, the basic version of the Typhoon-U meets class 3 standards of protection as per NATO-STANAG 4569, and the version with armored cab and load module meets class 4 of this standard (protection against 14.5 mm armor-piercing ammunition). Mine resistance is largely the same as that offered by the Typhoon-K (see above), with the front wheels, which most frequently set off mines, moving outside the frame profile. Thanks to these mine-resistance measures, the Typhoon vehicles have ten times the protection level of a standard truck. It is equivalent to NATO protection class 3 as per STANAG 4569 (explosive device of up to 8 kg [17.6 lbs.] of TNT detonated beneath the driver's cab).

Steps were also taken to reduce the visual and electronic signatures. These include coatings of Cape material, camouflage nets, and antiradar mats made of rubber fabric. The engine compartment cover can be "flushed" with air to shield heat radiation.

Ural-63099 Typhoon-U, view from the front left. *zr.ru*

Ural-63099 Typhoon-U armored truck

There is no standard armament for the Typhoon vehicles, but they can be equipped with remote-control combat modules. There are also firing hatches for small arms in the windows.

The Typhoons are powered by a new six-cylinder, in-line, diesel, multifuel engine, with a YaMZ-5367 turbocharger producing 450 hp. A hydromechanical automatic transmission and a two-stage manual transfer case were also fitted. The 6×6 independent wheel suspension operates pneumohydraulically. Differential locks and the tire pressure system in conjunction with a powerful engine ensure high off-road capability. The Typhoons can ford water obstacles up to 1.8 m (5.9 ft.) deep, climb walls up to 0.6 m (2 ft.) high, and cross ditches up to 0.6 m (2 ft.) wide. They can reach speeds of up to 40–50 kph (25–31 mph) off-road and up to 105 kph (65 mph) on roads. Two 300-liter (79 gal.) fuel tanks guarantee a driving range of up to 1,400 km (870 mi.). An onboard monitoring system reports irregularities in the engine and drivetrain.

Ural-63099 Typhoon-U. *wikipedia.org*

Vityaz Multipurpose Tracked Vehicle

Now we come to vehicles of a very special kind, which are part of the equipment of the 80th and 200th Motorized Rifle Brigades in the snowy Far North of Russia; namely, the articulated multipurpose tracked carriers of the Vityaz (Warrior or Sword) family. They have unique off-road mobility and speed even in the most difficult terrain (swamps, deep snow, mountainous terrain) and are suitable for operations in extreme climatic conditions (+40°C to −50°C). The Vityaz family includes the DT-10P, DT-20P, and DT-30P amphibious transport vehicles, with a load capacity of 10, 20, and 30 tons, respectively, as well as the DT-10, DT-20, and DT-30 nonamphibious vehicles, with the same transport capacity.

Development of these multipurpose all-terrain vehicles, consisting of articulated tracked vehicles, began in the USSR in the 1970s; similarities with the vehicles produced by the Swedish company Hägglunds are probably not purely coincidental. In any case, leading Soviet science, research, and design offices were involved in their development. Series production ran from 1982 to 1986 at the Ishimbay Transport Machine-Building Plant, better known as the Vityaz Machine-Building Plant. All Vityaz vehicles consist of front and rear units, which are connected by a steering unit with an articulated joint. The front carrier accommodates the driver and the crew of four to seven, with the engine behind. The cabin has autonomous heating and ventilation systems that provide the crew with comfortable working conditions in all types of weather. The rear carrier can carry a wide variety of cargo or weapons. Vehicles in the first series were powered by a V-46-5S diesel engine, producing 710 hp. The more powerful DT-10PM and DT-30PM were equipped with liquid-cooled, four-stroke V, multifuel diesel engines with direct fuel injection and YaMZ-840.10 centrifugal compressors, which delivered 800 hp. The engine still starts at ambient temperatures of −50°C. The hydrodynamic four-speed transformer transmission with limited slip differential can be replaced by a six-speed automatic transmission. The brake system uses pneumatic band brakes. A swivel clutch was developed especially for the Vityaz family, which enables the front and rear units to rotate independently of each other in all planes. A characteristic feature is the hydraulic cylinders, which allow the vehicle parts to be pushed apart or together horizontally or vertically in any direction. The horizontal folding cylinders act as a pivoting device and ensure that the vehicle is very maneuverable. The vertical hydraulic cylinders are shock absorbers and ensure very smooth running. Thanks to the swivel coupling and hydraulic cylinders, the vehicle can climb vertical obstacles up to 1.5 m (4.9 ft.) and cross trenches up to 4 m (13 ft.) wide, thanks to the vertical-cylinder-blocking system. The swivel coupling also ensures maximum traction. The torsion-bar-sprung running gear comprises four wide metal tracks with welded steel crossbars and rubber pads, four drive sprockets, and ten road wheels on each side. The spacing of the crossbars contributes to

The DT-10P Vityaz articulated multipurpose tracked vehicle, front view from the right

The DT-10P Vityaz negotiating an obstacle

effective self-cleaning of the chain from dirt, snow, and ice. The design of the drive wheels prevents damage to the running gear at temperatures below 0°C.

The Vityaz reaches a maximum speed of 36 kph (22 mph) on roads and up to 4 kph (2.5 mph) in water. Fuel capacity is sufficient for a range of 500 km (310 mi.) on roads, but this can be increased through the installation of additional fuel tanks. The characteristics of the tracked running gear, the ability to overcome water obstacles, and the high degree of maneuverability under the most-difficult terrain conditions make the Vityaz models unique transport vehicles in snowy and swampy regions, covering long distances that are inaccessible to other ground vehicles. Even Santa Claus in Rovaniemi, Finland, is said to have ordered a Vityaz.

Back to the development of Russian armored units. In the first decades of the twenty-first century, the Russian Ministry of Defense assumed that Russia had "no enemies in the West." The Russian Federation undertook large-scale reductions of its armed forces and created mixed brigades optimized for fighting terrorist groups. Troops were also redeployed from the western borders to the interior of the country. This created a zone hundreds of kilometers

The DT-10P Vityaz articulated multipurpose tracked vehicle

wide in the western part of Russia, in which only a fraction of the forces previously stationed there remained. At the same time, NATO continued its eastward expansion and moved ever closer to the Russians. NATO regularly conducts military exercises in the neighboring countries, the design and course of which point to the defense against possible Russian aggression.

In March 2014, relations between Russia and the NATO states were once again exacerbated by the annexation of Crimea. According to the then NATO secretary general Rasmussen, Russia was seen as a threat to Ukraine's sovereignty and, in particular, as a threat to European security as a whole. Rasmussen said that the alliance would continue to expand eastward and strengthen its presence in the alliance's eastern European member states. Rasmussen saw the events in Ukraine as a signal for European countries and NATO members to increase their military spending, and explained that Russia was currently behaving "more like an adversary than a partner." On April 1, 2014, NATO announced the end of cooperation with Russia.

The events in Ukraine led to a change in the overall military policy situation. The potential of Russian troops in the west in 2014 was clearly not sufficient to counter a new threat from the southwest. The maneuvers held from February 26 to March 3, 2014, which amounted to a review of the readiness of units of the western and central military districts (units of the 2nd, 6th, and 20th Armies) and included the command of the air forces and air defense, as well as units of the Northern and Baltic fleets (a total of about 150,000 troops), demonstrated Russia's inability to concentrate a sufficient grouping for actions against Ukraine (both defensive and offensive). The Russian 2nd Army was located southeast of the central regions of Russia (from Orenburg to Penza), and the 6th Army covered the northwest (roughly the Petersburg area and the Pskov region). A thin chain of tactical battalion groups assembled along the Russian-Ukrainian border (excluding Crimea) in early March comprised only around 10,000 soldiers. At the end of April, there were around 40,000 soldiers on the Russian-Ukrainian border (excluding Crimea), which was nowhere near enough to occupy a 1,900 km (1,178 mi.) front. Under these conditions, four new divisions were created in Russia, and the armies were "revived" as operational-strategic formations. Below is an overview of the current tank and motorized rifle divisions of the Russian army (2020).

2nd Taman Guards Motorized Rifle Division

Command and division headquarters
1st Guards Rifle Regiment, Unit No. 31135 (location: Kalininets)
15th Guards Rifle Regiment, Unit No. 31134 (location: Kalininets)
1st Guards Tank Regiment, Unit No. 58190 (location: Kalininets)
147th Guards Self-Propelled Artillery Regiment, Unit No. 73966 (location: Kalininets)
1117th Surface-to-Air Missile Regiment, Unit No. 51382 (location: Golitsnyo, Odintsovo District, Moscow Oblast)
1174th Independent Guards Antitank Battalion, Unit No. 51381 (location: Kalininets)
136th Independent Guards Reconnaissance Battalion, Unit No. 51387 (location: Kalininets)
211th Independent Guards Combat Engineer Battalion, Unit No. 77707 (location: Kalininets)
47th Independent Guards Telecommunications Battalion, Unit No. 56139 (location: Kalininets)
1063rd Independent Supply Battalion, Unit No. 56166 (location: Kalininets)
370th Independent Medical Battalion, Unit No. 57062 (location: Kalininets)
one independent company of unmanned aerial vehicles (drones, UAVs) (location: Kalininets)
one independent company for electronic warfare (location: Kalininets)
one independent recovery company (location: Kalininets)

Currently (2020), the division has finished equipping itself with BMP-2M infantry fighting vehicles with increased combat effectiveness, which have received the new Berezhok combat module. The module includes a 30 mm automatic cannon, a 7.62 mm machine gun, an automatic grenade launcher, and antitank missiles. In the future, the division will be equipped with Armata main battle tanks, Koalitsiya-SV self-propelled howitzers, Kurganets infantry fighting vehicles, Boomerang armored personnel carriers, and other state-of-the-art technology, as well as the latest fire control systems and drones. Relevant Russian media refer to the Taman division as the "division of the future."

Tanks of the 2nd Taman Guards Motorized Rifle Division on an exercise

Flag party of the 2nd Taman Guards Motorized Rifle Division during a parade

Motorized 3rd Guards Rifle Division

Command and division headquarters, Unit No. 54046 (location: Valuyki)
237th Guards Rifle Regiment, Unit No. 91726 (location: Zoloti)
245th Guards Rifle Regiment
252nd Guards Rifle Regiment, Unit No. 91711 (location: Boguchar)
752nd Motorized Rifle Regiment, Unit No. 34670 (location: Valuyki and Zoloti)
99th Guards Self-Propelled Artillery Regiment, Unit No. 91727 (location: Boguchar)
1143rd Surface-to-Air Missile Regiment (location: Belgorod region)
84th Independent Reconnaissance Battalion, Unit No. 22263 (location: Valuyki)
159th Independent Antitank Battalion
692nd Independent Telecommunications Battalion, Unit No. 22463 (location: Valuyki)
337th Independent Combat Engineer Battalion, Unit No. 91717 (location: Boguchar)
91st Independent Supply Battalion, Unit No. 54366 (location: Boguchar)
231st Independent Medical Battalion, Unit No. 83833 (location: Boguchar)
one independent company of unmanned aerial vehicles (drones)
one independent electronic-warfare company (location: Valuyki)
one independent NBC company

Main battle tanks and armored personnel carriers of the 3rd Guards Motorized Rifle Division during an exercise

4th Kantemirovskaya Guards Tank Division

Command and division headquarters (location: Naro-Fominsk)
12th Guards Tank Regiment, Unit No. 31985 (location: Naro-Fominsk)
13th Guards Tank Regiment, Unit No. 32010 (location: Naro-Fominsk)
423rd Guards Rifle Regiment, Unit No. 91701 (location: Naro-Fominsk)
275th Guards Self-Propeller Artillery Regiment, Unit No. 73941 (location: Naro-Fominsk)
538th Guards Surface-to-Air Missile Regiment, Unit No. 51383 (location: Naro-Fominsk)
37th Independent Reconnaissance Battalion, Unit No. 54919 (location: Naro-Fominsk)
413th Independent Telecommunications Battalion, Unit No. 56132 (location: Naro-Fominsk)
330th Independent Guards Combat Engineer Battalion, Unit No. 80808 (location: Naro-Fominsk)
1088th Independent Supply Battalion, Unit No. 56164 (location: Naro-Fominsk)
165th Independent Guards Medical Battalion, Unit No. 57069 (location: Naro-Fominsk)
one independent company of unmanned aerial vehicles (location: Naro-Fominsk)
one independent electronic-warfare company (location: Naro-Fominsk)
one independent NBC company (location: Naro-Fominsk)
one independent recovery company (location: Naro-Fominsk)
one independent military police company (location: Naro-Fominsk)

The Russian Defense Ministry decided to equip the division with updated T-80BVM main battle tanks with GAZ turbine engines. These power plants gave the T-80BVM exceptional speed and maneuverability. And the latest fire control system enabled the tank to engage ground and even aerial targets in any weather, day and night. According to experts, thanks to its new "jet" tanks, the 4th Division was particularly well suited to the European theater of war. The tank battalions and regiments could move very quickly and stood out on account of their great offensive and defensive capabilities.

A main battle tank of the 4th Kantemirovskaya Guards Tank Regiment during a winter exercise

42nd Motorized Guards Rifle Division

Command and division headquarters
(location: Khankala, Czech Republic)
291st Guards Rifle Regiment, Unit No. 65384
(location: Borsoi, Czech Republic)
70th Guards Rifle Regiment, Unit No. 71718
(location: Schali, Czech Republic)
71st Guards Rifle Regiment, Unit No. 16544
(location: Stanitsa Kalinovskaya, Czech Republic)
one independent tank battalion
(location: Czech Republic)
50th Guards Self-Propeller Artillery Regiment
(location: Schali, Czech Republic)
1203rd Guards Surface-to-Air Missile Regiment
(location: Czech Republic)
one independent reconnaissance battalion
(location: Khankala, Czech Republic)
one independent antitank battalion
478th Independent Telecommunications Battalion
539th Independent Combat Engineer Battalion
474th Independent Supply Battalion
106th Medical Battalion
one independent company of unmanned
aerial vehicles
one independent electronic-warfare company
one independent NBC company

A special feature of this division is the presence of a special antiterrorist battalion in each of the motorized rifle regiments. This enables the regiments to conduct "asymmetrical warfare" and to fight against irregular forces in addition to waging tactical warfare on the battlefield. Taking into consideration the special aspects of this type of warfare, the division was given only one tank battalion instead of a tank regiment.

BTR-82A of the 42nd Motorized Guards Rifle Division

90th Guards Tank Division

Command and division headquarters (Chebarkul)
6th Guards Rifle Regiment, Unit No. 93992 (location: Chebarkul)
80th Tank Regiment, Unit No. 87441 (location: Chebarkul)
239th Guards Tank Regiment, Unit No. 98547 (location: Chebarkul)
228th Motorized Rifle Regiment, Unit No. 22316 (location: Yekaterinburg)
400th Self-Propelled Artillery Regiment, Unit No. 15871 (location: Chebarkul)
one surface-to-air missile regiment (location: Chebarkul)
30th Independent Reconnaissance Battalion, Unit No. 17654 (location: Chebarkul)
351st Independent Combat Engineer Battalion, Unit No. 84975 (location: Chebarkul)
33rd Independent Telecommunications Battalion, Unit No. 94015 (location: Chelyabinsk region, Chebarkul)
1122nd Independent Supply Battalion, Unit No. 25481 (location: Chebarkul)
1st Company: ammunition
2nd Company: ammunition
3rd Company: fuel and lubricants
4th Company: supply (food, clothing, equipment)
5th Support Company with telecommunications platoon
26th Independent Medical Battalion, Unit No. 86000 (location: Chelyabinsk region, Chebarkul)

The division was the first unit to be fully equipped with the upgraded BMP-2M infantry fighting vehicle. Since 2019 the division has received new T-90M tanks (upgraded T-90A tanks, with increased firepower, improved targeting system, and better armor protection). The division is regarded as a kind of training and experimental unit for developing/testing new tactics and organizations.

Flag party of the 90th Guards Rifle Division during the march-past

127th Motorized Rifle Division

Command and division headquarters, Unit No. 44980 (location: Sergeyevska)
114th Guards Rifle Regiment, Unit No. 24776 (location: Ussuriysk)
394th Motorized Rifle Regiment, Unit No. 25573 (location: Sergeyevska)
872nd Self-Propelled Artillery Regiment, Unit No. 75234
77th Independent Reconnaissance Battalion
84th Independent Tank Battalion, Unit No. 82588
243rd Independent Combat Engineer Battalion, Unit No. 93580
928th independent Telecommunications Battalion, Unit No. 14241
42nd Independent Medical Battalion

The 127th Motorized Rifle Division was established in the Eastern Military District (Siberia) in 2018. The decision to establish the division was announced by the Ministry of Defense on May 25, 2018. The division headquarters and one of the motorized rifle regiments were formed from the 59th Motorized Rifle Brigade. Another motorized rifle regiment was formed from the 60th Motorized Rifle Brigade. The 59th and 60th Motorized Rifle Brigades were formed in 2009 from units of the disbanded 127th Machine Gun and Artillery Division.

144th Motorized Guards Rifle Regiment

Command and division headquarters (location: Yelnya, Smolensk region)
488th Motorized Rifle Regiment (location: Klintsy, Bryansk region): 31 T-72B3s, 129 BMP-2s, 18 122 mm 2S1 Gvozdika, 8 2S12 100 mm mortars, 4 9A34 Strela-10 surface-to-air missile launchers, 4 3SU 2S6M Tunguska self-propelled antiaircraft guns
182nd Motorized Rifle Regiment (location: Zaimishche, Bryansk Oblast)
254th Motorized Rifle Regiment (location: Yelnya)
228th Tank Regiment (location: Yelnya)
856th Guards Self-Propelled Artillery Regiment, Unit No. 23857 (location: Pochep, Bryansk region): 36 152 mm 2S19 Msta-S, 18 RS3O 2B17-1 Tornado-G multiple rocket launchers
1259th Surface-to-Air Missile Regiment
148th Independent Reconnaissance Battalion, Unit No. 23872 (location: Smolensk)
1281st Independent Antitank Battalion (location: Yelnya)
295th Independent Combat Engineer Battalion (location: Yelnya)
686th independent Telecommunications Battalion (location: Smolensk)
1032nd Independent Supply Battalion
one independent medical battalion
one independent company of unmanned aerial vehicles
one independent electronic-warfare company
one independent ABC company

Swearing-in of recruits of the 144th Motorized Rifle Division

150th Motorized Rifle Division

Command and division headquarters (Novocherkassk)
68th Guards Tank Regiment, Unit No. 91714 (location: Persianovskiy)
163rd Guards Tank Regiment, Unit No. 84839
102nd Motorized Rifle Regiment, Unit No. 91706 (location: Persianovskiy)
103rd Motorized Rifle Regiment, Unit No. 91708 (location: Rostov region, Novocherkassk)
381st Guards Artillery Regiment, Unit No. 24390
933rd Surface-to-Air Missile Regiment (location: Rostov region, Millerovo) (9K331M Tor-M2U surface-to-air missile launchers)
174th Independent Reconnaissance Battalion, Unit No. 22265 (location: Rostov region, Novocherkassk, Kadamovsky)
224th Independent Antitank Battalion
539th Independent Combat Engineer Battalion
258th Independent Telecommunications Battalion, Unit No. 84881 (location: Rostov region, Novocherkassk, Kadamovsky)
152nd Independent Supply Battalion, Unit No. 15272 (location: Rostov region, Novocherkassk, Kadamovsky)
195th Independent Medical Battalion
one independent unmanned aerial vehicle company
one independent ABC company
one independent electronic-warfare company
one independent repair company
one independent recovery company
one independent military police company

The division received new or upgraded combat equipment and a special structure: while a motorized rifle division usually consists of three rifle regiments and one tank regiment, the 150th Division was given two tank regiments and two motorized rifle regiments, making it a versatile hybrid—it can take on the tasks of both a motorized rifle division and a tank division. The unit does not have the numerical strength of a conventional motorized rifle division but surpasses a tank division in terms of firepower. The division was also designed for modern "high-tech warfare." At the beginning of 2020, there were reports that the Russian Ministry of Defense intended to set up a new motorized rifle division at the 11th Army Corps in the Kaliningrad region (formerly Königsberg, northern East Prussia). This division, which will presumably be assigned the number "1," will comprise (at least) the following units:

Ceremonial parade by units of the 150th Motorized Rifle Division

- 79th Independent Motorized Guards Rifle Brigade, Unit No. 90151 (location: Gusev/Gumbinnen)
- 7th Independent Motorized Guards Rifle Regiment, Unit No. 06414 (location: Kaliningrad/Königsberg)
- 11th Independent Tank Regiment (location: Gusev/ Gumbinnen)

The tank regiments of modern Russian tank and motorized rifle divisions have the following organization:

- Command/regimental headquarters
- 3 tank battalions
- 1 motorized rifle battalion
- 1 self-propelled-howitzer battalion
- 1 surface-to-air-missile battalion
- 1 sniper company
- 1 reconnaissance company
- 1 combat engineer company
- 1 telecommunications company
- 1 repair company
- 1 fire control and artillery reconnaissance battery under the artillery commander
- 1 ABC platoon

The tank regiments are equipped with T-72B3, T-72B3M, T-80BVM, and T-90M upgraded main battle tanks.

Organization of the self-propelled-artillery regiments of the tank and motorized rifle divisions:

- Command/regimental headquarters
- 2 self-propelled-howitzer battalions
- 1 rocket artillery battalion
- 1 fire control battery
- 1 artillery reconnaissance battery
- 1 repair company
- supply company
- command platoon

Organization of the antiaircraft regiments of the tank and motorized rifle divisions:

- Command/regimental headquarters
- 4 surface-to-air-missile batteries
- 1 technical battery
- 1 repair company
- supply company

The reconstituted divisions are the main components of the reconstituted tank armies and the five mixed armies. The 1st Tank, 20th Guards, and 20th Army are in the Western Military District; the 8th Guards and 58th Army in the Southern Military District; the 41st Army in the Central Military District; and the 5th Army in the Eastern Military District.

As a rule, in addition to the army command an army consists of the following:

- 1–3 mixed divisions
- 1–3 mixed brigades
- 1 artillery brigade
- 1 surface-to-air-missile brigade
- 1 independent reconnaissance brigade
- 1 logistics brigade
- 1 combat engineer regiment
- 1 NBC regiment

These armies are intended to fulfill offensive and defensive tasks and serve as a reserve. Their cores are made up of the tank and motorized rifle divisions. The tank and motorized rifle brigades are regarded as the operational shock troops of the armies. They are intended to penetrate the enemy's defenses, roll them up from behind, and serve as "army fire brigades" in defense. So-called supernova brigades have a balanced composition with increased striking power; they have fully fledged reconnaissance, rocket artillery, and antitank battalions.

Presentation of flags by the commander of the 1st Guards Tank Army, Major General A. Chaiko

T-72s in Syria

Taking into account its operational experiences in Syria, the Russian military has developed various tactics to increase the effectiveness of main battle tanks in combat, particularly in "asymmetric" conflicts. First and foremost, this includes the so-called tank carousel, which can consist of three, six, nine, or more main battle tanks. They move continuously in a circle—one fires, the other retreats to the rear and reloads, the third advances, and so on until the mission is completed or the ammunition has run out. The "carousel" is used when the strength and weaponry of the enemy is unknown or not precisely known—whether tanks, antitank missiles, or grenade launchers. The intense "harassing fire" of up to ten shots per minute forces the enemy to return fire and give themselves away. And then, camouflaged "sniper tanks" manned by specially trained crews lying in wait come into play. They identify the enemy and engage their position(s) with precise fire. The "tank carousel" is particularly effective in conjunction with the so-called Syrian wall, made of sand, earth, rubble, or similar materials with natural or purposely made "embrasures." The tanks move continuously along the parapet and fire through the "embrasure(s)" before taking cover behind the rampart after each shot. Since they are in constant motion, it is almost impossible to target and hit them. To

Russian T-72 main battle tank in action with the Syrian army

deceive enemy observers, the commander chooses a different "embrasure" each time, giving the enemy the impression that he is dealing with a larger number of tanks.

A single tank platoon can thus simulate an entire battalion. The only important thing is that the rampart covers the weak points that every tank has (mainly on its hull and running gear). Although the "carousel" is primarily a defensive tactic, it allows a quick transition to the attack or can create good conditions for it.

Another interesting tactic is the "tank trouser." The tank shoots alternately from two adjacent trenches—the main trench and the reserve trench. It does not stay in one place for more than three to five seconds. The tank "dives" into the trench, fires, engages reverse gear, and moves quickly to the next trench. The enemy's antitank defense has little or no time to react. The tanks can operate in pairs, determine their own speed, and change positions—the more chaotically, the better.

The well-known reference work *Military Balance* put the number of Russian main battle tanks in divisions and brigades at 2,780 in 2018. This estimate agrees quite well with an extrapolation based on reliable strength reports from some units—a total of 2,685 units. In this context, the overview of tank units and units of the modern Russian army on the website ALTYN73LIVEJORNAL.COM is of interest. It does not take into account those vehicles in depots or under repair or the Russian dual system, which "stores" tanks and equipment sets somewhere in the depths of the country in reserve bases so that they can be quickly supplied to the troops if necessary. Including these reserves, the Russian land forces are estimated to have 12,000–15,000 main battle tanks. Deputy Defense Minister D. V. Bulgakov commented on this in November 2017 in the newspaper *Krasnaya Zvezda*: "In the five-year period from 2012 to 2017, more than 25,000 new tanks and items of motor vehicle equipment and 4,000 items of modern missile and artillery weapons were delivered to the troops, making the Russian Federation the world leader in terms of the number of main battle tanks, infantry fighting vehicles, and multiple rocket launchers."

According to the general, eighty new types were introduced into service in five years, including rocket and artillery weapons, tanks, wheeled vehicles, special vehicles, etc. "The percentage [of systems] of modern technology today is over 50 percent," Bulgakov said, adding that defense industry companies had increased the serviceability of equipment to 98 percent: "Everything in our army is now on the move; everything is ready for use."

Currently (2020), the Russian tank forces are divided into tank divisions, tank brigades, and tank battalions of motorized rifle brigades. They are regarded by the Ministry of Defense as the core of the land forces. Their main tasks are

- in defense, in direct support of motorized rifle units during defensive operations or counterattacks; and
- on the offensive, in tactical-operational action into the depths of enemy territory.

The tank units are capable of acting independently day and night, breaking up strong enemy formations, overcoming radioactively contaminated zones, and forcing their way across water obstacles. They are also designed to withstand superior enemy forces.

The technical base of the Russian tank fleet is formed by the T-72 and T-80 main battle tanks, which were developed and built during the Soviet era and upgraded to the T-72B3 (or B3M) and T-80BVM standard. There are also a number of T-90Ms. The tank arm has high hopes for the promising Armata family in the form of the T-14 main battle tank, the T-15 heavy infantry fighting vehicle, and the T-16 armored recovery vehicle, as well as other modern developments. In addition, the Armata family is to be joined by a heavy armored vehicle with increased firepower, which is already being marketed as a "tank killer." Thanks to innovative digital network systems, the Armata family of vehicles can interact with one other and with other vehicles, units, and formations on the battlefield to an unprecedented extent. In principle, the Russian tank arm does not differ significantly from its predecessors in the Second World War in terms of the structure of its formations. However, the armaments company UVS (Uralvagonzavod) has proposed (probably not entirely unselfishly) a new mixed structure in which T-14s, T-15s, T-16s, self-propelled howitzers, and mine-clearing and other special vehicles work more closely together in one formation.

As for the Armata infantry fighting vehicles, they are able for the first time to accompany main battle tanks with an equal level of protection. Old thin-walled infantry fighting vehicles and armored personnel carriers cannot follow the T-14 without having to fear heavy losses. In addition, the T-15, armed with a 57 mm gun, can engage secondary targets such as antitank weapons, infantry fighting vehicles, combat drones, and helicopters and can virtually keep them away from the T-14, so that the main battle tank can concentrate on its main task—engaging the enemy's main battle tanks.

Tanks and motorized infantry during the final parade of Exercise West, 2018

In 2018, a procurement contract was signed for the delivery of a total of 132 Armata vehicles to the armed forces. According to a statement by the then deputy minister of defense, Yuri Borisov, in February 2018, the delivery includes two "battalion sets" of T-14s and one "battalion set" of T-15s to the motorized 2nd Taman Guards Rifle Division, which is to test the vehicles in the battalion and division framework and develop new tactics and organizations for them. The division will also serve as a training and instruction unit for other formations.

Nevertheless, the Russian tank fleet still consists mainly of the three main types—the T-72, T-80, and T-90 and modified versions of them. From 1985 to 1996, the T-72B in its three variants, the T-72B, T-72B1, and T-72B model 1989, was the most common. Starting in 1998, the armaments manufacturer Uralvagonzavod worked on further combat upgrades of the T-72B. It delivered the T-72BA from 1998 to 2005 and the T-72B3 from 2011 to 2015. The T-72B3s built from 2016 onward differ considerably from older T-72B3s, which is why they bear the unofficial designation T-72B3 Model 2016 or T-72B3M.

The T-80 main battle tank is represented by the T-80BV and T-80U versions (manufactured 1983–98). Vehicles modernized from 2005 onward are known as the T-80BVM and T-80UE-1.

T-90A (2004–10) and T-90M main battle tanks (from 2019) form the smallest tank group—apart from the T-14—especially since production batches from 2011 to 2019 were not delivered to the troops, who received another batch of brand-new T-90Ms only in 2020.

In the last ten years, the Russian armed forces have deployed thirty-nine new tank battalions, thirty-two of which have been stationed in the west and south. The total number of main battle tanks has almost doubled since then. Deliveries from industry were not sufficient to equip the new units; in addition to transfers from the military districts, it was therefore necessary to transfer vehicles from the brigades of the central and eastern military districts. The tank industry has greatly accelerated the pace of modernization of older types. While from 1998 to 2010 it brought around 150 T-72Bs and T-80Us up to the level of T-72BAs and T-80UE-1s, from 2011 to 2020 the troops received more than 600 T-72B3s, 300 T-72B3Ms, and 60 T-80BVMs. After a break of around ten years, the delivery of new tanks was resumed. The units listed below have a total of 2,685 main battle tanks. The proportion of new and upgraded vehicles (manufactured in 2000 and later) is approximately 45 percent or 1,200 vehicles.

One small "tidbit" should not go unmentioned at this point: Uralvagonzavod received an order from the Ministry of Defense to resume production of the T-34/85. These veterans are to be used for "ceremonial and representative tasks" and to appeal to the "military patriotism" of the younger generation. The Russian Ministry of Defense plans to create an entire T-34 regiment in the Moscow region and to establish a T-34 battalion in each military district. In addition, one company per division and each armored school are to be equipped with a T-34 company, and each brigade with a T-34 platoon. The T-34s are to make public appearances primarily during the annual "Victory Parades" on May 9 and at various "military patriotic events." A total of four hundred T-34/85s are to be built, for which the Ministry of Defense is providing over ten billion rubles. At the request of the ministry, Uralvagonzavod is also to examine the possibilities of reproducing other "oldies"—SU-100s, SU-76Ms, T-34/76s, IS-2Ms, IS-3Ms, and even T-35s. The only thing missing is German competition in the form of Panzerkampfwagen IIIs and IVs, Tigers, and Panthers, because what would the most beautiful army be without opponents.

CHAPTER 8
RUSSIAN TANK FORCES IN THE WAR IN UKRAINE, 2022 TO PRESENT

The basis of the Russian troops that invaded Ukraine in February 2022 was battalion tactical groups (BTGs). The appearance of BTGs in the Russian army is associated with the reduction of the Russian armed forces in the early years of the 2000s. Then, under the pretext of increasing combat readiness and mobility, it was decided to reduce the divisions to the level of brigades. At the same time, there was a sharp reduction in the officer corps (from 355,000 in 2008 to 142,000 in 2011), and enrollment in military schools from 2009 to 2012 was stopped. Along with the insufficiently active recruitment of ordinary soldiers for contract service, this led to the fact that in 2013–14, instead of the planned fully combat-ready motorized rifle and tank brigades, it was possible to staff only reinforced battalions (battalion tactical groups) with officers, contract soldiers, and trained conscripts.

It should be noted here that the BTG is by no means a recent creation. For the first time, such formations were created in the Soviet army during the war in Afghanistan (1979–89), where they served as small, combat-ready rapid-deployment forces. During the first and second Chechen Wars (1994–96 and 1999–2009), such formations were formed on a temporary basis due to the lack of manpower and equipment to complete brigades and divisions.

In 2014–15, Russian battalion tactical groups were staffed with contract and conscript soldiers, but after 2017, when the number of contract soldiers in the RF armed forces greatly exceeded the quality of conscripts, BTGs have been staffed entirely on a contract basis. However, the remaining one to two battalions in motorized rifle brigades are still staffed with conscripts. In some brigades, there is a significant difference in the involvement of conscripts in combat training—they are more often left for household work, outfits, and guard duty, and BTG and contract units are more often involved in training.

At present, the BTG is defined as a temporary formation with high operational flexibility. The BTG is created to perform specific tasks in motorized rifle and tank brigades on the basis of one battalion and its assigned combat units, combat support units, and logistics and medical support units.

The basis of the BTG's firepower is combat units:

- 2 motorized rifle companies (about 200 people + 34 armored personnel carriers or infantry fighting vehicles)
- tank company (10 tanks)
- artillery battalion: there can be a howitzer battalion (18 guns), rocket (18 RS3Os), or mixed (12 guns + 6 rockets)
- antiaircraft missile battery (equipped with mobile short-range air defense systems and portable antiaircraft missile systems)
- sniper platoon
- platoon of antitank guided missiles

Depending on the tasks to be solved, additional forces can be attached to the BTG; for example, chemical- and radiological-reconnaissance units or flamethrower units. Combat support units serve to solve specific tasks. They include the following:

- special-forces unit
- reconnaissance units
- air controllers
- electronic-warfare platoon
- unmanned aerial vehicle (UAV) operator team

Battalion tactical group before the start of field exercises

Units of the battalion tactical group during exercises

The number of BTG personnel can vary from six hundred to nine hundred soldiers and officers. In total, it includes about two hundred units with a variety of equipment, using both combat and conventional transport. On the march, the BTG forms a column about 10 km long.

On August 10, 2021, speaking at the Youth Educational Forum "Territory of Meanings," the then minister of defense of the Russian Federation, Sergei Shoigu, said, "Today we actually have troops of constant readiness. Today we do not have someone to gather, to find; we have everything in constant readiness. We have such a formation—battalion tactical groups. These are the ones who, when the button is pressed, are ready to go out of the gate in an hour. We have 168 of them today, and this is a very high figure."

The minister spoke about the immediate groups, which are fully staffed, and there are no conscripts in them. In modern conditions, they must be formed in advance and are unified in composition and means of strengthening. They can hardly be called created for a specific task, but they are a universal working tool that can be used immediately. The number of BTGs corresponds to the possibilities of the budget, primarily in terms of staffing. The number of contract soldiers and sergeants should increase to 500,000 people in the future, which will increase the number of combat-ready groups.

For the invasion of Ukraine on February 24, 2022, Russia fielded 125 BTGs with a total of approximately 125,000 troops. At that time, it was 80 percent of all ground combat forces in Russia.

On September 21, the president of the Russian Federation, Vladimir Putin, announced partial mobilization, which, according to Sergei Shoigu, ended on October 28. During the campaign, 300,000 Russians were called up and 18,000 volunteers were recruited. As of early November, more than 80,000 of them had already been sent to the front in Ukraine.

The experience of using battalion tactical groups in combat operations in Ukraine has shown the advantages of these formations and revealed their disadvantages.

The advantages include such a quality of BTG as autonomy. If we are talking about a local conflict of low intensity, then the BTG, with the support of reconnaissance, tank escort, and a combined missile and artillery battalion, independently conducts combat operations for two or three days without additional support.

Ability to create reconnaissance and strike circuits that provide tactical interaction between unmanned aerial vehicles and fire reinforcement assets. This increases the speed of hitting targets and creates tactical superiority.

The main Russian combat tank in Ukraine is the T-72 B3M

The presence of large-caliber artillery weapons makes it possible to optimally combine the means of fire destruction of the enemy and ensures the breakthrough of his defenses. Among the advantages of the BTG is the ability to adjust the composition and size of the group, depending on the task.

During the early stages of the war in Ukraine, when the BTGs were dealing with relatively small enemy units largely disorganized by the surprise attack, the Russian BTGs achieved significant successes. Usually, the battle was preceded by reconnaissance using modern means of communication and unmanned aerial vehicles. Then the artillery came into action. Aviation also worked on the folded sectors of the front. At the last stage, infantry and tank units moved forward, which were supported by artillery fire.

However, as the resistance of the armed forces of Ukraine intensified and the transition from maneuver warfare to bloody positional battles increased, the shortcomings of the BTG also appeared. One of the main drawbacks was the low number of personnel. This limitation on the number of troops involved becomes a disadvantage when enemy formations have superiority in strength. Sometimes it happened that, having captured enemy positions, the group did not have enough forces to hold them and was forced to retreat. The fact is that the Ukrainian troops operated as part of well-staffed brigades, in terms of firepower and the number of personnel significantly superior to the Russian BTGs.

Battalion tactical group on the march

Tanks from one of the 125 battalion tactical groups enter the territory of Ukraine.

BTG losses are replenished at the expense of the personnel of the brigade, from the units of which the BTG was formed. The team, as a rule, is located in the place of permanent deployment. This means that the troops still need to get to the place before they start infiltrating the BTG structure.

Resources for medical care are extremely limited. In addition, there are often difficulties with the evacuation of the dead or wounded. This does not have the best effect on the morale of the fighters of the group.

The change in the nature of the war in Ukraine has led to the cessation of the deployment of the Russian armed forces in the form of BTGs. Currently, Russian troops operate as part of tank and motorized rifle brigades and divisions.

However, the brigade form of troop organization does not fully meet the requirements of the Russian military. Brigades were created in the Russian army with the expectation of conducting combat operations in local, low-intensity military conflicts against a poorly armed enemy. In the conditions of the war in Ukraine, the brigades did not show themselves in the best way. Their offensive capabilities were insufficient to overcome the organized defense of the enemy; the stability of the brigades in defense also made us expect more.

An unpleasant surprise for the command of the Russian army was the huge losses of armored vehicles. According to Western analysts, in particular, specialists from the British International Center for Strategic Studies (IISS), in just nine months since the beginning of hostilities in Ukraine, the losses of Russian tank forces amounted to 40 percent of their combat vehicles as of February 2022.

One of the reasons for such high losses is that BTGs often moved forward without proper aerial reconnaissance. This allowed enemy troops to occupy advantageous firing positions and shoot at Russian tank columns with artillery fire corrected by reconnaissance UAVs.

Another reason is the presence of modern antitank missile systems (ATGMs) in the enemy's possession. At the very beginning of hostilities, the United States supplied Ukraine with two thousand Javelin ATGMs and subsequently

Russian tank knocked out in Ukraine

sent the same number of such complexes to Ukraine. The trajectory of the Javelin missile, according to the manufacturer, Lockheed Martin, can be set so that the warhead explodes over the upper, most vulnerable armor of the tank.

Many Russian tanks are equipped with a reactive armor system, which, when detonated, is designed to absorb the impact of missiles. However, the Javelin is equipped with two warheads at once. One destroys the dynamic protection, then the second penetrates the tank armor itself.

The UK has sent Ukraine at least 3,600 new-generation NLAW antitank systems, which are also designed to explode over a relatively poorly protected tank turret from above.

A significant proportion of Russian tank losses are due to attacks by antitank kamikaze UAVs. These devices are controlled by operators located at a distance of up to several kilometers from the battlefield.

Kamikaze UAVs are equipped with an engine (internal combustion, electric, or jet) and are filled with a projectile (high-explosive fragmentation, cumulative, cumulative-fragmentation, cluster munition, etc.). They can loiter according to a given program or operator commands, transmitting an image of the environment to him via an optoelectronic communication channel. Due to the use of artificial-intelligence systems, they can independently find and destroy specified targets.

Features and advantages of kamikaze UAVs:

high accuracy of hitting the target
relative cheapness (compared to antiradio radar missiles, for example)
small dimensions
slowness
low collateral damage (low probability of accidental civilian casualties during pinpoint strikes)

At the same time, it is noteworthy that about half of Russian tank losses are not from being knocked out and destroyed by the enemy, but by vehicles that failed due to improper maintenance or were simply abandoned. For example, during the retreat from the Kharkov region, it often happened that the crew abandoned a completely serviceable tank because it ran out of fuel or the track came off.

A Russian tank abandoned during the retreat

To restore the combat capability of tank and motorized rifle formations, the command of the Russian army took a number of measures. First, mobile repair and restoration battalions were moved to the front line, which evacuate damaged equipment from the battlefield and repair it in the field. It is noteworthy that the repair is carried out by the aggregate method. For example, if there is a serious malfunction in the tank engine, then it is immediately replaced with a new one from the reserve fund, and the defective one is sent to the manufacturer.

Major repairs are carried out at tank repair plants. Since the capacities of the factories remaining after perestroika are not enough, the government of the Russian Federation decided to build two armored-vehicle repair plants in the Moscow region.

An important source of replenishment of the tank fleet of the Russian army is the storage bases for weapons and military equipment, which house thousands of tanks of various types, from T-54s to T-80s and T-72s. Since tanks, as a rule, are stored in open areas, their condition is far from combat readiness. For this reason, those in the best condition will be taken from storage for repair and refurbishing. This will make it possible to quickly increase the supply of additional vehicles to the troops.

It is also possible to increase the supply of equipment from Russian defense suppliers. On December 19, 2023, the minister of defense of the Russian Federation, Sergei Shoigu, announced that 1,530 new and modernized tanks and 3,518 armored personnel carriers and infantry fighting vehicles were produced that year. By comparison: for the whole of 2022, tank production in Russia amounted to five hundred vehicles.

The new vehicles presumably include about 350–400 T-90Ms and a small number of T-14s (single machines) manufactured in Nizhny Tagil (Uralvagonzavod). Heavily modernized are the T-72B3Ms and T-80BVMs produced in Omsk (Omsktransmash) and at the 61st Armored Repair Plant (BTRZ) in the Leningrad region, the T-72B3Ms in Nizhny Tagil, and the T-62Ms at the 103rd BTRZ in Chita; this totaled 1,100–1,200 vehicles.

It should be noted that the heavily modernized tank has such new components as the engine, suspension, weapons control systems, gun and auxiliary weapons, a set of additional armor, and more. In principle, a modernized tank is practically no different from a new one.

If there were no issues with the modernization and delivery of tanks of the T-72 and T-80 families to the combat zone, then the modernization of the obsolete T-62 caused bewilderment among many militaries. This medium tank was adopted by the Soviet army back in 1961 and was produced in large series until 1972. It should be borne in mind here that most of the tanks available at the various storage bases were upgraded to the T-62M and T-62MV versions in 1983–85. On the first of them, additional armor protection was installed on the turret, hull, and bottom (the level of protection of the turret from APS was 350 mm; from KS, 400–450 mm), along with rubber-fabric onboard anticumulative screens, antineutron liner on the tower, and 9K116-2 Sheksna guided weapons system. The V-55V engine was replaced by the more powerful V-55U, with a performance of 620 hp; a new Volna fire control system was installed (KTD-2 laser rangefinder, BV-62 ballistic computer, TShSM-41U sight and M1 Meteor stabilizer), as were the 902B "Cloud" smoke grenade launcher system and the "Soda" napalm protection system.

The modernized T-62M tank does not have explosive reactive armor units.

Some of the vehicles were equipped with an NSVT antiaircraft machine gun instead of the DShKM, and the barrel of the gun was equipped with a heat shield. The suspension was also modernized, and the track from the T-72 tank was introduced. In addition, the tank was equipped with an R-173 radio station and an R-173P radio receiver.

The T-62MV differs from the T-62M in the absence of additional armor protection for the turret and hull, which was compensated for by the installation of Kontakt-1 explosive reactive armor. The smoothbore semiautomatic 115 mm 2A20 tank gun, with forty-two rounds of ammunition, is a deadly weapon in capable hands. Its armor-piercing subcaliber and cumulative shells are capable of penetrating armor from 380 to 440 mm at distances of from 20 to 5,800 m.

The tank's ammunition includes 9M117M1-3 Arkan laser-guided missiles, which are part of the 9K116-2 Sheksna complex, which, after flying out of the tank barrel, are capable of penetrating armor up to 850 mm at distances from 100 to 6,000 m. Arkan reliably penetrates the armor of the American M1A1 Abrams, Israeli Merkava 3, and German Leopard 2, not to mention the Ukrainian Oplot T-84 from any angle of fire; at an angle of fire of more than 30°, it can penetrate the armor of the more protected M1A2 and AMX-56 Leclerc.

The modernized tanks are supposed to be used for fire support of infantry storming fortified positions. At the same time, it is very useful that the smoothbore 115 mm T-62 gun, unlike the rifled one, has a higher penetrating force due to the use of armor-piercing, feathered subcaliber shells and a higher (two times) muzzle velocity of their flight and is capable of destroying long-term reinforced concrete, stone, and brick structures, which can serve well in the assault and siege of fortress cities. For this purpose, the tank is equipped with a telescopic TSh2B-41 and TPN-1-41-11 periscope electro-optical night sights, as well as two machine guns to cut off enemy infantry and work on light armored targets (coaxial with a 7.62 mm PKT gun with a combat rate of fire of 250 rounds/min., and a turret antiaircraft 12.7 mm DShKM with a combat rate of fire of 125 rounds/min.).

The armor protection of the T-62MV tank is reinforced with explosive reactive armor units.

At the end of 2022, the Ministry of Defense of the Russian Federation issued a contract to the 103rd Armored Repair Plant, located in Chita, according to which the plant must supply the Russian army with up to eight hundred modernized T-62 tanks decommissioned from storage within three years. Thus, the supply of about twenty-two vehicles per month is implied.

The tactics of using combat vehicles entering the tank forces changed significantly. Today it is almost impossible to assemble a large tank force in one place. The modern battlefield is visible from space and other various means of reconnaissance. Widely used high-precision weapons—UAVs, ATGMs, and adjustable artillery ammunition—are extremely effective at hitting tanks. In addition, the evolution of the use of tanks was especially influenced by the development of helicopter technology. Attack helicopters have become one of the main tools for destroying armored vehicles.

For these reasons, during the first months of the Ukraine invasion it was possible to see long tank columns moving from one point to another, as well as the massive use of these vehicles in the capture of strongholds; however, mass attacks such as this are rare today. Tanks then began to be used as nomadic firing points. That is, the T-72 or T-80 becomes a free hunter that moves to threatened areas and suppresses attacks by the enemy on lightly armored vehicles with the support of infantry. The tactics of nomadic firing points became effective thanks to the appearance of modernized tanks.

New observation and aiming devices are being installed on Russian equipment that allow crews to identify targets at a relatively safe distance and strike at them. Sometimes tanks approach enemy positions if it is known that the enemy has weak antitank defenses. Tanks are also used as self-propelled-artillery mounts, camouflaging themselves on the ground and firing from closed firing positions. With this application, the firing range is 8–10 km.

Russian tanks are also used for direct fire when storming fortified enemy positions. With direct fire, the tank gun is capable of hitting the enemy at a distance of up to 3 km.

The safety of the tankers is provided by a cover group. As a rule, these are infantry units that track enemy drones and enemy movements. They are ready to join the battle if they notice Ukrainian groups armed with antitank systems approaching the tank.

Russian tankers have recently begun to use the tactics of firing at areas. Several tanks move to the firing position at once and hit the target at the same time. A simultaneous salvo of several guns is able to cover a large area. The principle of this operation is the same as that of rocket artillery. In this case, the adjustment no longer plays a special role—the spread of shells is quite large. Such firing is used if reconnaissance has detected the movement of large enemy groups.

During the course of hostilities, modern tanks encounter very advanced antitank weapons. At the same time, modern tanks were designed taking into account the experience of the Second World War and subsequent wars, when the overwhelming number of hits on the tank fell on strikes from the frontal projection. For this reason, it was this projection that accounted for the main strengthening of armor protection.

The radical difference between modern means of combating tanks is that now the blow to the tank is delivered from above in a horizontal projection. And the protection of the tank from above is only antifragmentation. It has the largest projection area and the minimum thickness. At the same time, there is no way to increase the thickness of the armor; otherwise the tank will weigh too much. Active protection systems (KAZ) of the Arena family could increase the protection of Russian tanks. These complexes have repeatedly confirmed their characteristics in tests but have not yet been adopted by the Russian army. Currently, work is underway on a new modification of the Arena-M.

The Arena-M complex, like its predecessors, is designed to intercept incoming antitank ammunition at a safe distance from the tank. This KAZ is developed on the basis of the experience and solutions of previous projects of the family but includes a number of new ideas. First of all, a fundamentally new architecture of the main units has been introduced, which simplifies the installation of the complex on the carrier tank and increases its survivability.

The new KAZ includes radar threat detection equipment, automatic control, and launchers with protective ammunition.

Tests of the complex have been going on for several years, and a specific situation remains in the field of domestic means of active protection of armored vehicles. A promising KAZ "Arena-M" has been developed and tested, which has already confirmed full compatibility with the modern T-72B3. On the other hand, so far we are talking only about tests of the complex; the timing of their completion and the time of launch into mass production are unknown. Meanwhile, the mass modernization of existing tanks continues without the use of active protection systems.

As passive protection against blows to the roof of a tank in battles in Ukraine, Russian tankers use improvised devices nicknamed "barbecues." These are mesh metal canopies that tankers began to make themselves in Syria in 2022.

The main purpose of the canopy is to protect the tank from shaped charges from kamikaze UAVs, to disperse the shaped-charge jet from an explosion over the turret, and to reduce the accuracy and force of the impact.

The appearance of these canopies on the battlefield was initially perceived as absurd. However, contrary to expectations, these improvised devices welded to the turrets of tanks proved to be highly effective in protecting against grenade launchers, antitank missile systems (ATGMs) such as the American Javelin and the British-Swedish NLAW, and the ubiquitous kamikaze UAVs.

One of the variants of passive protective devices of the "barbecue" type was the "turtle"-type device. As is known, when a Russian T-72 was knocked out and its turret lost the ability to rotate, the tankers decided that their vehicle could be used as an assault gun or as a demining vehicle. It was necessary to protect themselves only from kamikaze UAVs, for which the tank, which had lost its former mobility, would become easy prey.

Tank T-72 B3M, equipped with a protective "Barbecue" canopy

Protective canopy on a tank

A device of the "Turtle" type quite effectively protects tanks from attacks by kamikaze UAVs.

The T-72 was sheathed from top to bottom with sheets of tin. As it turned out, a simple sheathing with thin metal successfully protected the tank from kamikaze UAVs. This particular tank was involved in hostilities in the area around the settlement of Krasnogorovka. The T-72 escorted the column with the landing force to the city and returned back to the positions on its own.

Of course, a tank that looks like a turtle will not be able to become mass-produced, although three similar vehicles have already been spotted on the line of contact. Such a total hull plating is quite effective in protecting against kamikaze UAVs. But it deprives the tank of its main advantages—speed, maneuver, visibility, and turret rotation. But for solving some immediate problems, a tank with such protection is quite suitable.

Another way to protect against kamikaze UAVs is to equip tanks with electronic-warfare stations in the form both of simple jammers and more-expensive and more-complex systems. Such a more complex system should analyze the radio frequencies on which the enemy UAV is controlled, and put interference on these frequencies at the exact moment when the UAV is in the suppression zone.

As a promising means of clearing the sky over tanks, the introduction of UAVs in one form or another is considered—interceptors that provide physical destruction of kamikaze UAVs.

A very promising area is the use of a laser weapons to destroy kamikaze UAVs. Prototypes of such weapons are already being tested at training grounds.

A question is raised about the wider use of smoke screens over the battlefield, which hide positions and troop movements from the eyes of the enemy. After all, the ability to broadcast images from the battlefield live is a major factor in the current revolution in military affairs. And it is UAVs that provide such an opportunity.

Thus, it can be hoped that despite significant progress in the development of antitank weapons, the tank will retain its status as one of the key elements of the war.

Tanks with improvised protective devices of the Mangal type on the march

Russian tank with "turtle"-type protection

APPENDIX

LIST OF THE TANK UNITS OF THE MODERN RUSSIAN ARMY

NORTHERN FLEET

One independent tank battalion of the 200th Motorized Rifle Brigade. In 2011 it was equipped with T-72Bs, in 2012–13 it was reequipped with T-72B3s, and in 2018–19 it received T-80BVMs.

WESTERN MILITARY DISTRICT

One independent tank battalion of the 138th Motorized Rifle Brigade. In 2011 it was equipped with T-72Bs, and in 2012-13 it was reequipped with T-72B3s.

One independent tank battalion of the 25th Motorized Rifle Brigade. In 2012 it was equipped with T-80BVs, and in 2019 it was reequipped with T-72B3s.

One independent tank battalion of the 76th Airborne Division, which was formed in 2019 with T-72B-3s.

One independent tank battalion of the 79th Motorized Rifle Brigade. In 2011 it was equipped with T-72Bs, and conversion to the T-72B3M began in 2020.

The 11th Independent Tank Regiment of the 11th Army Corps—established in 2019 with three tank battalions. The I Battalion was equipped with T-72B3s; the other two battalions have not completed their training/formation (2019).

The 1st Tank Regiment of the 2nd Motorized Rifle Division—established in 2016 with three tank battalions. All are equipped with the T-72B3M.

One independent tank battalion of the 1st Motorized Rifle Regiment of the 2nd Motorized Rifle Division (until 2012, an independent tank battalion of the 5th Motorized Rifle Brigade). Equipped with the T-90A in 2011, and from 2020 with the T-90M.

One independent tank battalion of the 15th Motorized Rifle Regiment of the 2nd Motorized Rifle Division. Established in 2012 and equipped with the T-72B3.

One independent tank battalion of the 27th Motorized Rifle Brigade, formed with T-90A tanks in 2011.

The 12th Tank Regiment of the 27th Motorized Rifle Brigade (until 2012: 4th Tank Brigade), with a total of three tank battalions equipped with T-80Us and some T-80UE-1s.

The 13th Tank Regiment of the 4th Tank Division, established in 2012. Total of three tank battalions with T-80Us and some T-80EU-1s.

One independent tank battalion of the 423rd Motorized Rifle Regiment of the 4th Tank Division, formed in 2016 with T-80BVs and from 2020 equipped with T-80BVMs.

The 6th Tank Brigade, consisting of three tank battalions. In 2011 it received the T-80BV. It converted to the T-72B3 in 2012–13 and to the T-72B3M in 2018–19.

The 59th Tank Regiment of the 144th Motorized Rifle Division, established in 2019. A total of three tank battalions with T-72Bs.

One independent tank battalion of the 488th Motorized Rifle Regiment of the 144th Motorized Rifle Division (until 2016, an independent tank battalion of the 28th Motorized Rifle Brigade). In 2011 it was equipped with T-72BAs, which starting in 2013 were partially replaced by T-72B3s.

One independent tank battalion of the 254th Motorized Rifle Regiment of the 144th Motorized Rifle Division, established in 2019. The battalion has not completed its formation and will probably receive T-72Bs.

The 237th Tank Regiment of the 3rd Motorized Rifle Division, established in 2017. Three tank battalions equipped with T-72Bs.

One independent tank battalion of the 252nd Motorized Rifle Regiment of the 3rd Motorized Rifle Division (until 2016, an independent tank battalion of the 9th Motorized Rifle Brigade). In 2011 it was equipped with the T-80BV, and in 2013 it was reequipped with T 72B3s.

One independent tank battalion of the 752nd Motorized Rifle Regiment of the 3rd Motorized Rifle Division (until 2016, an independent tank battalion of the 23rd Motorized Rifle Brigade). In 2011 it was equipped with the T-72B (prior to that with the T-72BA).

SOUTHERN MILITARY DISTRICT

The 68th Tank Regiment of the 150th Motorized Rifle Division, established in 2016. Three tank battalions equipped with the T-72B3M.

The 163rd Tank Regiment of the 150th Motorized Rifle Division, established in 2018. Three tank battalions equipped with the T-72B.

One independent tank battalion of the 103rd Motorized Rifle Regiment of the 150th Motorized Rifle Division, established in 2016 and equipped with the T-72B.

One independent tank battalion of the 103rd Motorized Rifle Regiment of the 150th Motorized Rifle Division is in the formation phase. It will probably receive the T-72B.

One independent tank battalion of the 20th Motorized Rifle Brigade, equipped with the T-90A in 2011.

One independent tank battalion of the 136th Motorized Rifle Brigade, equipped with the T-90A in 2011.

One independent tank battalion of the 70th Motorized Rifle Regiment of the 42nd Motorized Rifle Division (until 2017, an independent tank battalion of the 17th Motorized Rifle Brigade), equipped with T-72B3s in 2011.

One independent tank battalion of the 71st Motorized Rifle Regiment of the 42nd Motorized Rifle Division (until 2017, an independent tank battalion of the 18th Motorized Rifle Brigade), equipped with T-72Bs in 2011 and reequipped with the T-72B3 in 2013.

One independent tank battalion of the 42nd Motorized Rifle Division, established in 2017 and equipped with the T-72B3.

One independent tank battalion of the 19th Motorized Rifle Brigade, equipped with T-90A tanks in 2011.

One independent tank battalion of the 205th Motorized Rifle Brigade. Equipped with T-72B tanks in 2011 and reequipped with the T-72B3 in 2012–13.

One independent tank battalion of the 4th Military Base, equipped with T-72Bs in 2011.

One independent tank battalion of the 102nd Military Base, equipped with T-72Bs in 2011.

One independent tank battalion of the 7th Airborne Division, which was established in 2019 with T-72B3 tanks.

One independent tank battalion of the 56th Airborne Division, which was established in 2019 with T-72B3 tanks.

One independent tank battalion of the 126th Coastal Defense Brigade, established in 2014 and equipped with the T-72B3.

One independent tank battalion of the 7th Military Base, equipped with T-90As in 2011. Reequipped with the T-72B3 in 2016.

One independent tank battalion of the 555th Air Force Group in the Arabian Republic of Syria. Established in 2015 and equipped with materiel from the battalion of the 7th Military Base (T-90As).

CENTRAL MILITARY DISTRICT

Two independent tank battalions of the 21st Motorized Rifle Brigade. Equipped with the T-72BA in 2011 and starting in 2013–14 partially reequipped with the T-72B3.

One independent tank battalion of the 35th Motorized Rifle Brigade, equipped with T-72Bs from 2011.

One independent tank battalion of the 74th Motorized Rifle Brigade. Equipped with T-72Bs in 2011 and reequipped on T-72B3s in 2014–15.

One independent tank battalion of the 228th Motorized Rifle Regiment of the 90th Tank Division (until 2017, an independent tank battalion of the 32nd Motorized Rifle Brigade). Equipped with T-72Bas in 2011, and from 2020 with T-72B3Ms.

The 239th Tank Regiment of the 90th Tank Division (until 2017, the 7th Tank Brigade). Three tank battalions, equipped with T-72Bs in 2011.

The 6th Tank Regiment of the Tank Division, established in 2017. Three tank battalions equipped with T-72Bs.

The 80th Tank Regiment of the 90th Tank Division, established in 2017. Three tank battalions equipped with T-72Bs.

One independent tank battalion of the 201st Military base; created in 2016 from three independent tank companies. Equipped with T-72Avs in 2011 and partially reequipped with T-72Bs in 2016.

EASTERN MILITARY DISTRICT

One tank brigade with three tank battalions, which were equipped with T-72B tanks in 2011.

One independent tank battalion of the 36th Motorized Rifle Brigade. Equipped with T-72Bs in 2011 and reequipped with T-72B3s in 2013–14.

One independent tank battalion of the 37th Motorized Rifle Brigade. Equipped with T-72Bs in 2011 and reequipped with T-72B3s in 2013–14.

One independent tank battalion of the 38th Motorized Rifle Brigade. Equipped with T-80BV tanks in 2011 and reequipped with T-72B3s in 2013–14 and with T-80BVs in 2019.

One independent tank battalion of the 69th Covering Brigade. Equipped with T-80BV tanks in 2011 and reequipped with T-72Bs in 2013–14 and with T-80BVs in 2019.

One independent tank battalion of the 64th Motorized Rifle Brigade. Equipped with T-80BVs in 2011 and reequipped with T-72B3s in 2013–14 and with T-80BVs in 2019.

One independent tank battalion of the 39th Motorized Rifle Brigade. Equipped with T-80BVs in 2011 and reequipped with T-72B3s in 2013–14 and with T-80BVs in 2019.

One independent tank battalion of the 57th Motorized Rifle Brigade. Equipped with T-80BVs in 2011.

One independent tank battalion of the 60th Motorized Rifle Brigade. Equipped with T-80BV tanks in 2011 and reequipped with T-72Bs in 2013–14.

One independent tank battalion of the 114th Motorized Rifle Regiment of the 127th Motorized Rifle Division (until 2019, an independent tank battalion of the 70th Motorized Rifle Brigade). Equipped with T-80BV tanks in 2011 and reequipped with T-72Bs in 2014.

One independent tank battalion of the 394th Motorized Rifle Regiment of the 127th Motorized Rifle Division (until 2019, an independent tank battalion of the 59th Motorized Rifle Brigade). Equipped with T-80BV tanks in 2011 and reequipped with T-72Bs in 2014.

The 84th Independent Tank battalion of the 127th Motorized Rifle Division. Established in 2019 and equipped with T-72B tanks.

One independent tank company of the 46th Machine Gun and Artillery Regiment of the 18th Machine Gun and Artillery Division. Equipped with T-80BVs in 2011 and reequipped with T-72Bs in 2014.

One independent tank company of the 49th Machine Gun and Artillery Regiment of the 18th Machine Gun and Artillery Division. Equipped with T-80BVs in 2011 and reequipped with T-72Bs in 2014.

One independent tank company of the 83rd Airborne Brigade. Established in 2018 with T-72B3 tanks.

One independent tank company of the 40th Naval Infantry Brigade. Established in 2018 with T-80BV tanks.

One independent tank company of the 155th Naval Infantry Brigade. Established in 2014 with T-80BV tanks and reequipped with T-72Bs in 2019.

SCHOOLS

The training of tank officers takes place at the Tank School in Kazan, at the Omsk Institute of Automobile and Tank Technology in Omsk, and at the combined weapons schools in Moscow and the Far East. Tank Training Center 212 and the Training Centers for Motorized Rifle Units 56, 467, 473, and 392 also train prospective tankers. The total number of training vehicles is at least four hundred main battle tanks of all types (except for the T-90).